NON-CONTACT WARFARE

An Appraisal of China's Military Capabilities

NON-CONTACT WARFARE

An Appraisal of China's Military Capabilities

Brigadier Vivek Verma

UNITED SERVICE INSTITUTION OF INDIA
NEW DELHI

PENTAGON PRESS LLP

Non-Contact Warfare: An Appraisal of China's Military Capabilities *By Brigadier Vivek Verma*

First Published in 2021

ISBN 978-93-90095-16-2

Published by
PENTAGON PRESS LLP
206, Peacock Lane, Shahpur Jat,
New Delhi-110049
Phones: 011-64706243, 26491568
Telefax: 011-26490600
email: rajan@pentagonpress.in
website: www.pentagonpress.in

Printed at Aegean Offset Printers, Greater Noida, U.P.

Contents

Foreword

We are living in a world of endless contests and conflicts. The non-traditional security threats have expanded in scope while traditional security has become more lethal and autonomous. The operating environment across multiple domains of land, sea, deep sea, air, space, and cyberspace has broadened the strategic space. Technology has transformed the ability to influence the outcomes. Now winning is more important than victory, and the violence-force correlation is testing security discourse. The future of warfare had never been so dynamic and profound. Defining 'Non-Contact Warfare' and distinguishing it with the other terms used over the past four decades like irregular warfare, unconventional warfare, unrestricted warfare, hybrid warfare, and generational warfare, therefore becomes important.

The study of China's non-contact warfare capability is significant as the Communist Party of China (CPC) is unique. It has a state and an Army (the People's Liberation Army or PLA). The symbiotic approach of the Party and Army combine over the last seven decades has made the country self-reliant economically, thus fuelling the Chinese Dream. It knows that it has to create strategic opportunities and prevent strategic friction with the US and the West. The PLA reforms ushered in by Xi Jinping in October 2013 was to transform the PLA structures and strategies by adopting a well-crafted whole-of-a-nation approach. The doctrinal push by the CPC to avoid confrontation and contest the competition through non-contact means is therefore purposeful. It allows it to keep the conflict below the threshold level. It also helps the PLA to establish peace at the strategic level while continuing with its aggressive design at the operational and tactical level through 'active defence' and 'three warfares' strategy.

'Non-Contact Warfare: An Appraisal of China's Military Capabilities' authored by Brigadier Vivek Verma is an essential resource for the policy planners to understand the nuances of non-contact warfare. It shows how China's military is building its capability to play the game in the non-military and military 'kinetic and non-kinetic' arena. Brigadier Vivek Verma has provided an insight into PLA's non-contact warfare doctrinal precepts, and increasing capability development concisely. PLA's increasing capability in non-contact warfare has a direct implication on India's security. The recommendations provided in the book need careful examination. India needs a whole-of-a-government approach to deal with China's non-contact warfare capabilities. While the last war was about jointmanship between the services, the next war will be about the civil-military integration. The words by Alvin and Heidi Toffler in their book 'War and Anti-War' remains relevant, "if the war was ever too important to be left to generals, it is now too important to be left to the ignorant – whether they wear the uniform or not."

New Delhi
13 July 2020

Major General BK Sharma, AVSM, SM (Retd)**
Director, United Services Institute of India

Acknowledgements

The metamorphosis from soldier to scholar and from scholar to an author is an arduous journey. This journey cannot be traversed without a mentor and a guide, organisational support, critique from professionals, good wishes from friends and above all, the unstinted support from the family. The United Services Institute of India, New Delhi, as India's oldest think tank has a unique distinction of moulding and promoting scholar warriors. The wealth of experience resident within the institute and numerous interactions from professionals from other countries has been beneficial in crystallising thoughts on a subject where there are more talks than written work. Traversing an uncharted territory of non-contact warfare without a mentor and guide like Major General Rajiv Narayanan, AVSM, VSM (Retd) would have been unfathomable. His experience, patience and incisive remarks have been invaluable in steering the research and writing.

I want to express my special thanks to Lieutenant General SP Kochhar, AVSM**, SM, VSM (Retd), former Signal Officer-in-Chief, Lieutenant General SL Narasimhan, PVSM, AVSM*, VSM (Retd), Director General, Centre for Contemporary Chinese Studies and member National Security Advisory Board, Lieutenant General Vinod G. Khandare, PVSM, AVSM, SM (Retd), Military Advisor to the National Security Council Secretariat for their critique and counsel. It has helped me to streamline my book.

I am thankful to Lieutenant General PK Singh, PVSM, AVSM (Retd), former Director USI and Major General BK Sharma, AVSM, SM** (Retd), Director, USI, who motivated me with their presence during my presentations on the subject. They provided me with the opportunity to visit Taiwan that not only enriched my understanding of the Chinese non-contact warfare methods but also provided an insight into the cross-strait relationship.

My deep sense of gratitude to my seniors and colleagues at USI-Lieutenant General GS Katoch, PVSM, AVSM, VSM (Retd), Major General RPS Bhadauria (Retd), Brigadier Narender Kumar (Retd), Major General Sanjeev Chauhan, YSM, Dr Roshan Khaniejo, Major General SB Asthana, SM, VSM (Retd), Major General PK Goswami, VSM (Retd). Their advice and comments were vital for my project. I am also thankful to Brigadier Ashish Chhibber, Colonel Kunwar Nihar, Colonel Sanjeev Chopra and Colonel Anurag Jyoti for their invaluable inputs and for being the sounding board.

I am extremely indebted to late Brigadier Gurmeet Kanwal (Retd), former Director Centre for Land Warfare Studies and my commanding officer whose guidance was like a beacon to me. Losing him has been the biggest loss to me both personally and professionally. I am also grateful to Dr Monika Chansoria and Major General Dhruv Katoch, SM, VSM (Retd), former Director Centre for Land Warfare Studies whose critical comments on my synopsis immensely helped me. I am grateful to Dr. W Selvamurthy, Distinguished Scientist and former Chief Controller, R&D (Life Sciences & International Cooperation) at DRDO and President of Amity Science, Technology and Innovation Foundation and Director General for Amity Directorate of Science and Innovation at the Amity University, Noida, for his encouragement in pursuing a topic that is current and relevant in current context.

I will be failing in my duties if I do not extend my appreciation to the library and administrative staff at the USI who kept me charged with the flow of materials and fluids. I am also thankful to library staff at my old establishment at CLAWS, New Delhi.

Typically, after thanking those who helped in the creation of a book, the author adds a final note of thanks to his wife and children. I am not an exception. The lockdown due to COVID-19 confined me to my home and exposed my wife, Swastika, and my two little daughters, Vartika and Varalika, to my idiosyncrasies. Probably, they understood that patience, understanding and good humour are required as the man in the house retreats into research and pecks away at his computer. Tasks get undone, and the tolerance is tested when an obscure event captures imagination and dinner table conversations get mired into it. I am equally thankful to my parents for their encouragement.

During my stint with the Botswana Defence Force, one of my colleagues distilled to me the essence of life and our obligations towards society. The words are still afresh in my memory, "plant trees, build a pond, have children and above all write a book" and I found this an opportune time to make my contributions. Here is the book. I am thankful to my publisher for their faith in this book.

JAI HIND!

Preface

When the project to carry out the appraisal of 'China's People's Liberation Army (PLA) Increasing Non-contact Warfare Capabilities' was assigned to me, it sent me looking for the definition in the glossary of military terms. Sometimes lack of definitions provides the freedom to explore and draw conclusions. However, it comes with added caveat, as the definition arrived at forms the foundation over which the entire project depends. Thus, understanding the evolution of non-contact warfare was an essential imperative. The exploration of the nature of war (what is war) and changing character warfare (how it is fought) require a clear conceptual distinction between war and conflict. If war develops in the womb of politics and the strategy dictates its manifestation, then it throws up questions as to what lies at the heart of strategic formulation? A close examination of the contemporary conflict situations post World War II has been taken to contextualise the shifting landscape of security. Chapter One, therefore, attempts to develop the understanding of the non-contact warfare by exploring the strategies and technological developments during the Cold War and Post-Cold War conflicts. It has tried to postulate the definition for the 'non-contact warfare' and attempted to determine the key attributes which will be used while orchestrating non-contact warfare. The core instrumentality of threat and use of force to achieve political outcomes have been examined and how technology evolution is tripping doctrinal cycle has been captured. Challenge confronting a security planner is the ability to distinguish what is strategic and how and where the force should be used.

Last four decades of relentless effort nuanced by China by hiding its intentions and biding its time has helped it to gallop the economic ladder.

It has been able to bridge the dominance divide with the US. The world riding the Toffler's 'Third Wave' and flattened by the technology and management tools remains divided by ideas and identities. However, the disruptions by asymmetric means have given hope to countries like China to contest the war by other means. While the non-contact warfare embraces military, trans-military and non-military domains, however, the book examines only the military manifestation of non-contact warfare. Chapter Two, therefore tries to examine how China's PLA has adapted non-contact warfare in evolving its security doctrine? An analysis of classical Chinese texts, contemporary writings by the sinologists and Chinese writers, speeches of China's leadership and government reports and white papers have been carried out to fathom what Beijing wants. It also examines how it is likely to use non-contact warfare means to reduce strategic friction and improve strategic opportunity to achieve its millennium goal of building a great modern socialist country. The chapter has also tried to study Chinese strategic behaviour and its doctrinal precepts based on its visualisation of the future wars, the threat from 'American hegemonistic design' and how the new strategic concepts can counter new-generation threats. It has looked at Chinese strategists' assertion of defeating the superior through the adoption of superior strategy, structures and operational simulations while recommending discreet methods of countering America's global alliance system by favourably managing the 'Shi' – a Chinese method of gauging strategic situationism.

Chapter Three and Four examine the Chinese kinetic and non-kinetic non-contact warfare capabilities as part of PLA's preparation for military struggle. Given the PLA's global role to defend China's interest frontier that recognises no territorial boundary, places immense resource and responsibility on PLA. The chapters have tried to bring forth how PLA pushed into reform by Xi Jinping in 2016 has gone about revising its organisational, doctrinal and equipping norms. Informatisation, as the soul of force development points to a systematic approach, put in place by the PLA to improve its situational awareness and ability to influence the outcome of conflict through non-lethal and lethal means.

To make war one needs to find a reason. If trade and tariff war was not enough an excuse for the Sino-US conflict, the threat of a pandemic from the COVID-19 virus has given enough ammunition to understand the non-contact warfare. Chapter Five tries to look at the ways China aims to avoid entering into "Thucydides trap"* – where the triptych of fear, anger and emotions may ignite Sino-US conflict. Navigating the non-contact methods of warfare is probably the way out for China, where the principles of 'active defence in the new era' and 'three warfares' will be practised. For China defending its core interests of social stability and global interests are important. Hence, the chapter looks at China's capacity to project its soft power and ability to fight the battle of depth. The use of influence operations, strengthening of cyber architecture and exploring the new frontier of cognitive security are some of the issues that have been discussed. The ability to control and manipulate narrative and the utility of its magic weapon, the United Front Works Department, have also been contextualised. Beijing knows that orchestration of non-contact warfare is heavily dependent on situational awareness and development of anti-technologies like hypersonic and anti-satellite systems. It aims to disrupt the US Global Information Grid. The importance of 'war control' or escalation mechanism in Chinese doctrine has been highlighted to show how PLA would like to confine the crisis from spiralling out into conflict. The nuclear and non-nuclear deterrence capabilities and related complexities have also been discussed. To keep the conflict at sub-threshold level, PLA's ability to nuance grey-zone warfare, use civil-military fusion doctrine and develop disruptive technologies are some of the other issues that have also been evaluated.

Chapter Six looks at the implication for India, given the Chinese doctrinal and force developmental dynamics. While the PLA force development may be an outcome to balance the US dominance, nonetheless it provides it with better capability when compared with countries along its periphery. The intent is the reflection of capability, and if the capability exists the intent may change. Hence, amidst changing Chinese strategic discourse and security landscape, India will need to firewall its security interests. The chapter dwells on the challenges that India is confronted with and argues why India will need to have a whole-of-a-government approach to counter the threat from China. As Chanakya in 'The

*In the book, 'Destined for War', Professor Graham Allison explains a deadly pattern of structural stress that results when a rising power challenges a ruling one. He draws the inspiration from Thucydide, the famous Greek historian who in 'The History of the Peloponnesian War' wrote: "What made war inevitable was the growth of Athenian power (rising power) and the fear which this caused in Sparta (the dominant power)".

Arthashastra' said, "deliberations should not be unduly delayed once an opportunity for action arises".

At a time when I started writing the book, I never realised that the world would be confronted with contagion like the COVID-19. Biological warfare, an important element of non-contact warfare, that was so far ensconced within wraps of doctrinal and developmental dialogue will come out in open to script the future strategic discourse. With the signs of strain showing across the globe in handling the pandemic, the battle lines, however, have already emerged between the US and China. Chances of direct confrontation may not be the immediate goal. However, the recipe for orchestrating non-contact warfare is ripe. Non-contact warfare finds its applicability across all domains and escalation matrix. It looks at targeting adversary's sensitivities and vulnerabilities as it intends to keep the response calibrated and in accordance with the escalation matrix to remain ahead in the game of domination. Winning along each ladder of escalation is essential to extract favourable outcomes. Disruption, denial, distortion, disempowerment, destabilisation and destruction are few themes that the world is likely to witness as the dominance strategy using non-contact warfare gets unfolded.

The book is an earnest attempt to provide security planners with the basic framework of Chinese PLA's capability development and doctrinal deployment in the fields of non-contact warfare. The future study on Chinese economic predatory policies, lawfare to promote and safeguard Chinese interests and development of disruptive and new-age technologies will help in understanding Chinese methods of cultivating and harnessing leverages to influence the outcomes across multiple domains in the non-contact warfare scenario.

I hope the book will be of help to readers and will stimulate policy debate, discussion and implementation.

New Delhi **Brigadier Vivek Verma**
July 2020

List of Abbreviations

4 GW	Fourth Generation Warfare
5 GW	Fifth Generation Warfare
6 GW	Sixth Generation Warfare
A2AD	Anti-Access Area-Denial
AAM	Air to Air Missile
ADIZ	Air Defence Identification Zone
AESA	Active Electronically Scanned Array
AEW&C	Airborne Early Warning and Control
AIP	Air Independent Power
AMMS	Academy of Military Medical Science
AMS	Academy of Military Science
APT3	Advance Persistent Threat
ARPANET	Advance Research Projects Agency Network
ASAT	Anti-Satellite System
ASBM	Anti-Ship Ballistics Missile
ASCM	Anti-Ship Cruise Missile
ASuW	Anti-Submarine Warfare
ASW	Anti-Ship Warfare
AVIC	Aviation Industry Corporation of China
AWACS	Airborne Warning and Control System
BDA	Battle Damage Assessment
Bn	Battalion
BRI	Belt and Road Initiative
BWC	Biological Weapons Convention
C2	Command and Control

C4ISR	Command, Control, Computers, Communications, Information, Surveillance and Reconnaissance
CAG	Comptroller and Auditor General
CASC	China Aerospace Science and Technology Corporation
CASIC	China Aerospace Science and Industry Corporation
CAST	China Academy of Space Technology
CATOBAR	Catapult Assisted Take-off but Arrested Recovery
CBRN	Chemical, Biological, Radiological and Nuclear
CDS	Chief of Defence Staff
CENTCOM	US Central Command
CEP	Circular Error of Probability
CETC	China Electronics Technology Group Corporation
CFACC	Combined Forces Air Component Commander
CGTN	China Global Television Network
CHEOS	China High-Resolution Earth Observation System
CICC	China Institute of Command and Control
CICIR	China Institutes of Contemporary International Relations
CIDCA	China International Development Cooperation Agency
CLAWS	Centre for Land Warfare Studies
CMC	Central Military Commission
CMI	Civil-Military Integration
CNA	Computer Network Attack
CNE	Computer Network Exploitation
CNP	Comprehensive National Power
COMSAT	Communication Satellite
COVID	Corona Virus Disease
CPC	Communist Party of China
CRISPR	Clustered Regularly Interspaced Short Palindromic Repeat
CSIC	China Ship Building Industry Corporation
CSSA	Chinese Student and Scholars Association
CSSC	China State Ship Building Corporation
CWC	Chemical Weapons Convention
DARPA	Defence Advanced Research Projects Agency
DIME	Diplomatic, Intelligence, Military and Economy
DIUx	Defence Innovation Unit Experimental
DMA	Department of Military Affairs

DNA	Deoxyribonucleic Acid
DPC	Defence Planning Committee
DRDO	Defence Research and Development Organisation
ECM	Electronic Counter Measure
EDCA	Enhanced Defence Cooperation Agreement
EEZ	Exclusive Economic Zone
EMP	Electro-Magnetic Pulse
EMSM	Electro-Magnetic Spectrum Management
EO	Electro-Optical
ERP	Economic Recovery Plan
EW	Electronic Warfare
FDI	Foreign Direct Investment
FONOP	Freedom of Navigation Operations
GAD	General Armament Department
GDP	Gross Domestic Product
GLCM	Ground-Launched Cruise Missile
GNP	Gross National Product
GNSS	Global Navigation and Surveillance Systems
GPD	General Political Department
GPS	Global Positioning System
GSD	General Staff Department
HADR	Human Assistance and Disaster Relief
HALE	High Altitude Long Endurance
HF	High Frequency
HGV	Hyper Glide Vehicle
HUMINT	Human Intelligence
ICBM	Inter-Continental Ballistics Missile
ICT	Information and Communications Technology
IDSA	Institute for Defence and Strategic Analysis
IED	Improvised Explosive Device
IFV	Infantry Fighting Vehicle
IIR	Imaging Infrared
IME	Institute of Microbiology and Epidemiology
IMF	International Monetary Fund
INEW	Integrated Network Electronic Warfare
INF	Intermediate-Range Nuclear Forces

INS	Initial Navigation System
IO	Information Operations
IRBM	Intermediate-Range Ballistic Missile
ISI	Inter-Services Intelligence
ISIS	Islamic State in Iraq and Syria
ISR	Intelligence, Surveillance and Reconnaissance
JOCC	Joint Operations Command Centre
JSD	Joint Staff Department
JSD-NEB	Joint Staff Department Network-Electronic Bureau
KLA	Kosovo Liberation Army
KSM	Key Starting Materials
LACM	Land Attack Cruise Missile
LEO	Low Earth Orbit
LGB	Laser Guided Bomb
LHA	Amphibious Assault Ship
LIBP	Lanzhou Institute of Biological Produces
LPAR	Long Phased Array Radars
LPD	Landing Platform Dock
LTIPP	Long Term Integrated Perspective Plan
LTTE	Liberation Tigers of Tamil Eelam
MALE	Medium Altitude Long Endurance
MEO	Medium Earth Orbit
MietY	Ministry of Electronics and Information Technology
MIIT	Ministry of Industry and Information Technology
MIRV	Multiple Independent Re-entry Vehicle
MLPS	Multi-level Protection Scheme
MLRS	Multi-Barrel Rocket System
MNC	Multi National Corporation
MOAB	Mother of All Bomb
MoD	Ministry of Defence
MR	Military Region
MRBM	Medium-Range Ballistic Missile
MSME	Micro, Small and Medium Enterprise
MTR	Military Technological Revolution
NATO	North Atlantic Treaty Organisation
NDRC	National Development and Reform Commission

NDS	National Defence Strategy
NDU	National Defence University
NDWP	National Defence White Paper
NEP	New Education Policy
NIPRNET	Non-Classified Internet Protocol Router Network
NITI	National Institution for Transforming India
NLOS	Non-Line of Sight
NPC	National People's Congress
NPR	Nuclear Posture Review
NQI	National Quantum Initiative
NSA	National Security Advisor
NSC	National Security Commission
NSD	Network Systems Department
NUDT	National University of Defence Technology
OODA	Observe, Orient, Decide and Act
OPCW	Organisation for the Prohibition of Chemical Weapons
ORBAT	Order of Battle
ORF	Observer Research Foundation
OTH	Over the Horizon
PAPF	People's Armed Police Force
PGM	Precision Guided Munitions
PIMED	Political, Intelligence, Military, Economy and Diplomacy
PLA	People's Liberation Army
PLAAF	People's Liberation Army Air Force
PLAN	People's Liberation Army Navy
PLANMC	People's Liberation Army Navy Marine Corps
PLARF	People's Liberation Army Rocket Force
PLASAF	People's Liberation Army Second Artillery Force
PLASSF	People's Liberation Strategic Support Force
PME	Professional Military Education
PMS	People's Military Struggle
PRC	People's Republic of China
Psyops	Psychological Operations
R&AW	Research and Analysis Wing
RMA	Revolution in Military Affairs
ROC	Republic of China

RRF	Rapid Reaction Force
RV	Reentry Vehicle
SAL	Semi-Active Laser
SALT	Strategic Arms Limitation Talks
SAM	Surface to Air Missile
SATCOM	Satellite Communications
SCM	Supply Chain Management
SDI	Strategic Defence Initiative
SIGINT	Signal Intelligence
SLOC	Sea Lines of Communications
SMS	Science of Military Strategy
SOF	Special Operations Force
SPG	Strategic Policy Group
SQUID	Super-conducting Quantum Interference Device
SSBN	Ship Submersible Ballistic Nuclear
SSD	Space Systems Department
SSN	Submersible Ship Nuclear
START	Strategic Arms Reduction Treaty
TCAF	Theatre Command Air Force
THAAD	Terminal High Altitude Area Defence
TLAM	Tomahawk Land Attack Missile
TPP	Trans-Pacific Partnership
TRAI	Telecom Regulatory Authority of India
TST	Time Sensitive Targets
TT&C	Telemetry, Tracking and Control
UAV	Unmanned Aerial Vehicle
UCAV	Unmanned Combat Aerial Vehicle
UFWD	United Front Works Department
USAID	US Agency for International Development
USI	United Services Institute
UUCV	Unmanned Under-water Combat Vehicle
WMD	Weapons of Mass Destruction
XUAR	Xinjiang Uyghur Autonomous Region

1

Understanding the Non-Contact Warfare

Nothing we imagine is absolutely impossible.

– **David Hume, 1739**

WAR IN TIME WARP

Fall of Belgium and France in 1940 and Loss of Mosul in 2014

War is the product of its age; however, it has uncanny similarity. The fall of Belgium and France to the German blitzkrieg during 1940 on the commencement of World War II and loss of Mosul in 2014 by the Iraqi forces supported by American to the Islamic State in Iraq and Syria (ISIS) militia bear resemblance. It shows how the well-trained forces can capitulate to an effective and well-targeted operation directed against the leadership and the population.

Before commencement of World War II, Belgium and France planned elaborate obstacle systems. Five million French Army equipped with modern tanks and artillery manned the fortified Maginot line. The French conceived this defensive system after careful study of past wars with Germany. It convinced the Belgian and French generals that the defences were impregnable. However, the 2.5 million Nazi soldiers attacked the Allies where they did not expect. Instead of attacking the formidable obstacle line, the Germans chose to launch a daring campaign through neutral Holland and Belgium with the staggering attack on France through the Ardennes – a hilly and heavily forested area on the German-Belgian-French border. Thus, bypassing and overturning the formidable defence of Maginot-line.[1] The German plan relied on surprise Blitzkrieg ('lightning war') techniques. Synergised application of parachute detachments, swarming raids by aircraft, speed of the armoured vehicles supported by radio and capable propaganda machinery targeted the population and made them flee with fear. War was about the use of mobility, lethality and propaganda to instil fear in the minds of the people and make the leadership redundant.

The operational environment in 2014 of Mosul town was however different. 25,000 Iraqi Forces supported by American state-of-art vehicles and systems guarded Mosul garrison. The deep-rooted sectarian mistrust between the Shia majority and the Sunni minority had fractured the society in Mosul. Sunni civilians trust on soldiers and police were even less. The fractured society with pervasive mistrust provided an ideal condition for exploitation by the ISIS militia. Mobile phones which banned during Saddam Hussein reign were available freely. Phone-obsessed and internet savvy Iraqi teenagers became willing spies and recruits to well-crafted ISIS online forum coordinated via messaging service. ISIS pre-empted their vanguard action through twitter storm "#AllEyesOnISIS", which went viral. The images of ISIS fighters inspired Sunni men to indulge in terror acts as they openly supported the ISIS invaders. The ensuing events consumed the Shia, Christian and Kurdish neighbours with fear. Out of 25,000 Iraqi forces stationed in the Garrison about 10,000 Iraqi troops with smartphones witnessed the atrocities and could track the invading ISIS publicised advance. Even before the ISIS arrived, the soldiers were gripped with fear and abandoned their weapons and vehicles followed by the city's police and more than half-million civilians. The invading force of 1500 ISIS fighters had overwhelmed the town without even fighting. The remaining soldiers and officials became fodder for the online distribution of propaganda material.[2] ISIS posted pictures of captured arsenals and state-of-art American vehicles and half a dozen Black Hawk helicopters. For the first time, the armed non-state actors openly challenged and defeated a conventional military force.

While Germans blitzkrieg harnessed swarming air raids, fast armoured cars, radio and credible propaganda, ISIS integrated internet and Instagram filters on smartphone platforms. The war moved beyond the scope of hackers, malicious malware creators, financial disruptions and outages to another dimension of digital war. In the Mosul war, there was no hacking done. A viral campaign strategy was used to overwhelm the residents of Mosul and provided good publicity to ISIS to open militant recruitment franchise across the globe. ISIS propaganda spurred "lone wolf" attack from Paris to Sydney and brought to fore the role of the armed non-state actor in waging war. It introduced a new actor to the inter-state conflict where the state was fighting a non-state actor which had the ambition to establish Caliphate. Information highway was available to everyone to harness and exploit their interests.

Contextualising the two wars separated by time and space is to argue that the nature and character of warfare are changing. Both these wars questioned the global systems and employed the tools of their time to contest the superior opponents. The Thucydidean triptych of fear, anger and emotions that holds the motive for belligerent behaviour and codified as honour and interest remain relevant even today. It is being used by the parties in conflict to suit their strategy as a by-product of 'ends-ways-means' concept. It raises a pertinent question whether the nature of war has changed over a period of time? It also brings into focus how technology and new actors like armed non-state actors and civil security firms will alter the character or methods of warfighting? An evaluation of the types of conflict the world is faced helps in determining whether violence will remain the main ingredient of war, or is it giving way to alternate means? Will the 'war of interest' and 'war of ideology' add wings to the 'war by intervention, denial and disruptions' across multiple domains? Will the 'massing of force' give way to 'massing of effects' and in such an eventuality where will centre of gravity lie? How will the expansion of security from traditional to non-traditional security domain affect the distinction between war and conflict and the essential question of victory and winning? Exploring the answers to these questions through theoretical framework and prism of events will help us in conceptualising the future of warfare.

WAR, CONFLICTS AND METHODS OF WARFARE

War and Conflict

War has been the only constant which has not faded away with time. In the last 3,450 years of recorded history, only 268 have seen no war.[3] A look at the world's transition points at the end of Napoleonic wars in 1815,

World War I in 1919, World War II in 1945 and Cold War in 1991 have one thing in common – they have profoundly impacted the evolution of world politics and the behaviour of states. It will be hard to fathom the development of the modern nation-state systems in the absence of a pattern of warfare practised during these wars. As Tilly argued, "war made states and the states made war".[4] "While every war has a cause and a purpose",[5] wars have primarily been about wealth generation and dominance.

It may be prudent to look at the 'theoretical thinking' as articulated by Alan Sears, a Canadian Sociologist. 19th century witnessed the birth of new ideas and ideologies propounded by great military and social thinkers who shaped the regimes across Europe and the world. Post-French Revolution the regime change took place in Europe at varying speed. It changed from dynastic rule to regimes that took on the characteristics of national democracy. It replaced the right for the existence of the dynastic system with the rights of a nation to exist.[6] It led to the creation of a new international order which was guided by interests and power equations. It created an anarchic system in which nation-state vied with each other for national survival.[7] It gave rise to the concept of standing armies, total war, decisive battles and disarming of the enemies as a form to contest the established international order. The experience of actual war, however, began to reveal some unsettling developments. While the nation-state provided a capable vehicle for organising mass–mobilisation, the involvement of varied elements of society to support the war effort created vulnerabilities. While preparing for the war, the soldiers were trained to endure rigours of combat while civilians were left unprepared. Hence, the thought emerged that an attack on the civil population can result in the collapse of a nation. Gumplowicz, the father of Conflict Theory, in his book 'Outlines of Sociology' published in 1884, identified that engineering a conflict along "class, race or ethnic" considerations was therefore possible. He expanded on Marx's ideas by arguing that war and conquest are the basis of civilisations. He believed that cultural and ethnic conflicts led to states being identified and defined by a dominant group that had power over other groups. The conflict was thus about power projections in which the coercion was used as a last resort. The conflict was triggered when the interests of individuals or groups were antagonistic, and they conflict with status or power.[8]

Conflict, as seen by the sociologist, was different than seen by the strategists. For strategists, the conflict is not the relentless confrontation between enemies and nor is synonymous with the crisis. It is not a zero-sum game in which one party's gains are the other party's losses. The violence helped in distinguishing between war and conflict as war needed to be violent while it was not mandatory in case of conflicts. Hence, the relations between violence and conflict demand clarification. In certain phases, a conflict may be controlled and limited and hence does not call for violent methods to be used. However, in certain circumstances when the levers of escalation control erode, then the conflict impels it towards other rationales of war.[9] Thomas Schelling points out that messages which convey an appeal for an end to the conflict can take on the appearance of brutal and extreme violence – like the use of an atomic bomb on Hiroshima and Nagasaki.

The element of violence in war separates it from other forms of intergroup and interstate conflict. Most of the studies have been centred on interstate wars, especially between great powers or powerful states. The sustained and coordinated violence we observe over the last century has added new actors to interstate conflicts. It has been observed that states while fighting each other are also engaged in fighting the home-grown and extra-territorial challengers. There are many situations in which a State (the foreign State) will use force on the territory of another State (the territorial State) but where that force may not be primarily directed at the territorial State, but rather it is directed at a non-State armed group based in that State. For instance, the use of force by Israel in Lebanon was directed at the Hezbollah and therefore is also known as Israel–Hezbollah War in 2006. In most of these cases, the attack by the State on a non-State group abroad represents an extension of a pre-existing conflict. In some cases, the interstate war may result in multiple conflict scenario engaging multiple actors and states. The Gulf War 2003 which started as an interstate war between coalition force led by the US and Iraqi government of Saddam Hussein, translated into a domestic insurgency against an external state (coalition force), a civil war between Shia and Sunni for the control of Iraq, a war of secession from Iraq by Kurds and international intervention by Iran, Turkey, the US and ISIS.

Hedley Bull describes war as "organised violence carried on by political units against each other for political motives".[10] Levy and Jackson have also defined war as "sustained, coordinated violence between political organisations".[11] The war here is an instrument applied by states in a controlled, rational manner for political purposes. Hence, application of force leading to violence is the key to initiate war. It indicates that violence must be reciprocated for it to qualify as war as it is between two political organisations. Thus, war is the joint outcome of the behaviour of two or more actors. If the target of the initial violence does not fight back, then it does not qualify as a war. It explains why some rivalries, conflicts, or disputes lead to war while others do not is an important question.[12] The proponent of this school felt that the "Cold War" between the US and the Soviet Union was a rivalry and not a war as it did not escalate to war. They further illustrate that the Arab – Israeli conflict since the foundation of Israel in 1948, as a frequent low-level military activity rather than a continuous war except for the wars of 1948, 1956, 1967, 1973 and 1982, Israeli conflicts in Lebanon in 2006 and Gaza in 2008–09.[13] Another example of distinguishing war has been the Israel bombing of Iraqi nuclear reactor in 1981. It is seen as a preventive strike as Iraq did not respond militarily because it was already engaged in a war with Iran. The point proffered is that conflicts of interests and rivalries are fairly common, whereas wars are not. Hence, it is important to understand the distinction that separates war from conflict or rivalry.

C. Wright Mills, the founder of modern conflict theory, viewed social structures as an outcome of the conflict between people with differing interests and resources. According to him, individuals and resources are influenced by these social structures and the unequal distribution of power and resources in society. Mills argued that the interests of power elites were opposed to those of the common people. He propounded that the policies framed by the power elite resulted in "increased escalation of the conflict, production of weapons of mass destruction, and possibly the annihilation of the human race."[14] Gene Sharp, founder of Albert Einstein Institution and acknowledged as "Clausewitz of nonviolent warfare" advocates that the power is not monolithic. According to him political power, the power of any state—regardless of its particular structural organisation—ultimately derives from the subjects of the state. Power structure relies upon the citizens' obedience to the ruler(s) orders. If they do not obey, leaders have no power. According to Gene Sharp, in most political systems, war and other violence serve as an "ultimate sanction."[15] Ultimately, the violence used by state and non-state actors is with a purpose to influence the adversary's behaviour. It is in consonance with Clausewitz thoughts on the war that has transcended centuries and remain relevant to the practitioners of defence and diplomacy. According to him, "it is an act of force to compel our enemy to do our will."[16] He argues that there is no logical limit to the application of force as opposing sides will take reciprocal actions which would lead to extreme actions.

Rupert Smith, a retired British General Officer and author of the book 'The Utility of Force: The Art of War in the Modern World', disagrees with Clausewitz. He asserts that "we are living in a world of confrontations and conflicts rather than one of war and peace; one in which the clear categories of security and defence—the basic purposes for which force is used—have merged."[17] He goes on to argue that a paradigm shift in war has occurred. This paradigm shift is from interstate industrial wars to war amongst the people. War 'ends' are now focussed on societies and not states, with media platforms bringing the fighting into our living rooms. These conditions have made conflicts timeless with battle directed at not losing the troops while trying to achieve the military objective.

Additionally, emerging threats are exploiting new technologies and finding new uses for old technologies, with opposing sides frequently being non-state actors. He argues that war is no longer a massive event that achieves well defined political objectives. Despite his many cogent arguments, it is difficult to move past Smith's statement that war no longer exists, as many of Smith's assertions are based upon his restrictive interpretation of Clausewitz's definitions. Nonetheless, his assertion that "the militaries of our states must become the 'impressionists' of conflict; they must learn to use their 'Realist' tools—or in this case, the weapons and training of industrial war—to achieve a new outcome"[18] is relevant and has been the cornerstone of the NATO transformation. Smith downplays and artificially restricts the applicability of Clausewitz's theory of 'limited war' to 'war amongst the people'. He argues that instead of war, we now conduct operations which are the outcome of political confrontations. Yet, we look for a definitive military victory to resolve a political problem, rather than one that contributes and supports the resolution of the matter by other means.[19]

War and Politics

Clausewitz assertion that "war is not an independent phenomenon, but the continuation of politics by different means"[20] still resonate the security discourse. If politics is the womb in which war develops and the politics is defined as the actions or activities related to achieving and using power in a country or society, then the argument narrows down to what is power.

It has given rise to the concept of national power which is primarily a sum of natural and social resources available to a nation in the pursuit of national objectives. Niccolò Machiavelli and Hans Morgenthau considered power as an inherent goal for states to achieve as the use of power according to them dictate the global order. Most of the significant strategic plans are political, and it uses a combination of various elements of national power to draw out a campaign plan. Once the political elements enter the separate components of a campaign, it will radiate its influence and impact the outcome of warfare as "there can be no question of a purely military evaluation of a great strategic issue, nor of a purely military scheme to solve it."[21] According to this point of view, all strategic issues will be evaluated based on the relevance and ability of various elements of national power or comprehensive national power (CNP) – as ascribed by China – to compete, contest, deter and defeat. For many years, the acronym DIME (diplomatic, informational, military, and economic) has described the instruments of power.[22] However, there is a much wider array of agencies now involved in the development and implementation of national security policy. Multiple domains like diplomacy, economic, information, intelligence, legal, cultural, ecology, political and military are being used to promote national interests. A whole-of-government effort might better define the instruments of power. Influence has been the major contributor to exercising the will of the nation. Applications of elements of national power have led to the classification of terms such as soft power, hard power and smart power. Joseph Nye suggests that the most effective strategies in foreign policy today require a mix of hard and soft power resources or smart-power.[23]

According to western strategic thinking, the strategy has been about the end-way-means concept. The strategy looks at "how (way or concept) leadership will use the power (means or resources) available to the state to exercise control over sets of circumstances and geographic locations to achieve objectives (ends) that support state interests."[24] Hence, strategy provides direction for the coercive or persuasive use of power to achieve specified political objectives which by nature is proactive. It also attempts to control the environment as opposed to reacting to it. The strategy is not crisis management but a planned affair because crisis management happens in the absence of strategy or when the strategy fails. Thus, the premise of a theory of strategy is that strategy is proactive and anticipatory.

Beyond the western construct of war and use of power to attain the end state, the Chinese and Indian views of war are more related to realpolitik. In the 'Art of War', Sun Tzu treats the political, diplomatic, and logistical preparation for war, warfighting, and the handling of the aftermath of war as integral parts of the art of war. In this broad framework, the art of war is, in essence, the process of diplomacy; warfighting is only diplomacy by other means. In the Indian context, Chanakya in his book 'Arthshashtra' dated around 2nd century BCE lays out the political treatise and describes that the 'yuddha' or war are of three kinds. 1) Prakash-yuddha (or open fight) conduct is guided by the place, time, terrain and the opposition. 2) Kuta-yuddha (or concealed warfare) talked about the use of commonly recognised tactics on the battlefield. 3) Tusnim-yuddha (or silent-fighting) implied the use of secret agents for enticing enemy officers or killing them. It further adds that when the conqueror is superior in strength, and the season and terrain are favourable, he should resort to open warfare. If he is not superior to the enemy, and the terrain and season are unfavourable Kuta-yuddha is recommended.[25] It does highlight the use of asymmetry in warfare by use of rebellion within the enemy's rank and file or drawing him into a war by night.[26] According to Colonel PK Gautam, the 'Arthshashtra' is about just war, and Chanakya prophesied all types of war to which a kingdom should be prepared for.[27]

The threats, aspirations and balance of power have been the key ingredients which fuel competitions, rivalries and conflicts. Policies or strategies formulated to guide the contest is now being driven by technology. Technology has always impacted the tools and tactics of how we fight, and this trend is poised to continue. The use of the atom bomb brought the end to the deadly World War II, but it opened the world to a new form of war known as 'Cold War'. George Orwell, while coining the term "Cold War" in his 1945 article "You and the Atom" predicted that the nuclear arms is likely to put an end to large-scale wars but will prolong a "peace that is no peace".[28] The world is set to witness endless conflicts creating conditions for conflagrations and confrontations with cataclysmic catastrophe. Cold War era and the post-cold war era provide threads to this change in the character of warfare. Looking at the fatalities from 1989-2017 based on Uppsala Conflict Data Programme; it is evident that the casualties have increased post-2014. State-based violence still remains the primary cause of deaths as it comprises almost 80 per cent of the total fatalities while non-state violence remains 14 per cent. If the types of conflict are accessed, it shows that the one-sided and non-state violence gained currency after 1989.[29]

EXAMINING CONFLICTS DURING COLD WAR

Cold War and post-Cold War define the period existing post World War II. The engagement of major world powers like the US, the Soviet Union and the Russian and the Chinese in various conflict situations provide an insight into the changing character of warfare and how the entry of new actors, niche technologies and new domains have expanded the security discourse and their outcomes. The critical subject of enquiry, therefore, will remain as to how the conflict outcomes shaped by the contact warfare is being gradually replaced or complemented by non-contact methods to achieve massing of effects? How disruptions and denial are redefining the "kill chains" and how dynamic lethal and non-lethal responses are dictating the force calibrations?

Cold War: Breeding Ground for Doctrines

George Orwell directly referred to the Cold War as the ideological confrontation between the Soviet Union and the Western powers. It was a war that did not involve direct military confrontation. It was pursued primarily through political actions, economical aids, propagandas and proxy surrogate or satellite states. The technology was the main driver driving economic growth as well as fuelling arms race. It primarily drove ideology power contest in which both nation-states were paranoid not to lose the power status gained by them at the end of World War II. It helped in the creation of bipolar world order. Strategy and doctrines were evolved to dominate the strategic competition through the use of various elements of national power and resources.

1945-1950: Political Warfare and Competitive Strategy

The strain between the western Allies and the Soviet Union started surfacing even before World War II concluded. The quest to control Germany gave rise to the Morgenthau Plan (the JCS 1067)[30] in April 1945, which aimed at the removal of Germany's ability to wage war. The Soviet Union plan to start political parties on their side of Germany on 10 June 1945 took western allies by surprise and turned the discourse from de-Nazification to de-Communism of Germany. To stave off the financial crisis afflicting Britain and Germany due to the weakening of economies and strong communist challenges in France, Austria, and Italy compelled the US to restructure European recovery plan. On 05 June 1947, the Marshall Plan or the JCS 1779 replaced the Morgenthau Plan that aimed at making Germany stable, productive, and not doing the same thing that led to Hitler's rise. In May 1948, George Kennan, an American diplomat, proposed containment policy against Soviet expansion. He ascribed 'Political Warfare' as a tool and defined it as "the employment of all the means at a nation's command, short of war, to achieve its national objectives. Such operations are both overt and covert. They range from such overt actions as political alliances, economic measures ... and 'white' propaganda to such covert operations as clandestine support of 'friendly' foreign elements, 'black' psychological warfare and even encouragement of underground resistance in hostile states."[31] Thus, putting in motion an amalgam off multi-domain measures to contain the spread of Soviet influence beyond the Eastern Bloc countries. In 1947 the Soviet unveiled their Molotov Plan (officially the Economic Recovery Programme) to counter the US containment plan. It aimed to rebuild the countries in Europe and Asia that were aligned to the Soviet Union politically and economically. It was seen as one of the first elements of communist integration, as it removed trade barriers and set up institutions to coordinate the socialist economy on a continental level. Political Warfare got translated into containment strategy, thus laying the foundation of competitive strategy. The competitive strategy led to the practising of dominance battles and favoured the use of developmental economics to divide the world along ideological grounds.

The creation of the World Bank, International Monetary Fund (IMF) as part of the Bretton Woods monetary system[32] was to create surrogate and client state. Economic gratification enmeshed into the intelligence operation was used for regime control. However, both superpowers looked at the technology for the panacea. Revolutionising the military space was given more importance than the economic space. The US Air Force created special "Pilotless Aircraft Branch" in 1946, taking note of US General Henry "Hap" Arnold declaration that he had made at the end of World War II, "the next war will be fought by aeroplanes with no men in them at all".[33] By 1950 the 'Firebees' drones were developed by Ryan Aeronautical Company.[34] In the meantime, the 1949 nuclear explosion carried out by the Soviet Union compelled the western powers to look at the cost of atomic misadventure and search for new thresholds of war.

1951-1975: Deterrence and New Space Domain

Korean Conflict – 1950 to 1953

The rivalry between the superpowers led to wars in foreign countries, as was displayed during the Korean War in 1950 that lasted for three years. Similar to Germany, Korea was divided along 38th parallel with North Korea (aligned with the People's Republic of China and Russia) and South Korea (aligned with the US). The Korean War brought to fore the capitalist and communist rivalry with the Soviet Union and China on one side and Western Allies on the other. Truman doctrine laid the ground rule for a limited war under a nuclear overhang. However, the restraint posed by the atomic nations (the US and the Soviet Union) on both sides ensured that the conflict ended in a stalemate. The debate on the need for 'victory or winning' emerged on the menu of the planners and new contest scenarios developed.

Cuban Missile Crisis – 1962

In October 1962 Cuban Missile Crisis locked the leaders of the US and the Soviet Union in a tense 13-day political and military standoff over the installation of nuclear-armed Soviet missiles on Cuba, just 90 miles from US shores. The crisis almost brought the world to the brink of destruction but had far-reaching ramifications. It established the coercive diplomacy as a tool to crisis resolution. The dangers of nuclear fallout led to the refining of the doctrine of deterrence as a means of conflict management. The overarching lesson of this strategy was aimed at shaping the thinking of the potential aggressor. It assessed the actions that would raise the costs and risks of an attack and primarily followed two approaches – deterrence by denial or by punishment.[35] The deterrence either direct (own) or extended (with allies) looked at using the threat of military response and use of non-military threats like economic sanctions, diplomatic exclusion, or information operations.[36] Thus, deterrence was seen as "dissuasion by means of threat".[37] In real-world situations, the US often combines threats and inducements depending on the status of the state. However, while dealing with peer rival as was seen during the Cuban crisis, some form of reassurance is almost always part of any successful dissuasion strategy.

Technology Travails: Space, Nuclear, Missiles, Drones and Internet

The Soviet Union launched Sputnik 1 on 04 October 1957 using inter-continental ballistic missile (ICBM). It stirred the American response to start the Explorer 1 on 31 March 1958. The first manned mission by Russian

Lt. Yuri Gagarin in Vostok 1 on 12 April 1961 was followed by American crewed mission on 20 February 1962. The manned and unmanned mission to outer space gained prominence by 1969. By 01 November 1968, the ICBM design was completed, and by 1973 it was fielded[38] giving rise to the militarisation of space and the nuclear arms race.

The famed 1960 Soviet shoot-down of an American U-2 spy plane propelled new technological contest. The Soviet engineers drew blueprints of satellite killers based on the emerging threat from spy satellites, particularly the American Satellite Interceptor, or SAINT project, developed at the end of the 1950s and publicly disclosed in 1960.[39] The incident also prompted the US to develop long-range surveillance drone 'Lightning Bugs' which flew pre-programmed routes. The aim was to enhance the credibility of operations without risking lives,[40] and by 1964 these drones were fielded against "denied area" across cold war battlefield in Cuba, North Korea and China. The 1962 Cuban missile crisis also triggered the need for networking the geographically displaced nuclear assets within the US. The ARPANET, a pioneering network for sharing digital resources among geographically separated computers, was conceptualised. In 1968 BBN Technologies built the first routers to make the ARPANET operational, and its initial demonstration in 1969 led to the birth of the Internet, whose world-changing consequences unfold daily today.

Space and the nuclear arms race spurred treaties like Outer Space Treaty 1967, Seabed Arms Control Treaty 1971, Anti-Ballistic Missile Treaty 1972 and Strategic Arms Limitation Talks (SALT 1) 1972. All the treaties intended to deny access of weapons of mass destruction (WMD) to the other technologically inferior countries. An exclusive club came into existence to control resources and proliferation of technology.

Space and under-sea exploration unlocked the communication and television boom, making information more accessible. Space emerged as a new domain which was militarised by the superpowers to gain access over their overseas bases. Integration of technological space provided by Alan Turing computational framework set the world of computers abuzz. By 1975, programmers like Bill Gates and Paul Allen founded a start-up company called Microsoft to get "a computer on every desktop and in every home" while Steve Jobs and Steve Wozniak found Apple Computer Company. It laid the foundation of the information age.

1975-1990: War by Other Means and Emergence of New Actors

The US twenty years of misadventure (1955 to 1975) in Vietnam, Laos and Cambodia and Russian invasion in Afghanistan in 1979 pitted the superpowers against the armed militia. Soviet support to Viet Cong resulted in American pull-out amidst adverse televised public opinion at home affecting the military psyche of the nation. American-Pakistani support to Taliban militia ended the Soviet occupation of Afghanistan and paved the way for the establishment of Taliban government in Kabul. The defeat of superpowers to the armed militia in guerrilla warfare provided strategists fodder for countering strong nations by proxies. It strengthened the narrative among nations to use proxy war as a tool to engage and bleed countries. Pakistan used the Taliban and terrorists employed during the Soviet occupation of Afghanistan as strategic assets and redirected them to India to wage a proxy war. The operation was with the intent to bleed India through a thousand cuts. The doctrines of irregular warfare, proxy warfare, information warfare and asymmetric warfare started gaining grounds. It was during the same time the concept of Fourth Generation warfare (4GW) was introduced into American military thinking through an article in the Marine Corps Gazette published in 1989. According to it, 4GW aimed at using highly disaggregated forces (guerrillas, terrorists, and the like) managed by non-state actors to undermine conventional forces.[41] The 4GW talked about widely dispersed and largely undefined nonlinear battlefronts that blurred the distinction between 'civilian' and 'military'. The 4GW model of warfare introduced a new class of international force—the non-state actors. It surmised that the state-to-state conflict would decline while conflicts between state-based armies and non-state actors will increase.[42] However, the theory did not take into account the possibility of the non-state actors themselves challenging the nation-state existence.

The 4GW gave birth to the generational model of warfare discourse. US Marine Lieutenant Colonel Stanton Coerr contended that "Fifth Generation Warfare (5GW) is what happens when the world's disaffected direct their desperation fastened with the idea of opportunism rather than purely ideological and the battlefield looks at targeting people and the political will.[43] For the fifth-generation fighters' weapon of choice is a political stalemate as these fighters win by not losing, while we lose by not winning."[44]

The loss to inferior and irregular forced the super-powers to review their strategy and military preparedness. They again looked at the technology for the answers. Soviet termed their technological development as the Military Technological Revolution (MTR) while the US called it the Revolution in Military Affairs (RMA). The Cold War period witnessed a dramatic expansion of state-funded science and technology research with government and military patronage. The prime focus was on national security—the space rush to mount surveillance to remain ahead in the strategic awareness game fuelled the arms race. The electronics and information and communications technologies led the charge. The multitude of surveillance devices came into existence – from tiny portable to space-based spy satellites scanned, spotted and geo-referenced potential targets. It germinated the concept of Strategic Defence Initiative (SDI), commonly called the Star Wars programme. However, the US Defence Advanced Research Projects Agency (DARPA) driven development of network systems like Global Positioning System (GPS) added to the intelligence, positional and precision warfare. The deployment of military technology for civilian use helped the multi-national corporates (MNC) in streamlining their challenges of supply chain management (SCM), thus boosting their productivity. Hence, monetising of the military technology for civil use laid the foundation of civil-military collaborations. It gave impetus to the development of dual-use technologies, and MNCs emerged as new actors in the business of security.

Increase in Violence

The fallout of the arms race was ominous. The report, 'Soviet Military Power 1985' declassified by the Pentagon showed that the Soviet Union was spending almost 15-17% of Gross National Product (GNP) by 1983 on weapon development and procurement. Despite 1981 oil glut that triggered the strain in the economy, the arms race continued unabated. It prompted the Office of Net Assessment under Andrew Marshal to forecast the collapse of the Soviet Union. The collapse of the Berlin Wall in 1989 set the Soviet implosion into motion. The role of geo-economics in shaping the world order was championed as the model of new warfare by political scientists. For the first time, the non-contact method led to the capitulation of a leading power. The 'end state' defined by economics was triggered by mass-scale protests, initially across the Soviet Union and soon it engulfed the communist nations around the world including the pro-democracy movement in China's Tiananmen Square. Phenomena of protests and social engineering to change the regime thus found its place in the lists of waging non-contact wars.

The Cold War managed to prove that the international system is anarchic; the possibility of war is always present. The spectrum of conflict was defined, and small wars, proxy wars and the new non-contact warfare filled the space between stable peace and nuclear wars (refer Figure 1.1). For almost half a century, the world lived within the shadow of the threat of a 'Third World War' with a nuclear overhang and learnt to use non-contact methods to succeed in a contest or conflict. The period also witnessed the miniaturisation of gadgets through semiconductor and technology integration. New cellular communication platforms that allowed communication on the go, revolutionised the information age through embedded technologies.

Figure 1.1: Spectrum of Conflict

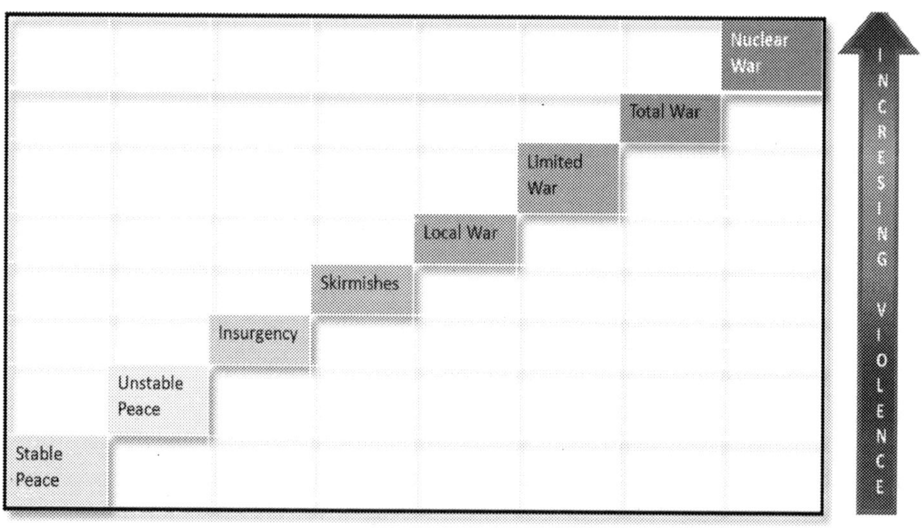

EXAMINING POST-COLD WAR CONFLICTS

1991 – Collapse of Soviet Union, Gulf War I and 6th Generation Warfare (6GW)

The Collapse of the Soviet Union: Protest Dynamics as Realistic Alternatives
According to Henry Kissinger in his book 'Diplomacy', "the Cold War

had begun at a time when America was expecting an era of peace. And the Cold War ended at a moment when America was girding itself for a new era of protracted conflict. The Soviet empire collapsed even more suddenly than it had erupted beyond its borders."[45] 1991 set into motion a new world order that was accompanied by chaos, collapse and catastrophe. The opening of the Iron Curtain in the Soviet Union saw the entry of CNN as the first non-Soviet broadcaster in Moscow. The winds of democratic waves within the Soviet empire was set-off by the elections for the new Congress of People's Deputies. Uncensored debates witnessed by the people on their TV where the Communist leadership was being questioned and held accountable fuelled the protest across the communist world. In Poland, the Communist government toppled, and the chain reaction for the dissolution of the Soviet Union was set by the Baltic States. The power of protest that engulfed the world gave fodder for future discourse to social scientists like Gene Sharp to probe into other alternatives of regime change. In his book 'There Are Realistic Alternatives' he lists out 198 methods in which the people and economic actions can be leveraged to generate pressure on the politico-military combine. According to him, the sole purpose of leveraging the people is to paralyse the governance structure. The unveiling of internet and digital technologies in 1991 boosted the capacity of influencing people through a targeted information campaign. The collapse of the Soviet Union reaffirmed the idea that war can be won without weapons or blood-bath.

Gulf War I - 1991: Emergence of 6GW

The turn of events in the Soviet Union kept the US focused on handling the impending catastrophe. At the same time, the epicentre of conflict emerged in West Asia in the form of Iraq invasion into Kuwait on 02 August 1990. The failure of deterrence caused by the US ambassador's ambiguous statements to Saddam Hussein that the US had no official view on his territorial disputes with Kuwait emboldened Saddam to precipitate Kuwait invasion.[46] Throughout the 1980s, Pentagon merely looked at the Iranian contingency and turned a blind eye to Saddam Hussein's arsenal acquisition for which he was investing close to 35 per cent of the GNP.[47] The US by 1990 was more or less an undisputed leader in a unipolar world and was thus the architect of planning and execution of Operation Desert Storm (commonly known as the Gulf War I).

Operation Desert storm began with a six weeks air campaign from

16 January to 23 February 1991 in which the Coalition forces fielded approximately 2700 modern combat aircraft. They flew over 110,000 sorties of all types (combat, combat support, surveillance and battlefield logistics), averaging 2,560 sorties a day. Key targets included Iraqi main force units, air defences, command and control nodes, and critical infrastructure. The Iraqi Air Force, the sixth-largest in the world, collapsed by the end of the first week, without producing any tangible results for its country. When the ground phase of the war began on February 24, it lasted for only one hundred hours. The outcome could only be described as lopsided. Forty-two Iraqi divisions were rendered ineffective, including 3,700 tanks, 2,400 armoured vehicles and 2,600 artillery pieces. Approximately 20,000 to 30,000 Iraq soldiers were killed as compared to only 293 allied military personnel.

On the night 23/24 February when the ground offensive rolled out, the Defence Secretary Dick Cheney called for forty-eight-hour information blackout and "pool system was used in Gulf war not to facilitate news coverage but to control it."[48] The control was evident as Pentagon sanitised the reporting for war. When the war was over on 28 February 1991, the militaries around the world took note of the arrival of RMA. The networked war also demonstrated night fighting, guidance and precision capabilities of the Americans and laid the foundation of the networked world. The same year, in August 1991, World-Wide-Web was released for the public.[49] It accelerated the cyber-security aspects of anti-virus programming industry also. Technology and anti-technology platforms thus created were supposed to guide the information age. The number of technology companies came into existence in the US and western world to harness the new wealth brought about by the globalisation of economic activities. The expensive star war programme was incubated in the absence of a real competitor. Cyber emerged as a new domain with ICT as its backbone.

Russian defence analyst General Slipchenko was quick to classify it as sixth-generation warfare or 6GW.[50] He pointed that there will be increased reliance on contactless methods brought about by synergy of kinetic and non-kinetic platforms based on stealth, long-range precision platforms aided with Command, Control, Computers, Communication, Information, Surveillance and Reconnaissance (C4ISR) systems. It became evident that the kinetic non-contact lethal means would effectively shape the battlefield, and non-kinetic means using C4ISR systems to be used to shape the opinion of the leaders and masses.

The Kosovo Conflict - 1999: Small War with Big Lessons

The Kosovo war was a short war lasting three months, but it fundamentally altered the international politics. The conflict pitted military forces led by Serbian President Slobodan Milosevic, infamous for his murderous actions in the Bosnian conflict, against ethnic Albanian Kosovar insurgents and NATO forces. Kosovo raised severe concerns about NATO's military capability as the war plan made by General Wesley Clark, NATO's top commander at the time, to bombard Belgrade was hindered and scuttled by some NATO nations. Inability to address the centre of gravity of the Serbian forces yielded negligible results in the first two months of aerial campaign. Once the US stepped in with a changed strategy to bombard deep into the Serbian territory, shifted the momentum. The Serbian TV headquarters in Belgrade was bombed on 23 April 1999, killing 16 civilians, was with twin purpose to silence Serbian propaganda and disable the Serbian military command and control apparatus that kept Milosevic in power. Seventy-eight days of bombing forced Serbian troops to withdraw, and NATO ground troops led by British and Norwegian Special Forces supported by Kosovo Albanian rebel group known as Kosovo Liberation Army (KLA) swiftly moved in. Asymmetric elements like KLA added to the swiftness of NATO ground operations. The US had conducted the majority of air campaign with suppression of Serbian air defences using precision-guided strikes.[51] Again, the standoff precision weapon systems coupled with the use of asymmetric forces helped in the early culmination of operations.

The Kosovo conflict altered the global security discourse. Firstly, it set the precedence of unilateralism in the international relations after World War II as the bombing did not gain the approval of the UNSC. Secondly, it brought nationalism in security discourse which was cultivated and curated carefully by Russia and China in shaping mass opinion. Russian President Yelstin ambivalence in supporting the Serbian ally against the NATO-led airstrike due to economic compulsion resulted in Yeltsin losing his job to Vladimir Putin. In other instance, the targeting of Chinese embassy frayed nerves of Chinese who sought a formal apology from the American. However, the event was used by the Chinese government to use nationalism as a strategy of stoking victimisation and anti-American sentiments which it has been using selectively. Thirdly, it also started a conversation about the war for humanitarian intervention – a policy that echoed during Libyan and Syrian intervention by the US and NATO forces in 2011 and 2014 respectively.

9/11- Asymmetric Warfare and Collusivity of State and Armed Non-State Actors

The start of the 21st century witnessed the new avatar of non-state actors. They declared the war against the most powerful country in the world by killing more than 3,025 people on 11 September 2001 by using the hijacked commercial airliners to selectively target the World Trade Centre, the Pentagon, and Somerset County, Pennsylvania. America was attacked on its soil this time not by an enemy state but by armed non-state actors. Enraged US President George W. Bush Jr declared the global war against terrorism[52] least realising that the US was to fight its creation.

The 9/11 attack for the first time showcased that the non-state actors used Taliban ruled Afghanistan as a proxy and sponsoring state for their activities. The 9/11 Commission Report reveals how a decade of conflict in Afghanistan, from 1979 to 1989, allowed Islamist extremists to establish an eco-system of financial and arms network and a rallying point to recruit jihadists world-wide.[53] Osama bin Laden kept the ecosystem afloat and renamed his jihadist outfit Mektab-al-Khidmat as Al-Qaeda. This new organisation had its components of intelligence, military, financial, political, media affairs and propaganda cells. It also had an Advisory Council (Shura) made up of Osama's inner circle.[54]

Osama had carefully studied American debacle during 1983 suicide bombing in Beirut that killed 241 US marines, the 1993 attack on the World Trade Centre and the 1993 dragging of American marine in the street of Mogadishu that led to the termination of US Operation Restore Hope under public backlash. He knew the US inability to deal with the adverse public sentiments. Hence, from the confines of the Tora Bora rugged mountains in Afghanistan, he went about plotting events like Manila air plot in 1994, attacking the Israeli city of Eilat using Saudi fighter jets and 9/11. Khalid Sheikh Mohammed, a graduate from the US-North Carolina Agricultural and Technical State University,[55] was the principal architect of plotting these attacks. Osama extensively used the information age tools like satellite links, internet and computers to communicate with his cells. However, he used information armour of dispersion, covertness and stealth to cover his digital trail. He also realised that if one cannot hide or disperse, then it is better to bury and dig deep. Thus, Tora Bora rugged mountains provided him with the right refuge.

The day before the attack, Osama's deputies discussed the "big attack" day – "Two sticks, a dash and a cake with a stick down,"[56] a code for "9-11". By using computers, satellite communications and the Internet, Al-Qaeda pre-deployed its strike team in America and Canada where each cell could coordinate its action with others, even up to the last minute. At about the same time, back in Afghanistan, the Taliban scattered their small number of jet fighters and tanks into the countryside.[57] Al Qaeda and the Taliban, in other words, were coordinating military operations on a global scale bringing the collusive relationship between state and non-state actor to the forefront.

Al-Qaeda won on September 11, because it had information dominance. It knew where its targets were and manoeuvred to attack them. The 9/11 for the first time brought the organisational strength of the networked yet dispersed armed non-state actors in dealing with networked yet monolithic, hierarchical and centrally controlled organisations like the armed forces. It also showed their innovation in turning the non-military equipment into a lethal platform. Intercepting Al-Qaeda communications was hard as they knew how to hide in the torrent of digital data flow. Off-the-shelf availability of communication technology acted as a force multiplier in connecting remote cells. 'Asymmetric warfare' methods—strategies and tactics that avoid strengths head-on was mastered by Al-Qaeda during its campaign against the Soviet military. It used the skill to target US sensitivity using suicide missions. Asymmetric warfare also inspired other terrorist organisations like ISIS during the battle of Mosul in 2014.

Global War on Terrorism: Test of Technology, Terrain and Tactics

'Operation Enduring Freedom' launched by the allied forces led by America against Taliban governed Afghanistan in October 2001 was part of the 'Global War on Terror'. The original mission of war in Afghanistan was to destroy Al-Qaeda and remove the Taliban from power without getting into nation-building. However, George W. Bush, despite initial hesitation, went about assigning the task of nation-building to the overstretched military.[58] This entailed use of an expeditionary force to rapidly impose American will on the hostile foreign soil and then maintaining a robust presence to ensure the change is lasting. The new strategy implied an inextricable linkage between the post-conflict peace and the conduct of the combat operations. Thus, it looked at managing the stability operations until the formation of an alternate government structure in Afghanistan.

As a testbed and demonstration platform for futuristic visions, Afghanistan was the worst-case scenario. It was an austere theatre farthest from the US with an active embargo against Afghanistan's two major neighbours: Iran and Pakistan. The enemy was fleeting and unconventional. The terrain was rugged in the extreme. The infrastructure was almost non-existent. And finally, the surrounding region was unstable and characterised by a variety of competing interests. It challenged the US Air Force, Navy, Marines Corps, and Special Operations Forces (SOF) as the command centre was located in Tampa, Florida. The fight started on 07 October 2001 with an air campaign, and by 06 December 2001 Taliban forces were defeated, and Mullah Omar and the senior Taliban leadership fled Kandahar. The key notables which emerged from the war in Afghanistan are:

- The campaign plan by Lieutenant General David Barno, commander of military operations in Afghanistan from 2003 to 2005, recognised the Afghan people as the "centre of gravity" and specifically underscored the importance of non-military factors to enable reconstruction and good governance. However, Washington embraced these points only in 2009, when the military had shifted to counter-insurgency operations.[59]
- Integration of surveillance and combat unmanned platforms in the form of Predator armed with Hellfire missile and designated MQ-11 while reducing the risk to own troops raised the temptations for tailored killings even if that meant violations of sovereign rights of Pakistan. It laid the precedence concerning the principles of distinction and proportionality in the use of force using unmanned combat aerial vehicle (UCAV) for all future campaigns.
- Use of citizen surveillance technologies introduced to assist in the governance to discriminate between law-abiding citizens and the insurgents or terrorist had its ramifications. The massive surveillance programme mounted by the US in Afghanistan digitally mapped over 2.5 million out of 30 million Afghans.[60]

China co-opted this idea for social security measures at home and used it for exporting surveillance equipment to the authoritarian regime for population control.

- The standoff, lethal weapons like GBU-43/B bomb also known as Mother of all Bomb (MOAB)[61] have been useful in breaking the Taliban and Al-Qaeda command and control network tunnel complex in Afghanistan's eastern province of Nangarhar. Its smaller predecessor, the BLU-82, was used several times against the Taliban in late 2001, including during the battle of Tora Bora.[62] However, the demonstration of such weapon systems was also used as part of strategic messaging by the US to nations like Iran and North Korea regarding the US ability to strike their nuclear stockpile sites.
- The challenges of controlling operations in Afghanistan from CENTCOM HQ at Tampa, Florida, made the American realise the emphasis it has to give to the C4ISR mechanism for Gulf War II.

Gulf War II: Decisive Battle Elusive Conquest- Recalibrating Strategy

Removal of Saddam Hussein remained an unfinished agenda after the Gulf War I for the US administration. Sixty per cent of Iraq was declared as no flying zone for Iraqi aeroplanes, and helicopters and the US forces were engaged in a frustrating low-grade, undeclared war. When President George W. Bush Jr. took over the Presidency in January 2001, Iraq became his priority. A 'forward-leaning' strategy replaced Clinton's 'reflexive pullback' strategy. This implied activation of the credible trigger to initiate the Iraq invasion through a concerted Information Operations (IO).[63] Intelligence operatives were assigned the task to collect the proof of sanction violations and locations of WMD, and special forces on the ground were assigned to undertake destabilisation operations within Iraq. Bush took on himself to nurture the new narrative to garner international support which, according to Bob Woodward, was a "chronicle of continual dilemmas since the president was pursuing two simultaneous policies. He was planning for war, and he was conducting diplomacy aiming to avoid war."[64] Based on the political and military objectives, the Bush administration pushed the agenda of Iraqi Freedom. He labelled Iraq as the "Axis of Evil;"[65] got the security resolution passed in UN on 08 October

2002 holding Iraq in "material breach" of previous UN resolutions and set 17 March 2003 deadline for Iraqi compliance. On 09 March the first propaganda campaign kick-started. Almost 31,800,000 leaflets were dropped, and about 158 leaflet missions were flown.[66] Besides this, 306 hours of radio broadcast and 304 hours of TV broadcast was done.[67] 116 C4ISR targets which included ten media facilities, were engaged as part of information warfare physical attack.

On 19 March 2003, the special operations were launched once Saddam Hussein failed to comply with the ultimatum to leave Iraq. On 20 March, the decapacitation attack followed the ground offensive. For the first the time the space aspects were being coordinated by Combined Forces Air Component Commander (CFACC) who was designated, Space Coordinator. One of the tasks was to identify Time Sensitive Targets (TST) based on its fleeting nature and the sensitivity of the targets. Three types of targets were defined as TSTs: Leadership, WMD and Terrorists. A total of 156 TSTs were engaged. The dynamic targets were prosecuted using re-roled airborne aircraft. A total of 19,948 Guided Munitions including 802 Tomahawk Land Attack Missile (TLAM) and 562 Hellfire besides scores of smart munitions with Laser Guided Bombs (LGB) were used. Only 9251 unguided munitions were used.[68] Patriot Anti-Missile systems were fielded to protect the allied forces against Iraqi Scud missile attack, which effectively neutralised the first attack on 20 March 2003. Coalition forces launched the massive air campaign on 21 March with over 1700 air sorties and firing of 504 TLAM cruise missiles. Under absolute air supremacy, the ground forces swiftly reached Baghdad by 05 April 2003, and by 09 April the regime at Baghdad fell and major military operations ended by 14 April 2003.[69]

The technology aided the accomplishments of military operations, but it failed to leverage the people-centric stability operations. The key lessons that emerged:

- It is easy to gain a military victory as freedom of use of violence and means are at the disposal of the forces. However, more people-centric stability operations require restraint and hence need a different approach.
- IO, which emerged as the backbone for military operations had to be orchestrated by multiple stakeholders. For instance, intelligence and destabilisation operations by the special forces,

politician and diplomats were dealing with the building of international consensus, and even the military operations commenced with propaganda. Effective IO was feasible due to coordination that existed between the CIA's Special Activities Division and CENTCOM level.

- Unprecedented situational awareness formed the pivot for the launch of operations. Extensive catalogue of sensor systems, fusion and analysis facilities, dissemination systems, and competing operational concepts posed tremendous challenges.[70] Although the bandwidth deployed was almost 42 times more than Gulf War I (refer Figure 1.2) but was still less when it came to information sharing as the Battle Damage Assessment (BDA) centres operated from Tampa, Florida.

Figure 1.2: Bandwidth Requirement

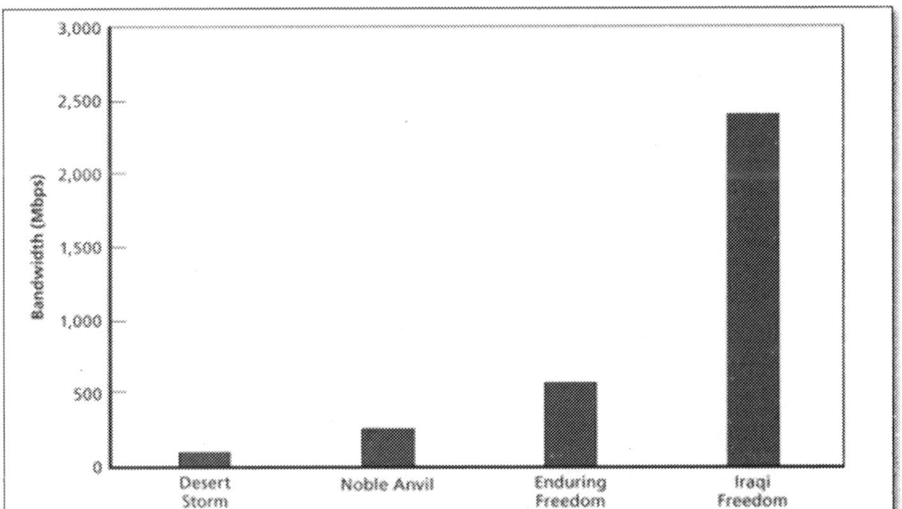

Source: RAND Report, 'Operation IRAQI FREEDOM: Decisive War, Elusive Peace,' p. 282.

- The proliferation of unmanned systems for surveillance and post-strike damage assistance aided by precision-guided systems also added to the effect-based operations. More than 12 types of UAVs were used – at a strategic level Global Hawk, with an operating range of 22,000 km was used. In contrast, Predator was used at the operational level with the task of locating WMD sites, SCUD-like missiles and hunt the high-value enemy personnel. Hunter, Pointer and Shadow were used at divisional and below level.

Silver Fox and Raven were used at battalion level and were equipped with chemical detection sensors.[71]

- The massing of effects was possible due to adaptive execution based on the critical intelligence provided by the Special Operations Force. It helped in urban warfare and while dealing with the Saddam Fedayeen.[72]
- Influence operation was incorporated to win the population and silence any misinformation campaign post-conflict. Wider access to the operational details was provided to about 2200 media reporters and 660 pooled/embedded media persons from newspaper and electronic media.[73] Operation Iraqi Freedom enabled the use of non-contact methods in shaping the global and local narrative.

The 2001 US Quadrennial Defence Review had listed IO to be developed as a core capability to meet new threats. Operation Iraqi Freedom enabled the mainstreaming of IO in military operations. IO was used to effectively control the information environment comprising of enemy forces, the Iraqi population and the Iraqi military. It usually relied on non-lethal means of influence, such as deception and psychological operations. Electronic warfare, computer network operations, and physical destruction were all used to deny or disrupt the Iraqi communication systems and flow of information. It brought about the integration of intelligence operatives, special forces and surveillance systems and was orchestrated across multiple domains to destabilise Saddam regime and force its capitulation. Once the objective was not realised then as part of the second phase, lethal kinetic operations were launched. The capture of Saddam fulfilled the military phase. The stability operations again reinforced the point that the population remains its the centre of gravity and if not addressed well will result in the protracted insurgency. A fact that has been worrying the US military planners.

RUSSIAN ROULETTE: GEORGIA, CRIMEA AND SYRIA

Russian Strategic Thoughts

The evolution of Russia's foreign policy in the mid-1990s was the by-product of Primakov doctrine. Evgenii Primakov, who in 1996 became the Minister of Foreign Affairs and Prime Minister in 1998, asserted for the restoration of Russia's great power status by restoring Russia's presence in regions where Moscow had been active. The 1999 Kosovo War altered the mood of Kremlin as it saw the war as infringement in its area of influence.

Russian defence analysts like Major General Vladimir Slipchenko spoke of "no-contact warfare" as the optimal form for 6GW necessitating major military reforms based on niche technology shaping information space[74] and a multi-domain approach to target military, economic and political system.[75] General Makhmut Gareev though endorsing the pursuit of non-contact capabilities underlined the need for contact warfare options also citing the outcome of urban warfare in Lebanon in 2006. He argued that coming decades would see a shift towards reliance upon indirect and asymmetric means to accomplish limited political ends through the use of information warfare and the RMA.[76]

Major General Alexander Vladimirov pointed out that there is a blurring of the boundary between war and peace and the emergence of the transitional state of insecurity hinged on fear and chaos. He predicted an eternal war which will question the existence rather than territory. War will aim to exert influence across multiple domains rather than destroy or annihilate as the strategy is no longer destruction. Hence, the direct use of military means, according to him, is not the most critical method. Instead, the strategy becomes the use of means for indirect action where the goal is to create organised chaos. The objectives seek to influence politicians, the military and the population directly. It aims to create internal collapse by influencing the opponent's national elite and undertake a proactive cultural war through various mass media and agents of influence, a war in depth using special forces and commercial irregular forces. He sees a contactless war continuing with varying degrees of intensity and on several concurrent lines of operation which will use remote means of warfare that reduce direct engagement. However, Special Forces and subversive units will operate in-depth in enemy territory.[77] Thus, according to him, the war will no longer involve purely military units but will see political synergy in dealing with the crisis or conflict. Wars waged within an opponent's territory will use subversive and diversionary operations that can complement remote attacks from land, the air, the seas and from space when the strategic and operational conditions are favourable. He forecasted a sharp increase in precision weapons, an increase in non-lethal means and unmanned military craft that can be autonomous and armed.

Operational and strategic mobility enhances the performance of weapon systems and platforms. He talks about a limited armed phase in future operations as the wars will be preceded by actions against nation's civil society, political leadership and population reinforced by information warfare and psychological warfare with reliance on diversionary operations.[78] This new form of warfare is endless and requires continuous preparation for war with varying intensity and centres of gravity to influence the operating environment to gain favourable strategic position.[79] The society is the target of psychological warfare, information warfare and agents of influence to weaken, destabilise and isolate it. Once the situation is favourable, then remote and specialist weapons from all dimensions and Special Forces along with asymmetric forces, carry out coordinated strikes. It aims to use combinations of kinetic and non-kinetic means to neutralise or incapacitate important political leadership, vital societal infrastructure, and military infrastructure across the operational area.[80] Soviet and Russian military theorists have a common tradition of belief in operations in depth[81] where science and technology influence the success of the war.[82]

The 1989 event remains embedded in the consciousness of Russian security analyst. It not only seeks coordination of Russian national, regional and international resources to provide synergistic effects but also looks at amalgamating civil resources with military capabilities to initiate surprising changes to influence Russian goals, means, methods and risks. In his February 2013 article General Gerasimov, clearly articulated that the rules of war have changed in terms of the scale of the casualties and destruction and "the catastrophic social, economic, and political consequences."[83] There is an increase in the role of non-military means to achieve political and strategic goals, and, in many cases, they have exceeded the power of force of weapons in their effectiveness. The distinct focus of the Russian military modernisation looks at 'non-contact warfare' instead of a close-range force on force engagements.

War of intervention at Kosovo and Iraq in 2003 by the US and NATO allies and series of colour revolutions in the former Soviet republics of Ukraine, Georgia, and Kyrgyzstan in 2003-2005 created moments of anxiousness in Russia. Putin saw new pro-west government in power in Ukraine and Georgia as threat. Russia alleged that the western powers have been "creating hotbeds of international instability and illegitimate use of force"[84] to implement their political, economic and military interest and not necessarily the interests of citizens or states where the revolutions occurred. The course of events across the last two decades shows dialectical development occurring sequentially and in parallel at the political, strategic, operational and tactical levels.[85] Leon Trotsky thought remains relevant in Russian context "where force is necessary, there it must be applied boldly, decisively and completely. But one must know the limitations of force; one must know when to blend force with a manoeuvre, a blow with an agreement."[86]

Georgian Conflict – 2008

In August 2008, Russia invaded Georgia after conflict broke out between the Georgian military and insurgents in the breakaway republic of South Ossetia. Russian tanks and soldiers drove out Georgian forces to the outskirts of the capital, Tbilisi. The use of force surprised the international community and demonstrated that Russia was willing to wield its influence in former Soviet space. The six-day war divided the EU more than it united. The EU mere commitment to Georgia's territorial integrity did not go down well with many Georgians. The EU report blamed Georgia of starting the war.[87] The lacklustre response of the Georgian government created a negative strategic, economic and psychological impact on Georgia and created internal divisiveness. These actions are in alignment with the concept of 6GW and Russian strategy of "reflexive control".[88] It also showed a breakthrough in the integration of cyber-warfare and other non-kinetic tools into a conventional strategy what some observers in the West have termed "hybrid warfare". The term has now become synonymous with Russian aggression. It signifies a style of warfare that combines the political, economic, social and kinetic means and methods in a kind of conflict that recognises no boundaries between the covert and overt war. Russia also concluded that it had lost the "media war," despite its successes on the ground.

Georgian experiment served as a wake-up call for Russia to reform and modernise its military and doctrine. "War does not stop; it occurs continuously in the form of preparation for war with varying intensity and centres of gravity."[89] The conflict was about militarily balancing against NATO, and definitely, Moscow is not keen for Tbilisi to join NATO.

Colour Revolution and Crimean Conflict – 2014

In the winter of 2011-2012, Russia witnessed its most massive protests since the 1990s. It coincided with Putin's decision to run for the presidency again. Putin and the state-controlled media portrayed these movements as western conspiracies, CIA plots funded by George Soros.[90] Putin campaign of "make Russia great again" was aimed at bolstering Russian image through a strategic combination of propaganda and geopolitical aggression. The term "Colour Revolution" was used by the Russian to describe the crisis in Ukraine. It was a ploy by the US and EU to wage a non-violent struggle to change power in Ukraine through outside manipulation of the population through protests in conjunction with political, economic, humanitarian and other non-military measures. It aimed at triggering destabilising revolutions as a means of serving the US and EU security interests at low cost and with negligible casualties. In 2013, Russian Chief of the General Staff, General Gerasimov while analysing the 'Arab Spring' and 'Colour Revolutions' pointed out that in 21st Century wars will increasingly use non-military methods and will target population and communications with the active deployment of special-operations forces.[91]

The November 2013 mass protests in Ukraine known as "Euromaidan" sparked when the Ukrainian government decided to suspend the signing of the agreement with the EU. Instead, it chose closer ties with Russia and the Eurasian Economic Union. The scope of the protests soon expanded, with calls for the resignation of President Viktor Yanukovych and his government. It called for joining EU and ended the rule of Viktor Yanukovych, who had the backing of Russia. It was a major breach of the zone of privileged control exercised by Russia around the Black Sea. By annexing Crimea in 2014, where its Black Sea Fleet is based, and by deploying forces in the southern Caucasus, Russia aims to maintain this region not merely as a strategic safeguard but also as an alternate transport corridor for its military and energy needs. It also provides strategic overreach to West Asia and the Mediterranean.

Shortly after Yanukovych was ousted, Russia employed a host of deception measures in Ukraine to conceal Russian involvement in the seizure of the territory. The political subversion with the insertion of intelligence agents and the Special Forces was attempted to dissuade outside intervention and exercised total control of public opinion. It created a safe sanctuaries for waging the proxy war. Russia engineered separatist violence as a convenient pretext to launch a full-scale multi-domain invasion to annex Ukraine's autonomous state of Crimea. On 27 February 2014, unmarked Russian Special Forces or the "little green men" who wore Russian military uniforms, without insignia, seized critical infrastructure in Crimea with almost no bloodshed. Ukrainian troops were contained through electronic eclipse – no electromagnetic communications including radio, cell-phone and television worked. It defeated Ukrainian UAVs and smart artillery munitions with electronic fuze. Command and control nodes identified by tracking electromagnetic emissions were targeted by Russian using their UCAV or massed artillery fire. Standoff massed area fires of artillery and the Multiple Launch Rocket System (MLRS) produced a new level of intensity in modern conventional combat. Data from the Ukraine conflict showed that artillery produced approximately 80 per cent of all casualties. The increased availability of overhead surveillance as overwatch systems, to suppress anti-tank defences.

Lawfare was used to legitimise the Russian annexation of Crimea. Crimean politicians dissolved the parliament and replaced their prime minister with a member of Crimea's Russian Unity party. In a swift referendum participated by 82 per cent of the Crimean population, 96 per cent favoured reuniting of Crimea with Russia, a claim made by Putin in his address to Duma on 18 March 2014.[92] Putin referred to Kosovo's unilateral separation from Serbia by the NATO countries as the precedence to justify Crimean independence legal. He quoted Article 2, Chapter 1 of the UN Charter, the UN International Court ruling, "general international law contains no prohibition on declarations of independence."[93]

Crimean War, thus, showcased the non-contact methods of a coordinated intelligence operation with the use of special forces to destabilise the country. It demonstrated eclipsing of the electromagnetic spectrum to subvert, disrupt and deny effective use of new-age systems of C4ISR. Lastly, it used lawfare, psychological warfare and opinion-shaping to project to the world the legal annexation of Crimea. A typical case of multi-domain operation.

Syrian Intervention – 2015

On 30 September 2015, the Russian turned the table on the US by entering into a war of intervention in Syria. On invitation from President Basharal-Assad, it undertook mission against the Syrian rebels. It was Russia's first military engagement outside the former Soviet Union since the Afghan War of the 1980s. The invitation from Assad gave credence to Russia to intervene as per international convention. It also embarked on influence operations to bring out the duplicitous role of the US in supporting Al-Qaeda in Syria. The charge was led in May 2016 by Russian minister Sergei Lavrov. Russia blocked any future UN resolution proposing military action against Assad,[94] thus cementing its relationship with Syria. Russian intervention in Syria was with three-fold intent: firstly, to come out of the international isolation caused due to Crimean annexation; secondly to provide stability in the North Caucasus region by stabilising the situation in West Asia and lastly to limit the American superpower status and restore Russian pride. Russia has used its presence in Syria to manipulate Shia-Sunni complexities. At the same time, it has leveraged its energy security and given a boost to its defence industry. It has been able to sell to Syria two diesel-electric submarines, fifty MiG-29 fighters and seventy-five IAK-30 training airplanes.[95] Unwilling to repeat the mistakes of the Soviet in Afghanistan and the US in Iraq, Russia is interested in a low-risk and low-budget operation that projects its image of transformed modern armed force capable of conducting complex operations. Russian aims to achieve decisive political outcomes with limited and overt use of stand-off devastating kinetic force.

Interference in the US Presidential Election – 2016

The events leading to the American Presidential election in 2016 brought to fore the extent of influence operation allegedly launched by Russia. On 03 July 2018, the Senate Select Committee on Intelligence initial investigation concluded that there were increased Russian activities in the run-up to the 2016 US presidential election with a motive to interfere in the US domestic politics. This escalation was made possible by cyber-espionage and cyber-driven covert influence operations, conducted as part of a broader "active measures" campaign that included overt messaging through Russian-controlled propaganda platforms. On examining the activities of the Internet Research Agency, the Committee uncovered an elaborate Russian effort to manipulate social media outlets to sow seeds of discordance and to interfere in the 2016 election and American society.

Russia has also identified information dominance as the essential elements in winning the non-contact warfare. It exploits ethnic-linguistic-class differences, corruption to compromise the leaders. Cyber-attacks are to compromise infrastructure and leaders. A RAND report estimates that Kremlin spent almost US$1.1 billion on mass media in 2014. These information operations were akin to the Soviet-era "active measures" with blends of attributed, affiliated, and non-attributed elements that exploited new realities of online and social media at an unprecedented scale. It sowed disinformation to erode trust in institutions. In one such instance, online social media falsified Ukrainian government documents to discredit the Ukrainian government's support to the war effort alleging that the Ukrainian government sold US-supplied weapons to Syria for personal gains.

Russian Roulette: Contouring Non-Contact Strategies

Russia is very sensitive to regime change as it fears that one day it may induce a Russian Spring. Georgia, Crimea, Ukraine and Syria are part of this jigsaw puzzle to create polycentric international order to balance the US across global levels. Russia has evolved a strategy of leveraging kinetics and non-kinetic means to persuade, dissuade and intimidate the adversary. Russian grand strategy seems to be aimed at controlling an uncontested sphere of influence in the post-Soviet region, assert Russian voice and influence globally and constrain the US.

The Russian roulette amidst Georgia-Crimea-Ukraine-Syria imbroglio and practising of political warfare for favourable regime change shows clear signs of non-contact warfare orchestration across multiple domains. Putin has repurposed the political warfare. The Kremlin's political warfare against democratic countries has evolved from overt to covert influence activities. It has been a classic case of probing weak spots, exploiting internal crises, and use force to change borders along its buffer region with NATO, an area which Russia calls its 'zone of privileged interest'. In the face of the challenge and mindful that the West is vastly more powerful, Russia has adopted a strategy of targeting the NATO unity and will to act, using a variety of non-contact means. To achieve its military strategy on the discount, Russia continues to rely on a hybrid or nonlinear, approach to modern warfare. It seeks to merge political warfare with conventional means. Along these lines, it plans to weaponize information, orchestrate third-party cyber-attacks against the government and civilian targets, carry out electronic warfare, and utilise local proxy volunteers as well as embed special forces and intelligence operative to undertake IO.

Grey zone operations by Moscow aims to create chaos within states it considers as part of its zone of privileged interest or against those whom it feels are likely to interfere or intervene in this zone. Plausible deniability to ambiguous attribution in cyberspace allows it to exploit it. Russia will also continue to exploit disagreements within NATO by sowing uncertainty and intervening in their political structures. Lawfare will be effectively used to contort international rules and norms to serve its will. It provides legitimacy and ethical status to the aggressive design as was seen during the referendum of Crimea.

Coercive deterrence and negotiated manipulation will form the tool kit to influence neighbours, create confusion amongst western allies and forge ties with countries inimical to western powers. Russia has also increased its exercises, training, and professionalism of its military forces in the region. The 2018 Exercise Vostok intended to display capabilities of Russian Forces in various contingencies and the foreign participation by countries like China and Mongolia indicated that it is not isolated

CHINESE CHECKERS: CONTEST BY OTHER MEANS

Managing Perceptions to Exploit Strategic Opportunity

China has hedged its growth to the sustained pursuit of strategic opportunity. The Chinese Communist Party (CPC) United Front Work Department (UFWD) is the agency responsible for coordinating influence operations both inside China and in foreign missions. Mao had claimed that military activity, party building and UFWD are China's three magic weapons. Xi'an incident of 12 December 1936, celebrated by China, is a testimony to the use of this magic weapon. During this period, CPC was facing the existential threat from the relentless Kuomintang campaign launched by Chiang Kai-shek. He regarded CPC as a bigger threat than the Japanese invasion. To prevent CPC decimation, Mao-Zhou combine subverted Kuomintang Nationalist Marshal Chang Hsueh-Liang, whose father was killed by the Japanese, along with General Yang Hucheng. At the behest of Mao, they detained their commander Chiang Kai-shek and forced him to sign a truce with communists.[96] So-called China's second reunification moment post-Xi'an incident gave time to the CPC to regroup itself while Kuomintang faced the brunt of the Sino-Japanese war.

At the end of World War II, Japanese which had captured Taiwan in 1895, returned the control of Taiwan to the Republic of China (ROC) led by Chiang Kai-shek. ROC began ruling China, including Taiwan. However, the celebration was short-lived for ROC as the CPC recommenced the civil war immediately after World War II taking Kuomintang and the Allies by surprise. It ultimately resulted in the creation of communist China in 1949. The government of ROC had to flee to Taiwan. However, ROC held China's seat on the UNSC and was recognised by many Western nations as the only Chinese government until 1971 when Mao sprung another surprise on ROC, keeping in league with his ability to exploit strategic opportunity and concept of 'active defence'.

The Ussuri River conflict of March 1969 set the stage for Sino-Soviet split and warming of Sino-US relations. Nixon-Kissinger combine intention was to defang the Soviets and use China as a counterweight. But it was Mao who wanted US assurance badly to prevent further fallout from Russian. He also recognised that improved relationship with the US advances China's "quest for additional recognition and entry into UN."[97] In 1971 China was successful in extracting the diplomatic recognition for itself while unseating ROC from the UN. Despite flexible interpretation, in April 1979, China persuaded the US to sign the Taiwan Relations Act[98] as the act diluted the cause of ROC, which had to contend with being called Taiwan. This act legally fulfilled China's national goal of mainstreaming into the international system.[99]

Tiananmen Crisis – 1989

The ideological drawdown in Moscow created waves in Tiananmen Square in April 1989. For seven week the protests kept China on the verge of social disobedience as it had spread like wildfire across almost 321 cities. The CPC ordered a military crackdown against the millions of youth protestors. The Peoples' Liberation Army (PLA) rushed in at least 30 divisions from five of the country's seven military regions amassing almost 250,000 troops to defeat the revolution. The suppression and oppression committed by the PLA were immortalised when the image of the defiant "Tank Man" in front of PLA tanks went viral on 05 June 1989. Crushing of the Tiananmen revolution of 1989 by employing PLA was Chinese way of demonstrating its assertiveness about addressing its core interests. It also showed the sensitiveness of Beijing towards social instability and demonstrated its resolve to employ the PLA if required.

Taiwan Crisis – 1995-96

Taiwan remained an unfinished agenda for CPC and reunification remains a core issue for it. CPC again displayed its assertiveness in 1995-96 over Taiwan issue precipitating the crisis. Enraged by the supply of 150 F-16 warplanes to Taiwan by the US in 1992, Beijing resorted to coercive diplomacy. Firstly, Jiang Zemin sent 'eight-point' proposal to Taiwan, urging them not to fight fellow brethren. Secondly, it accused the US of meddling with the internal affairs of China, as it considered Taiwan as its integral part, and intoned that it is open to use of force against any collaborator interfering in China's unification.[100] Between July 1995 and March 1996, China conducted four-phased military exercises and missile tests in the vicinity of the Taiwan Strait. With each phase, Beijing intensified the fire and manoeuvre exercise. In the last phase undertaken in March 1996, DF-15 missiles were directed approximately 50 miles away from Taiwan's busiest ports. Forty naval vessels, 260 aircraft, and an estimated 150,000 troops participated in the manoeuvres and included amphibious landing exercises and aerial bombing. The show of force was the message to deter Taiwan from pursuing independence from China and to the US to stop intervening. According to Andrew Scobell, "the crisis was a case of coercive diplomacy, the result of a civil-military consensus."[101]

Contest by Other Means

'Unrestricted Warfare', a book written by two PLA Senior Colonels, Qiao Liang and Wang Xiangsui, in February 1999 elaborates how the use of unconventional methods by the technologically inferior force will yield disproportionate success when directed against advance militaries. China has launched a concerted force modernisation programme based on mechanisation and informatisation. The central theme of the use of unconventional weapons and doctrines to overwhelm a superior adversary. It aims to improve its situational awareness through multi-arrayed guided surveillance systems in space and cyberspace. In contrast, improve its unmanned and stealth systems and long-range lethal precision systems for risk mitigation. US President Obama's 2011 "pivot to Asia" strategy has been seen by Chinese analysts as a containment strategy by the US to constrain China's rise. Hence, China has embarked on a large-scale influence operation led by its UFWD to secure Chinese political and business interests. It launched its Belt and Road Initiative (BRI) programme in 2013 to help it in creating coalitions and gain strategic space using its economic inducement programme. It aims to counter the American strategy of denial through asymmetric means and capability enhancement. Thus, China aims to use non-contact warfare as part of its war control strategy, an aspect that has been deliberated in Chapter 2.

CONTEXTUALISING NON-CONTACT WARFARE

Contextualising Theoretical and Existing Security Trends

A close look at the theoretical construct and security dynamics across the world points to a volatile, uncertain and complex international order where the major powers like the US, China and Russia are constantly engaged in a competitive slugfest. Alvin and Heidi Toffler in their book 'War and Anti-War' surmised that the war follows the wealth. Shifting security landscape from traditional to the non-traditional arena and new forms of warfare propagated by the security planners have changed the character of warfare. Show of restraint in the use of force has made the security experts look for alternate means of a contest. Non-military measures and to non-contact military measures are employed to influence the politico-military decision outcomes. It may use kinetic or non-kinetic and lethal or non-lethal means. Security trends discerned from the events evaluated so far show that the nations engaged in orchestrating competitive strategy are primarily looking at low-cost options with a focus on the use of smart power – a combination of soft and hard power. Balance of power game is still on display with dominance and counter-dominance strategy in play.

Dominance through Denial and Disruptions. According to American analysts, past two decades distracted Washington from its core military purpose, as it was embroiled in an endless war in Afghanistan and West Asia. The US 'National Defence Strategy 2018' (2018 NDS) is seen as a course correction to guide atrophying American and allied forces capability building that lost its edge to China and Russia. The US, by declaring China and Russia as its strategic competitor has unveiled the Cold War 2.0, however, with a difference. This time the US seeks to deal with multiple players besides China and Russia. It aims to deter 'rogue nations' of North Korea and Iran while defeating terrorist threats. The mantra of the US 2018 NDS is clear – 'compete, deter and win'.[102] It talks about the employment of both non-kinetic and kinetic means to coerce or subvert the competitive space across multiple domains through the use of economy and new technologies.[103] It seeks interagency synergy, use of lethal, agile force with advanced autonomous systems and resilient logistics capable of working in a multi-domain attack scenario. Denial and disruptions will be the critical components in a competitive strategy amongst competing powers, deterrence and asymmetric means will be the driving force between unequal powers.

Increase in Low-Cost State on State Conflict. The diverging interests among major powers, ongoing terrorist threats, the spread of lethal and disruptive technologies and continued frailty of impoverished nations will push for greater competition between nation-state. The world is likely to witness an increase in inter-state conflicts. The unilateralism by NATO may lead to a realignment of relationships between countries like Russia and China on the issues of common interests. A Syrian cauldron is a place where major powers are engaged in a low-cost game. The potential of conflict to spiral out is dependent on the outcomes and interests pursued by multiple actors in this conflict.

Balance of Influence. While the balance of power will remain relevant in the traditional security discourse, but it is the power of influence which pays dividend in the non-traditional security arena. For instance, the US has been trying hard to decouple itself from the protracted conflict in West Asia and Afghanistan, where it has sunk more than US$ 7 trillion. However, the competing powers and power elites within the region do not want the US to leave. The volatile situation in this area has set the stage where the US, despite its influencers, is finding difficult to manage the security situation. The game is being played both online and offline with people, society, ethnic groups besides multiple government agencies and officials.

'People' as the Centre of Gravity. The most important actors in the complex environment of conflict are human beings. Humans are known to make unpredictable choices and as such, are the most significant variable in any system. In the bipolar, industrial age of World War II, the numbers of human actors operating at the strategic level were far fewer than it is in today's multipolar, information age world. In present circumstances, any individual with Internet access can spur an immediate global crisis with the push of a button. The international community is navigating through this new array of non-traditional security threats. Chaos and complexities are affecting civil and military equally. The weaponization of social media platforms to script mass agitations and revolutions like the Arab Spring and Colour Revolution pose a challenge to the governance. Russian alleged interference in the US 2016 elections has opened up the debate on data sovereignty and opinion-shaping to manipulate the democratic processes.

The Weaponization of New Domains. The pace of RMA set-off by the Gulf Wars of 1991 and 2003 has given birth to a large array of niche technologies and new doctrines. The shift in operational doctrine from 'massing of forces' to 'massing of effects' with the quantum reduction in physical contact between adversarial forces has become the norm. The pace of technological reforms in the fields of stealth, stand-off precision targeting, networked ISR, autonomous systems have compelled major powers like the US, Russia and China to initiate defence reforms. The overlapping of traditional battlespace of land, seas, air and outer space with the non-battlespace like technological space (cyber and electromagnetic space), social spaces (politics, economics and culture) and cognitive space of human mind[104] has ensured that virtually every space is being contested with battlefield significance. Access to digital information has led to the erosion of borders and empowerment of individuals and non-state organisations, including terrorists, organised criminals, non-governmental organisations (NGOs), and MNCs. Simply said, today's environment is exponentially more complex, and the trend is likely to continue. Any domain with an ability to influence has the potential of being weaponised.

Non-Attribution, Diffused Situation and Invisible Warriors. The greater accessibility to instruments of war with a variety of actors like states, non-state and sub-state entities (terrorist groups, trans-criminal networks, insurgent forces, mercenaries, and MNCs) and motivated individuals will increase conflict across domains. Criminal syndicates, private security agencies, influencers and wolf warriors may get deployed even before the combat forces. A diffused situation is likely to emerge as the distinctions between combatants and non-combatants is likely to become less meaningful as the numbers of participants will expand especially to avoid attribution. The means of conflict will be diverse and will vary across a wider spectrum. It will range from non-contact capabilities, such as economic coercion, cyber-attacks, and IO, to use of advanced military capabilities comprising of stand-off, stealth, lethal weapon system across multiple domains, to include space and cyberspace.

Complex Governance and Military Response. The diversity will challenge the government to deal with the contingencies. Disruptions will test the government response mechanism as there will be an increasing emphasis by states and non-state groups, on disrupting critical infrastructures, societal cohesion, and government functions. Defeating enemy forces in the combat zone through traditional military means will be of lesser priority as long as other ways can help in achieving dominance. It is likely to blur the boundary between war and peace and will trigger endless competition and numerous contingencies. The desired outcome is intimately linked with the question of whether winning is important or victory. Non-contact non-lethal and lethal methods will play an essential role in guiding future conflicts. Adversaries are likely to rampantly use them to surprise, embroil, embattle and degrade the capabilities.

Defining Non-Contact Warfare

Non-contact warfare poses an important question – how do we know that we are at war? The competitive strategies and penetrative properties of new technologies available with the state and non-state groups, and even individuals are good enough to create a crisis. Remote and invisible means and methods can be used to perpetuate the crisis. The armed attack may not only define the 21st-century war but can be triggered by other hostile actions designed to weaken a state. Thus, the argument goes, a nation may be at war without knowing it and without knowing precisely who the enemy is. Strategic futurists have speculated that this may take the form of cyber-attacks from unidentified sources, engineered economic crises, engineered public protests or even pandemics. Major General Rajiv Narayanan, Distinguished Fellow at the USI of India, finds the world oscillating between 4GW (guerrilla warfare and use of non-state actors), 5GW (non-contact warfare enabled due to digitisation) and the 6GW (aimed at manipulating the space-time loop based on extreme electronic deception).[105]

Lieutenant General Devender Kumar, former Signal Officer-in-Chief of Indian Army, was the first to define the non-contact warfare in the Indian context. According to him, non-contact warfare "involves the application of all national capabilities in an integrated manner, while ensuring minimum physical contact of own forces, to conduct distant operations to achieve a quick, decisive victory by disrupting, denying and destroying the enemy's war-waging potential and his command and control systems through remote delivery of destructive kinetic energy and soft power by relentless information operations".[106] This definition is more military-centric and focuses on information warfare, missile warfare, remote warfare and robotics.

The world has been devising a strategy of winning without fighting. Hence, the hosts of terms like hybrid warfare, unrestricted warfare, asymmetric warfare, information warfare, political warfare have gained currency. The advent of Information and Communication Technologies (ICT) has connected people, economy and governments as never before. The economy has been the engine of growth and has been impacting people, government and military alike. Hence, it has been considered as a new pillar to the existing 'Government-Military-Population' Trinity model propounded by Clausewitz (refer Figure 1.3). Technology is fuelling not only growth but competition and conflict. According to a Chinese analyst, Gao Heng, the 'Battle of Depth' has been put in place with the marriage of Internet with communication platforms. The digital world, with its penetration into all aspect of governance, economy and society has for the first-time exposed people, political leadership, governance structures and economy to the forefront of the frontiers to be guarded. Unlike conventional warfare, where the focus was to defeat the military or the leader (refer Figure 1.3), the non-contact war aims at making the military irrelevant or enhance its capability by shaping the environment.

Figure 1.3: Conventional Warfare Vs Non-Contact Warfare

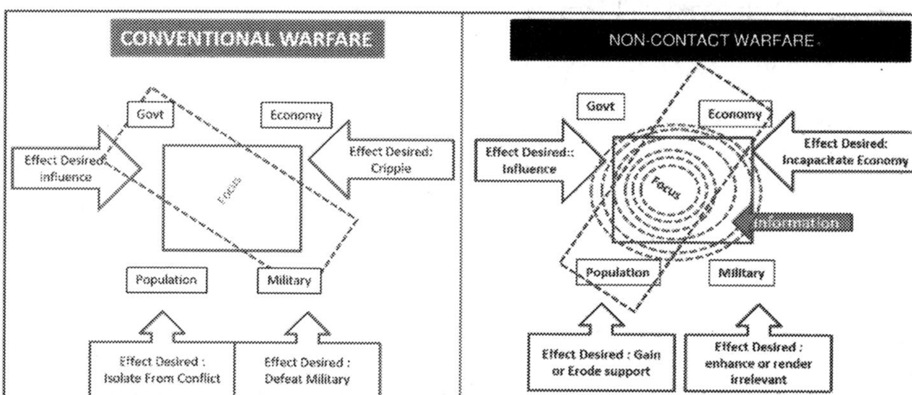

Source: Modification to Clausewitz model to include economy as the additional pillar. Refer to Lieutenant Colonel Brett W. Andersen, Clausewitz's Continued Relevance and Foundation for Educating Critical Thinking Skills, Strategy Research Project, United States Army War College, Carlisle, 22 March 2012, p.4, accessed from https://apps.dtic.mil/dtic/tr/fulltext/u2/a560832.pdf

Non-Contact warfare, therefore, can be broadly defined as the form of warfare in which states seeks to employ all elements of national power and the non-state groups attempt to leverage their influence across multiple domains to target adversary's population, sovereignty, governance structures and economy through non-military or military non-kinetic and kinetic means to intimidate, paralyse or denude its politico-military response capabilities and enable winning without fighting or fight with minimum use of physical contact of own forces. Non-contact warfare can be non-lethal or lethal and looks at addressing adversary's sensitivities and vulnerabilities in both non-military and military domains. The intent is to keep the response measured and calibrated along the desired escalation matrix to remain ahead in the game of domination. Winning along each ladder of escalation is essential to extract favourable outcomes.

Orchestrating Non-Contact Warfare

Non-contact warfare looks at employing denial, deceptions or disinformation to undermine the adversary's orientation within the OODA (Observe, Orient, Decide and Act) loop (refer Figure 1.4). Orientation is the first level where this game is played as it is the fulcrum of Boyd's OODA Loop.[107] It shapes the way we interact with the environment—hence the way we observe is, the way we decide, and act. Orientation shapes the character of the loops and affects future orientation as it targets the mind. The goal is to collapse adversary's system into confusion and disorder, causing it to over or under-react to activity that appears simultaneously menacing as well as ambiguous, chaotic, or misleading. The relentless IO is part of the narrative build-up, and use of force through standoff means is part of re-emphasising the narrative. Non-contact warfare finds its applicability across all domains and escalation matrix. The complexities involved in orchestrating it need a higher degree of situational awareness and inter-agency coordination.

Deterrence, disruption, denial, distortion, disempowerment, destabilization and destruction are some of the themes that will be used to coerce or compel the aggressor to abide by the international rule-based norms. Dominance strategy aims to remain ahead in across economic and technological realm with a balanced political disposition, capability-based security force, robust legislations. It leverages its presence within the adversaries' systems for generating better acceptability across the intended zone or area. For a competing power, the challenge will be to either accelerate economic and technological progress or create disruptions or impediments across domain by external or internal means to dislocate and divert efforts. Unequal powers will attempt to forge alliances to remain relevant or if isolated, will resort to asymmetrical methods to create decision dilemmas for the superior strength in exercising force. Conflict initiated by unequal power may be born out of its motivation, misperception or the ability to attack the vulnerabilities of the stronger state. The equations between dominant force, competing power and unequal power is based on the context in which the comparison is conducted. For instance, in the case of the US, Russia, and China are the competing powers while Iran, North Korea and non-state actors are unequal powers. However, when China applies the same in the Asian context, then Japan and India emerge as competing powers while ASEAN neighbours are the unequal powers. Beyond the rationality lies the "crazy state" like Taliban ruled Afghanistan which had extremely non-rational ideologies and leaders who are willing to use force to realise their goals. Application of non-contact warfare in various contingencies needs more in-depth analysis of instruments available to orchestrate such operations.

Figure 1.4: OODA Loop Domination in a Non-Contact Scenario

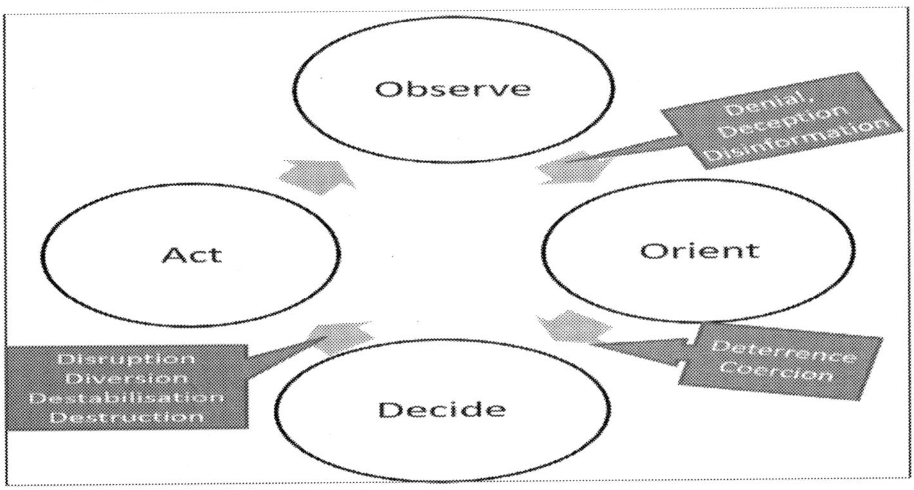

The security landscape changes are usually attributed to the transition from a bipolar to a multipolar world. Still, it may be more appropriate to associate today's challenges with the transition from the industrial to the information age to knowledge age. The strategy in the narrow sense may be about security, but in a broader understanding of political context, it refers to power and sovereign issues. The idea of traditional security has expanded and given way to non-traditional security calculus. Strategy as the bridge connecting the worlds of politics and military power is no more an exclusive idea. The threat and use of force to achieve political outcome may be guiding the strategy, but what is strategic is dictated by how and where the force is used. The domain in which the contest is being shaped will indicate what are the strategic assets in use. The contest can be strategized as controlled radiation of influences to securitise own vulnerabilities yet exploit the vulnerability of opponents. In this phenomenon, the opposing parties have structured response and measures and follow a rational escalation ladder up to the desired threshold level after which it may collapse precipitating disorder or lead to compromise thus building peace and reducing risks of escalation. At times, the contest can commence with a precipitous action with an intent to trigger radial disruptions and disorder across selected or multiple domains causing crisis leading to chaos. It can be a deliberate effort or maybe an outcome created due to black swan events like a pandemic, which has a larger effect on the masses and thus create complexities and uncertainties in the response mechanism. The chaos may either compel to adopt measures to contain its spread or may trigger catastrophic outcome leading to severe and irreversible damage to the parties in the contest.

Figure 1.5: Orchestration of Contest

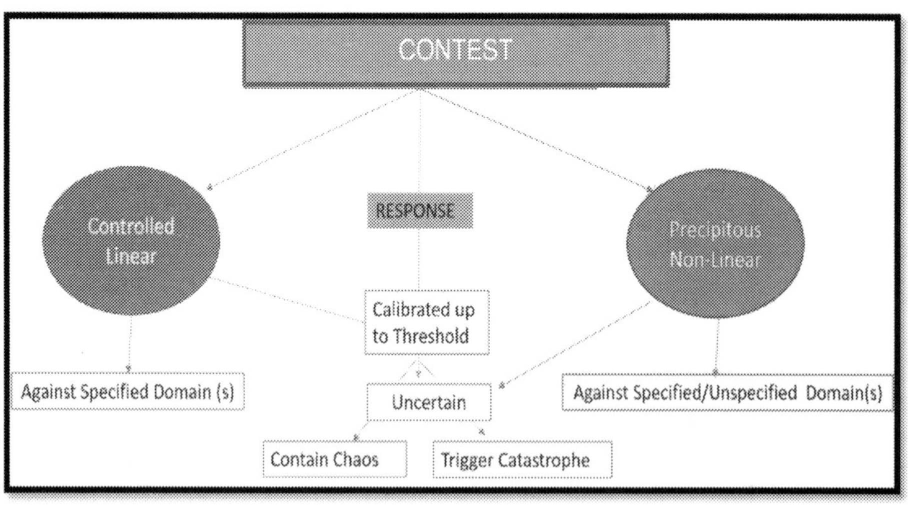

The distinction between contact warfare and non-contact warfare lies in the primary target source. While conventional warfare is primarily aimed at the government and military, the non-contact warfare looks at population and economy to influence the government and make military irrelevant. The victory in the case of conventional operations is sine-quo-non. However, in a non-contact warfare domain, the effect can be measured based on the goal envisaged to be achieved. The role of conventional forces as the nation last responder will be tested due to the fluidity of the operational environment. The breakdown of governance structure may create conditions where the probability of the armed forces being sucked into a subsidiary role may increase. Non-contact response and asymmetric response to conventional superiority are where non-contact warfare will play a pivotal role – typically, American 'Full Spectrum Dominance' and Chinese 'Unrestricted Warfare'. The scope of non-contact warfare thus covers a vast spectrum – from the threat of use of force to the disproportionate use of non-contact lethal force.

KEY ATTRIBUTES OF NON-CONTACT WARFARE

The orchestration of non-contact warfare requires specific attributes which need closer examination as they help us in understanding the way the game will be played and how some of the domains are likely to be contested. It will also help us in understanding the way the capability building and force structuring by the world major military powers are undertaken.

Kinetic and Non-Kinetic Prevalence

Non-Contact Warfare will be waged through a well-devised escalation matrix. Minimum physical contact of own forces is desired as the reliance is on the conduct of distant operations through use kinetic and non-kinetic means. The non-kinetic means look at the methods of shaping opinion or decision cycle of the OODA loop. Information war will play a lead role in shaping battlespace across the continuum of conflict. It will aim to deceive, deny, disrupt and disorientate the governance structures, thereby creating the crisis in decision making. Kinetic capabilities will be used to degrade, deter and restrict response actions or alter the OODA cycle. The US co-opted the capability of non-contact and autonomous means as part of its RMA in its fiscal year 2004–2009 Defence Planning Guidance. It directed the services to improve IO capabilities.[108] The penetration of digital space provided a platform to initiate battle deep inside adversary's territory or organisations. Stuxnet and series of protests across the world and the regime change brought about by Arab Spring during 2010-2011 brought the focus back to the non-kinetic methods of executing the warfare. However, Ukraine and Syrian conflict again established close coordination in executing operation using both kinetic and non-kinetic means.

Selection of Aim

All conflicts are born out of the dispute, and the resolution of dispute is dependent on the outcomes desired. Hence, the selection of aim, like any other principles of war, is also an essential facet of non-contact warfare. However, unlike military operations which are time-bound and exercised over limited space, the non-contact warfare arena is dictated by the players in the contest and their ability to shape the competitive space. Hence, while deciding the aim, outcomes for each domain and agencies employed for executing it will have to be defined on a visualised timeline.

Persistent Situational Awareness

Non-Contact Warfare is likely to manifest across multiple-domain and will test the governance structure of a country. The country which adapts agility in its governance and can communicate across various agencies seamlessly will be the one which emerges as the winner. The pre-requisite, therefore, is to keep the OODA loop clear of distortion and disruptions. The purity in observation is consequently important to have an unbiased orientation. It means that the state will have to invest in collection, collation, synthesising, interpreting, analysing and disseminating intelligence to the appropriate levels for implementation and execution across sectors identified by the governments as critical or important. Situational awareness about every single aspect which impinges on national security becomes important. Hence, related technologies will be important to ensure that the situational modelling and appropriate response options are integrated at all levels. Situational awareness is, therefore, necessary for self-preservation.

Unity of Planning and Monitoring

Non-contact warfare is waged across multiple domains. The group of experts should assess the themes of national interests and emerging threats. Before evolving a detailed plan, future scenarios and capability requirements need careful examination. It necessitates that all stakeholders are incorporated into the planning stage. The unity of planning ensures resource optimisation and ease of coordination as all stakeholders are aware of the challenges and opportunities across the escalation ladder. The dispersed execution by each stakeholder necessitates that the periodic monitoring and analysis is carried out at the highest level of execution. Situational awareness and flow of information are vital to ensure correct planning and execution.

Information Control

As already discussed, the first phase of non-contact warfare is likely to be played at the orientation stage. Hence, the situational overlays available will be essential to help in decision making. Information is the primary enabler to swing the influence. While the information available through situational awareness will dictate the decision making; the ability to pollute the adversary's data will be key to gain information ascendency. The contest of information operations by the opponents will be the order of the day. Methods likely to be employed will be by either denying the access to information, deceiving the opponent about the information content by planting ruses, remaining incognito or using other deception measures. In an era marked by competition and dominance, the potential adversaries endeavour to keep their competitive challenges below the combat threshold. Ability to launch relentless IO has increased with the digital explosion and cyber penetrative capability. The ability to influence is now effectively democratised since any individual or group can influence large numbers of others in a short time based on data and device accessibility. Finally, the incognito methods have resulted in influence generation without attribution. It has fundamentally challenged the traditional news media's function as gatekeepers and agenda setters.[109] Interactions within the information environment are rapidly evolving, and old models are becoming irrelevant faster than new ones can be developed. The result is the uncertainty that leaves one exposed to dangerous influences without proper defences. Controlling information purity is, therefore, an important facet for a responsive decision support system.

Non-Military Influencers

Agile Governance. The non-contact warfare aims at undermining the political and executive class through a sustained IO. The governance capacity can be denuded by the corrupt and compromised officials and institutions putting the people at risk, thus increasing societal cavity and instability. The non-military measures of disrupting the critical infrastructures are just a scenario to test the agility of governance. The population as the centre of gravity is subjected to enormous influence and is being encased in cultural and ethnic echo chambers to manipulate their behaviour to affect the Governance. Organised crime, influenced and funded through the trans-national cartel, can be used as a proxy to show the government in poor light. Protests dynamics may be used to disrupt the developmental works. An agile governance system needs to look at firewalling such attempts through effective use of law and order agencies.

Economic Influence and Outreach. Influence operations are being countered at multiple levels by various nation-states. As regards economic influence is concerned, it has been aided by globalisation which is more of an industrial action than a social one. Driven by technology such as the internet and network, it employs the management tools for the optimising the resources to unlock the value chain. It has been able to grid-lock the world financial institutions and businesses through digital system and data has emerged as the new wealth source. Guarding and monetising it has created vulnerabilities. According to the World Economic Forum 2019, data breaches and cyberattacks are the top global risks alongside natural disasters and climate change as increased connectivity in society and rapidly evolving threats are leaving the world open to damaging large-scale cyberattacks. While economic sanctions, embargoes, trade and tariff war are available as a means of deterrence to influence errant behaviour, economic ambushes and predatory measures are used to gain financial access and creation of client state through economic inducements.

Lawfare. Attrition may be at the heart of warfare, but, the collateral damage takes away credit from successful military operations due to legal issues surrounding the peace support operations. Lawfare, if handled well, can alter the outcome of the conflict. Russian-Georgia War of 2008 shows how the war findings of EU blamed Georgia for starting the war, thus giving higher moral ground to Russia. Similarly, the Crimean annexation of 2014 through a deftly planned referendum was the Russian method of legitimising the annexation. New technologies are testing old treaties like the 1967 Outer Space treaty. The provisions within the old treaty are found inadequate to deal with militarisation and weaponisation of space.

Similarly, the governance models and legislative mechanisms are too slow to evolve and understand the direction of technology development and its implications on humanity and world order. With mega-corporations leading the research and security discourse, the state institutions if not armed with legal provisions, will find it challenging to exercise oversight on norms development, regulation and law-making. Domains that lack natural borders such as outer space, the deep oceans, cyberspace and bio-spaces are likely to lead future conflicts due to lack of consensus to create international legal frameworks. It is so because nations with "first mover" advantage seek to defend their interest. The concept of securitisation by a security actor invoking the principle of necessity as a way of getting around legal or moral restraints is fraught with legislation tangles. It will test the relationships between partners and predators.

Deterrence

Deterrence is a broader multifaceted influence process which aims at strategic stability. The logic of deterrence has moved out of the nuclear realm to other areas like cyber and the use of lethal non-conventional weapons. Many older questions of rational choice theory and ethics apply with renewed force in a post-Cold War world. For security planners, it is crucial to work out deterrence mechanism if the threat of attack cannot be traced back to the country or entity that launched it. The mechanism to handle the actions of enemies that are highly unpredictable and decentralised is vital. It is equally important to examine whether the issue of threats of kinetic action to deter the primary actors who are brutal and threaten the lives of the people or undertake cyberattack compromising the lives of people, legitimate. Given the complexities of modern warfare, the challenges of the deterrent theory need revisit so that deterrence remains a relevant, reliable and realistic national security concept in the 21st century. According to the US Strategic Command, deterrence will remain a core concept of national security policy, "because the prevention of war is preferable to the waging of it."[110] The Pentagon advocates "Tailored Deterrence"[111] campaigns during peacetime to expand the range of deterrence. It aims to assimilate the behavioural pattern of the aggressors based on their identities, interests and decision-making process. Implementing deterrent and compelling strategies are among the most critical tasks of the national security decision-maker. With more nuclear-armed countries and proliferation of new non-nuclear-weapon technologies such as ballistic missile defence, anti-satellite weapons, precision-strike missile technology, and biotechnology systems is likely to create diverse deterrence relationships and will add to the tool kit of non-contact warfare. Deterrence has always been a tool of war avoidance and fits in well with the non-contact warfare concept.

Escalation Control

The US, Russia and China competition are dominated by the 'nation first' approach where each country is locked in a dominance and counter-dominance strategy. It entails the effective management of potential confrontations. The risks of escalation get complicated when more numbers of nations with WMD jump into the fray because the escalation options are dependent on the intelligence, about the capability and capacity of the adversary to absorb and retaliate against a given aggressive design. Escalation dominance is an area in which the nations want to operate. It is derived based on the cost-benefit analysis of each action and reaction.[112] Escalation deals mostly with the 'political' use of force, although the military uses of political techniques need considerations. "The potential, as well as the actual, uses of force in both peace and war can be for defence, denial, punishment, destruction, warning, bargaining, fining, deterrence, and so on".[113] The PLA has focused on escalation control, and in their writings, it tends to use the terms like "war control", "crisis management", "crisis control", "war situation control" and "war termination".[114]

In an era where the world strategic landscape is getting competitive due to dominance-disruption dialogue, the escalation models are no more going to be bilateral. A multi-dimensional approach necessitated due to non-contact warfare play a lead role in the escalation continuum. Events like 'black swan' and 'grey rhinos' will test the pitch of the escalation ladder.[115] COVID-19 pandemic, engulfing the world since the beginning of 2020, is one such instance which has tested the non-military escalation control levers. The world economy is in a tailspin and creating global destabilisation. The turn of events in June 2020 indicates drawing of battle lines in military sphere too as the aggressiveness by China grows in the South China Sea and along the high Himalayas.

Technology Trends and Non-Contact Warfare

The RMA debate of the 1990s highlighted that while technology provided the raw materials for military revolutions but entrepreneurship, and organisational adaptation based on doctrine development sparked these revolutions.[116] Based on the issues discussed earlier, the development trends of military-relevant technology can be organised into four categories. The first trend is about sensors, as these help us in building the situational awareness by gathering data of relevance for future operations. The second trend comprises the computer and communications systems as it processes the data into intelligence and the distribution and carrier mechanism over which the IO is going to ride. The third category looks at the critical enabling technologies that enhance the lethality and reach of the weapon platforms. The fourth trend relates to key disabling, disrupting and destructive technologies. It may range from nonlethal weapons of various kinds to biological pathogens and other weapons of mass destruction, to lasers and particle beams, to rail guns and long-range kinetic strike systems, to enabling technologies such as nanomaterials and additive printing or 3D manufacturing.

Sensors based situational awareness and use of IO applications using Internet of Things (IoT), Artificial Intelligence (AI), Robotics, autonomous systems are data intensive. They are primarily guided by the electromagnetic systems, computers and communications wedded together in the cyber domain. Data is the wealth-ware or the heart of the operational systems. Space-based satellites and deep-sea communication cables provide the platforms through which bulk of the traffic is flowing. However, all these systems are vulnerable to electronic warfare systems, software shortcomings or severe solar storms that happen once in a century.[117] The sensor technology enhancement with quantum computing will be something that will test the ability of military platform remaining incognito or invisible as it will be able to pick up a needle from the haystack. However, it opens up possibilities of using and repurposing the civilian use platforms for targeting as was done during the 9/11 attack.

Propulsion, guidance and control systems are the ones which are driving the weapon platform development that includes stand-off range, accuracy, speed and means of delivery. Other areas which have made the systems invisible or difficult to be detected are in the sphere of stealth, noise reduction and metamaterials,[118] nanomaterials[119] and "bespoke"[120] materials.

The disabling, disrupting and destructive technologies in the non-lethal arena aims to embed the devices to gain pervasive presence in the targeted country, thus creating difficulties for the people, businesses and the government. Additive technologies reduce the timeframe for fielding the weapon prototypes. Its availability with non-state actors has security ramifications for the governments. Deterrence concept ensures that the penchant for lethal systems will remain. WMD like the chemical, biological, radiological and nuclear (CBRN) remain part of the arsenal of major powers, and they have no intention to do away with them. The difficulty in verifying the global spread of coronavirus, COVID-19, has brought the discussion on secret development of biological agents into the centre stage.

The world is now witnessing the fourth industrial revolution. The battlefield implications in domains of sensors, autonomous systems guided by robotics, hypersonic systems, reusable rockets, biological pathogens and bespoke materials may develop faster than visualised. The new strategic capabilities across four technological categories mentioned above could incentivise risk-taking and aggressive behaviour. The participation of corporates in designing security solutions add to the complexity and increases the canvas for playing the non-contact warfare game. In other words, the strategic space for contesting non-contact warfare has increased due to new technologies and the participation by the non-state groups. Enhanced capacity to operate at speed puts security actors into a constant state of high alert and forces societies and state to live with uncertainty. Under these conditions, war by mistake – either through over-confidence in one's own ability to win or because of exaggerated threat perception – becomes more likely. It puts the polycentric world order in a period of strategic destabilisation. It aggravates the balance of power contest. Developing deterrence solutions to thwart attempts by adversaries, including non-state actors, will compound the technology- anti-technology game. With technology tripping the doctrinal cycles, it is essential to formulate doctrines for the emerging technologies so that it can lead to early adoption and absorption of technologies.

Conclusion: Non-Contact Warfare and China

Post-World War II, there was a deep belief that the advent of nuclear weapons had transformed the war so completely, that the idea of waging conventional warfare was questioned. However, the Korean conflict proved that the conflict is feasible within the nuclear threshold. A brief look into the conflicts of the last century has shown that amidst changing geo-political and geo-economic environment, a contest for dominance is being waged. While the US seeks to retain its dominance of the world order, the competing powers like Russia and China are looking to alter the status. The world riding the Toffler's 'Third Wave' and flattened by the technology and management tools remains divided by ideas and identities. The unipolar world emerging from the shadows of cold war created an operational environment in which the competing powers felt disenfranchised, marginalised and aggrieved in selective application of rule-based international order. Despite the quicksands of Iraq and Afghanistan that the US military finds itself into, the RMA created by a combination of new technologies and doctrines has been shaping the post-Cold War era conflicts. It has created global instability. However, the disruptions by asymmetric means have given hope to countries like China to contest the war by other means, and it has drawn its lessons from the 'Unrestricted Warfare'.

The key attributes of the non-contact warfare make it evident that the emerging warfare has been about the increasing use of non-military means and covert methods for applying appropriate force so that the conflict remains within the threshold and does not necessitate a military response. It is more targeted at the adversary's perceptions and society. Information confrontations are the new arena where the contest is happening while the hard power is being retained to win along the escalation ladder. Winning is now by disrupting the political, societal and economic harmony by using the military and non-military means across multiple domains – land, sea, air, space, CBRN and cyberspace.

Last four decades of relentless effort nuanced by China by hiding its intentions and biding its time has helped it to gallop the economic ladder. It has been able to bridge the dominance divide with the US. It has also compelled the US to recalibrate its national security strategy in 2018. Naming China has a strategic competitor to resurrect its atrophying capability; the US has forced China to review its defence strategy and hasten its reforms. China which has so far managed the period of strategic opportunity, finds itself entering the period of strategic friction. The outbreak of pandemic – COVID-19, which emanated from Wuhan in China and has engulfed the world has created strategic destabilisation across the globe. However, as the Chinese proverb goes, when the wind changes direction, there are some who build walls and those who build windmills. It is therefore imperative to assess how Chinese has adapted non-contact warfare in its security doctrine to exploit the strategic opportunity.

NOTES

1 Lanza, C.C. (1941, June). *The Fall of Belgium.* Retrieved January 29, 2020, *The Field Artillery Journal*, Vol. 31, No. 6, pp.346-351, https://sill-www.army.mil/firesbulletin/archives/1941/JUN_1941/JUN_1941_FULL_EDITION.pdf.

2 Singer, P.W., Like War: The Weaponization of Social Media, Daily Books, USA , 2018, pp.10-21

3 Durrant, Will and Ariel, The Lessons of History, Simon and Schuster Paperbacks, New York, 1996, p.79.

4 Tilly, Charles, " Reflections on the History of European State Making . ", In Charles Tilly, ed., *The Formation of National States in Western Europe,* Princeton, NJ : Princeton University Press, 1975, p.42.

5 Heuser, Beatrice, "The Evolution of Strategy", Cambridge University Press, 2010, p.11.

6 Jan Willem Honig, "The Idea of Total War from Clausewitz to Ludendorff", in The Pacific War as Total War: Proceedings of the 2011 International Forum on War History, National Institute for Defence Studies, Tokyo, 2012, p. 34.

7 Honig, Jan Willem Honig, 'Totalitarianism and Realism: Hans Morgenthau's German Years', *Security Studies*, 5, 2 (Winter 1995), pp. 283-313.

8 Wieviorka, M. (2010). *Social conflict.* Retrieved March 11, 2020, from Sociopedia.isa: http://www.sagepub.net/isa/resources/pdf/Social%20Conflict%20-%20English.pdf

9 Ibid.

10 Hedley Bull, The Anarchical Society: A Study of Order in World Politics (New York: Columbia University Press, 1977), p. 184.

11 Levy, Jack S. and William R. Thompson, The Arc of War: Origins, Escalation, and Transformation, University of Chicago Press, 2011, p.4.

12 Ibid.

13 Ibid.

14 Knapp, P. (1994). One World – Many Worlds: Contemporary Sociological Theory, Harper Collins College Div, Retrieved: March, 25, 2019 pp. 228–246.

15 Sharp, Gene, There are Realistic Alternatives, Albert Einstein Institution, Boston, USA, 2003, pp.2-3.

16 Ibid.

17 Rupert Smith, The Utility of Force: The Art of War in the Modern World, (New York City: Vintage, 2005) pp.3, 20, 410-15.

18 Ibid.

19 Ibid.

20 C. von Clausewitz, On War, M. Howard and P. Paret (eds and trans.), Princeton University Press, Princeton, 1976, p. 75.

21 US Army War College Guide, National Security Issues – Army War College. (2012). Retrieved July 3, 2020, from https://publications.armywarcollege.edu/pubs/2182.pdf.

22 Peter C. Phillips and Charles S. Corcoran, Harnessing America's Power: National Security Structure for the 21st Century, Joint Forces Quaterly, Issue 63, 4th quarter 2011, pp.38-40.

23 Joseph Nye, Soft Power: The Means to Success in World Politics, Public Affairs :New York, 2004.

24 Yarger, Harry R., Strategic Theory For The 21st Century: The Little Book On Big Strategy, Strategic Studies Institute, US Army War College, Carlisle, February 2006, accessed on 08 February 2019 from https://www.files.ethz.ch/isn/20753/Strategic%20Theory%20for%20the%2021st%20Century.pdf.

25 R.P. Kangle, The Kautilya Arthasastra, Part 3: A Study, Delhi, Motilal Banarsidass, 1986, pp.258-259.

26 Dikshitar, V.R. (1999). *War in Ancient India.* New Delhi: Genesis Publishing Pvt Ltd., p.87.

27 *Workshop on Kautilya: Creating Strategic Vocabulary.* (2013, April 09). Retrieved March 12, 2020, from IDSA: https://idsa.in/event/WorkshoponKautilyaCreatingStrategicVocabulary.

28 George Orwell, You and the Atom Bomb, *Tribune*, 19 October 1945, https://blog.oup.com/2015/10/george-orwell-cold-war/.

29 Uppsala Conflict Data Programme, Department of Peace and Conflict Research, Uppsala University, Accessed on 17 June 2020, https://ucdp.uu.se/downloads/charts/.

30 JCS 1067, U.S. Directive to General Eisenhower on Military Rule of Germany, 17 October, 1945, US Department of State Bulletin, Accessed on 14 December 2018, https://controhistoria.files.wordpress.com/2017/02/joint-chief-staff-1067.pdf.

31 269. Policy Planning Staff Memorandum, National Archives and Records Administration, RG 273, Office of Historian, Department of State, The US, Washington, May 4, 1948, Accessed online on 13 December 2018, https://history.state.gov/historicaldocuments/frus1945-50Intel/d269.

32 Post-war reconstruction and development in the Golden Age of Capitalism, accessed from https://www.un.org/development/desa/dpad/wp-content/uploads/sites/45/WESS_2017_ch2.pdf.

33 Spinetta, Lawrence. (10 November 2010), *The Rise of Unmanned Aircraft*, Published Online at: http://www.historynet.com/the-rise-of-unmanned-aircraft.htm#sthash.buUvlv45.dpuf, Accessed on 26 January 2015.

34 Ian G.R. Shaw (2014). *"The Rise of the Predator Empire: Tracing the History of U.S. Drones"*, *Understanding Empire,* https://understandingempire.wordpress.com/2-0-a-brief-history-of-u-s-drones/ retrieved on 25 January 2015.

35 Mazarr, Michael J., Understanding Deterrence, Perspective 2018, RAND Corporation. Accessed on 17 January 2018 from https://www.rand.org/pubs/perspectives/PE295.html.

36 Freedman, Lawrence, Deterrence, London: Polity Press, 2004, pp. 26–27, 36–40.

37 Paul Huth and Bruce Russett, "Deterrence Failure and Crisis Escalation," International Studies Quarterly, Vol. 32, No. 1, March 1988, pp. 30 & 42.

38 Ibid.

39 Anatoly Zak, The Hidden History of the Soviet Satellite-Killer, Popular Mechanics, Online, 01 November 2013 accessed from https://www.popularmechanics.com/space/satellites/a9620/the-hidden-history-of-the-soviet-satellite-killer-16108970/.

40 Ibid.

41 William S. Lind, Colonel Keith Nightengale (USA), Captain John F. Schmitt (USMC), Colonel Joseph W. Sutton (USA), and Lieutenant Colonel Gary I. Wilson (USMCR), The Changing Face of War: Into the Fourth Generation, Marine Corps Gazette, October 1989, Pages 22-26.

42 Ibid.

43 Lt. Col. Stanton Coerr, How To Win A 'Fifth-Generation' War, Marine Gazette accessed on 09 February 2019 from https://www.wired.com/2009/01/how-to-win-a-fi/.
44 Ibid.
45 Kissinger, H. (1995). *Diplomacy.* New York: Simon & Schuster, p.1159.
46 Roger Cohen and Claudio Gatti, In the Eye of Storm- The Life of Norman Schwarzkopf, Natraj Publishers, New Delhi, 2004, pp.183-184.
47 Ibid.
48 Ibid, pp.269-270.
49 McPherson, Stephanie Sammartino, Tim Berners-Lee:Inventor of World Wide Web, Twenty-First Century Books, 2009.
50 Major-General Vladimir Slipchenko Views Possible US 'Non-Contact' War on Iraq", Vremya Novostei, October 5, 2002.
51 Cameron Abadi, The Small War That Wasn't: Why the Kosovo conflict still matters today, Foreign Policy Online, 22 January 2019, https://www.scribd.com/article/397549617/The-Small-War-That-Wasn-t.
52 President George W. Bush, public radio address, 2030, 11 September 2001, Capitol, Washington, DC. Transcript from http:/www.whitehouse.gov/ews/eleases/001/9/0010911-16.html, accessed 15 July 2003.
53 Ibid, pp. 52-56.
54 Ibid.
55 9/11 Commission Report submitted by the National Commission on Terrorists Attacks Upon the US under Public Law 107-306, 27 November 2002, pp.145-150, accessed on 22 January 2019 from https://govinfo.library.unt.edu/911/report/911Report_Ch2.pdf.
56 The Mastermind – CBS News. https://www.cbsnews.com/news/the-mastermind/
57 Berkowitz, Bruce, The New Face Of War, The Free Press, New York, pp.27-30.
58 On candidate George W. Bush's opposition to nation-building, see his remarks in the second presidential de- bate, October 11, 2000, accessed 24 January 2019, http://www.debates.org/?page=october-11-2000-debate-transcript.
59 Ambassador Ronald E. Neumann, Washington Goes to War, in 'Our Latest Longest War', Ed. Colonel Aaron B. O'Connell, The University of Chicago Press Chicago, 2017, pp.78-82.
60 Biometrics in Afghanistan: The eyes have it- *Biometric data and the Afghan war, 07* July 2012 accessed on 24 January 2019 from https://www.economist.com/asia/2012/07/07/the-eyes-have-it.
61 It is the most powerful bomb in America's non-nuclear inventory, weighing about 22,000 pounds and carrying an explosive yield of about 11 tons of TNT. With its blast area of nearly a mile in all directions, it was designed primarily as a weapon to clear concentrations of fairly soft defences. It works by creating blast overpressure rather than by direct explosive effect. It can only be used in relatively uncontested air space because it has to be dropped close to the target by a lumbering cargo plane, such as a C-130 or C-17.
62 The Mother of All Bombs: America Drops Its Most Powerful Non-Nuclear Bomb on Afghanistan, Economists, 14 April 2017, online edition accessed from https://www.economist.com/united-states/2017/04/14/america-drops-its-most-powerful-non-nuclear-bomb-on-afghanistan?zid=312&ah=da4ed4425e74339883d473adf5773841.

63 Pentagon lists electronic warfare, psychological operations, military deception, operations security, and computer network operations as the core activities of IO.
64 Ibid.
65 President Bush's first State of the Union address, delivered to Congress on 29 January 2002 night, accessed on 29 January 2019 from http://edition.cnn.com/2002/ALLPOLITICS/01/29/bush.speech.txt/.
66 Report by Lt Gen T. Michael Moseley, USAF Commander, Operation IRAQI FREEDOM, by the Numbers Assessment and Analysis Division, 30 April 2003, accessed on 30 January 2019 from https://media.defense.gov/2013/Jun/13/2001329960/-1/-1/0/uscentaf_oif_report_30apr2003.pdf.
67 Ibid.
68 Ibid.
69 Ibid.
70 Ibid, pp. 269-270.
71 Ibid, pp. 263-267.
72 Fedayeen Saddam was founded by Saddam's son Uday in 1995 to protect them. The organisation operated outside legal structures and had a strength between 18,000 and 40,000 troops recruited from regions loyal to Saddam. https://www.globalsecurity.org/intell/world/iraq/fedayeen.htm.
73 Ibid, pp. 305-310.
74 "Major-General Vladimir Slipchenko Views Possible US 'Non-Contact' War on Iraq", Vremya Novostei, October 5, 2002.
75 Mattsson, Peter A., Russian Military Thinking – A New Generation of Warfare, Journal on Baltic Security, Volume 1, Issue 1, 2015.
76 Makhmut Gareev, If War Comes Tomorrow?: The Contours of Future Armed Conflict (Cass Series on Soviet Military Theory and Practice)" (Paperback), Routledge, 1998.
77 Vladimirov, Alexander, General Theory of War, 2013 via Baltic Defence College Journal on Baltic Security, 2015, p. 66.
78 Kipp, Jacob W, op.cit.
79 Vinogradov, V.A., Trends in the Conduct of Operations in a Major War, Military Thought No. 4, 2013.
80 Mattsson, Peter A., op.cit.
81 Ogarkov, SN, The Deep Operation Battle, ed. Frank Cass, The Evolution of Soviet Operational Art, 1927-1991, Vol. 2. London, 1995, pp. 199.
82 Savkin, V., The Basic Principles of Operational Art and Tactics. A Soviet View, University Press of the Pacific, Honolulu, 2002.
83 Mckew, M.K. (2017, May 9). *The Gerasimov Doctrine.* Retrieved June 17, 2020, from The Politico: https://www.politico.eu/article/new-battles-cyberwarfare-russia/.
84 Speech and Following Discussion at the Munich conference on Security Policy, 10 February 2007, Official Internet Resources of the President of Russia, accessed on 01 February 2019 from https://en.kremlin.ru/events/president/transcript/24034.
85 Peter A. Mattsson, Russian Military Thinking – A New Generation Of Warfare, Journal on Baltic Security Vol 1, Issue 1, 2015.
86 Galeotti, M. (2018, November 29). *(Mis)Understanding Russia's two 'hybrid wars'* . Retrieved from www.eurozine.com: https://www.eurozine.com/misunderstanding-russias-two-hybrid-wars/.
87 Valasek, Tomas., What Does The War In Georgia Mean For Eu Foreign Policy?, Centre for European Reform, Briefing Note, Accessed on 04 February 2019 from https://

www.cer.eu/sites/default/files/publications/attachments/pdf/2011/briefing_georgia_15aug08_tv-1136.pdf.

88 This concept aims at conveying to the adversary specially prepared information to incline him to voluntarily make the predetermined decision desired by the initiator of the action.

89 Russia's Border Marking in Georgia Is Part of Broader Strategy, Commentaries, The Jamestown Foundation, 24 July 2015, accessed on 03 February 2019 from https://jamestown.org/russias-border-marking-in-georgia-is-part-of-broader-strategy/.

90 Sophie Pinkham, How Annexing Crimea Allowed Putin to Claim He had made Russia Great Again, *The Guardian Online*, 22 March 2017, accessed on 03 February 2019 from https://www.theguardian.com/commentisfree/2017/mar/22/annexing-crimea-putin-make-russia-great-again.

91 General Valery Gerasimov, The Value of Science In Prediction accessed online from blog of Mark Galeotti on 12 December 2018, https://inmoscowsshadows.wordpress.com/2014/07/06/the-gerasimov-doctrine-and-russian-non-linear-war/.

92 Address by President of the Russian Federation, Vladimir Putin to State Duma Deputies, Federation Council members, heads of Russian regions and civil society representatives in the Kremlin, Moscow, 18 March 2014, accessed on 03 February 2019 http://en.kremlin.ru/events/president/news/20603.

93 Ibid.

94 Agata W³odkowska-Bagan, Syria in Russia's Foreign Policy in the 21st Century, Teka Kom. Politol. Stos. Miêdzynar. – OL PAN, 2017, 12/1, 27–40,

95 E. Barry, "As Nations Line Up Against Syrian Government, Russia Sides Firmly With", The New York Times, 27.01.2012, http://www.nytimes.com/2012/01/28/world/europe/russia-sidesfirmly-with-assad-government-in-syria.html?_r=0 [accessed: 14.08.2016].

96 Chinese Embassy in Australia, 2006. *China marks 70th anniversary of Xi'an Incident*. 13 December. Accessed December 01, 2019. http://au.chineseembassy.org/eng/xw/t283333.htm.

97 Central Intelligence Agency. 19 April 1971. "Intelligence Memoranda – Ping Pong Diplomacy." CIA Intelligence Report, Department of Intelligence, Washington DC. Accessed December 02, 2019. https://www.cia.gov/library/readingroom/docs/LOC-HAK-114-7-3-4.pdf.

98 Ibid, p.356.

99 Ibid, p.387.

100 Scobell, Andrew, China's Use of Military Force: Beyond the Great Wall and the Long March, Cambridge University Press, Year, 2003, pp.175-176.

101 Ibid.

102 Sharpening the American Military's Competitive Edge, Summary of 2018 National Defense Strategy of The United States of America, Department of Defense, United States of America, pp.1-2.

103 Ibid.

104 Qiao Liang and Wang Xiangsui, Unrestricted Warfare, Beijing: PLA Literature and Arts Publishing House, February 1999 pp.41-44, 205.

105 Maj Gen Rajiv Narayanan, Evolution of Warfare and Technology -1, Indian Defence Industries, 08 December 2018, accessed from https://indiandefenceindustries.in/evolution-of-warfare-1.

106 Kumar, Davinder, 'No Contact Warfare and the China Factor', Scholar Warrior, Spring 2014, Published by Centre for Land Warfare Studies, pp.76-78.

107 Robert Coram, Boyd The Fighter Pilot Who Changed the Art of War, Hachette Book Group, New York, 2002, and Col John Boyd presentation on Patterns of Conflict.

108 Nick Cook, Military Priorities and Future Warfare, Jane's Defence Weekly, September 11, 2002.

109 Rand Waltzman, "The Weaponization of the Information Environment," American Foreign Policy Council Defense Technology Program Brief, September 2015.

110 Kevin Chilton and Greg Weaver, Waging Deterrence in the Twenty-First Century Strategic Studies Quarterly, 2009 accessed from https://www.law.upenn.edu/live/files/1363-waging-deterrence-in-the-21st-century-chilton.

111 President George W. Bush's administration introduced the term tailored deterrence into U.S. national policy documents in 2006 with the release of the administration's second National Security Strategy and Quadrennial Defence Review. These documents represented a major shift in national security policy, as President Bush's 2002 NSS had downplayed the effectiveness of deterrence and advocated preventive war to remove threats from rogue states.

112 Kahn, Herman. On Escalation: Metaphors and Scenarios, Frederick A. Praeger: New York, 1965, p.30.

113 Ibid, pp.40-41.

114 Alison A. Kaufman, Daniel Harnett, Managing Conflict: Examining Recent PLA Writings on Escalation Control, CNA China Studies, February 2016, pp. iii, 10-11.

115 The 2007/9 Global Financial Crisis is well-described as a black swan event, a term coined by contrarian risk manager, Nassim Taleb, as a low probability but high impact event. Michele Wucker, in his book "The Gray Rhino: How to Recognise and Act on the Obvious Dangers We Ignore", St Martin Press, 2016 defines the grey rhino as the highly probable, high impact yet neglected threat, which when it charges, can cause severe damage. She includes in that category issues such as climate change, terrorism, financial stress and social unrest. Accessed from https://www.thestar.com.my/business/business-news/2017/07/22/from-black-swans-to-grey-rhinos/#fRIgTJ8KgpliAhIr.99.

116 O'Hanlon, M. (2018). *Forecasting Change in Military Technology 2020-2040*. Washington, D.C.: The Brookings Institution, p. 4.

117 Ibid, p.17.

118 Composite artificial materials assembled from various types of constituent elements like metals and Plastics.

119 Material with dimensions on the order of one-billionth of a metre.

120 Customised material with specific chemical and atomic structures and compositions.

2

Non-Contact Warfare and China's Security Doctrine

Renewing war conceptions is more important than weapon renewal.[1]

– Lieutenant General Liu Yazhou,
Deputy Political Commissar of the PLA Air Force

STRATEGIC MANOEUVRING

What Beijing Wants?

2012 was the period of strategic manoeuvres witnessed by the world. The shifting of world economic and strategic centre to Asia-Pacific prompted Obama's administration to put in place "Pivot to East Asia" regional strategy. It sought to expand American presence within the Asia-pacific by forging closer military, trade and people-to-people ties with Indo-Pacific states to leverage the world's new political and economic centre of gravity. Washington attempted to bolster US presence in the region by creating Trans-Pacific Partnership (TPP) which involved agreements with 12 Pacific Rim countries. Besides transforming tariffs and trade standards to generate an additional trade of US$225 billion for the world economy by 2015.[2] It also aimed to strengthen military ties through forming the Enhanced Defence Cooperation Agreement that was perceived by China as a "containment policy" directed against it.

While the US rebalancing strategy was taking shape, China was undergoing the power transition from Hu Jintao to Xi Jinping in November 2012. At the 18th National Congress, Communist Party of China (CPC) declared its aim of building a moderately prosperous society by 2020.[3] The goal hinged on economic and social development, and it recognised that China's prosperity depended on deepening of reforms and adoption of a sustainable economic growth model and ability to deal with the US.

The US was always seen by the Chinese with scepticism, especially after the Tiananmen pro-democracy unrest of 1989.[4] In 2013, the PLA National Defence University produced the Chinese film "Silent Contest" that portrayed the US as China's enemy. The film suggested that the US was trying to subvert China through five avenues: 1) undermining China politically, 2) engaging in cultural infiltration, 3) warfare in terms of ideas, 4) the training of fifth column agents and 5) the fostering of opposition forces within China.[5] The film's intended audiences were the domestic military and civilian constituencies. The movie contextualised the contest of China and the US in a non-contact arena.

In 2013 PLA's prestigious Academy of Military Science (AMS) released the "Science of Military Strategy" (SMS) a capstone doctrinal publication of the Chinese PLA. The publication categorically highlighted the hegemonistic design of the US and suggested the strategic adjustments to be made by China. According to it, the non-contact, and non-linear operations directed at the depth areas without attacking the enemy may get manifested more often. The time and space for people to adjust and adapt will be critical as physical strikes combined with psychological shocks will be used to magnify the effectiveness of deterrence. Compared with the traditional winning that believes in annihilating the enemy, the new war looks at paralysing the enemy.[6] The publication also set into motion the PLA reforms.

Over the past 40 years, and arguably since the founding of the People's Republic of China in 1949, its rulers appear to have had three strategic objectives: First and foremost, to preserve the power of the CPC. Secondly, to restore China to what the regime sees as its proper, historic status as the dominant power through economic and social development. Thirdly, to become a global player with power, prestige and influence at par with, and eventually superior to, that of the US for which they need to modernise the military. Hence, the core interest of China is to preserve the party and its ideology for which it requires a strong military to keep control on people and stave off outside influence which may be inimical in polluting the party ideology. People, propaganda, and PLA are the three pillars that the CPC seeks to control. Hence, China's governance structure aims to make the CPC all-powerful and looks at balancing the military influence within the party framework.

Reforms to Make CPC Powerful

Constitutionally the CPC is the supreme ruler. It commands state institutions, and the National People's Congress (NPC) and local People's Congresses are subject to CPC directives and control. CPC dominates the party system; as the eight so-called democratic parties that are officially recognised are subordinated to them. Though the constitution talks about the rule of law, the CPC remains above the law. It has been willing to engage in only what is officially referred to as "governing the country according to law." The priorities are clear for the Xi administration to ensure the supremacy of CPC.

The measure of reforms unleashed by Xi has resulted in consternation within the party circle, especially with the anti-corruption drive launched against almost 100,000 corrupt officials[7]. To extend Xi's grip of power, China's NPC passed a constitutional amendment in March 2018 abolishing the nation's presidential two-term limit,[8] thereby paving the way for President Xi Jinping to seek a third term once his second term finishes in 2022. Such a move has extended Xi's power, and he has been able to deal with anti-corruption drive more rigorously by enacting new investigative agency, National Supervisory Law and Commissions. According to Chinese media, the constitutional amendment allows "stability and consistency" in governance, which is a requirement for advancing reform. According to them, Xi is the right man to do so.

Tightening of CPC-PLA Linkages

In a period of perceived internal and external challenges faced by the CPC, the foremost priority for Xi after strengthening the CPC and his status was to tighten the CPC-PLA linkage as he felt that party control over PLA was atrophying. The PLA has always been a "Party's army," which must follow the CPC's instructions and defend its interests. The conscience of the past events plays significantly on the mind of Chinese planners. The issue surrounding refusal by local PLA units to use force against the student protesters during the 1989 Tiananmen crackdown remains at large.[9] With the revived concerns regarding lobbying by some PLA officers for transforming the PLA from the armed wing of the CPC into a "national army", which if true could represent a serious threat to Party's survival.[10] Chinese analysts have been critical of the 1991 Soviet military coup which they suggest was partially the result of the Soviet Communist Party's loosening grip over the military.[11]

In October 2013, at the third plenum of the 18th Party Congress, Xi Jinping declared his intention to overhaul the military's command structure, adjust the size and composition of the services and strengthen civil-military cooperation.[12] In his 2014 speech at Gutian, a site where CPC established the principle of Party control over the PLA in 1929, Xi targeted corrupt officials at the helm of affairs like Guo Boxiong and Xu Caihou, CMC vice-chairmen under Hu Jintao. He urged the PLA to develop officers both loyal to the Party and capable of "leading soldiers to fight and win battles."[13]

"Two Big Gaps", "Two Inabilities" and "Three Whether"

Improving the combat strength has become a significant focus for the PLA as it believes that there still exists the "Two Big Gaps" and "Two Inabilities" when it comes to comparison with advanced global peers. The article carried in a Chinese-origin, English-language reference published in 2016 pointed to the Chinese armed forces inability of waging modern warfare and lack of command skills for modern warfare amongst its officers.[14] The "Three Whether" is an assessment first seen in 2014 that questions the PLA's leadership loyalty to the party and competence to lead forces and emerge victoriously.[15] Hence, on 01 January 2016, the CMC issued a blueprint for the PLA reform. In November 2017 a new guideline was published by the CMC calling for total loyalty of the armed forces to Xi Jinping. Thus, by seeking total allegiance of the PLA, strengthening the leadership with disciplinary and discretionary powers, Xi is in an unenviable position to drive government reorganisation.

China's Defence Policies

The US force structuring has always affected China's defence policy. China's 2019 National Defence White Paper (NDWP) on 'National Defence Policy in New Era' is a direct reflection of China's concern over US 2018 National Defence Strategy (NDS). China has been closely following on the heel of the US economic manoeuvring and military capacity and capability development. Its continuous evolution of military strategy from "people's war" to "local war under high-technology conditions" to "informationized warfare" has been the outcome of its unceasing observation of the major wars in Iraq, Kosovo and Afghanistan and wars of intervention in Libya and Syria. The lethal effectiveness of information-enabled precision-strike weapons and highly mobile forces has forced PLA to review the application of its strategic concept of "active defence" in an information age. How has China adapted this non-contact warfare in developing its doctrinal construct is therefore essential. China has been publishing its white paper on defence for over last two decades, yet the defence policy seems shrouded in secrecy. Hence, demystifying it helps us to understand the reform trajectory, strategic behaviour pattern and more importantly, its intent.

Chinese Strategic Discourse Development

For Chinese, strategic thinking and related writings precede the generations of strategic concepts. PLA published a book on the subject titled 'Analysis of China's Strategic Culture' which explores Chinese strategic culture and contrasts it with western strategic culture. In the words of Lieutenant General Li Jijun, the former Vice President of the Chinese Academy of Military Sciences (AMS), "Culture is the root and foundation of strategy. .... Each country or nation's strategic culture cannot but bear the imprint of cultural traditions, which, in a subconscious and complex way, prescribes and defines strategy making." [16]

An analysis of classical Chinese texts and historical events by the western scholars' points to the fact that Chinese prefer realpolitik, the use of force or coercive diplomacy and a tendency to justify the use of force as purely defensive.[17] Classical texts like Sun Tzu's 'The Art of War', the most influential and widely read of China's ancient texts, emphasises the role of military force in international relations. According to it, "warfare is the greatest affair of the state". It is ambivalent about employing violence but feels coercion is better to bring about subjugation as Sun Tzu says "one who excels at employing the military subjugates other people's armies without engaging in the battle."[18] He further says, "No country has ever profited from protracted fighting."[19] He emphasises deception or stratagem and proffers strategic defence as the means for a materially inferior to defeat a superior enemy. Sun Tzu's 'The Art of War' and 'Methods of Sima' are some of the classics that resonate across the consciousness of Chinese planners as these handbooks tell how to fight a war- if war cannot be avoided. It is much against the US concept where strategy is seen as the use or threat of force, to achieve not just the goal of victory in the war but to achieve national strategic goals. The PLA strategy, while drawing their thoughts from the classics, seems more influenced by the Soviet military, which looks at strategy as a means to prevent wars through military means.[20]

The PLA writings have grasped the experiences and lessons of previous strategic practices like Fuller's "mechanised war" theory, Douhet's "air supremacy" theory, Germany's "blitzkrieg" theory, the Soviet Union's "great warfare" theory, etc. The term 'strategy' has been modified with time. In 1956 strategy was defined as, "the highest department of military academia, that studied leadership and progress of the armed struggle or ways to go to war."[21] The 1987 definition called it a, "guide for the overall situation of war".[22] It was further modified in 1999 to read as "planning and guidance of the overall situation of military struggle."[23] 2007 Second Military Encyclopaedia of China Military Strategy defined Chinese strategy in the new period based on the country's comprehensive strength. Guided by the idea of 'active defence' which forms the basis of winning local wars under informatised conditions. Military strategy, according to it, is about "planning and guiding the construction and use of armed forces in the overall situation of military struggle." 2011 PLA dictionary defined military strategy as the "set of fangzhen and stratagem that guides the comprehensive war effort".[24] The SMS 2013 further adds that military strategy is subservient to national strategy and the general situation of national development.[25] By the end 20th century, the term 'war' was dropped from the definition and replaced by 'struggle' to help justify subsequent military operation as a self-defence option. It aligns with the Chinese narrative of peaceful rise without alarming the world obsessed with war.

The strategic engagement by China is the product of the responsibilities and legitimacy it attaches based on the historical continuum of thought and the ingrained political culture preached by the CPC. The interrelationship between legitimacy, power, authority and struggle has been the guiding the strategy practised by Xi and his predecessors to fulfil state obligations to steer the country and its people. Contextualising challenges and the resilience of the Chinese state throughout its dynamic history is the recipe which is being fed by CPC as a rallying point. It builds the bogey of nationalism whether during the Taiwan Strait crisis or bombing of the Chinese embassy in Belgrade in 1999. Controlled nationalism helps CPC to cope with the external and internal challenges as it sees it as a glue which binds it against divisive agenda propagated by the west. For China, opinion-shaping and psychological conditioning is an important facet and party has used it effectively since its inception. Hence, CPC driven strategic discourse aims at internal stability and capability to deal with hegemons using non-contact methods till such time it attains the balance of power.

Component of China's Three-Tiered Strategy

According to SMS 2013, China has divided its strategic system into three levels – national strategy, military strategy and theatre operations. The national strategy is planning and guidance for the overall situation of China's national security strategy and the national development strategy. These focuses on supporting socialism with Chinese characteristics through consolidation of state power and social stability to achieve the goal of building a well-off society and enable the great rejuvenation of the Chinese nation. National strategy forms the basis for formulating military strategy.

Military strategy is the second level of the strategic system structure. China's expanding footprints across the globe has resulted in the expansion of its military missions too. The military strategy, therefore, focuses beyond its core task of 'winning local wars under the conditions of informatisation' as part of traditional security. It also handles various non-traditional security threats that may emanate beyond territorial jurisdiction in the ocean, space and network electromagnetic space.

The service or theatre strategy is the third level of strategic architecture and is subordinate to military strategy. The main tasks are to formulate unified guidance in force construction and deployment based on the strategic direction. Under the conditions of informatisation, military strategy and theatre strategy is required to focus on unified strategic objectives and plan for joint operations based on system-based combat capability. Planning and guidance for the use of overall forces are also closely connected with the overall situation of national security and development and thus have dual attributes.

China's Strategic Assessment

Washington sees China's growing economic and military ascendance as a policy of asserting power through an all-of-nation long-term strategy. It feels that the PLA's military modernisation programme is to counter the US Indo-Pacific strategy in the near-term and displacement of the US to achieve global pre-eminence in the future.[26] Pentagon aims to create an operational environment where it can outmanoeuvre its competitors and counter their coercion and subversion efforts. It intends using the concept of unpredictability by integrating the actions of US agencies in coordination with allies and partners.[27] The Sino-US rivalry looks at increasing the competitive space. The US intends to bring a series of combined actions by employing all national power to include Departments of State, Treasury, Justice, Energy, Homeland Security, Commerce, USAID, as well as the Intelligence Community, law enforcement, and others. It seeks to counteract Chinese coercive acts by identifying and addressing the vulnerabilities in the areas of economic, technology and information. It is working on long-term strategic competition with "seamless integration of multiple elements of national power—diplomacy, information, economics, finance, intelligence, law enforcement, and military."[28] The US strategic approach spells out the need for more lethal force, strong alliances, technological innovations, and the ability to achieve decisive military advantages.

The thrust of the US force modernisation shows its inclination to catch up on its capability building in the areas of the cyber, aerospace and maritime while retaining the credible deterrence capability in the nuclear domain. Arguably the most far-reaching change in the US 2018 NDS is its emphasis on conventional deterrence by denial, a fundamentally different approach to "all-domain dominance" model that the US military has grown used to in the post-Cold War era.[29] The US policies and strategies like the 2017 National Security Strategy, 2018 NDS, 2018 Nuclear Posture Review and 2019 Missile Defense Review have been the product of this US belief. The US 2018 NDS declaring China and Russia as the principal strategic competitor has provoked China to come out with an NDWP. On 24 July 2019 China released its NDWP called, 'China's National Defence in the New Era'. It blamed Washington's hegemonic unilateralism and power play in Asia-Pacific responsible for undermining the regional strategic balance and global security.[30] China feels that the increase in America defence expenditure for building additional capacity in nuclear, outer space, cyber and missile defence,[31] the Indo-Pacific Strategy and the deployment of the Terminal High Altitude Area Defence (THAAD) system in South Korea has added to the strategic instability. The US alliance partners like Japan and Australia policy recalibration has also compelled China to issue a stern warning to all the peripheral states involved in disputes with it over territorial issues to respect historical facts and seek a peaceful solution. China now feels that it is entering the period of strategic friction with the international community and, in particular, with nations on China's periphery.[32]

China being a strategic competitor to the US, finds itself engaged across all spectrum of war. The concept of deterrence, degradation and denial employed by the US against a nuclear power state like China calls for restrained retaliation to manage the competition and conflict escalation. To maintain the force credibility and superiority, it needs to preserve its economic and technological dominance to navigate the international power play. Chinese 2019 NDWP is an outcome of the continued pressure brought about by the US through trade and technology war, and no wonder China sees these powerplays as creating grounds for informationised warfare through non-contact methods.

The 2015 NDWP on China's Military Strategy ruled out world war in the immediate future. It reckoned that new threats from neo-interventionism, the international competition for the redistribution of power, rights and interests, terrorism and "Hotspot issues" may portend itself in small-scale wars, conflicts and crises. However, it did not factor the black swan event like the COVID-19 pandemic, which has caused global strategic destabilisation and has potential to marginalise China's growing influence. The 2019 NDWP establishes that socialism with Chinese characteristics has entered a new period where peace trends may be irreversible, but the world is not yet a tranquil place. While the 2015 NDWP had surmised that the world "faces both immediate and potential threats of local wars" the 2019 NDWP talks of "informationized warfare" and goes on to add that the "intelligent warfare" is in the horizon. China is overly worried about the US pursuit of military superiority through RMA and institutional innovations. With the task of mechanisation in the final lap, China feels that its military security may be confronted with risks from technology surprises and growing technological generation gap from Washington. China is thus looking for bridging the capability cavity through its identified millennium goals.

National and Military Strategic Goals for the Millennium

National Goals. The 13th Five-Year Plan (2016–2020) for China's Economic and Social Development has lauded the efforts made by CPC to steer the country through the 2008 financial crisis. China has emerged as an economic power due to improved economic structure and faster transformation of the growth model. China is now the world's second-largest economy.[33] Past two decades of the new millennium has given the strategic opportunity for China to grow. Xi during the 19th CPC Congress on 18 October 2017 laid out the strategic goals for the millennium for China. It aims to build a moderately prosperous society by 2025; and build a great modern socialist country that is prosperous, strong, democratic, culturally advanced and harmonious by 2050.[34,35]

Military Goals. The longer-term vision for military transformation finds its mention in 2019 NDWP on 'China's National Defence in the New Era'. These are:

- To generally achieve mechanisation by the year 2020 with significantly enhanced informationisation and greatly improved strategic capabilities.
- To comprehensively advance the modernisation of military theory, organisational structure, military personnel, and weaponry and equipment in step with the modernisation of the country and complete the modernisation of national defence and the military by 2035.
- To fully transform the people's armed forces into world-class forces by the mid-21st century.

PLA Missions and Strategic Tasks

In China, the publication of defence policy falls under the purview of the central leadership. For years, China did not have a formal national security strategy nor had an organisation dedicated to formulating one.[36] With the focus on making the ministries and bureaucracies accountable for successful implementation of the reforms, the 3rd Plenary Session of the 18th Central Committee in November 2013 established the National Security Commission. In 2015 China issued its NDWP on 'China's Military Strategy'. In April 2018 in the review meeting of the Commission, Xi proclaimed that the commission had solved many national security problems that "had long remained unsolved, and achieved tasks that had long remained undone."[37] It is a comprehensive body to coordinate Xi's broad vision for national security. While the details are more obscure, however, the Chinese analysts point that the wide-ranging national security laws passed since 2015 are part of deliberation by this body. The 2019 NDWP on 'China's National Defence in New Era' has been a step to bridge the policy gap between national defence aims and the military tasks (refer Table 2.1).

Table 2.1: China's National Defence Aim and Tasks of PLA

*National Defence Aim**	*Tasks of PLA***
• To deter and resist aggression	• To maintain strategic deterrence and carry out nuclear counterattack
• To safeguard national sovereignty, unity, territorial integrity and security; • To safeguard China's maritime rights and interests	• To deal with a wide range of military threats and emergencies to adequately safeguard the sovereignty and security of China's territorial land, air and sea
• To oppose and contain "Taiwan independence"	• To resolutely safeguard the unification of the motherland
• To safeguard national political security, people's security and social stability • To crackdown on proponents of separatist movements such as "Tibet independence" and "East Turkistan"	• To strengthen efforts in operations against infiltration, separatism and terrorism to maintain China's political security and social stability
• To safeguard China's security interests in outer space, cyberspace and electromagnetic space	• To safeguard China's security and interests in new domains
• To safeguard China's overseas interests	• To safeguard the overseas interests
• To support the sustainable development of the country	• To perform emergency rescue and disaster relief, rights and interest's protection, guard duties, and support for national economic and social development. • To participate in regional and international security cooperation and maintain regional and world peace

Sources: *The State Council Information Office of PRC.2019. "China's National Defense in the New Era." July. White Paper, Foreign Languages Press Co. Ltd, Beijing, China.
**The State Council Information Office of the People's Republic of China. 2015. "China's Military Strategy." May. Accessed April 09, 2018. http://eng.mod.gov.cn/Press/2015-05/26/content_4586805.htm.

China's national defence aims given in 2019 NDWP succeed tasks of PLA enunciated in 2015 NDWP thus plugging the strategic dissonance. The national defence aims and tasks are aligned with China's core interests.

The PLA has been nominated as the lead agency to work on doctrinal issues for all security contingencies, including protecting the overseas interests. The priority is clear- internal political stability and reunification of Taiwan remain the prime agenda. Domination of near and far seas to protect its maritime and overseas interests comes next. Sovereign issues remain essential to it – whether it is on the land, air or maritime border or in the niche field of data, deep sea or outer space. Developing situational awareness and deterrence capability as war avoidance and war control measures is something which is of prime concern to PLA. Avoiding conflict and extending the period of strategic opportunity to bridge the capability gap with competing power is its priority. Within this ambit, it is likely to play the game in a non-obtrusive zone by extending its influence across PIMED. Thus, it is likely to refine its non-contact warfare methods to keep the contest within the manageable threshold and should the conflict arise it should possess requisite levers to douse the conflagration from going beyond control based on war control philosophy.

Trends in PLA Capabilities and Force Structures

SMS 2013 edition gives inputs on how China visualises the contemporary wars will shape future wars and how the new strategic concepts will counter new-generation threats. It also opines that the revolution in technology has fundamentally changed the traditional relationship between matter, energy and information. Information systems have replaced the mechanised combat platform and have become the centre and multiplier of combat power generation. 'Information flow' guides the 'material flow' and 'energy flow' while 'information chain' supports 'command chain' and control the 'strike chain'. It lists significant trends which will impact the way the war develops.

- **Confrontation of systems**. SMS 2013 looks at combat systems and war systems as two subsets and finds system confrontation a reality the facing the world. It talks of system confrontation as a basic form of confrontation, especially with IT penetrating across politics, economy, law, public opinion and other fields of governance. China is concerned about the US strategy of striking the system integrity and stability first with an intent to deteriorate the system performance leading to system paralysis causing disorder of procedures and functional decline. China, like the US, therefore, also advocates targeting the centre of gravity at the start of the conflict to accelerate the process of war, and control war risks and costs.

- **Stand-off precision strike as the determining method of operation**. Mechanical technology and ICT has enabled modern wars to be conducted remotely. Seeking is no more regarded as part of the tactical pursuit. The availability of lethal and accurate medium and long-range precision strike system has made seeking part of strategic pursuit by its ability to execute decisive missions deep inside enemy territory. Networking has improved the versatility of engagement across multiple domains of land, sea, air and space. Based on the perspective of war practice, the superior side uses a large number of distant weapons to implement asymmetric, non-contact, non-linear full depth precision strike. It is capable of incapacitating huge mechanised force. SMS 2013 quotes the US Army "Assessment Report" of 2010 that advocated enhancement of the long-range strike and surveillance capability for the US forces, a fact that the 2018 NDS reinforced. SMS 2013 concurs with the US development plan, and calls for the development of five-dimensional long-range warfare capabilities covering land, sea, air, space and net, and establish a global strike system thus stirring the arms race.
- **Combat power enhancement through a networked military information system**. Networked systems have transformed the combat efficiency of combat operations. Situational awareness and ability to share it across information highway with multiple stakeholders and platforms have added to the speed in mission execution and responsive survivability. Covert and overt forces are now in sync to orchestrate desired effects at the point of application. China seems enamoured by the US plans of building a global, networked and full-spectrum joint force which it feels is necessary for the PLA too. Beijing sees 5G, which is claimed to support the network of network as the gamechanger. However, it has given rise to techno-nationalism and has increased the Sino-US tensions. Huawei leading the 5G charge from China is in the centre of the storm. 5G and AI allow for the integration of information and kill-power that allows for soft killing and hard destruction. Implementation of high-intensity information attack, interference and suppression operations integrated by the

network and energy may result in disruption of spatial situational awareness and enhancing the kill-capabilities. The situational awareness could be affected by either eclipsing the systems like over-the-horizon radar and ISR nodes across land, air and sea and communication relay platform or engaging them in electronic warfare by using operational deception and disruption platforms. It is aiming to improve the firepower strike systems accuracy by installing a target tracking system through data link and navigation and positioning electronic equipment.

- **Expansion of area of operation from three-dimensions to five-dimensions**. The combat space has been enhanced from the existing three dimensions of land, sea and air to five dimensions to include space and cyberspace additionally. The battlefield dominance is now about space control and network extension. Space is the new strategic high ground, and space-based information support and support systems are the indispensable strategic support of the version of information warfare. According to SMS 2013, in the recent local wars of the US military, 100 per cent of navigation and positioning, and more than 90 per cent of communications rely on satellites. Emphasis is to vigorously develop military aerospace technology and space weapon systems to strengthen space warfare on the lines of the US military "Global Rapid Conventional Strike System."
- **The fast-movers dominate the slow-movers**. The combat rhythm is time-dependent and is to be orchestrated based on the situational matrix. According to SMS 2013, information warfare is a time-controlled affair. Taking into the context of the former US Secretary of Defence Cohen analogy that the modern wars are likely to be orchestrated along "perception-decision-action" or OODA cycle as alluded in Chapter 1. Operational superiority aims to exploit the OODA cycle to control the initiative timely based on time-sensitivity of the target and the speed by which it can be engaged or disabled. In the war of influence, time control and space control complement each other, unlike traditional operation where space and time can be traded.
- **Unmanned, invisible and inaudible wars are emerging**. The emerging wars are likely to be "unmanned, invisible and silent" based on the development trends related to precision, remoteness,

and networking. Intelligent technologies lead to miniaturisation and evolution of stealthiest technologies for the multi-dimensional battlefield. New concept weapons such as electromagnetic guns, high-energy laser, unmanned systems, microwaves, biological and other technologies will alter the decibel of military operations.

Chinese strategic and military planners have emphasised the need to continually innovate strategic guidance, operational thoughts and response mechanism arising from the RMA for capability development to seize the strategic initiative and realise its millennium goals.

China's Strategic Guidelines and People's Military Struggle

In China, the 'military-strategic guidelines' acts as the foundation for China's national military strategy. The PLA's glossary of military terms defines it as the "core and collected embodiment of military strategy".[38] It primarily enunciates how China will fight the next war and contains both general and specific principles about the process of military operations. A strategic guideline helps in deciding the People's Military Struggle (PMS) based on the identification of strategic opponent, the main strategic direction and the basic guiding thought for campaigns and operations.[39]

Xi while addressing the 90th-anniversary parade of the PLA in October 2019, reiterated that while China would not indulge in invasion and expansion, but at the same time it would not allow any piece of Chinese territory to separate from China. The mandate for PLA, therefore, is to manage crises comprehensively, and resolutely deter and win wars. It approaches the mandate by adopting a balanced war preparation and war prevention posture, rights protection and stability maintenance, deterrence and warfighting, operations in peace and wartime, and employment of military forces in non-war military operations during peacetime.[40] Thus, China intends pursuing the path of development by increasing its interests in evolving the concepts of deterrence, crisis management, war control and containment. It intends employing war control methods through all the elements of comprehensive national power to shape the international environment and prevent unintended escalation, thus putting China in a favourable position. Its scope covers pre-war crisis control, operational control during war, and stability control after the war. 'Active defence' remains the cornerstone of PLA under the new situation according to 2015 NDWP.

Readjusting 'Active Defence' in the New Era

China's military strategic guideline since the founding of the PRC in 1949 has been 'active defence' which is based on its long-term practice of revolutionary wars and aimed at strengthening its national sovereignty. While engaging in a protracted battle as was seen against Japan or Kuomintang in the 1930s, the 'active defence' talks about experiencing strategic defence, strategic stalemate and three phases of strategic counterattack. All along the process, it advocates defensive campaign, but while engaging in the offensive phase, it looks for long-lasting strategies and quick-decision battles of battles. Trading space for time and once the time is ripe seize initiative through the relentless campaign.

Periodically the review of the military strategic guideline is carried out by the CMC. After the formation of PRC in 1949, it modified the national aim as national security and development. In April 1952, the PLA Deputy Chief of Staff proposed laying the boundary of the country in entirety. He pulled out the Chinese controversial 1938 map of 'China's shame' to buttress his point. The map shows the 'lost' Chinese territories to include not only the Russian Far East, the Ryukyus, Taiwan and the South China Sea, but also Korea, Vietnam, Cambodia, Laos, Thailand, the Malay Peninsula and Singapore, Myanmar, Nepal, parts of India and most of Central Asia.[41]

In March 1956, the CMC ratified the report on "Strategic Guidelines for Defending the Motherland and Issues of National Defence Construction."[42] The peoples' war was to contest large scale aggression with the main strategic direction being the US and Japan with an intent to trade space for time using positional defences and fight the enemy deep into the battle-zone.[43] In the early 1960s, China faced a unique challenge. The breakdown of relations with the Soviet, the grim border situation with India, and the threat from the US impacted Mao Zedong assessment. He was apprehensive of a joint attack by the US, the Soviet Union and India. Hence, he called for a general policy to cope with the multi-direction attack.[44] By September 1961, the PLA strength grew by approximately three hundred thousand to three million.[45] Based on the risk analysis it attacked India in November 1962 to secure its Southern borders and crush any secessionist movement in Tibet while deflecting public attention from the failure of the Great Leap movement launched by Mao. The 'Flexible Response Strategy' by the US in 1963 compelled China to plan to fight an "early, major, nuclear war" and hastened China to go nuclear by 1964.[46] However, the US intervention in Vietnam in 1965, the internal strife within CPC due to commitment of PLA in the cultural revolution and the worsening Sino-Soviet relation post-1967 made Mao seriously consider about the threat of war. It forced him to make economic recalibration towards industrialisation to meet the war preparation efforts. As the gestation period for industrial production was large; hence, he reposed his reliance on the strategy of luring the enemy deep. To mitigate the stress on the PLA, Mao revisited its foreign policy to lure the Americans by posing to act as a counterweight to Russia and extracted the promise for entry into the UN.[47] Mao-Nixon bonhomie helped China to successfully extract the diplomatic recognition for itself in 1971 while unseating Republic of China (ROC) from the UN. It helped China in strengthening its strategic defence, and it could concentrate on dealing with the Soviet threat as the main strategic direction shifted to the North.

The Arab-Israel conflict of 1973 gave an idea to the Chinese to review their strategy to deal with the Soviet in the context of the limited war between nuclear nations[48] and marked the strategic transformation of PLA armed forces. However, it was not until 1985 when the transformation was set into motion. After Gorbachev's 1986 speech at Vladivostok, the Soviet began withdrawing troops deployed in the Russian Far East resulted in the reduction of Soviet threat. Hence, the 1988 strategic guideline was more general, identifying a kind of war and not an adversary as the focus of planning – "dealing with local wars and armed conflicts" was set as a task for military struggle.[49]

The events of the 1990s, like the technological demonstration in the form of Gulf War I and the collapse of the Soviet Union, altered the strategic situation. In 1993, Jiang Zemin put the PLA on the path of modernisation by renewing the strategic military guideline as "winning local wars in conditions of modern technology, particularly high technology."[50] The goals of the strategy were to "defend national territorial sovereignty and maritime rights and interests, safeguard the reunification of the motherland and social stability, and provide strong security guarantees for reform and opening, and modernisation."[51] The strategic guiding thought in the new guideline stressed how to achieve these goals: "Foster strengths and avoid weaknesses, be flexible in handling emergencies, deter wars, and win wars."[52] Thus, Jiang laid the foundation of crisis management and strategic deterrence in the strategic construct of PLA while pointing out that China's military strategy should "be subordinate to and serve the nation's development strategy... accelerate the quality building of our army, and strive to raise our army's emergency combat capability."[53]

Gao Heng, a Chinese analyst, in his article in 1995 on "future military trends" made a profound observation on the west led Grand Strategy. He observed, "preparing for war in-depth" as the basis of the Grand Strategy and added that the US and other Western countries had dropped the strategic programmes like Star Wars in favour of creating a strategic programme for the information highway. According to him, this major revolution in military affairs regardless of its speed will turn "the whole globe into a unified battlefield".[54] He talked of intercontinental missiles, planes, warships and tanks to become information weapons.

In 2003, when Hu Jintao took over the reins in China, Gulf War II demonstrated the capability of networked-centric war and its ability to influence the battlefield. Lessons learnt from the previous wars were revisited and "New Historic Mission" was promulgated by Hu in 2004. The strategic guideline was modified as "winning Local Wars under Informationised Condition." The economic growth supported the quest for scientific and military innovation and indigenisation of defence industrial base. It also augmented PLA's role as a diplomatic and military instrument and as a custodian of China's global interests besides preserving the "period of strategic opportunity" for China's development.

The PLA counter-piracy operations in the Gulf of Aden since 2009, non-combatant evacuations in Libya and Yemen, and expanded peacekeeping operations in Africa under UN auspices, have been part of China's vision of expanding PLA activities to support its growing global influence. China's establishment of the first overseas military base in Djibouti in 2017 is against its policy of not stationing troops or setting up military bases in any foreign country made in its first defence white paper issued in 1998. Forward bases are following the footsteps of forward defence an aspect of 'active defence' strategy readjusted to the evolving geopolitical realities.

2001 NDWP saw China's borders and coasts as the strategic first-line or front line. However, 2013 NDWP called for pushing the first line away from China's borders and coasts to ensure that battle is fought away from the homeland. To implement the strategic military guideline of 'active defence' in the new situation, Chinese 2015 NDWP made the strategic guidance more "forward-looking" through innovative doctrines and force development in critical security domains. The arduous task, according to it, is "to safeguard its national unification, territorial integrity and development interests."

Xi Jinping has pushed in the reform to realign the PLA priorities in line with the new era reality. The 2019 NDWP reinforces it by adding nuclear, space and cyber into its sovereign domain, thereby authorising the PLA to ensure their security. It calls for the development of relevant technologies to enhance the survivability of space-based information resources while strengthening situational awareness through the resolute cyber defence. Thus, the scope of 'winning Local Wars under Informatisation' looks at the multi-domain scenario (refer to Table 2.2 for PLA Doctrine Evolution and Likely Employment). Its force design is reflected in its defence reforms (for details refer to Chapter 3). It has created a Strategic Support Force to oversee its space and cyber capabilities and redesignated the PLA Second Artillery Force (PLASAF) as the PLA Rocket Force (PLARF) to handle the missile defence and nuclear security issues. China aims to fight the new era war with an informationised platform riding on its ability to firewall its own information space and looks at seizing the initiative in the information domain through its ambitious 5G information highway.

Table 2.2: PLA Doctrine Evolution and Likely Employment

Period	*Doctrine*	*Spectrum*	*Duration*	*Operational Conduct*	*Technologies*	*Domains*
Pre-1985	People's War	Across complete Spectrum	Protracted	Massed employment of manpower and firepower	World War II vintage equipment	Land and air
Post-1985	Winning Local Wars under Modern Conditions	Limited Wars	Short wars – seek QBQR[#]	Rapid Reaction (EFSA*) and forward defence, Gain Initiative	Limited Mobility in air and ground	Land and Air
1993	Local Wars under High Tech Conditions	Limited within War Zone	Short War seek QBQR	Rapid Reaction (EFSA) and forward defence	Limited Mechanisation, Missile and & Electronic Warfare	Land, Air, Sea and Electronic Domain
2004	Local Wars under Informatisation	Limited within War Zone	Short War QBQR	Rapid Reaction, informatised EFSA, Near Sea superiority	Mechanised, Limited networked long-range, precision systems	Land, Air, Sea, Space, Cyberspace

Period	*Doctrine*	*Spectrum*	*Duration*	*Operational Conduct*	*Technologies*	*Domains*
2019	Winning Local Wars under Informatisation	Across complete spectrum within War Zone	Protracted QBQR through measured effective control	Rapid Reaction, informatised EFSA, overseas domination	Mechanised, long-range, precision networked autonomous platform with AI and Robotics	Multi-Domain across PIMED $
In future	Intelligent War	Across complete spectrum	Protracted. QBQR through dynamic effective control	Tailored defence and offence through Informatised EFSA	AI or Cognitive Intelligence-driven long-range, precision, autonomous systems	Multi-Domain across PIMED $

QBQR- Quick Battle Quick Resolution
*EFSA- Elite Forces and Sharp Arm
$ PIMED – Political, Information, Military, Economic and Diplomacy

According to the 2019 NDWP, the strategic concepts of 'active defence' work within the realm of "strategic defence and operational and tactical offence and adherence to the principles of defence, self-defence and post-emptive strike." It is categorical in specifying that China will not initiate the war but will surely respond if attacked. Thus, it gives a lot of importance on the ability to contain and win wars through the adoption of 'active defence' strategy with no change in its application. The essential point for PMS is to win informationised local wars besides highlighting the maritime military struggle.[55] China is overly concerned about the situational awareness gap against with the US created due to "the new landscape of strategic competition, the new demands of national security, and new developments in modern warfare".[56] Its committed nuclear policy of 'No First Use' at any time and under any circumstances, and not using or threatening to use nuclear weapons against non-nuclear-weapon states or nuclear-weapon-free zones unconditionally places the PLA in a challenging situation.[57] The PLA interprets 'active defence' to include both de-escalation and seizing the initiative hence it looks to control significant crises, properly handle possible chain reactions effectively, and firmly safeguard the country's territorial sovereignty, integrity and security. China banks heavily on creating strategic deterrence. It also looks at creating conventional strategic parity through the development of kinetic capabilities in terms of missile development, stealth and autonomous platforms.

PLA abandoned the continental mindset and emphasised on developing maritime, cyber, space and nuclear capabilities based on networked systems featuring information dominance, precision strikes and joint operations. The expanded security concepts combine both internal and international issues; looking at people and diasporas, overseas enterprises and interests crucial for the development of China. The 2019 NDWP looks at dominating the far seas to prevent any reinforcements as part of its A2AD strategy.

China is trying to explore strategies to deal with the US strategy of denial. US 2018 NDS assertion of increasing the competitive space for adversaries has prompted Xi to relook at the domains which need to be managed and protected. Accordingly, he broadened the security domains to include 11 fields: political, territorial, military, economic, cultural, social, scientific and technological, informational, ecological, financial, and nuclear domains.[58] Security interests have also expanded into the Open Ocean, Outer Space, and Cyberspace. Thus, addressing various facets of defence across multiple domains has been incorporated by China.

PLA has the responsibility of innovating strategies and tactics to deal with 'informationised warfare' and look into the 'intelligent warfare' using the concept of 'active defence'. The concept of 'active defence' also looks at the core issues fundamental to expanding economic interests and associated threats. Although the threat of invasion to China is remote, however, the global informationised network systems have expanded the non-contact threats related to space assets and state cyber and communication infrastructures. It allows both lethal and non-lethal threats to paralyse China's military capabilities and undermine its economic growth engines. Thus, 'active defence' measures in Chinese context look at countering the threats by dominating new and emerging domains while planning for forces capable of operating from beyond its borders and occupying new avenues in terms of time, space and technology. Beijing is aware of the resource constraints in matching the US capabilities and is looking at reforms vigorously to trim the forces and generate revenues to pursue modernisation.

China's security interests in the new era have blurred the lines between civilian and military tasks. The increasing complexity of security has guided China to look at civil and military fusion in security policy formulation and given impetus to the reforms which are being vigorously pushed by Xi at the helm of CMC. 'Active defence' therefore, does not remain within the confines of the military alone. Non-contact nonprovocative methods are the areas of exploration for the PLA while building its coercive and deterrent capabilities.

The Military Strategic Guideline of 'Active Defence'. The 2015 NDWP lists out the strategic military guideline of 'active defence' in the new situation and clearly states the principles which China's armed forces will uphold. These include:[59]

- To prevent crises, deter and win wars in accordance with the national strategic goals by incorporating a holistic view of national security.
- To foster a strategic posture favourable to China's peaceful development. The national defence policy aims to coordinate political, military, economic and diplomatic work so that it can positively cope with comprehensive security threats.
- To safeguard national territorial sovereignty and maritime rights and interests and maintain security and stability within and along China's periphery.
- To endeavour to seize the strategic initiative in the military struggle, proactively plan for military struggle in all directions and domains, and grasp the opportunities to accelerate military building, reform and development.
- To employ strategies and tactics featuring flexibility and mobility, give full play to the overall effectiveness of joint operations, concentrate superior forces, and make integrated use of all operational means and methods.
- To ensure proper responses while dealing with most complex and challenging scenarios.
- To enrich the contents, ways and means of the concept of people's war through focused war mobilisation from human resources to science and technology.
- To actively expand military and security cooperation, deepen military relations with major powers, neighbouring countries and other developing countries, and promote the establishment of a regional framework for security and cooperation.

PLA STRATEGIC CONCEPTS

What will constitute a victory for China in a conflict 'short of war' will dictate its strategic choices. To enrich the 'active defence' in a new era, the focus of PLA is to effectively respond to the dual strategic needs of war threats and safeguarding the expanding national interests while handling internal stability. It has significant relationships with war and control, war and non-war situations. Based on disputes, the strategic control function of military power is activated to help in maintaining and prolonging the period of national development. While continuing to support the core functions of "strategy of war", the PLA is also attached to the needs of diversified applications. It enriches the development of local warfare under the conditions of informatisation through a carefully crafted strategic concept for promulgating the 'active defence' policy.

Local Wars

The SMS 1999 defines the peacetime and local war strategy in the context of Local Wars under High Tech Conditions. According to it the word 'peacetime,' does not mean the absence of future conflict, but only the low likelihood of a general war. Peacetime strategy includes deterrence operations and crisis management as well as local war.[60] While the local war is seen as a strategic problem manifesting during peacetime, it is limited in objectives and area of application and put a premium on joint operations.[61] High-tech local wars are characterised as being highly intense, mobile and destructive.[62] The types of operations in the local war include blockades, amphibious assaults, counter-offensive campaigns, and precision strikes.

The prosecution of local wars looks at six principles or guidelines. The first is to prepare in many directions and any activity to respond to contingencies flexibly. It entails quick reaction and focused training. The second is to combine the offence and defence to seize the initiative. Unlike total war, the local war under high tech conditions being intense and fast requires larger content of offensive operations to seize the initiative. The third aspect deals with integrated operations for key point attacks which aims at attacking enemy war systems through an integrated force. Key point attack refers to addressing the centre of gravity using the "Elite Force and Sharp Arms" to establish superiority against an opponent using the best suitable force. The fourth issue calls for quick decisions but prepares for a protracted conflict. It underlines the need of speed to enable "quick battle quick resolution" before the international pressure mounts. Thus, lethal kinetic high mobility operations provide the necessary edge to gain strategic superiority. The fifth principle talks of the use of CNP through "overall planning to win victory through coordinated efforts." While from the military perspective, the scope of local war may be limited for the military, but it is broad at the national level, and include political, information, diplomacy and economic means too. Lastly, it states that since the high-tech local war will be complex and quick, therefore there is a need for "unified leadership, centralised command."

The SMS 2013 stresses on the PLA's ability to contain the exaggeration of war into an uncontrollable stage and the massive financial or logistical burdens a prolonged war may impose on a country's economy. The use of high-tech weapons and combatting systems makes wars extremely costly and may threaten the government. Therefore, the PLA's ability to control the exaggeration of war is important for drawing benefits of strategic opportunity. The controllability of conflicts requires the PLA to apply strategies with high efficiency and high flexibility.

The SMS 2013 sets the goals of local wars to empirically reflect the limited political goals, limited military goals, and limited economic goals. The end states desired are as under:[63]

- Moderate magnitudes of war. Instead of threatening the survival or completely eradicating the adversary's military capability, there is a need to focus on forcing the adversary to compromise.
- Limited areas of war. War should be confined to a region rather than covering the entire nation.
- Differentiated targets of striking. Effort should be expanded in striking the targets of strategic importance in supporting war execution and sustainment, such as military-political leaders' residence, military commanding centre, high-tech weapons base, and critical logistic base.
- It prioritises the use of conventional weapons over weapons of mass destruction.
- It looks for short duration war through effective control.

Forward Defence or Frontline Defence

Forward defence aims at expanding the battlespace beyond China's borders to increase China's strategic depth. It redefines China's foundational concept of 'active defence'. China's 'active defence' strategy adjusted in the past was always as part of a defensive strategy for national territory and looked at fighting within or on the borders. However, the SMS 2013 breaks the mould and talks about enlarging of the defences of the national territory to forward defence. It is primarily due to the expansion of Chinese national interest. The struggle faced by China to counter the West-led containment strategy has resulted in China to emphasize on retaining control in interstate conflict over maritime, polar, space and network domain and global commons.

It also assesses the global trend towards informatised long-range combat systems where the need to defend further away from territorial/ coastal boundaries is required to ensure sufficient strategic depth. The risk of invasion inside China is remote. Hence, the SMS 2013 talks of threat "from a traditional land invasion to space, air-sea and network-air integrated non-contact strikes" and how China has to deal with a strong adversary with "comprehensive distant war superiority in maritime direction."[64] While highlighting the difficulty in engaging from land or near seas, it suggests the need to expand the scope of warfare for the implementation of "outwardly oriented defensive operations."[65] It aims to push the strategic frontier to the surroundings, from land to sea, from air to space, from tangible space to intangible space while taking into account the physical and virtual fields. The strategic frontier expansion looks at radiating from inland theatre to the outside while naval theatre to extend from near seas to the ocean.

To implement frontier defence, SMS 2013 highlights that offensive operations need to be undertaken based on a solid defence. Since the 1990s, the asymmetric, non-contact, non-linear operations have blurred the boundaries between offensive and defensive operations. Hence, it feels that in the coming wars, the strategic attack may be regarded as an essential type of 'active defence', especially because of all arms and services integration.[66] While implementing frontier defence, it highlights the strategic needs of progressive operations, and rely on local joint operations as a necessary form of combat as China's interest expansion is centred around its periphery and entangled with external conflicts.[67] Thus, unlike the three-phased strategic operations witnessed during the revolutionary era, it may be replaced with a concurrent orchestration of strategic defence, strategic stalemate and strategic offensive or counter-attack based on situational awareness and need to seize the initiative. Reliance on the remote long-distance warfare, which is essentially integrated joint warfare under 'the condition of informatisation', tests China's military capabilities. Thus, it argues that the use of asymmetric combat or creation of strong points allows it to enhance strategic delivery and overseas support capabilities. It aims to deal with complex and challenging situations through an integrated mechanism of deterrence and war control. Through transformation, it intends to undertake capability remodelling, thereby accelerating the promotion of PLA from a homeland defence force to a frontier defence force.

Strategic Space

The SMS 2013 defines "strategic space" as "the area required by the nation or state to resist foreign interference and aggression and safeguard their survival and development."[68] While similar to forward defence, the main contention lies in area were the combat operation will be conducted. Thus, the strategic area encompasses not only the area of interest but also an area where China would like to influence the operations. "The national game is competition around maximising national interests."[69] With China's interest expanding globally, the need for it to acquire strategic space across the world is also gaining momentum. Its basing requirement at Djibouti and its keen interest in acquiring the ports all along in the Indian Ocean from Gwadar to Hambantota to Kyaukpyu are pointers to its keenness to extend the strategic space. With the Belt and Road Initiative (BRI) in the Central Asian Republic region gaining traction it may well have its eyes set on land-base. With space and deep-sea gaining prominence both from harnessing the global common and security standpoint; China has plans to seek strategic space in these areas too. The information networks are another area which China wants to dominate as it feels vulnerable due to IT supply chain infiltration. Lack of core technologies limits China's ability to defend against such attacks.[70]

Effective Control

According to SMS 2013, "if war is politics, then peace is greater politics." Hence, when the world oscillates between war and peace with new strategic choices at the disposal of the nations, then the variable forces and controlled violence are likely to impact the controlling of war situations. China realises that it has to do a lot to influence international opinion. Hence, its roadmap propagates "adherence to Yin and Yang[71] to maintain obscurity and actively make a difference"[72] in shaping the international surrounding in a controlled, flexible and gradual way. To resolve security pressure, it aims to expand national interests and maximise the transformation in the world into opportunities.[73]

China acknowledges that while its CNP has increased but it lacks strategic capabilities, especially for operations beyond the sovereign boundary.[74] The SMS 2013 is categorical in highlighting the premium in fighting short wars or avoiding wars that would have the propensity to escalate and become protracted. Given the narrative of peaceful development being pursued by China, the paper notes that in such an eventuality, China's fight must be actively controlled to reduce the risks of war. Dynamic and complex security challenges, especially the increasingly prominent non-traditional security threats, have frequently affected the overall situation of national development and security. The contradictions, frictions and struggles that are encountered rely more on non-military means such as politics, economy and diplomacy. Still, the military as the pillar to safeguard national sovereignty, security, and territorial integrity, relies on effective control. It is not only a strategic guide for combat operations but also a military deterrent and non-war military operations. The shift in the approach of PLA is evident: [75] (1) from "emphasising 'defence' to emphasising 'control'," (2) from "emphasising 'war' to emphasising 'power'," and (3) from "seeking 'victory' to winning first." Thus, effective control seeks to achieve all objectives of war but without resorting to combat if possible.

It looks at using three components to manage effective control. The first is "creating situations" which implies "creating a strategic situation advantageous for internal stability and external expansion and a long period of order and security. The core lies in the strategic balance, a stable periphery and opposing separatism to promote unity."[76] It examines the engagement policies and concept of strategic deterrence while dealing with hegemons like the US or its allies. The second component looks at "preventing and controlling crises." China realises that the competition and crisis build confrontations and has the potential to upset the period of strategic opportunity into a period of strategic friction and finally lead to strategic danger, thus upsetting its rise. Hence, it looks at creating deterrence and evolving non-military actions to prevent spiralling of crisis.

It talks that crisis could be exploited by seizing opportunities and quotes the instance of democratic reforms in Tibet in 1963 after the outbreak of the rebellion in Lhasa. The third component talks of "controlling war situations" which may happen once the peace overtures are damaged. It talks of controlling the escalation matrix by making sure that the favourable situation on the battlefield does not expand political goals and escalate the war while at the same time, end the war in a controlled manner.

Strategic Posture or Layout

"Strategic posture" is defined as "carrying out overall development activities of strategic forces and resources to achieve strategic goals."[77] Thus, it implies the overall deployment of military capabilities to gain the strategic initiative and create a favourable strategic situation. It calls for force disposition to enable control of key nodes. It translates into a structured force to meet contingency based on the strategic direction which has been done by theaterisation of commands in the 2016 PLA reforms. The intertwined traditional and non-traditional threats require China to improve its capabilities against the main adversaries and safeguard its global interests in maritime, space and information domains. The change in the character of war towards Informatisation has compelled China to abandon "its traditional emphasis on ground war and territorial defence in favour of joint, long-distance and offensive-focused approaches."[78]

SMS 2013 identifies four transformations. The first is "functional versatility" which allows strategic posture to deal with traditional and non-traditional threats and multi-domain ability to operate. It looks at gaining strategic deterrence ability in peacetime and capability of a rapid reaction during a crisis. The second is "multidimensional integration" that seeks multi-domain posture as it feels that the networked integration of forces across land, sea, air and space impinges on strategic freedom of operations. The third is "internal and external unity" which refers to shifting of internal security to the periphery while externally look at overseas strategic support areas to guard the national interest. Lastly, the "integrated coordination" looks at jointmanship to improve response mechanism and resource optimisation. As long as the roots of war do not die, responding to the threat of war is always the top priority of the PLA.

Conditions of Informatisation

The SMS 2013 postulates that the growing importance and sophistication of information technology will play a significant role in the non-contact wars.[79] Chinese scholars predict that the future informatised wars may involve, "the danger of being the target of high-technological warfare, such as air-naval, air-space, and space-cyber wars. The threat from the east is more severe than that from the west, the threat from the sea is more severe than that from the ground; the threat from space and the cyber network is gradually becoming true."[80] SMS 2013 further adds that the probability of conducting military operations to protect rights and limited overseas war operations is ever increasing. The most severe war threat is a large-scale strategic sudden attack launched by a strong adversary, which aims at destroying our war potential to force.[81] The PLA is, therefore, undergoing a transformation from "war strategy" to "historic mission strategy," from "contingency-based strategy" to "capability-based strategy."[82]

SMS 2013 stresses the need to gain information supremacy as it feels that control of information is the foundation of seizing initiatives in battle. In the space arena, it advises to target high-cost systems and undertake "uneasy development of space weapon technology, to create superiority in a localised area to hit and destroy critical targets of the enemy's space system." On the military-civilian dual use of space system, it highlights the need to protect the safety of civilian space assets, and use civilian space system to enhance the capability of the military space system. Regarding the characteristics that space activity requires support from the surface, it insists on using multiple methods in various domains including land, sea, air, space, cyberspace, and electromagnetic to disrupt the communication system which could cut the connection between space and the earth. Thus, the enemy will not be able to operate its space system, thus atrophying it's command and control systems.

The Beginning of Non-contact Warfare

The changing character of warfare post advent of informationisation and ability to integrate surveillance and reconnaissance platform with the kill chain performing their tasks at stand-off ranges have provoked discussions within China's NDU on non-contact warfare. Replacing the concept of 'massing of force' to 'massing of effects' through targeted killing or disabling the capability by the precise and accurate strike has been seen as one major shift. The second is the altering of the concept of distance in a battlefield. The transparency over the depth areas through ISR means and ability to hit over large range has added deterrence to the list of conventional forces as security lies in deterring the enemy giving impetus to the development of lethal long-range weaponry. "Distance is no longer an obstacle on the battlefield. It meets the inherent requirement for non-contact joint firepower attacks in informatised war. It is the essence of an informatised battlefield."[83] The third issues deal with the ability to avoid detection and attribution. The lists of necessary capabilities that a country needs to have for non-contact warfare thus include unmanned weapons, making "invisible arms" such as stealth fighter jets and bombers, "integrating offence with defence" through theatre missile defence, and dominating outer space.[84]

There is also a discussion on the use of non-contact means in contact warfare in a tactical realm. Artillery engagements are one issue which has been examined especially in an active scenario besides the use of fighter jets for air raids or surgical strikes. The paper also talks of strike operations beyond detection range and over the horizon surveillance using a combination of radars and missiles in an integrated joint engagement mode.[85]

The cyber domain is another area which favours non-contact warfare. PLA is working on improving its cyber capabilities in the field of computer network exploitation (CNE) and computer network attack (CNA) besides reinforcing its C4ISR architecture besides key missile and strategic assets like electricity grid, transportation grid and financial systems. China knows that future warfare will not entail invasion into its territory, but the penetration will take place in its policies. The local informationised war will look for quick outcomes. It will necessitate the involvement of a full spectrum of integrated operations across multiple domains and the ability to use asymmetric means to balance the effects and end the conflict through effective control.

Development of Non-War Military Operations

SMS 2013 gives a detailed and copious account on the development and practice of the theory of non-war military operation. According to it, globalisation and emergence of non-traditional threats have diversified the security product and has led to the division of military operations into two categories: war and non-war. For both, the US and China, homeland security is the highest priority. According to the definition given in the new edition of 'Military Language of the Chinese PLA' non-war operations are "armed military actions undertaken by forces to safeguard national security and development interests that do not directly constitute war move. It includes counter-terrorism and stability maintenance, disaster relief, protection of rights and interests, security alert, international peacekeeping, international rescue and other operations."[86] The PLA non-war military operations in the narrow sense mainly focus on maintaining national security, social stability and deterrence. However, in the broader sense, it includes all such actions in which military participates in as long as it is not a declared war. According to SMS 2013, German Berlin crisis, the Cuban missile crisis, Iran hostage crisis are typical non-war military operations. In the 'new era,' the traditional security threats have diminished, and the non-traditional security threats are gaining ground. China has been following the US and NATO discourse on non-war military action theory or in other words 'military operations other than war'- the principles of non-war, non-violence, unconventional military operations and special wars. SMS 2013 also refers to Indian "Disaster Management Law" as part of India's non-war military operations.[87]

The non-war military operations have been dovetailed with the political structure of China since the time of revolutionary war. Xi'an incident of 1936 (refer Chapter 1) is one such instance which changed the destiny of CPC without firing a bullet. PLA has worked alongside the CPC in its internal and external operations during the period of Great Leap movement and Cultural Revolution. President, as the head of the CMC, provides a unique ability to China to bring about civil-military synergy in non-war operations. PLA recognises non-war military operations as an essential means of fulfilling the new mission and an effective way to support the expansion of interests and strategic opportunity. It is a powerful tool for maintaining world peace with the non-war forming basic attribute of non-war military operations. However, once the war breaks out, it gets subsumed in the wartime agenda. The vast array of tasks helps PLA to enhance its skills in diverse areas from cognitive to incognitive domains to information and logistics support areas to handle the crisis. To harness skill sets for non-war forces, PLA has embarked on hiring civilians in its organisation.

Non-war military operations revolve around the country's military, political, economic, diplomatic, and social needs. PLA has classified non-war military operations based on the nature of operations which varies in scope, degree and conduct. These are:[88]

- **Confrontational Actions**. It includes anti-terrorism, armed anti-narcotics, combating transnational crime, anti-piracy and to stop social riots, targeting individuals and groups that are mostly hostile to China and may be directly related to social stability and the national security. The scope of action is mostly limited, and the purpose of the action is to eliminate threats before it turns violent. The degree of confrontation and the intensity of actions is dependent on the situational awareness and ability to coerce and strike.
- **Law Enforcement Actions**. It mainly includes border and coastal defence blockade, aerial blockade, sea rights protection, escort, security alert, international peacekeeping, military patrol, etc. The scope of action is mostly within the country or on the disputed areas and global hotspots. The purpose of the operation is to adopt a rational, beneficial and economical military rights protection and law enforcement activities in response to larger-scale organized provocations that endanger security and development. To curb the escalation and expansion of the situation, eliminate significant factors of instability and restore the usual security environment and social order.
- **Rescue Operations Actions**. It mainly includes emergency rescue and disaster relief (natural disasters, major rescue and disposal of nuclear, chemical and biological accidents, etc.), evacuation of overseas Chinese, medical assistance, etc. The scope of the action environment is fairly complex, with many unpredictable and uncontrollable factors.
- **Cooperative Actions**. It mainly manifests in international joint military exercises, military diplomacy, military aid, demonstration of improved joint operational capabilities to deter common opponents, control real and potential crises, and stabilize the situation in the region.

The above four types of military operations include multiple types of operations. The first one contains certain use of force and the possibility of upgrading, but the use of force is low in strength and cannot be used as a layer of war. The last three types focus on peacetime benefits in the long run and are more frequently used. The strategic guiding principles for non-war military operations formulated by PLA is as under: [89]

- **High-level decision-making and macro coordination**. Non-war military operations usually have complex backgrounds, unpredictable evolution and significant impacts due to associated global emergencies. Hence, it is executed within a certain time and space. The coordination made by the Party Central Committee and the CMC provides unity of command and enables unambiguous execution.
- **Grasp the initiative and classification guidance**. Non-war military operations envisage that the participating troops should be conversant with laws and requirements of the mission. It should be able to grasp the intentions in the shortest possible time. It should synchronize mobilisation and manoeuvres proactively by establishing links with relevant local authorities depending on the type of operational action.
- **Responsive and flexible response**. According to the situational analysis, the PLA troop is required to make a comprehensive evaluation and judgement and decide on the scope and escalation control measures.
- **Limited goals and powerful control**. Major non-war military operations have their broad political, economic, military and social influences, sometimes with a significant international fallout. It is more so in case of the confrontational operations. Non-war military operations advocate determining the actions to meet the given objectives by making rational response strategy.
- **Act in accordance with the law**. Non-war military operations aim to proceed under the guidance of national policies and within the framework of legal principles and regulations. However, it gives enough choice of action to deal with hardened elements, especially in case of handling resistance movements and unlawful assemblies.

Deterrence and Coercion

The traditional Chinese military philosophy dictates that to subdue the enemy without fighting is the acme of skill. SMS 2013 emphasises on the use of deterrence to prevent adversaries from taking war actions against China. It defines military deterrence as, "strategic operation, with the threat to use or the actual use of the military capability to influence the adversary's strategic judgments. It is done by making the adversary feel difficult to achieve anticipated targets or the cost, may exceed the benefits, and is conducted by countries or political groups for certain political goals. In accordance with different criteria, military deterrence can be categorized as conventional or nuclear, space or nuclear, direct or indirect, regular or contingent, operational or non-operational, and local or global."[90]

Deterrence is the use of potential violence instead of friendly negotiation and political compromises; its fundamental executive method being an imposing threat. According to SMS 2013, the three critical components to achieve the goals of deterrence are "magnitude of deterrence, determination, and information conveyance." It calls for widening the 'spectrum' of military strategy from the traditional 'war strategy' into a 'strategy that fulfils the PLA's historic missions'. Increasing conventional and intertwined unconventional threats affect the survival of nation-state. It recommends the strategic use of military force at peaceful times and emphasizes the strategic function of military deterrence and non-war military actions. The methods to be employed intend to "increase the number of strategic options and enhance strategic flexibility, to prevent war, win war, secure stability and defend interests."[91]

The PLA strives to build reliable and credible deterrence capacity. Its main objectives are:[92]

- To secure the strategic opportunity for development as the goal of deterrence.
- Preventing and containing crisis as the focus of the operation.
- To enhance the capability of military struggle as the foundation of deterrence.
- To win local wars under the conditions of informatisation as the core of deterrence.
- To join military and civilian capability as the way to increase the deterrence capacity.

Strategically, military deterrence is a subset of the strategy of 'active defence'. China seeks to deter small wars, thus to prevent more massive conflicts, based on self-defensiveness, and strategic limitedness. "It is an active counteraction to the invasive actions which infringe China's interests. It is not offensive or pre-emptive." China aims to build up a system of deterrence with the following forces:[93]

- Small but strong and effective nuclear force.
- Informatised conventional operational force.
- Information warfare force which could be advantageous in a local information confrontation.
- Flexible and various space force.
- Innovative and developmental civilian deterrence force.

China's promulgation of Air Defence Identification Zone (ADIZ)[94] on 23 November 2013 in the East China Sea covered the Japanese-controlled Senkaku Islands (Diaoyu Islands), and Socotra Rock, claimed by South Korea. It was an act of practising coercion. Despite hard balling by Japan and the US, China was able to compel most of the states, including South Korea, to comply with the guidelines within a month of the declaration. The ADIZ episode has posed challenges for the US and the countries in maritime dispute in the South China Sea into the quandary. It has made them wonder whether China is going to impose it in the South China Sea where it is again engaged in a dispute with much weaker ASEAN nations.

The deterrence strategy is hinged on creating more uncertainty in the minds of adversaries. The emergence of new deterrence forces, based on new technology such as information, cyberspace, space, and new-material technologies is intending to increase more uncertainty when the adversary is evaluating the military capabilities. The credibility of deterrence is enhanced by constructing asymmetrical methods of deterrence.

Asymmetric Warfare: Defeating the Superior with Inferior

China has drawn lessons from history and past to create a concept of defeating a powerful opponent with a weak force. Chinese prefer realpolitik, the use of force or coercive diplomacy and a tendency to justify the use of force as purely defensive.[95] Mao used the historical materials from the Yin, Zhou, Ming, and Qing dynasties to explain that war is a competition to win superior subjective initiatives between the commanders of two forces backed by financial capacity and military strength. The correctness or incorrectness of the subjective factor will turn the inferior into the superior, or passivity into an initiative, or vice versa. We can conclude from Mao that the key to defeating the powerful with a weak force is making the most of subjective initiative.[96]

According to SMS 2013, under the conditions of informatisation, the battlefield situation changes rapidly, seizing the initiative of the battlefield makes the struggle for power extremely fierce. China realises its capability gap against the US and recognises that it is challenging for the weaker side to defeat the powerful in a high-tech war and recommends three initiatives to tackle the disadvantages. Firstly, by creating a superior structure that can function by integrating armed operations with non-armed operations. Secondly, by having a superior strategy and it draws its lesson from Yom Kippur war where a disadvantageous Israel could turn the table on Egyptian through superior strategy. Thirdly, it calls for adopting superior operational methods like non-linear employment of troops and resources to break the rhythm of operations. It also looks at anti-technologies to deal with technological superiority. Space and cyberspace domains thus become crucial in the theorization of China's military strategy to create asymmetry against an enemy and favour China's position.

SMS 2013 theorises that the advantage of adhering to asymmetrical warfare lies in its high flexibility and ability to create conditions "to seize the war initiative, and to use favourable condition/posture to compensate the inferiority in equipment...dare to use military deterrence, particularly the new methods of struggle in the fields of space and cyberspace, to impair the enemy's war commanding system."[97] Asymmetric warfare attempts to play along with time and space dynamics. In terms of time, it uses pre-emption and speed to affect the enemy OODA loop relentlessly. Spatially, it attempts to gain advantage through extensive penetration, gaining positional advancement by expanding space of action while limiting and compressing the enemy options.

Practising Xing and Shi

Xing and shi are two core ideas that anchor Chinese strategic thinking. In modern Chinese, xing and shi used together refer to a "situation of any shape, of any scope." Xing is the idea of a situation or configuration, "as it develops and takes shape before our eyes as a relation of forces."[98] The potential of the situation cannot be predicted in advance. It can only be detected since it changes all the time. Shi is the concept of potential, which is implied by that situation. It can be made to work in one's favour, or one can be positioned to be favoured by it. The key to Chinese strategy is to rely on the inherent potential of the situation. It is known as "strategic situationism."[99] Shi is "to fall between the static and the dynamic." The polysemy of the word adds ambivalence which makes it fascinating to discern and apply. Sun Tzu described 'Shi' in 'The Art of War' as the art of influencing the enemy by creating such situations that makes him conform to his design. A skilled strategist is required to ensure victory over a superior by "the alignment of forces" or "propensity of things to happen."[100] Michael Pillsbury, in his book 'The Hundred-Year Marathon', illustrates how 'Shi' has been wedded to Chinese strategy. Shi and Chinese grand strategy follow China's most iconic board games, 'wei qi'[101] rules of encirclement by which it looks at building its coalition while simultaneously undermining the opponent. A significant component or feature of 'Shi' is called 'wu wei', which means to get other nations to do your work for you. For instance, China has developed Pakistan as a meaningful proxy against India, while BRI is one of the methods being employed by Beijing to create a coalition of nations who can work for them.

Francois Jullien, a French sinologist, provides a deeper understanding of the Chinese concept of 'shi' meaning disposition or circumstance, power or potential. He examines the twin themes of efficacy and strategy to look beyond Western ways of thinking. He establishes efficacy as a central tenet of strategy. According to him, it can be explained in three parts. The first is the logic of manipulation contrasting between strategic and political mechanisms. While in the first instance, the aim may be to destroy the enemy's power of resistance while at the other case, it has no qualms in exterminating any subject once he becomes an obstacle.[102] Hence, in the context of shi, power relations are more important than human virtues. The second aspect of efficacy does not necessarily mean confrontation. It looks at the strategic opportunity to turn the tide. Xi'an incident of 1936 brings to fore Mao's strategy of using the Kuomintang Marshal to arrest Chiang Kai-shek, their leader, and force him to sign the truce with the communists. This incident forced Kuomintang to redirect its energy towards Japanese and gave time to Mao to reorganise the communist party for its 1945 civil uprising. Finally, efficacy does not depend on personality because political position operates as a power relation. The position of the sovereign can be defensive; it can also become an instrument of totalitarianism.[103]

Souring of Sino-Soviet relation during the 1950s and 1960s is seen by some Chinese strategists of Deng Era as the inability of the Chinese leaders to perceive 'Shi' correctly as the Soviets discovered China's intention of usurping the USSR's leadership of the Communist world. Hence China failed to extract further foreign investment, trade opportunities, military technology, or political support from the Soviet Union.[104] Stung by their failure to master 'Shi' in their relations with the Soviets; China turned to the US. It was Mao who made first overtures to scout Nixon-Kissinger in building the bridge.[105] Henry Kissinger, in his book 'On China' highlights how China uses 'Shi' as an attribute to deal with war and crises and points out how it has used it against the US. According to him, China's relationship with the US is one of the combative coexistence.[106] Pillsbury points out how for past four decades China has "used American technology, foreign investment, political support, and access to America's domestic market for Chinese products—without tipping off the Americans to China's larger ambitions."[107] Chinese strategists have been recommending discreet methods of countering America's global alliance system while building an alternative alliance for itself. Hence, while examining the crisis, conflict or collaboration build-up, it is imperative to the monitoring of indicators to identify the direction of 'Shi'.

'Shi' is also used to assess the balance of power. This measurement was used during the Warring States period to convince their opponents to concede just by showing the quantitative calculations to opponents, thus dooming them to defeat.[108] Quantitative measurements play a vital role in Chinese military and intelligence services to determine how China compares with its geopolitical competitors. It helps in analysing the time China will take to overtake its opponent- a typical game of 'wei qi' for courting coalitions and capabilities. For China, non-contact warfare provides an opportunity to minimise the strategic friction, thus allowing it to pursue its capability enhancement and alliance building goals- an essential facet for managing 'shi' and playing 'wei qi'.

Three Warfare: Scheming Security Narrative

The Chinese 'three warfares' strategy consists of public opinion warfare, psychological warfare and legal warfare. They form the critical components of China's strategic approach both in peacetime and wartime alike. The 'three warfares' is engaged in a perceptual preparation of the battlefield that is critical to advancing Chinese interests. PLA texts on military strategy like the SMS 2013, the 2015 NDWP, teaching material by the NDU 'An Introduction to Public Opinion Warfare, Psychological Warfare and Legal Warfare' illustrate the extent to which 'three warfares' is integrated into the PLA's strategic thinking and officers' curricula.[109] The three warfares is an inherent part of the national strategy as it aims to increase China's soft power and acceptability. Greater informationisation helps it in permeating across the continuum of military struggle and especially across the non-war military operations and is executed by an amalgam of uniformed PLA and civilian.[110] Each element of 'three warfares' operates through the perceptual presence and relies upon the efficacy of information. Public opinion warfare and legal warfare primarily operate at the strategic level of warfare, whereas psychological warfare is at the campaign and tactical levels.[111]

- **Public Opinion Warfare**. It involves shaping domestic and international public opinion through various forms of media to weaken the adversary's will to fight. It propagates through first information release advantage and its active guidance to preserve the public opinion battlefield or use target source within the enemy's country to create confusion if not able to correct the narrative. It was used by PLA during the Doklam crisis against India in 2017 and is also while fighting the perception battle related to COVID-19 or the "Wuhan Virus".
- **Legal Warfare**. It envisions the use of all aspects of the law, including national law, international law, and the requirements of war, to secure seizing "legal principle superiority" and delegitimize an adversary. In the context of the South China, Sea Arbitration ruling 2016 China twisted interpretations of international law to oppose the Philippines' position and seek to delegitimize the arbitration process. Legal Warfare aims at discerning prospective problems before they arise and provide a legal pretext for military action to safeguard national sovereignty and territorial integrity. It is, therefore, a unique blend of the traditional military component of coercion and persuasion to consolidate China's interests.
- **Psychological Warfare**. It seeks to undermine an adversary's combat power, resolve, and decision-making while exacerbating internal disputes to cause the enemy to divide into factions.

China has been actively using the 'three warfares' strategy—media, psychological and legal warfare against countries with which it has dispute. The Chinese policy of encirclement of India can be viewed through the prism of 'three warfares' where Beijing has not shied away from using its economic muscle to spread its influence in South Asia. It has used Pakistan as a proxy to undermine Indian influence in the region. The 'three warfares' strategy attempts to extend conventional war dynamics into the political domain, as is evident in its Taiwan engagement. A slow-moving and surreptitious ploy, the strategy is designed to subdue nations with the dispute with China without ever needing to fight. The 'three warfares' strategy is looking deeply into the fault lines. Social engineering is a concept which can be well utilised for popular mobilisation dynamics using a web of cyber tools, political subversion, creation and preparation of underground militia or workers. Beijing has realised the 'three warfare' strategy is well designed for democracies due to readily available fault line aided by the ever-pervasive internet within the society – a prerequisite to launching the non-contact warfare.

Practising Grey-Zone Contest

Over the past few years, numerous observers have drawn attention to the challenges that acts of creeping coercion pose to the international order. Global powers' shared predilection has compounded these concerns for so-called grey-zone strategies, a combination of information operations, political and economic coercion, cyber and space operations, and provocation by state-controlled forces. China has demonstrated a finely tuned risk calculus to expand its sphere of influence and sovereignty across multiple domains. 'Grey Zone' refers to a space in the peace-conflict continuum in which the operating environment by the aggressors is kept ambiguous. It leverages non-attribution to achieve strategic objectives while limiting counteractions by other nation-states. The methods for engaging adversaries in that environment have much in common with the political warfare that was predominant during the Cold War years that advocated the use of CNP to achieve its national objectives in a conflict 'short of war'. A combination of overt and covert measures is adopted to realise the laid-out objectives. The overt actions may include white propaganda, political alliances, and economic programmes. In contrast, covert operations may consist of clandestine support of 'friendly' foreign elements, 'black' psychological warfare, and even encouragement of underground resistance in hostile states.[112]

There has been growing interest in grey-zone operations that leverage existing social movements and nonviolent civil resistance based social revolution. A study of 323 resistance movements whose objective was regime change or expulsion of a foreign occupation force between 1900 and 2006 suggest that strategy of "nonviolent resistance against authoritarian regimes were twice as likely to succeed as violent movements" and China seems to be fully aware of it.[113] Russian influence in the US Presidential election has also shown the vulnerabilities of democratic processes.

A Grey-Zone win may not be a win in the classic warfare sense. Still, it does provide the government positional advantage, namely the ability to influence partners, populations, and threats toward the achievement of regional or strategic objectives. Specifically, Grey-Zone control helps in retaining decision space, maximizing desirable strategic options, or merely denying an adversary a decisive positional advantage.

Conclusion

China's national security efforts are intended to advance several core objectives of meeting its millennium goal of Chinese rejuvenation. To ensure that the goal is realised it looks at perpetuating the CPC's rule. It feels that the US policy of promoting democracy may undermine it by bringing social instability or by containing China's economic growth through external measures. It is equally aware of the penetrative power of cyber and space to influence its citizen and diaspora. It is facing the problems brought about by black swan events like pandemic (COVID-19) that has stressed all economic sectors, government and party structures. China is equally aware of the capability cavity which exists between it and the US-led western powers.

For the past four decades, China has been engaged in transforming it's military enjoying the 'period of strategic opportunity.' It has expounded its interest across the globe while transforming society through socio-economic leverage. As China enters the 'new era' as christened in 2019 NDWP, it is facing the headwind from the US and its allies. It has adopted a slew of measures to localise the contest threshold by engaging in non-contact warfare in non-military and non-lethal domains so that threshold of conflict remain manageable, and the strategic opportunity of growth is not lost.

The SMS 2013 and series of NDWP points that Beijing is modernising and reforming its doctrines to ensure that it can keep the external environment calm by moderating the magnitude of conflict so that it can exercise effective control. To navigate through the period of uncertainty and strategic destabilisation, it aims to improve situational awareness. 'Active Defence' has incorporated deterrence and coercion as part of non-contact warfare, and China sees its utility in extending it into conventional and nuclear warfare affairs. Its "three warfares" strategy aims to employ influence outcomes keeping the conflict localised. Ability to dominate the information space helps it to secure its overseas and outer-space areas by forward deployment to increase the strategic space.

A glance of the doctrinal shift in the PLA strategy shows that China is confident of its external environment. Still, it also recognises that it has entered the 'period of strategic friction' with the US. It is aware that its credible conventional and nuclear deterrent capability rules out any invasion to its border. It knows that it has to surmount protracted US competitive strategy and has to be prepared for contest in the emerging domains of the cyber-space-deep sea while safeguarding its economic development and preserving its core interests. For dealing with the superior power like the US, it is looking at increasing its balance of power through capability development, contingency-based deployment and asymmetric measures. However, while dealing with other nation-states, it is likely to employ the strategy of coercion through inducement or intimidation.

The force development trend of the PLA according to 2019 NDWP is "driven by the new round of technological and industrial revolution, the application of cutting-edge technologies such as AI, quantum information, big data, cloud computing and the Internet of Things (IoT) is gathering pace in the military field...new and high-tech military technologies based on IT are developing rapidly. There is a prevailing trend to develop long-range precision, intelligent, stealthy or unmanned weaponry and equipment."[114] The growing strength of comprehensive national power has enhanced its risk resistance capacity and capability of winning the informationised war. It throws the door open for the contest with non-contact means. The reading of conflict situation and applying the escalation control means for crisis mitigation will see a display of non-contact warfare strategy which PLA has carefully built.

NOTES

1 2005. "Interview with Lt Gen Liu Yazhou of the Air Force of the People's Liberation Army." *Heartland: Eurasia Review of Geoploitics* (Cassan Press) 1/2005: p.28. Accessed

September 14, 2019. http://temi.repubblica.it/limes-heartland/china-america-the-great-game/748.

2 "Remo, Amy R. *Gov't to pursue PH inclusion in TPP.* 17 September 2016. https://business.inquirer.net/215035/govt-to-pursue-ph-inclusion-in-tpp (accessed September 14, 2019).

3 People's Daily Online. *What does 18th CPC National Congress tell the world?* 08 December 2012. http://en.people.cn/102774/8051340.html (accessed September 14, 2019).

4 Pillsbury, Michael. (2015). *The Hundred-Year marathon: China's Secret Strategy to replace America as the Global Superpower.* New York: Henry Colt and Company., p.104.

5 Jingjing, Huang. (2013). *Silent Contest Silenced.* 17 November. Accessed February 17, 2019. http://www.globaltimes.cn/content/825489.shtml.

6 Academy of Military Sciences. (2013). *The Science of Military Strategy.* Edited by Sun Zhaoli. Beijing : Military Science Press, pp. 87-98.

7 Hickey, Dennis V. *Xi Jinping and the Removal of Presidential Term Limits in China.* Vers. PacNet #29. April 20, 2018. Dennis V. https://www.pacforum.org/analysis/pacnet-29-xi-jinping-and-removal-presidential-term-limits-china (accessed August 29, 2019).

8 Yunyi, Li Ruohan and Bai. *China adopts Constitutional amendment* . March 11, 2018. http://www.globaltimes.cn/content/1092805.shtml. (accessed August 29, 2019).

9 Andrew J. Nathan and Perry Link, eds., The Tiananmen Papers, New York: Public Affairs, 2001.

10 Scobell, Andrew. "China's Evolving Civil-Military Relations: Creeping Guojiahua." *Armed Forces & Society 31, no. 2,* January 2005: pp.227–244.

11 Wan, William. *In China, Soviet Union's Failure Drives Decisions on Reform.* March 23, 2013. William www.washingtonpost.com/world/asia_pacific/in-china-soviet-unions-failure-drives-decisions-on-reform/2013/03/23/9c090012-92ef-11e2-ba5 (accessed August 29, 2019).

12 2013. *CPC Central Committee Decision on Deepening of Reforms for Major Issues.* 15 November. Accessed February 19, 2019. http://news.xinhuanet.com/politics/2013-11/15/c_118164235.htm.

13 Mulvenon, James C. (2015). "Hotel Gutian: We Haven't Had That Spirit Here Since 1929." no. 46, Winter 2015, China Leadership Monitor. Accessed February 17, 2019," accessed from www.hoover.org/sites/default/files/research/docs/clm46jm.pdf.

14 Blasko, Dennis J. ""PLA Weaknesses and Xi's Concerns about PLA Capabilities."" *U.S.-China Economic and Security Review Commission.* February 07, 2019. https://www.uscc.gov/sites/default/files/Blasko_USCC%20Testimony_FINAL.pdf (accessed December 26, 2019).

15 Ibid.

16 Jijun, Li, Traditional Military Thinking and the Defense Strategy of China, *Letort Paper No. 1,* Carlisle Barracks, PA, Strategic Studies Institute, 29 August 1997.

17 Gilboy, George J; Heginbotham, Eric, *Chinese and Indian Strategic Behaviour: Growing Power and Alarm,* New Delhi: Cambridge University Press, 2012 p.32.

18 Sawyer, Ralph, *Sun Tzu Art of War,* New York, Basic Books, 1994, pp.173-179.

19 Ibid.

20 Academy of Military Sciences. (2013). *The Science of Military Strategy.* Edited by Sun Zhaoli. Beijing : Military Science Press, pp.12-18.

21 Ibid.

22 Ibid.

23 Ibid.

24 Ibid.
25 Ibid.
26 *Summary of the National Defense Strategy of The USA.* Policy, Washington: Department of Defence, 2018.
27 Ibid.
28 Ibid.
29 Colby, Elbridge A. *Testimony Before the Senate Armed Services Committee Hearing on Implementation of the National Defense Strategy.* 29 January 2019. https://www.armed-services.senate.gov/imo/media/doc/Colby_01-29-2019.pdf, p.4 (accessed August 28, 2019).
30 *China's National Defense in the New Era.* White Paper, Beijing, China,: The State Council Information Office of PRC, Foreign Languages Press Co. Ltd., 24 July 2019.
31 Ibid.
32 Tuosheng, Zhang. ""A Study of China's Behavior in International Military and Security Crises" [Zhongguo Junshi Anquan Weiji Xingwei Yanjiu]." *World Economics and Politics [Shijie Jingji yu Zhengzhi],* April 14, 2011, : pp. 103–121.
33 Central Committee of the Communist . 2016. *The 13th Five-Year Plan for Economic and Social Development of the People's Republic of China.* Five Year Plan, Beijing: Central Compilation and Translation Press.
34 "Full Text of Xi Jinping's Report at the 19th CPC National Congress." *www.xinhuanet.com/english.* November 03, 2017. www.xinhuanet.com/english/special/2017-11/03/c_136725942.htm . (accessed July 24, 2019).
35 *Xi Jingping during 19th CPC National Congress .* October 18, 2017. Xi Jingpin during 19th http://www.xinhuanet.com/english/2017-10/18/c_136689568.htm. (accessed November 16, 2018).
36 Timothy R. Heatth, Chapter 1: An Overview of China's Military Strategy, Joe McReynolds Ed. China's Evolving Military Strategy, Jamestwn Foundation, Washington, 2017, p.13.
37 Mai, Jun. (2018). *Xi Jinping claims progress on national security in meeting of secretive commission.* 20 April. Accessed May 18, 2020. https://www.scmp.com/news/china/policies-politics/article/2142505/xi-jinping-claims-progress-national-security-meeting.
38 Fravel, M. Taylor. "China's New Military Strategy: Winning Informationized Local Wars," */jamestown.org; China Brief Online, Volume XV's Issue 13 s.* July 2, 2015,. https://jamestown.org/wp-content/uploads/2015/07/China_Brief_Vol_15_ Issue13.pdf?x95163 (accessed September 12, 2019).
39 Ibid.
40 Ibid.
41 Wade, Geoff. *China's six wars in the next 50 years.* November 26, 2013. https://www.aspistrategist.org.au/chinas-six-wars-in-the-next-50-years/ (accessed December 30, 2019).
42 Academy of Military Sciences. (2013). *The Science of Military Strategy.* Edited by Sun Zhaoli. Beijing : Military Science Press, pp.44-46.
43 Fravel, M. Taylor. (2019). *Active Defense: China's Military Strategy since 1949.* New Jersey: Princeton University Press., p.72.
44 Academy of Military Sciences. (2013). *The Science of Military Strategy.* Edited by Sun Zhaoli. Beijing: Military Science Press, pp.44-46.

45 Fravel, M. Taylor. (2019). *Active Defense: China's Military Strategy since 1949.* New Jersey: Princeton University Press, pp. 72-88
46 Ibid.
47 Central Intelligence Agency. (19 April 1971). "Intelligence Memoranda – Ping Pong Diplomacy." CIA Intelligence Report, Department of Intelligence, Washington DC. Accessed December 02, 2019. https://www.cia.gov/library/readingroom/docs/LOC-HAK-114-7-3-4.pdf.
48 Fravel, M. Taylor. (2019). *Active Defense: China's Military Strategy since 1949.* New Jersey: Princeton University Press, pp.145-155.
49 Ibid.
50 The State Council Information Office of the People's Republic of China. (2015). "China's Military Strategy." May. Accessed April 09, 2018. http://eng.mod.gov.cn/Press/2015-05/26/content_4586805.htm>.
51 Jiang Zemin, *Jiang Zemin wenxuan* [Jiang Zemin's Selected Works], Vol. 1 (Beijing: Renmin Chubanshe, 2006), p. 285.
52 Ibid.
53 Ibid.
54 Feng, Guo. (September 1998). "Future Trends in Military." In *Chinese Views of Future Warfare*, by Michael Pillsbury, 85-94. Washington DC: National Defense University Press.
55 *China's National Defense in the New Era.* White Paper, Beijing, China,: The State Council Information Office of PRC, Foreign Languages Press Co. Ltd.
56 Ibid.
57 Ibid.
58 Xi Jinping Speaks at Politburo Study Session on Security," Xinhua, April 15, 2014.
59 The State Council Information Office of the People's Republic of China. (2015). "China's Military Strategy." May. Accessed April 09, 2018. http://eng.mod.gov.cn/Press/2015-05/26/content_4586805.htm.
60 Fravel, M. Taylor. (December 2005). "The Evolution of China's Military Strategy: Comparing the 1987 and 1999 Editions of Zhanlüexue." In *China's Revolution in Doctrinal Affairs*, by James Mulvenon and David M. Finkelstein, Virginia: The CNA Corporation. Wang, pp. 79-100.
61 Ibid.
62 Ibid.
63 Academy of Military Sciences. (2013). *The Science of Military Strategy.* Edited by Sun Zhaoli. Beijing : Military Science Press, pp.103-110.
64 Fravel, M. Taylor. "Chapter 2: China's Changing Approach to Military Strategy: The Science of Military Strategy from 2001 and 2013." In *China's Evolving Military Strategy*, by M. Taylor Fravel, edited by Joe McReynolds. Washington DC: The Jamestown Foundation, January 2017, pp.55-58.
65 Ibid.
66 Academy of Military Sciences. (2013). *The Science of Military Strategy.* Edited by Sun Zhaoli. Beijing : Military Science Press, pp.103-110.
67 Ibid.
68 Ibid.
69 Ibid.
70 Fravel, M. Taylor. "Chapter 2: China's Changing Approach to Military Strategy: The Science of Military Strategy from 2001 and 2013." In *China's Evolving Military Strategy*,

by M. Taylor Fravel, edited by Joe McReynolds. Washington DC: The Jamestown Foundation, January 2017, pp.59-60.

71 The meaning of yin and yang is that the universe is governed by a cosmic duality, sets of two opposing and complementing principles or cosmic energies that can be observed in nature.

72 Academy of Military Sciences. (2013). *The Science of Military Strategy.* Edited by Sun Zhaoli. Beijing : Military Science Press, pp.114-120.

73 Ibid.

74 Fravel, M. Taylor. "Chapter 2: China's Changing Approach to Military Strategy: The Science of Military Strategy from 2001 and 2013." In *China's Evolving Military Strategy*, by M. Taylor Fravel, edited by Joe McReynolds. Washington DC: The Jamestown Foundation, January 2017, pp.60-61.

75 Ibid.

76 Ibid.

77 Ibid.

78 Ibid, pp.64-65.

79 Academy of Military Sciences. (2013). *The Science of Military Strategy.* Edited by Sun Zhaoli. Beijing : Military Science Press, pp.93-98.

80 Ibid.

81 Ibid, p.100.

82 Cheng, D. (2009). Prospects for China's Military Space Efforts. In Kamphausen, R., Lai, D. & Scobell, A. (Eds.). Beyond the Strait: PLA Missions Other Than Taiwan. U.S. Army War College.

83 Zhaonian, Pan. (05 October 2013). "Strategic Thinking for Battlefield Construction in Joint Operations Under Informatized Conditions." *China Military Science [Zhongguo Junshi Kexue].* quoted in Timothy R. Heath, Kristen Gunness, Cortez A. Cooper. 2016. *The PLA and China's Rejuvination.* Santa Monica, California: RAND Corporation., p.36.

84 Timothy R. Heath, Kristen Gunness, Cortez A. Cooper. (2016). *The PLA and China's Rejuvination.* Santa Monica, California: RAND Corporation., p.36.

85 Ibid.

86 Academy of Military Sciences. (2013). *The Science of Military Strategy.* Edited by Sun Zhaoli. Beijing : Military Science Press, pp.154-155.

87 Ibid, p.159.

88 Ibid, pp.162-165.

89 Ibid, pp.166-168.

90 Ibid, pp.124.

91 Ibid pp.116-117.

92 Ibid.

93 Ibid.

94 An area of international airspace bordering a state's territorial airspace in which a state specifies additional aircraft identification requirements.

95 George J. Gilboy and Heginbotham, Eric. (2012). *Chinese and Indian Strategic Behaviour: Growing Power and Alarm.* New Delhi: Cambridge University Press, p.32.

96 Senior Colonel *Shen Kuiguan DIALETICS of Defeating the Superior with Inferior, Air Force Command Institute, Beijing; his paper originally appeared in* China Military Science *(Winter 1994)*

97 Ibid.

98 Jullien, F. (1999). The Propensity of Things Toward a History of Efficacy in China. New York, NY: Zone Books, p.16.

99 Ibid.

100 Lai, David. (01 May 2004). *Go Approach to Mastering China's Strategic Concept, Shi.* U.S. Army War College Strategic Studies Institute . http://www.strategicstudies institute.army.mil/pubs/display.cfm?pubID=378.

101 'Wei Qi' translated literally, means "encirclement board." An iconic Chinese game played during the Warring States period. The purpose of the game is to encircle the other player's pieces rather than annihilation. To win, you must entice the opponent by opening up new positions while deceptively encircling him, hoping the opponent will not notice your true strategy. The player who designs multiple positions of encirclement and counter-encirclement so that the degree of the encirclement is not apparent to the other wins.

102 Ibid.

103 Ibid.

104 Ibid.

105 Ibid.

106 Henry Kissinger. (2011). *On China.* New York: Penguin Press, p.235.

107 Pillsbury, Michael. (2015). *The Hundred-Year marathon: China's Secret Strategy to replace America as the Global Superpower.* New York: Henry Colt and Company, pp.47-55.

108 Gottlieb, Thomas M. (1977). *Chinese Foreign Policy Factionalism and the Origins of the Strategic Triangle.* Santa Monica, CA: RAND Corporation. http://www.rand.org/pubs/reports/R1902.html.

109 Kania, Elsa. (2016). "The PLA's Latest Strategic Thinking on the Three Warfares." *China Brief,* Vol. 16, Isuue 13, Jamestown Foundation, August 22. Accessed September 13, 2019. https://jamestown.org/program/the-plas-latest-strategic-thinking-on-the-three-warfares/.

110 Ibid.

111 Ibid.

112 269. Policy Planning Staff Memorandum, National Archives and Records Administration, RG 273, Office of Historian, Department of State, The United States, Washington, May 4, 1948, Accessed online on 13 December 2018, https://history.state.gov/historicaldocuments/frus1945-50Intel/d269.

113 Stephan, Erica Chenoweth and Maria J. (2014). "Drop Your Weapons: When and Why Civil Resistance Works." *Foreign Affairs 93,* No. 4, July/August : 94–106.

114 *China's National Defense in the New Era.* White Paper, Beijing, China,: The State Council Information Office of PRC, Foreign Languages Press Co. Ltd., 24 July 2019.

3

PLA's Kinetic Non-Contact Warfare Capabilities

The structure follows strategy.

—**Alfred D. Chandler**

PLA'S REFORM ANALYSIS

Showcasing Capability

On the seventieth anniversary of its founding on 01 October 2019, China in its military parade, exhibited the PLA's strength by displaying its strategic weapon systems. 2019 parade was exceptional for the number and assortment of new, high-tech weapons showcased.[1] The carefully choreographed parade was to popularise China's emerging warfighting doctrine. The political messaging was primarily to show the might of China to guard against the foreign intervention forces. While it may be directed against the US Indo-Pacific strategy, but it had overtones for the countries in China's neighbourhood also. It emphasised China's technological growth and its focus on informationized armed forces working on kinetic and non-kinetic systems intended to bolster China's capacity and capability building riding on reforms. The significant capabilities demonstrated during the parade were:

- Thrust to augment its precision-guided strike complex with improved ISR capabilities.

- Ability to wage effective electronic warfare by disrupting communication and information networks, threatening situational awareness and precision targeting.
- Hypersonic systems to challenge the existing air and missile defences systems.
- To increase the undersea situational awareness, challenging the dominance of US submarines.
- Bolster its deterrence capability by displaying new and upgraded nuclear delivery systems with mobile intercontinental ballistic missiles (ICBM) and submarine-launched ballistic missiles (SLBM). Moreover, the display served to highlight the technical sophistication and modernity of China's strategic missile force, a central consideration in Chinese nuclear decision making.

The showcasing of the capability by China was part of the four decades of its carefully crafted and sustained force development plan. The thawing of the Sino-US relationship in April 1979 with the promulgation of Taiwan Relationship Act gave the boost to the Chinese planners to carefully manage the flow of 'Shi' (refer Chapter 2 for details). It aimed at modernising China despite its ideological differences with the West. The trajectory of Chinese force development gives its intent of power play.

China's Guidelines for PLA's Force Development

Xi Jinping has empowered himself through a slew of the constitutional amendment and has struck at the bureaucratic opposition to reform by breaking up the four general departments (previously described as "independent kingdoms"), reducing their institutional power of the previously dominant ground forces and removing disloyal and corrupt PLA officer corps.[2] The PLA is tasked to upgrade and develop the strategic concept of people's war. The People's Military Struggle (PMS) as referred in 2015, NDWP on China's military strategy, requires it to be enmeshed with political, economic, diplomatic, cultural and legal endeavours. Here the strategies and tactics can be used in a comprehensive way to prevent and defuse crises and deter conflicts and winning wars.[3] The national defence policy pushes for the RMA with Chinese characteristics to attain informationisation through clear undermentioned guidelines for force development:[4]

- Establish rapid and efficient modern centralised and unified national defence mobilisation system in a phased manner.

- Joint operations should form the cornerstone of the PLA operational strengths.
- The PLA Army (PLAA) to move from regional defence to trans-regional mobility, and improve its capabilities in air-ground integrated operations, long-distance manoeuvres, rapid assaults and special operations.
- The PLA Navy (PLAN) to implement the gradual extension of the strategic depth for offshore defensive operations and enhance its capabilities in integrated maritime operations and nuclear counterattacks.
- The PLA Air Force (PLAAF) to speed up its transition from territorial air defence to both offensive and defensive operations by increasing its capabilities in the airstrike, air and missile defence, ISR and strategic projection.
- The PLA Rocket Force (PLARF) to progressively improve its force structure of having both nuclear and conventional missiles and raising its capabilities in strategic deterrence and conventional strike under conditions of informtionisation.
- The critical domain of outer space to provide strategic assurance for national and international development. It aimed to improve space situational awareness, safeguard space assets and enhances the capacity to safely enter, exit and openly use outer space.[5]
- PLA to safeguard "national cyber sovereignty, information security and social stability"[6] to enable economic growth and social development.
- Step up the economy, science and technology, information and innovation content in all forms of people's war and develop new strategies and tactics for people's war in conditions of informtionisation.

The 2019 NDWP provides the vision for the evolution of war from informationized warfare to intelligent warfare. The PLA is keen to complete the informatisation phase as it feels that its rise will be constrained if not contested. Hence, it is aiming to create tailored and targeted response-ability to defuse and deter crisis and conflicts. The reforms aim to bridge the strategic gaps in weapon, force and doctrine development.

Setting the Tone of Reforms

Xi while steering the fourth meeting of the Leading Group for further reforms on 18 August 2014, urged the relevant central departments to "appropriately handle the relationship between reform and the formulation, revision and abolishment of laws...define effective measures, and coordinate and set the pace of implementation to advance reforms."[7] Xi Jinping, on assuming office took two important decisions to bring greater coherence in the conduct of China's national security policy. In 2015, an expansive National Security Law was passed to strengthen the role of central authorities. In the same year, the CPC established a new National Security Commission (NSC) to combine efforts of various departments under the CPC guidance. The Commission's purview appears to encompass domestic stability and external security, a much wider scope than the US National Security Council.[8] President Xi, Premier Li Keqiang, and NPC Chairman lead the Commission. The NSC's mission to take care of national security suggests that they will be the key players to steer the national discourse. In April 2018, in the review meeting of the Commission, President Xi Jinping complimented the Commission for having solved many national security problems that had remained unsolved and undone."[9]

Xi has linked the reforms to the rule of law and quoted Wang Anshi, a Song Dynasty statesman, who said, "when the law of the land under heaven is good, there will be order in the land under heaven."[10] He has embarked on enforcing the rule of law "scrutiny" and "audit" within party organs, administrative and judicial set up. He has not spared even media and public. The seriousness to reform China intense. Xi Jinping has elevated Wang Huning, Director of the Policy Research Office of the CPC Central Committee in the 18th Central Committee of Politburo to Director of CPC Comprehensively Deepening Reforms Commission in the 19th Central Committee to Politburo Standing Committee position. Thus, the legal muscle has been given to the CPC by Xi to control and steer the reforms.

Structural Reorganisation: Boost to Non-Contact Component

The reforms dissolved the four general departments and created an expanded revamped CMC with 15 functional organs established directly under it. The reform centralised the command and control in the CMC and its chairman with the new Joint Staff Department (JSD) given the responsibility for supervising joint operations. The CMC now oversees a dual command structure where services are responsible for force construction, and five theatre commands are responsible for conventional joint operations in their respective regions. Strategic Support Force and Rocket Force fall outside this bifurcated arrangement, maintaining responsibility for their force construction and strategic operations.[11] The reorganisation of the PLA is complete. Transitioning the Military Region (MR) system to a more joint Theatre Command structure (refer to Figure 3.1) is oriented to improve inter-service operability and enhance the CPC control. The Jinan, Nanjing and Guangzhou MR have been spared, as they focused on the disputed East China Sea, the Taiwan Strait and the South China Sea. However, the Beijing and Shenyang MR has been merged, and so has the Lanzhou and Chengdu MR, reducing the country's seven MR to five Theatre Command. The operational control over the ground, naval, air, and conventional Rocket Force units is now being exercised by these five joints Theatre Command within their areas of responsibility. Now, the PLA services are principally responsible to the CMC for manning, equipping, and training activities. At the same time, the theatres assume operational control of forces under the supreme command of the CMC.

The reorganisation has led to the establishment of a distinct PLA Army headquarters, a Joint Logistics Support Force, granting of military service status to the PLARF (formerly Second Artillery Force), and creation of Strategic Support Force. It thus consolidates many intelligence, space, cyber and electronic warfare organs and responsibilities (refer Figures 3.1 and 3.2). It promotes joint organisations in PLAN and PLAAF and re-engineering of logistics and support systems. Ground force and air force units have all been reorganised into a standardised "group army/corps-brigade-battalion" structure. The previous 18 Group Armies have been reorganised into 13 new ones. The PLA has completed its downsizing of 300,000 officers and troops, cutting over 1,000 units and 30 per cent of commissioned officers.[12] According to 2019 NDWP, there has been 25 per cent cut at regiment and above level and 50 per cent at non-combat units' level. PLA Army has been the main looser, and the PLAN and PLARF have been the leading gainer in this reform. The thrust of the reform appears to give priority to the non-contact content during restructuring besides synergising the command and control structure with strict oversight.

Reforming Command and Control (C2)

In October 2017, 19th Party Congress reduced the size of the CMC to integrate joint command structures for speedier strategic decision making with increased political oversight. It has eliminated the bottlenecks in the flow of strategic direction from CMC to the theatre commands. The role of the Service Headquarters has been reduced to the administrative task of force management. Thus, the reform has made the PLA theatre commands ready for joint operations along strategic directions. All-encompassing resources have been assigned to it less the nuclear and strategic support force which will be allocated based on the operational requirements. The C2 has been harmonised by the creation of Joint Operations Command Centres (JOCC) at CMC and theatre level by drawing officers from all arms and services. The CMC JOCC coordinates the efforts of the five theatre commands. The theatre-level JOCCs are responsible for all operations in their area of responsibility including maintaining situational awareness, evaluating doctrinal issues through joint exercises, and providing communications hub to link theatre commanders with service component commanders and forces.[13] The Joint Staff Department (JSD) has assumed all responsibilities which were earlier with the General Staff Department (GSD) for combat planning, command and control support, and formulating strategy and requirements.[14] In contrast, other departments have assumed other aspects of mobilisation, training and administration. The joint C2 structure mirrors Western-style force structuring.

Though in principle, the reforms have removed the service headquarters from operations, in practice, all of them have held onto some operational command responsibilities. PLA Army headquarters retains the responsibility for border and coastal defence. Similarly, PLAN headquarters supervises the counter-piracy patrols in the Gulf of Aden, and the PLAAF headquarters retain centralised control of bomber, transport, and airborne assets. The Rocket Force has operational control over strategic forces.[15]

The PLA is fielding new technologies to improve commanders' situational awareness by sharing information on robust, redundant communication networks and advanced automated command systems, such as its Integrated Command Platform, with units at lower echelons across the force.[16] As these command automation tools get integrated, it will significantly enhance the PLA's flexibility and responsiveness.

Figure 3.1: PLA Structure Prior to 2016 Reform

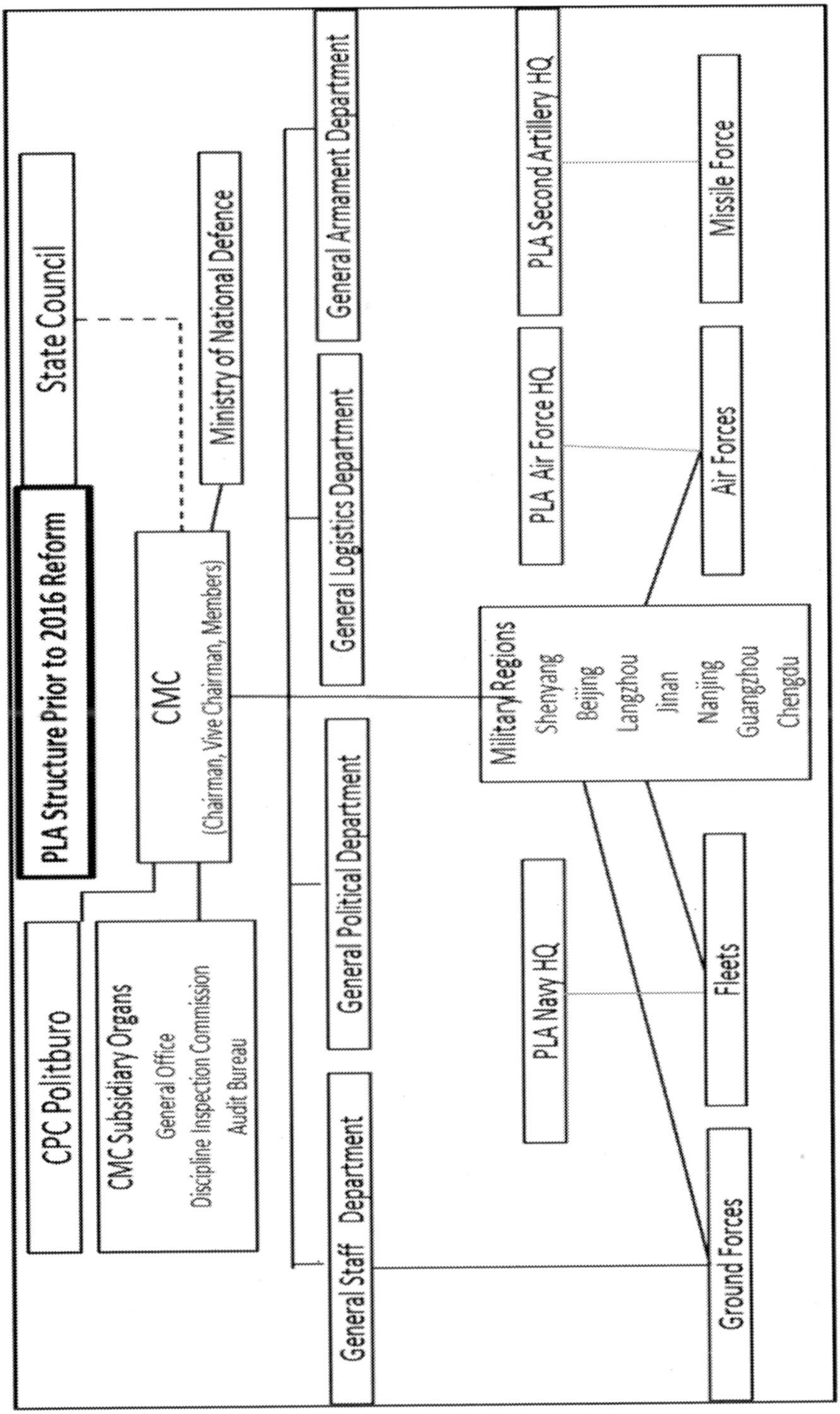

Figure 3.2: PLA structure after 2016 Reforms

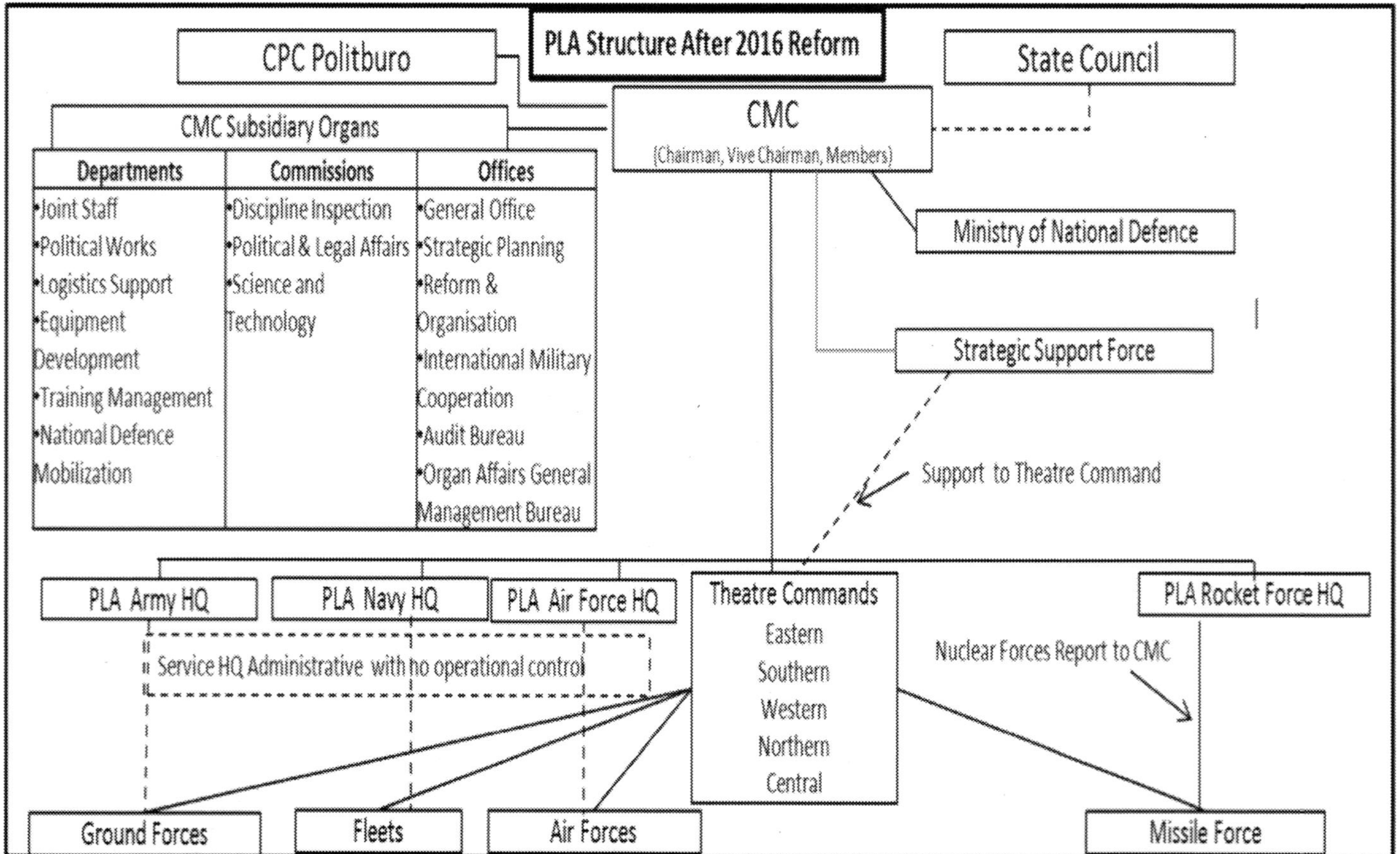

Examining Kinetic Domain

PLAAF and PLARF are the movers and shakers in the strategic kinetic domain while the PLA Army and PLAN operate at the operational and tactical level. PLAAF and PLARF form the mainstay of kinetic warfare fulcrum of China. According to SMS 2013, PLARF will serve as the core component of China's strategic deterrent and its role will increase with improvements in its nuclear and conventional missile capabilities. For PLARF, the conventional missile is the primary weapon. The long-range, rapid response, high precision and strong deep penetration capabilities with multiple lethal payloads make it more favourable non-contact weapon systems as compared to other conventional weapons. 2019 October parade display of equipment was done by China to demonstrate PLARF capacity and capability. PLAAF, on the other hand, operates at the strategic and operational level. It has tailor-made missions which primarily looks after the air-defence, undertake offensive air operations such as joint fire strikes, part of blockade or island landing operations besides Human Assistance and Disaster Relief (HADR) missions. The information operation force looks at effective suppression and destruction using 'soft kill' or 'hard kill' options. The PLA Army and PLAN while looking at the border and maritime security has invested in developing long-range lethal systems while honing the grey zone operational art as part of conflict management approach.

PLA Rocket Force: Core Force for Strategic Deterrence

The PLA Second Artillery Force (PLASAF) was renamed as the PLA Rocket Force (PLARF) in late 2015 as part of military reforms. The force was elevated to a full-service level and received the designation junzhong or service.[17] It puts it on equal footing with the PLA Army, Navy, and Air Force.[18] PLARF is the Strategic Missile Forces with more than 120,000 personnel. It organises and commands its troops to launch nuclear counterattacks with strategic missiles and to conduct operations with conventional missiles. The PLASAF was formed in July 1966, shortly before the PRC test-fired its first nuclear-capable ballistic missile. It had always been responsible for China's land-based nuclear-armed missiles and their nuclear deterrence mission, and this responsibility will continue for the PLARF. Starting from the mid-1980s, the PLASAF pursued the task of 'dual deterrence and dual operations', meaning it was to maintain both nuclear and conventional missiles, a mandate under which the PLASAF dramatically expanded and diversified its conventional forces.

PLARF Missions

At the inauguration ceremony for the PLARF in December 2015, Xi Jinping articulated the need for the PLARF to 'possess both nuclear and conventional capabilities' and be prepared to conduct 'comprehensive deterrence and warfighting' operations.[19] While the requirement is not new, but the emphasis on 'comprehensive deterrence and warfighting' is significant. This comprehensiveness includes a geographic element that requires the PLARF to be able to fight and deter enemies across different regions and distances.[20] But it also consists of a domain element that requires the PLARF to conduct operations across land, sea, aerospace and electromagnetic spectrums.[21] The 2019 NDWP reiterated the mission and called for deterring wars in all battle-spaces having taken into account the US 2018 Nuclear Posture Review (NPR). However, the US withdrawal from Intermediate-Range Nuclear Forces (INF) Treaty on 02 August 2019 and expiry of New Strategic Arms Reduction Treaty (START) in February 2021 will add pressure on China to review its deterrence posture. The newly-emphasised requirement for the PLARF remains to prepare for 'comprehensive deterrence and warfighting' operations. It suggests that the force is expected to execute, either independently or as part of a joint effort, a diverse range of warfighting and deterrence operations while championing its stated policy of "No First Use." The elevation of the PLARF will undoubtedly help the service to improve China's strategic missile forces.[22] Chinese rapidly modernising nuclear forces have considerably increased the credibility of its nuclear deterrent. The PLARF has two vital missions: strategic deterrence and conventional warfighting.

Strategic Deterrence

SMS 2013 describes PLARF as the core force for strategic deterrence with a conventional missile as the primary weapons and principal component of PLA's long-range conventional strike force. The Chinese interpretation of term deterrence is closer in meaning to what Thomas Schelling referred to as "coercion," as it encompasses both deterrence and compellence. PLA strategists believe that of strategic deterrence entails not only nuclear deterrence, which is essential for responding to the most severe threats to

Chinese national security interests but also conventional deterrence, which provides China's leaders more flexibility in the employment of resources. Notably, China's conventional deterrence is becoming more effective and credible, especially because of its long-range strike capabilities. China's conception of strategic deterrence also includes deterrence in space and information domains, and since PLARF makes use of both the domains, a symbiotic relationship exists between the three.

In peacetime, the PLARF supports strategic deterrence objectives in several ways, including displaying new missiles in military parades, participating in military exercises, or revealing missiles when an adversary's satellites are passing overhead. During the PRC's 70th-anniversary military parade on 01 October 2019, Beijing undoubtedly signalled its growing nuclear deterrent capability and credibility by displaying newly developed DF-17's hypersonic glide vehicle technology which could make the ballistic missile defence of the US ineffective. DF-41 ICBM with a range of 12,000 to 15,000 km was also displayed to showcase the Chinese capability of reaching the US mainland.[23] As part of strategic deterrence, the PLARF has developed the credible nuclear second-strike capability to deter nuclear attacks or coercion against China. The Chinese strategists stress the importance of linking deterrence actions to political objectives. The combination of nuclear and conventional missiles according to 2015 NDWP gives PLARF the ability to transform itself in the direction of informtionisation, enhance the safety, reliability and effectiveness of missile systems for strategic deterrence and nuclear counterattack through the use of medium and long-range precision strikes. Hence, PLARF is an ideal instrument for strategic deterrence operations because of its ability to launch rapidly, penetrate enemy missile defence systems, and destroy key targets.

Warfighting

The PLARF prepares for two major types of warfighting campaigns: the nuclear counterattack campaign and the conventional missile strike campaign. In keeping with China's NFU policy, the nuclear counterattack campaign is the only type of nuclear strike campaign discussed in Chinese military publications. They also state that such a campaign could be carried out independently by the PLARF or as a major part of a "joint nuclear counterattack campaign" involving the other services like the PLAN, which currently deploys four out of a total projected eight Type 094 *Jin*-class

SSBNs. The PLAAF which appears poised to regain a nuclear role for its bomber force, which would provide China with a credible nuclear triad.[24] In any case, the nuclear counterattack campaign requires the survivability of the missile force and the ability to strike key enemy targets, and it would be executed strictly under the authority of the highest level of China's leadership. Chinese military publications also indicate that the nuclear counterattack campaign could be a large-scale or small-scale nuclear counterattack campaign and could consist of both initial nuclear strikes and follow-on nuclear strikes. The use of nuclear weapons will be dependent on the need to deter further escalation or launch follow-on strikes if required.[25]

In a crisis or conflict situation, the PLARF can conduct higher-intensity deterrence operations, such as raising the readiness level of missile units, conducting exercise launches, or carrying out warning strikes. Significantly, even though China officially maintains a strict nuclear NFU policy, some PLA publications suggest that "lowering the nuclear threshold" could deter an enemy from launching conventional attacks against certain types of strategic targets. However, the Chinese strategists see nuclear deterrence as relevant in any crisis or conflict involving a nuclear-armed adversary, especially if the strategic deterrence fails, and China comes under nuclear attack. In such an eventuality the PLARF is responsible for carrying out a nuclear counterattack. As part of its conventional warfighting role, the PLARF is mandated to conduct standoff medium-, and long-range precision engagements strike with land-based missiles against key strategic and operational targets of the enemy. PLA missile strategy stipulates the use of its conventional missile force against high-threat and high-value enemy targets, such as C4ISR, anti-air, and logistics systems.

The PLARF's view, its conventional strike precision weapons are part of Elite Force Sharp Arms, and part of deterrence arsenal against the US as the conventional ballistic and cruise missiles can serve as an instrument of coercive diplomacy.[26] The land-based conventional missiles give it an added advantage in terms of deep penetration in a short span. Even with the diversification of the long-range strike capability PLARF conventional force development is primarily focused on countering not only the US developmental dynamics but also other nations in possession of missiles. China feels that by extending its capability in deterrence field, it will be able to extend its period of strategic opportunity as the deterrence adds to calming the external environment.

The PLA of 2019 has made rapid advancement in its capabilities and readiness development over the past two decades ago. However, according to Dennis J. Blasko, "when Chinese leaders state there is a gap of at least two to three decades between their capabilities and those of advanced militaries, they over-simply the actual situation. In certain areas, such as some categories of ballistic and cruise missiles, air defence, electronic warfare, and cyber capabilities, the PLA ranks among the world's leaders."[27]

PLARF Organisational Construct

Comprehensive deterrence and warfighting are the strategic requirements for the PLARF. It suggests that the PLARF is required to possess a full spectrum of missile capabilities. It would require advanced missile technologies, appropriate doctrines and critical supporting systems, such as command and control, communications, intelligence, reconnaissance, targeting and tracking platforms.[28]

According to 2015 NDWP, the PLARF commands the missile bases, training bases, specialised support units, academies and research institutions. It possesses a series of "Dong Feng" ballistic missiles and "Chang Jian" cruise missiles. The PLARF has organised force-on-force evaluation-oriented training and training based on operational plans at brigade and regiment levels, strengthened training for joint strikes. According to Military Balance 2019, the PLARF remains organised in a series of corps leader- grade 'bases', numbering nine in total. Six of them (bases 61–66) command the force's operational missile brigades, while the other three handle warhead storage and transport (67 Base), specialist engineering (68 Base) and test and training (69 Base). Each missile base has between three and five subordinate missile brigades, with most bases operating a mix of conventional and nuclear brigades. The exception is Base 61 (formerly Base 51), which operates only conventional missiles and may have up to eight missile brigades.[29] The multiple new missile brigades formed during 2017 are now beginning to take shape, with some resultant relocation of units and changes to equipment and missions. The two new brigades formed in 64 and 66 bases are likely to be road-mobile intercontinental ballistic missile (ICBM) units- one may be responsible for the still-developmental DF-41 (CH-SS-X-20) ICBM into service and the other probably to equip either the DF-31A(G) ICBM or additional DF-41s. Both of these missiles are capable of deploying multiple independently targetable re-entry vehicles. The new brigades would mark the first expansion of the PLARF's road-mobile ICBM fleet in nearly a decade. In late 2017, media reports described two test firings of a new developmental short-range ballistic missile or MRBM, reportedly with a hypersonic glide-vehicle payload. Reportedly this missile may have the PLA designation DF-17.[30]

Over the past two decades, China has modernised and expanded the size of its nuclear and conventional missile forces. It has greatly improved the Rocket Force's ability to conduct the deterrence operations and missile strike campaigns outlined earlier. Tables 3.1 and 3.2 provides the details of missile brigade holdings, likely equipment holding and characteristics.

Table 3.1: Surface-to-Surface Missiles

ICBM Brigade with Equipment	*IRBM & MRBM Brigade with Equipment*	*SRBM & GLCM Brigade with Equipment*
1 ICBM brigade with DF-4*	2 IRBM brigade with DF-26$	4 SRBM brigade with DF-11A
2 ICBM brigade with DF-5A*	2 MRBM brigade with DF-16	2 SRBM brigade with DF-15B
1 ICBM brigade with DF-5B*	6 MRBM brigade with DF-21A/E$	2 GLCM brigade with CJ-10/CJ-10A
1 ICBM brigade with DF-31*	2 MRBM brigade with DF-21C#	
2 ICBM brigade with DF-31A/A(G)*	2 MRBM brigade with DF-21D#	
5+ SSM brigade (Under Raising)		

Legend: * - Nuclear; $ - Dual Role (Convention and Nuclear); # - ASBM

Source: 15 February 2019. *Military Balance.* https://doi.org/10.1080/04597222.2018. 1561021, pp. 235-236.

Table 3.2: PLARF Missile Types

Sl.	*System*	*Type*	*Warhead*	*Propellant*	*Deployment Mode*	*Max Range in km*
1	CSS-3/DF-4	ICBM	Nuclear	Liquid	ROTL**	5,500+
2	CSS-4/DF-5	ICBM	Nuclear	Liquid	Silo	12,000-13,000
3	CSS-7/DF-11A	SRBM	Conventional	Solid	Mobile	300-600
4	CSS-6/DF-15B	SRBM	Conventional	Solid	Mobile	600-850+
5	CSS-11/DF-16	MRBM	Conventional	Solid	Mobile	800-1,000
6	CSS-5/DF-21A/21E	MRBM	Nuclear and Conventional Variants	Solid	Mobile	1,500-1,750+
7	CSS-5 Mod-5/DF-21D	ASBM	Conventional	Solid	Mobile	1,500+
8	DF-26	IRBM	Nuclear and Conventional Variants	Solid	Mobile	4,000
9	CSS-10/DF-31	ICBM	Nuclear	Solid	Mobile	7,200-11,200
10	CJ-10	GLCM	Conventional	Solid	Mobile	1500+

Within PLARF organisational structure, the base is responsible for command and control of the assets, and it passes down through brigades, battalions, companies, and platoons.[31] Though most of China's missile bases command both nuclear and conventional brigades, however, their command and control arrangements are separate. While the nuclear units are believed to report directly to the CMC, the conventional units may be operating under the theatre commands.[32] There are indications of personnel from PLARF posted with the theatre commands as staff officers.[33] The structure of brigades differs for fixed-site missiles and mobile missiles, as well as for conventional and nuclear missiles. Thus, the number of missiles per brigade may vary greatly between conventional missile brigades (up to 36 launchers with up to 6 missiles per launcher), mobile nuclear-armed missile brigades (between 6 and 12 missile launchers per brigade), and fixed-site nuclear-armed missiles (6 or fewer silos).[34]

PLARF Force Building

To build a lean and effective force in accordance with the development of military science and technology, the PLARF strives to raise the informtionisation level of its weaponry and equipment. The focus of development is to enhance the safety and reliability, and improve its capabilities in protection, rapid reaction, penetration, damage and precision strike. After several decades of development, it has created a weaponry and equipment system with both nuclear and conventional missiles, both solid-fuelled and liquid-fuelled missiles, different launching ranges and various types of warheads.

Nuclear Missile Force Modernisation

The key drivers of PLARF have been the threats posed by advances in US ISR, precision strike and missile defence capabilities.[35] China describes its desired force structure as a "lean and effective" nuclear deterrent, one that is capable of ensuring retaliation following an enemy attack against China.[36] The US Department of Defence reports that China is "developing and testing several new variants of missiles, forming additional missile units, retiring or upgrading older missile systems; and developing methods to counter ballistic missile defences."[37] According to the Pentagon, "China's ICBM arsenal to date consists of approximately 75–100 ICBMs."[38] It includes the silo-based DF-5A, the silo-based DF-5B equipped with MIRVs, the road-mobile DF-31 and DF-31A, and the older, shorter-range DF-4.

PLARF nuclear missile force modernisation continues to focus on enhancing survivability and countering missile defence developments.[39] Recent examples of this continuing effort include the new DF-31AG ICBMs, which feature improved launchers and greater mobility.[40] The PLARF also deploys nuclear medium-range ballistic missiles (MRBMs) and IRBMs for regional deterrence and strike missions.[41] The deployment of the DF-26 IRBM, which has nuclear and conventional precision strike capabilities, as well as a conventional anti-ship version, is another significant development in PLARF modernisation.[42] China has also developed an extensive network of tunnels to conceal its operations and enhance its survivability. For example, a June 2017 Chinese media report highlighted the release of a PLARF video depicting an ICBM brigade's participation in a "month-long underground survival exercise in an unidentified facility 'beneath mountains."[43]

Conventional Missile Force Modernisation

Meanwhile, modernisation of the PLARF conventional missiles has focused on expanding the range, enhancing their accuracy and ability to overcome enemy missile defence systems, and improving the rapid-response capabilities of missile units. According to the US Department of Defence, the PLARF deploys DF-16, conventional DF-21 MRBMs, and the DF-21D anti-ship ballistic missile (ASBM)[44] (for range and characteristics refer to Table 3.2). In addition, the PLARF has about 1,200 short-range ballistic missiles a large number of short-range ballistic missiles (SRBMs), comprising of the DF-11 and DF-15, and many CJ-10 ground-launched cruise missiles with a range of about 1,500 km.[45] Doctrine for conventionally armed missiles emphasises pre-emptive strike as compared to "No First Use" nuclear strike. The career progression within PLARF points out that experience with conventionally armed missile units is more likely to lead to a senior leadership position than officers who have served in units tasked with primarily regional or strategic nuclear missions.[46]

Conventional MRBMs have found their way in the PLARF inventory to allow it to orchestrate precision strikes against land targets and naval ships (including aircraft carriers) operating between Chinese shores and the first island chain.[47] The CSS-5 Mod-5/DF-21D with a range exceeding 1,500 kilometres has a manoeuvrable warhead. The new MRBM DF-16G unveiled in 2017, features high accuracy, short preparation time, and an improved manoeuvrable terminal stage that can better infiltrate missile defence systems.

China has developed the DF-26 intermediate-range ballistic missile (IRBM) which is capable of conducting precision strikes against ground targets and contributes to China's counter intervention posture in the Indo-Pacific region. During the 2015 parade, official public statements also referenced a nuclear version of the DF-26, which, if it has the same guidance capabilities, would give China its first nuclear precision-strike capability against theatre targets.

China's 2015 NDWP states that the PLARF will strengthen its capabilities for strategic deterrence and nuclear counterattack, as well as improve its conventional precision strike capabilities. Additionally, the white paper indicates that it will meet its vital requirement of being lean and effective by possessing both nuclear and conventional missiles."[48] The PLARF will also strive "to transform itself in the direction of informtionisation,[49] press forward with independent innovations in weaponry and equipment, enhance the safety, reliability and effectiveness of systems besides improving the force structure of both nuclear and conventional capabilities."[50]

The modern trends in missile systems are for the use of solid propellants as it reduces the logistical requirements and improves the simplicity of operation. Multiple-stage missiles, with each stage having its independent propulsion system, are more efficient for longer-range missions. ICBMs characteristically have two or three stages, with powerful liquid-propellant engines or solid-propellant motors to propel the payload toward its target, and a post-boost vehicle with a much smaller propulsion system. Some long-range ballistic missiles carry multiple independent re-entry vehicles (MIRV), with up to 10 re-entry vehicles (RV) per missile. RV re-enter the Earth's atmosphere at very high velocities, on the order of 4-5 miles per second at ICBM ranges.[51]

Dong Feng (DF) - 41(CSS-X-20). The DF-41 has a range of 12,000-15,000 km with a capability to target the continental US. The DF-41 is solid propelled and can carry a payload of up to 2500 kg. The DF-41 missile is carried by Tian HTF5980 special wheeled chassis with 16×16 configuration.[52] While the DF-41 is still under development, China has flight-tested it numerous times since July 2012 including the South China Sea and in the Gobi desert in 2017.[53] The DF-41 can carry up to 10 MIRVs with nuclear warheads. Its development as rail-mobile systems makes it harder for tracking and difficult to verify the number as the movements of the missile may be disguised as passenger trains. It can also use tunnels for protection from satellites and as secure storage and loading facilities for the missiles.[54] The road-mobile versions are extremely survivable due to their ability to stay protected inside of tunnel facilities and can be moved to nearby launch positions during a crisis.

Cruise Missile Development

The interest in cruise missile increased following the success of US Tomahawk cruise missiles. Cruise missiles are usually categorised by the intended mission and launch mode (instead of a maximum range). The two broadest categories are LACM and Anti-Ship Cruise Missiles (ASCM). LACM guidance is generally in three phases- launch, midcourse, and terminal. In the launch phase, a missile is guided only by the inertial navigation system. In the midcourse phase, the missile is guided by the inertial navigation system. It can be updated by one or more of the following systems- a radar-based terrain contour matching system, radar or optical scene matching system, and a satellite navigation system such as the US GPS or the Chinese BeiDou system. The terminal guidance phase begins as the missile enters the target area and uses either more accurate scene matching or a terminal seeker (usually an optical or radar-based sensor). It can be launched from an aircraft, ship, submarine, or ground-based launcher. The researchers at Nanjing Army Command College claim that the trend in anti-ship missile development will be towards stealth, high velocity, and high manoeuvrability.

CJ-10 (DH-10) Ground-Launched Cruise Missile (GLCM). CJ-10 (DH-10) is the first of the Chinese Chang Jian series of long-range missiles and LACMs. This cruise missile has a range of over 1,500 km and enhances targeting options. GLCMs and air-launched LACM provide critical operational and planning flexibility. These weapons improve the survivability of Chinese aircrews while complicating an adversary's air and missile defence problem.[55] In addition to incremental improvements, gains from adapting existing missile systems to new platforms (for example, creating an air-launched variant of the DH-10) and to new targets (for example, creating an anti-ship variant of the DH-10) are likely. Mastery of real-time targeting could help the PLA to achieve significant operational breakthroughs.

Hyper Glide Vehicle (HGV) - DF 17/ DF ZH. The basic design of Hypersonic weapons incorporates the speed of a ballistic missile with the manoeuvring capabilities of a cruise missile. Hypersonic weapons refer to weapons that travel faster than Mach 5 and have the capability to manoeuvre during the entire flight. Though the designed speed of the hypersonic missile is faster than sound, its advantage lies in its enhanced manoeuvrability and smooth flight path. It is much harder to track than that of traditional missiles.[56] China is developing HGVs for the PLARF – the DF-17 which first appeared in public in Beijing on 01 October 2019. Defeating the ballistic defence systems deployed by the US is China's priority, and hence it has given the development of HGVs a high priority.[57,58] The DF-17 is a two-stage weapon with a rocket booster and a high-speed gliding warhead. The DF-17 reportedly can strike targets over a distance of nearly a thousand miles. Its speed and flat trajectory could complicate interception attempts.[59] Theoretically, DF-17 can penetrate the US-made missile shields in the region. Still, analysts like Tom Karako are sceptical of its efficacy as he feels that the system to be effective needs complete kill-chain components like airborne sensors.[60] DF-ZF, another hypersonic glide vehicle known in the US as the WU-14, has undergone more than a half dozen development tests between 2014 to 2016.[61] The DF-ZF, the current system under development, is expected to reach nearly Mach 10 at the last stage of a missile and is being compared with the US hypersonic cruise vehicle programme driven by DARPA.

Supersonic Speeds cruise missile programmes are likely to undergo incredible advancement over the next two or three decades. Supersonic ASCMs present challenges that include areas such as size and weight, anti-interference, and stealth. Additionally, future combat will involve more than just one type of weapon or unit fighting, thereby requiring ASCMs to have multipurpose functions. China is exploring to develop LACMs, which have ranges longer than the existing ASCMs, to attack ships at sea. If it is achieved, the aircraft could fire cruise missiles from outside the SAM envelope of US warships. China has already fielded a LACM, the YJ-63, with a 200 km range and is replacing it with YJ-18 variants of 540 Km range. Indications exist that an anti-ship variant of the DH-10 LACM with a range of 3,000 km could be in the early stage of development.

Tactical Nuclear Delivery? A Subject of Speculation

The Soviet navy has emphasised the employment of nuclear-armed cruise missiles against US carrier strike groups during the Cold War. The US and the Soviet Union/Russia have developed and deployed such missiles, but these are now being discarded due to vintage. Several American analysts are of the view that China might also pursue nuclear cruise missiles in the future. Despite the absence of major technological barriers, no concrete evidence suggests that it is pursuing this ambition. China would face several non-technological barriers in developing and deploying nuclear-armed cruise missiles, which would increase substantial command and control issues, be inconsistent with current nuclear doctrine, and cause undesirable international reactions. The CPC Committee of the PLAAF suggests that while the strategic air forces in some nations possess nuclear cruise missiles, but no nation dares to cross that threshold easily, as the main mission of nuclear weapons is 'strategic deterrence'. But the possibility of China possessing it cannot be entirely ruled out.

A US analyst, for instance, hints that the new ballistic and air-and ground-launched cruise missiles give Beijing a better survivable and flexible nuclear force. Rear Admiral Michael McDevitt, of US Navy, goes so far as to assess that the PLAN is likely already "arm[ing] nuclear attack submarines with nuclear-tipped cruise missiles"[62] and may be influenced by the Russian navy. Reflecting on modern Russian navy, the PLAN publication Modern Navy notes that the nuclear-powered general-purpose attack Akula-class submarine Gepard (launched in 2001) can carry 24 nuclear-armed cruise missiles. Chinese researcher has explored the advantages of nuclear-tipped cruise missiles and the options to increase its lethality. According to the PLAN Naval Armaments Department Senior Captain Liu Yang, the special anti-aircraft carrier mission is under development. Various types of warheads like "low-weight nuclear burst warhead", "fuel-air explosive warhead" or "special type warhead" that can meet the requirements for attacking an aircraft carrier is being explored.[63] Liu's affiliation with major PLAN weapons testing community at Wuhan and citation of only Chinese sources suggest that these concepts may be under serious consideration and development.[64]

PLAN-PLARF Integration Challenges

Ballistic and cruise missiles will remain an offensive weapon of choice because of their relatively low operating costs, their potential to penetrate defence systems. Matching them with capable guidance sensors and secure communication link adds to precision capability. PLARF, as the main custodian of strategic deterrence, will continue to review the US 2018 NPR and planned allocation of budget for the missile development programme.

The growing PLA emphasis on conducting conventional joint operations might seek to expand the PLARF arsenal and missions. China's relatively restrained nuclear strategy may limit the growth potential of the nuclear mission. At the same time, its conventional operations can more easily justify an expansion in force size and mission set. In the nuclear realm, the PLARF maintains a comparative advantage over the other services. The need to maintain a "lean and effective" nuclear deterrent may imply a cap on the size of nuclear forces, but it also may like to seek and capitalise on its unique nuclear role in other ways. To execute an integrated operation, the PLARF may wish to take over operational control of PLAN nuclear *Jin*-class SSBNs[65] and PLAAF bomber force on the pretext that these services have little or no experience in controlling nuclear weapons. It would like to assume the complete charge of the triad under one umbrella.

PLA AIR FORCE: STRATEGIC ROLE AND CAPABILITY DEVELOPMENT

PLAAF New Role

The PLAAF is one of the largest air force in the Asian region and the third-largest in the world. It has more than 2,500 total aircraft (excluding UAVs or trainers) and 1,700 combat aircraft. Pre 1999 PLAAF was the mainstay of national territorial air defence, with the Army, Navy, and People's Armed Police Force (PAPF) all undertook some territorial air defence responsibilities. The PLAAF exercised unified command over complete air defence components. However, Gulf War II and the 1999 Kosovo war had a major bearing on PLAAF restructuring. Two major changes affected PLAAF in 2004- PLAAF commander was granted a place in the CMC, and PLAAF received its first service-specific strategy.[66]

The 2015 NDWP added additional responsibilities and capabilities to the existing list. It called PLAAF to shift its focus from territorial air defence to both defence and offence and build an air-space defence force structure that can meet the requirements of informatised operations. The expanded role for the PLAAF to look into far seas and deep inside land boundaries of countries like India entails that it must seamlessly integrate situational awareness and standoff platforms. Hence, the PLAAF composed of aviation, ground air defence, radar, airborne and electronic countermeasures (ECM) arms is required to meet the strategic tasks that focus on reconnaissance and early warning, airstrike, air and missile defence, and strategic projection. The PLAAF is engaged in developing advanced weaponry and equipment such as new-generation fighters, bombers and new-types of ground-to-air missiles and radar systems to improve its early warning, command and communications networks. It raises its strategic early warning, strategic deterrence and long-distance airstrike capabilities besides boosting its capabilities for air and missile defence, information counter-measures, airborne operations, strategic projection and comprehensive support (refer Table 3.3).

Table 3.3: PLAAF Role and Capability Development

Period	*Role*	*Capability being developed*
Pre-1999	Territorial Air Defence	Early Warning and Air Defence
2004	Territorial Air Defence with both offensive and defensive capability	1. Improving strategic early warning, command and communications networks 2. Raising strategic deterrence 3. Increase long-distance airstrike
2015	Shift focus to both defence and offence and build an air-space defence force structure	1. Air and missile defence 2. Information counter-measures 3. Strategic Projection

PLAAF New Missions

The SMS 2015 provides the peep into the air and space integration with both attack and defence capability. It talks about five strategic missions:

- Participate in the primary "strategic direction." It is based on theatre strategy and dovetails strategic offensive and strategic air-raids.
- Conduct homeland air defence. It is to uphold the nation's territorial airspace, including ADIZ through monitoring of air activities.
- Safeguard China's border and maritime rights and interests. It is consonance with the earlier role of PLAAF in support of PLA Army and PLAN.
- Conduct emergency and disaster relief operations and assist in maintaining domestic stability. It looks at non-war military

operations of HADR and confrontation operations striking at the terrorists or secessionists.

- Conduct foreign exchanges in support of military diplomacy and cooperative security measures.

Operational Capability Under Development

PLAAF is developing one command information system to integrate five forces and seven operational capabilities (refer to Table 3.4). Informatisation and joint operations are crucial for PLAAF's air and space integration, and the command information system covers the PLAAF strategic space activity. It looks at space-based information platform that integrates air, space and land domains that covers from strategic campaign to tactical level operations. The system of systems includes Chinese-designated 4th-generation aircraft, aerial refuelling, long-range reconnaissance aircraft, AEW&C aircraft, UAVs and guided munitions. Future systems to incorporate could include strategic bomber and air and space integrated equipment like near-space strike weapons and airborne laser weapons.

Table 3.4: PLAFF System. Forces and Operational Capabilities

One System	*Five Forces*	*Seven Operational Capabilities*
Command Information System	Air Offensive Forces	Medium and Long-range precision strike
	Air Defence/Anti-Missile Forces	Air defence and anti-missile system-of-systems with three-line control structure spanning (coastal-First Island Chain- Second Island Chain)
	Reconnaissance, early warning and surveillance forces	Noted for PLAAF's various operational capabilities
	Information Operations	Information Assistance Support
		Electronic Warfare and Network Warfare capability
	Strategic Transport Force	Air strategic projection capabilities
		Airborne forces operational capabilities

Source: L. Garafola, Cristina. "Chapter 3: The Evolution of PLAAF Mission, Roles and Requirements." In *China's Evolving Military Strategy*, by Joe McReynolds, 74-100. Washington DC: The Jameston Foundation, January 2017, p.83.

The primary strategic direction operations are mainly for integrated fire strikes, blockade operations and island landing operations. It forms part of the strategic offensive and air raids in an informationised condition. PLAAF is looking at long-range strike capability as its global interests expand and limited bases available to it to operate. It includes medium and long-term air precision strike with a focus to reach remote combat capabilities of 3000 Km or the ability to strike second island chain and the majority of areas in the Indian subcontinent. Air to air refuelling meets the requirement of extended range operations. It is also pursuing to extend the range of LACM in case of a contested air-defence zone, and deep penetration is not feasible. The use of engagement of targets beyond detection ranges adds to the deterrence capabilities of PLAAF.

Strategic delivery is another area being focussed by PLA as part of its power projection capability and to support PLA-wide ranging contingency operations. In recent years, PLAAF has begun to develop nascent expeditionary capabilities. China is aware of the political sensitivities associated with designing an "expeditionary force" modelled on the US doctrine. However, it does recognise the importance of such operations for out of nation contingency operations. The SMS 2013 discusses requirements for conveying forces abroad to carry out the PLAAF's core missions probably a Taiwan or Tibet contingency.[67] However, most of the activity has consisted of non-war missions, and a substantial portion of PLAAF operations abroad have comprised of HADR, a non-combatant evacuation operation, and personnel recovery missions involving transport aircraft. China's increasing economic and strategic interest gets reflected in its expeditionary capabilities' development. To protect its overseas interests, China aims to promote social stability in countries featuring large Chinese investments, counter threats to its overseas personnel and investments.

The homeland air defence being multi-directional operations deals with strategic early warning, monitoring of air space sovereignty and implementation of ADIZ. The SMS 2015 note that the resource spent in air-defence will be greater than offensive means. SMS 2013 does not elaborate on the coordinating tasks with PLA Army and PLAN for safeguarding the rights and interests.

The task of maintaining domestic stability in case of terrorist or serious crime-related incident entails the use of a drone or airstrike for conducting operations. It was reported on 02 August 2015 as China considered the use of the drone to kill Myanmar drug lord.[68] SMS 2013 states that PLAAF should have information operations force capable of effective suppression and destruction via both soft-kill and hard-kill of opponents' information systems. However, with the Raising of PLASSF, some of these functions will now be delegated to them. However, it is not clear how will PLASFF coordinate the operations with PLAAF.

The PLAAF role for space and outer space may be limited or shared with PLASSF and PLARF. SMS 2013 talks of air and space deterrence and discusses the gradual development of the deterrent role of controlling space from the air.

Organisational Reforms

In 2017, the PLAAF reorganised its force structure to include the establishment of at least six new airbases and restructuring the subordinate regiments into brigades by disbanding fighter and fighter-bomber divisions. The PLAAF's consolidated seven former Military Region Air Forces (MRAFs) into five Theatre Command Air Forces (TCAFs) in early 2016. The PLAAF also relocated or subordinated some units to different theatre commands and re-designated as the 15th Airborne Corps as the PLA Airborne Corps.[69]

Airborne Corps

The PLA 15th Airborne Corps based in Xiaogan, Hubei province, was composed of three divisions (the 43rd, 44th and 45th) has been renamed simply the Airborne Corps.[70] In the 1990s, it served as a rapid reaction force (RRF) and part of the strategic reserve. After the restructuring of the military in 2017, the four-tier commanding system (corps-division-regiment-battalion) has been flattened to three tiers (corps-brigade-battalion) and placed under the air arm of the Central Theatre Command. PLA Airborne Corps consists of six airborne brigades, a special operations brigade, an aviation brigade, and a support brigade.[71] Although some of its subordinate units have moved to the Northern Theatre Command, the Airborne Corps is still in Hubei province and is the major provider of mobile support from the air.

The PLA Airborne Corps' primary purpose is to carry out operations including parachute, aircraft landing, and mixed parachute and aircraft landing. According to PLA Army doctrine, the main advantage of airborne operations is to "cut across ground defence lines and topographical obstacles to unfold attacks directly inside the enemy disposition."[72] These operations support main operational efforts to seize and hold important targets and areas in the enemy's rear (such as airfields and bridges), block an enemy's retreat and reinforcement and conduct raids on key targets in the enemy's depth.[73] In the recent years, the Airborne Corps has also been practising parachuting at altitudes of over 4,600 meters for Tibet contingency. This domestic training has reportedly increased the ability of airborne forces to operate in a wide variety of climates and terrain. According to one report, all the servicemen of the Airborne Corps, irrespective of gender and age, from generals to the rank and file, can jump from five aircraft models over nine types of terrain and open double parachutes, among other things, and are ready to perform.[74]

Equipment Development

The PLAAF has embarked on a series of a development programme that improves its reach and accuracy. To enhance its engagement efficiencies, it has tried to invest in platforms that improve its early warning, provides better fixation of targets, ability to engage at longer ranges stealthily. A glance at Table 3.5 gives the array of development being undertaken by PLAAF to improve its armoury. The PLAAF classifies its aircraft as J-series for the fighter, H-series for the bomber, JH-series for fighter-bomber, Y-series for the transport, KJ-series for the AEW&C aircraft and Z-series for the helicopters.

Table 3.5: Details of Chinese Manned Aircraft – Fighter/Bombers/ AEW&C

Chinese Manned Aircraft	*US Generation*	*Mission/Role*	*Status*	*AESA Radar*	*Long-Range A/A Missiles*	*Off-Bore-sight A/A Missiles*	*Precision-Guided Munitions*	*Speed*
J-7	2nd	Fighter	Operational					Mach 2
J-8	3rd	Fighter	Operational		x			Mach 2
Su-30	4th	Fighter	Operational		x	x	x	Mach 2
J-10A	4th	Multirole	Operational				x	Mach1.8
J-11B	4th	Multirole	Operational		x	x		Mach 2
J-10B	4th	Multirole	Operational		x	x	x	Mach 1.8
J-10C	4th	Multirole fighter		x	x	x	x	Mach 1.8
J-16	4th	Multirole fighter		x	x	x	x	Mach 2
Su 355	4th+	Multirole fighter	From Russia		x	x	x	Mach 2
J-20	5th	Multirole fighter	Development	x	x	x	x	Mach 2

Chinese Manned Aircraft	*US Generation*	*Mission/Role*	*Status*	*AESA Radar*	*Long-Range A/A Missiles*	*Off-Boresight A/A Missiles*	*Precision-Guided Munitions*	*Speed*
J-31	5th	Multirole fighter	Development	x	x	x	x	Mach 1.8
JH-7	N/A	Fighter Bomber	Operational				x	Mach 1.7
H-6	N/A	Bomber	Operational				x	Subsonic
Tactical	Next-Gen	Fighter-Bomber	Operational	x	x		x	
Strategic Bomber	Next-Gen	Long-Range Bomber	Development	x			x	
KJ-2000	N/A	AEW&C	Operational	x				Subsonic
KJ-200	N/A	AEW&C	Operational	x				Subsonic
KJ-500	N/A	AEW&C	Operational	x				Subsonic

Source: US Defense Intelligence Agency. 2019. *China Military Power: Modernising a Force to Fight and Win.* Intelligence Report, Washington DC. Accessed December 30, 2019. www.dia.mil/Military-Power-Publications, p.88

Bombers

China's bomber force comprises of variants of the H-6 Badger bomber. This Chinese-built airframe is the 10th design variant of the Soviet Tu-16 that began flying in 1952. The H-6K variant, are available in large numbers, integrates standoff weapons and features more efficient turbofan engines in redesigned wing roots.[75] This extended-range aircraft can carry six LACMs, providing the PLA with a long-range, standoff, precision-strike capability that can reach Guam. In 2017, it was spotted to have air to air refuelling probe.[76] Coupled with it is the development of CJ-20 (Changjian-20/Long Sword 20) LACM for mounting on the H-6 bomber[77] with a range of 2,200 kilometres makes it feasible for PLAAF to address the Indian Subcontinent and the second island chain. PLAAF annual military exercises have incorporated the incremental improvements of PLA power projection capabilities. In 2015 the PLAAF carried out four exercise training missions past the first island chain through the Bashi Channel, the northernmost passage of the Luzon Strait, and through the Miyako Strait closer to Japan.[78]

The PLAAF is developing new medium, and long-range stealth bombers called the H-20 to strike regional and global targets. Stealth technology continues to play a crucial role and it is likely to fructify no sooner than 2025.[79] These new bombers will come with full-spectrum upgrades compared with current operational bomber fleets and will employ many fifth-generation fighter technologies in their design having capabilities of both conventional and nuclear deterrence and strike missions. It is in direct competition with US Strategic Air Command assets like Boeing B-52, Rockwell B-1 and the Northrop Grumman B-2 Stealth Bomber, while Russia's Long-Range Aviation Command has the Tupolev Tu-160, Tu-95 and T-22M. China has overcome many technical difficulties in developing strategic bombers like engine, air inlet, material and stealth technology. The progress on the development of precise guided munitions is fast, and it has amassed experience in manufacturing the Y-20 military aircraft. The H-20 is being developed to cater for large-volume data fusion and transmission so that it can "serve as a C4ISR node and interact with large sensor platforms like UAV, early warning aircraft and strategic reconnaissance aircraft."[80] According to Military Balance 2019, the project has made significant progress. The H-20 is assumed to be a low-observable – possibly tailless – design, which could enter service from the latter half of the 2020s. Xian, a subsidiary of the Aviation Industry Corporation of China (AVIC), continues to build upgraded variants of the H-6 and is involved with the H-20 programme. Meanwhile, China and Ukraine have agreed to restart the production of the world's largest transport aircraft, the An-225 in 2019. With the capability to lift 254 tonnes of load, this aircraft improves global reach and strategic lift capability too.[81]

Fighters

The PLAAF still runs a large number of older second and third generation fighters, but it will probably have a majority fourth-generation force over by 2025. At least 600 fourth-generation fighters have been fielded by the PLAAF, and it is already developing fifth-generation fighters. What the US and Western militaries refer to as fourth-generation fighters, China refers to as third-generation. It is because the PLA never had first-generation fighters—its first fighter aircraft were second-generation fighters acquired from Russia.[82] Chinese J-10B/C, J-11B, and J-16 (Fourth-generation* fighter aircraft)—are generally characterised by the following:[83]

- Electronically or mechanically scanned multi-mode radars, passive infrared search and track systems.
- High-bandwidth communications and datalinks and identification friend or foe (IFF).
- Advanced electronic warfare (EW) avionics, including digital

jamming system, radar warning receiver, chaff/flare dispensers, and adaptive countermeasures.

- Advanced weapons, including long-range air-to-air missiles (AAMs), off-boresight short-range AAMs, LACMs, ASCMs, and precision-guided munitions (PGMs).

Passive electronically scanned array radar or active electronically scanned array (AESA) radar provides long-range detection. The electronically scanned radar beams allow automatic target acquisition, tracking of numerous targets simultaneously, and generate data for effective air-to-air and precision air-to-ground engagements. The Digital radio frequency memory (DRFM) jammers enable instantaneous smart jamming responses by automatically selecting jamming waveforms to counter a definite radar threat—significantly improving fighter aircraft survivability.

The evolving Chinese J-20 and FC-31/J-31 are commonly defined (Fifth-generation fighter aircraft) with network-centric warfare technology; potent air-to-air lethality and standoff attack capabilities in sensor-to-shooter operations. State-of-the-art technologies include:[84]

- To designs the aircraft with significant stealth, reduced radar and infrared signatures.
- Multiband EO long-range targeting systems.
- Sensor fusion.
- Advanced data links fusing data from air and ground networks.
- Internal carriage of off-boresight and long-range AAMs, LACMs, ASCMs, and PGMs.
- Sophisticated EW suites with advanced DRFM jammers and EO defensive systems.
- Super manoeuvrability and/or supercruise capability (ability to fly above Mach 1 with-out use of afterburner).

To meet the technological gap between the developmental phase has prompted PLAAF to acquire Russian Sukhoi Su-35 Flanker E. All 24 Su-35s in the initial order was to be delivered by the end of 2018 or early 2019. The deal included the acquisition of the export version of the Russian R-77-1 (AA-12B Adder) active-radar-guided medium-range air-to-air missile, an upgrade of the basic R-77. Delivery of this missile to the PLAAF has already begun. However, it is not clear whether the PLAAF will buy additional Su-35 aircraft, or if its operational experience with the type will lead it to favour its own defence industry's continuing development of a single-seat Flanker, the J-11D.[85]

China is no more reliant on Russian turbines to power its burgeoning fleet of combat aircraft. New-build production J-10C and J-20 aircraft are leaving the Chengdu factory with indigenous WS-10 'Taihang' engines installed. Previously these aircraft were delivered with variants of the Russian-produced Salyut AL-31 engine.[86]

Early Warning

The PLAAF and PLAN Aviation operate a range of airborne early warning and control (AEW&C) aircraft.[87] Besides the conventional threats, the Chinese have taken note of the dangers from drones after two major oil installations of Saudi Arabia were attacked by ten drones on 14 September 2019. China has already developed complete systems to counter-drone attacks and protect especially its strategic facilities. Keeping the conventional threats also in mind, China in the 1990s tried to mount the Israeli system on IL 76 but had to shelve the plan due to US intervention.[88] With IL 76 already procured China got down to the development of its AEW&C aircraft, such as China's KJ-2000 Mainring. The KJ2000, which uses a Russian airframe and indigenous Type 88 early warning radar, entered operation in the early 2000s but could develop just four aircraft. The lack of IL-76 airframes from Russia grounded the KJ-2000 too.[89]

Eleven KJ-200, variant of the KJ-2000 has been fielded -five to six each with PLAN and PLAAF.[90] The KJ-200 aircraft have mounted AESA radars also known as the "Silk Eye," designed by the CETC 38th Research Institute.[91] The KJ-200 also known as the Y-8W, supports electronically scanned phased-array antennas on a canoe-shaped fairing above the fuselage. The "balance beam," design provides limited full-sector coverage. Hence, KJ-500 aircraft with rotodome design has been equipped with three-sided AESA radar to overcome the limitations.[92] It entered into mass production in 2018[93] and about more than fifteen of them may be in operation across the PLAAF and PLAN. It has also been supplied to Pakistan as ZDK-03 and renamed as Karakorum Eagle operating from Masroor base, near Karachi. The KJ-600 currently under development is designed to provide an improved early warning capability and could be operated off China's new aircraft carrier.

KJ-200 and KJ-500 are force multipliers with the capabilities to detect, track, and target threats. These aircraft extend the range of a country's integrated air defence system network. In particular, these systems are better designed to detect low-altitude targets at greater standoff distances. For low-altitude detection strategic warning balloons equipped with large phased-array radar have also been used besides the fighter jets.[94]

China is likely to possess at least four ground-based, large phased-array radars (LPARs) for ballistic missile tracking. These LPARs are located near Huanan, Yiyuan, Hangzhou, and Korla.[95] Detection range is estimated to be 4,000 km with the capability to detect incoming missiles and to track satellites. Also, China's JL-1A and JY-27A radars have been assessed to be designed to address the threat of ballistic missiles.[96] Reportedly, the JL-1A is capable of precision tracking of multiple ballistic missiles. The JY-27A is a VHF active electronically scanned array (AESA) radar for long-range surveillance and guidance that is characterised as resistant to jamming.[97] Continued advances in radar technology will become vital enablers for the PLA's "system of systems" for future crisis or conflict scenarios through robust situational awareness overlays.

UAVs and UCAVs

The PLAN, PLAAF, PLARF and PLASSF operate many UAVs for early warning, reconnaissance, and surveillance, and the PLA is likely to continue expanding its employment of UAVs for these purposes. Since 2016 the PLA has improved its UAV capabilities and unveiled new aircraft that combine strike capability with aerial reconnaissance. Select platforms have been deployed in the South China Sea. China has also developed its first turbine-powered armed reconnaissance UAV, the Yunying (Cloud Shadow), and the armed ISR UAV GJ-1 (Gongji-1 or "Pterodactyl"), which has the capabilities for integrated reconnaissance and precision strike.[98]

The first unmanned Airborne Warning and Control System (AWACS) was displayed at the Zhuhai air show in 2018. The JY-300 Airborne Unmanned Early Warning Vehicle, which has a range of more than 1,000 km and a practical ceiling of more than 5,000 meters, is reportedly capable of detecting third-generation fighters at a distance of up to 50 km and may enter service.[99] Moreover, new HALE UAVs, including some that are stealthy, are variously under development and are beginning to be fielded, including the Shendiao, which could be employed for early warning.[100] Meanwhile, the Chinese defence industry is actively developing several high-altitude, solar-powered, and long-endurance UAVs like AVIC's Morning Star and China Aerospace Science and Technology Corporation's (CASC) Rainbow. It could enable persistent surveillance for months, at high altitudes and also in near space, thus providing an alternative to satellites with greater flexibility, including for sea area surveillance.[101]

The China Academy of Aerospace Electronics Technology has successfully tested Feihong-98 (FH-98), the largest unmanned transport aircraft, with a maximum payload of up to 1.5 tonnes at Baotou test site in China's Inner Mongolia region. It has been adapted from the prototype of the Shifei Y5B, a China-developed transport plane. The FH-98 has a maximum take-off weight of 5.25 tonnes, a maximum capacity of 1.5 tonnes and 15 cubic meters, a flight height of 4,500 meters, a cruising speed of 180 kilometres per hour, and a maximum range of 1,200 km. It needs a simple runway of 150-meters for take-offs and landings. With a longer voyage capability and a larger cargo load, the drone can effectively meet the needs of logistics transportation in remote areas and complex terrain conditions.[102] The PLAAF electronic countermeasures regiment is reportedly equipped with a reverse-engineered version of the Harpy, the ASN-301 anti-radiation loitering munition.[103] Developed by the Xi'an ASN Technology Group, was featured in the August 2017 parade that marked the 90th anniversary of the PLA's establishment, where it was shown in a fire unit that can consist of 54 drones.[104]

According to the Pentagon report, China plans to build 42,000 drones by 2023.[105] China has captured 74 per cent of the world drone market.[106] It undertook swarm flight of 119 UAVs in June 2017. China's future capabilities in swarm intelligence, military-use AI, will be enabled by high-level plans and extensive funding. China's new national roadmap for artificial intelligence advances an ambitious agenda for the development of this critical emerging technology through 2030.[107]

Air Defence

Surface-to-Air Missiles. The PLAAF possesses one of the largest advanced long-range SAM systems in the world. It has a combination of Russian-sourced SA-20 (S-300PMU1/2) battalions and indigenously produced CSA-9 (HQ-9) battalions. In early 2018, China has started receiving the S-400/ Triumph SAM system from Russia to improve its strategic air defence systems as a follow-on to the SA-20. The PLAAF may simultaneously develop its domestically produced CSA-X-19 (HQ-19) to provide the basis for a ballistic missile defence capability.[108] China is advancing a new ballistic missile interceptor, the HQ-19, as part of deployed missile defence system. HQ-19 interceptor is likely to be armed with a kinetic kill vehicle and will be able to target ballistic missiles and satellites in lower-earth orbit. The HQ-19 is a significantly updated variant of the HQ-9, a long-range surface-to-air missile that has a limited capacity to hit short-range ballistic missiles up to 500 km in range.[109] HQ-26 and the HQ-29 are other Chinese air and missile defence systems under development with a range of 2,000 km.[110] HQ-18, missile system has been developed by China, which is reverse engineering of Russian S-300V series. The HQ-18 is a highly-capable, hypersonic air and missile defence system but relatively little information is known publicly about the differences between the two systems."[111]

Counter Drone/UAV. China Aerospace Science and Industry Corporation (CASIC) has developed a counter-drone system. It consists of multiple weapons and equipment, including land-based rockets and drone-hunting drones that can shoot huge webs and vehicle-based detection devices.[112] China also has rifle-shaped counter-drone devices, which "shoot" jamming signals that will disrupt drones, bringing about either a forced landing or divert an intruding drone, a Shanghai-based weapons manufacturer told the Global Times.[113]

Laser Systems. China has been developing laser-related equipment both for kinetic lethal and non-lethal surveillance mode. In May 2018 the Pentagon claimed that military-grade laser pointers injured two US pilots shone into their eyes from China's navy base in Djibouti. Though Beijing denied the allegations, it brought to fore the fielding of laser weapons developed by China Academy of Engineering Physics. The laser systems range from low-powered tactical beam emitters to a high-energy strategic weapons system to counter airborne and space-borne threats. In 2016 during the G20 summit in Hangzhou China fielded its "Silent Hunter" laser weapon system to safeguard against the drone. Developed by China Poly Technologies, it has three variants – 10 Kilo-watts, 20 Kilo-watts and 30 Kilo-watts. It uses a directional-emission high-energy laser to quickly intercept many kinds of aerial targets, such as photoelectric guidance equipment, drones, guided bombs, and mortars. The 10 Kilo-watts system can destroy UAVs, within a range of 200 to 2,000 meters while the 30 Kilo-watts laser can engage targets at 4000 metres. Guorong-I anti-drone systems developed by Guorong Technology, China Electronics Technology Group and the Public Security Bureau is a short-range ground-to-air laser weapon system. It can detect radar, electro-optical interference device and high-power laser ejector that can shoot down a UAV.

Strategic Transport

The aviation industry of China continues to test its Y-20 large transport aircraft with 66 metric tonnes load and an estimated range of 3700 to 5200 Km. It aims to supplement and eventually replace China's small fleet of strategic airlift assets, which includes a limited number of Russian-made Il-76 aircraft. The maiden flight by Y-20 was conducted in early 2013 by using the same Russian engines as the Il-76. The Y-20 large military transport aircraft support airborne C2, logistics, paradrop, aerial refuelling, and strategic reconnaissance operations as well as HADR.[114] The PLAAF's primary transport units are the 13th Transport Division has three regiments: the 37th Air Regiment and the 38th Air Regiment are equipped with medium-capacity transports, and the 39th Air Regiment is equipped with the current mainstay of the PLAAF's heavy-lift aircraft, the Il-76. The division also has a small number of all-female aircrews[115]—the 4th Transport Division from the former Chengdu Military Region. A separate former Beijing MRAF division is responsible for transportation of high-profile dignitaries.[116] Most of the PLAAF's light aircraft like Y-5s, Y-7s, Y-11s, and Y-12s are assigned to independent transportation units in the different Theatre Command Air Forces.

Smart/ Intelligent/Precision Weapons

China is developing smart, intelligent, and precision ammunition with surgical strike capability since 2007 like KD-88 having an IR TV guidance system and an estimated range of about 110 km with a capability to hit small targets.[117] The other state-of-the-art arsenal in use is the supersonic Russian and Chinese made anti-radiation missiles (KH 31P, YJ-91) for operational use with SU-30, JH 7A and J-11 attacks, laser-guided and satellite-guided bombs (onboard Q-5 aircraft). It is estimated that almost all the modern aircraft of PLAAF today are capable of carrying the PGMs.

Capability Development

Revitalised Nuclear Deterrence and Strike Mission. The PLAAF follows its "strategic air force" vision to revitalize its nuclear deterrence and the associated nuclear capabilities as it modernises its bomber force. China demonstrated a more assertive posture concerning Taiwan and the East China Sea. In May 2018, the PLAAF flew H-6K bombers and Su-35 Flanker E combat aircraft around Taiwan. These 'training flights', as the PLA put it, were an attempt to discourage Taipei from making any moves towards independence.[118] These actions offer new strategic signalling options and an additional layer of nuclear strike options in the region. With nuclear force capability, PLAAF has plans to join PLARF to bolster China's strategic deterrence.

Aerial Assault Gyroplane. Lieying or Falcon gyroplane debuted at the 2019 China's National Day parade. Manufactured by a private company Shaanxi Baoji Special Vehicle Manufacturing, this bizarre-looking gyroplane can carry two commandos with their communications equipment and weapons. It has a range of 690 km, a ceiling of 5,300 meters, a take-off weight of 560 kg, and can operate in temperatures as low as minus 36 Celsius. It caters for deep insertion and conduct of stealth reconnaissance missions. It is tough to be detected by radar because of its size and ability to glide if required.[119] It is being touted as the success of China's civil-military integration.

PLAAF has borrowed the concept of a global strike from the US and the Russian Air Force and contends that the intelligence sensors deployed in space increase its extent of air defence umbrella. The inclusion of pre-emptive strikes within China's official strategy of 'active defence' indicates that PLAAF and PLARF will try and complement each other for strategic and operational environment shaping. The aim will be to dominate the air, space and cyberspace while executing offensive and defensive tasks.

PLA ARMY KINETIC COMPONENTS

A 915,000 strong PLA Army is the world's largest standing ground force. Military reforms ushered in the creation of a separate PLA Army head-quarters for the first time besides restructuring to a corps-brigade-battalion force structure. The new combined-arms brigades were designed for better agility and response mechanism through a C4ISR system to guide joint operations and interoperability issues. 2006 NDWP laid out five folded aim for the Army: move from regional defence to trans-regional mobility, improve air-ground integrated capabilities, undertake long-distance manoeuvres, rapid assaults and special operations. The 2008 NDWP gave guidelines for equipment development that looked to gradually informatise main battle weapon systems. The mechanisation of the main battle weapon systems like tanks, artillery and air defence pieces were to be achieved along with improvement in the areas of rapid detection, target location, friend-or-foe identification and precision strikes. The combat platforms have been successfully developed, and the proportion and number of precision-guided munitions are on the rise. The 2010 NDWP gave the trajectory to the PLA Army modernisation. The focus was digitisation, mechanisation and improved mobility of amphibious and airborne assault forces. PLA Army, while looking at sovereignty and territorial issues is also entrusted with the CPC's mission of managing political security and social stability. Besides undertaking all-encompassing defensive and offensive manoeuvres, the critical areas from non-contact warfare that is being addressed by the PLA Army are:

- Firepower strike options.
- Special operations for both conventional and sub-conventional.

In the kinetic arena following guidelines were given in 2010 NDWP:

- All artillery components (weapons, equipment, and ammunition) to possess higher levels of informationised strike system capable of executing missions at the operational and tactical level. It demanded precision-based integrated reconnaissance, control, strike and assessment capabilities.
- The air defence components of radar, command information systems and medium and high-altitude ground-to-air missiles systems should possess better interception capability and missile defence operations.
- The PLA Army aviation wing to be armed with upgraded attack helicopters to act as a main-battle assault force coupled with modularized grouping with transport and service helicopters to enhance force projection and support missions significantly.

Examining Firepower Strike Options

Beijing is obsessed with the anti-intervention strategy, especially in the context of the US and the western power-driven Indo-Pacific strategy. The firepower strike options look at the use of the kill chain mechanism at its disposal ranging from artillery to rocket force to air defence systems. The reliance on the C4ISR and electronic warfare countermeasures are for system integration and early response mechanism.

Artillery and Multi-barrel Launcher Rockets System (MLRS)

China continues to develop modern artillery systems aimed at advancing the mechanisation of PLA Army artillery while integrating information systems to increase lethality and precision. The primary systems are the PHL03 300-mm SP MLRS, the PLZ05 155- mm SP gun/howitzer, and two tracked and two-wheeled 122-mm artillery systems. These new systems are likely to replace almost all towed artillery. The exception to this modernisation trend is PLA Army coastal defence artillery, which will continue using towed Type 59-1 130-mm guns and Type 66 152-mm howitzers. According to Military Balance 2019, PLA Army artillery holds almost 8954 pieces[120] of artillery weapons systems with thrust on SP systems and MLRS (refer Table 3.6). Given the PLA training priority for joint and trans-regional theatre training, since 2014, artillery and air defence brigades have undertaken training in transregional exercises as part of below-the-neck-reform.[121] The critical areas of development are in tune with the 2010 NDWP guidelines.

Table 3.6: Details of PLA Army Artillery Holdings

Type	*Calibre*	*Quantity*	*Remarks*
SP Guns Holding -2120			
PLZ-89	122mm	500	in store 200 PLZ85/70
PLZ-07A	122mm	350	
PLZ-07B	122mm	150	Amphibious Role
PCL-09	122mm	300	Truck Mounted
PLL-09	122mm	350	8x8APC Wheeled
PLZ82/83	152mm	150	in store 200
PLZ-05	155 mm	320	
Towed Guns Holding-1234			
PL-96(D-30)	122mm	500	in store 2800 PL54-1
PL-59	130mm	234	
PL-66(D-20)	152mm	500	
MRLHolding -1550			
PHL81/90	122mm	550	in store 700 PHL-81
PHL-11	122mm	350	
PHZ-89	122mm	375	
PHZ-11	122mm	100	
PHL-03	300mm	175	

Source: Military Balance 2019

PLA is convinced that while it may be lagging in informatisation field but it has the edge over the US as far as conventional artillery and rocket systems are concerned. Its development also takes into account two critical areas for the employment of the weapon systems – Taiwan and Tibet. It is aiming to achieve 100 Km range with conventional artillery system while it is looking at a range over 200 Km for the MLRS. An analysis of the gun systems in use and development points to the growing urge to dominate.

Evaluating the Current PLA Artillery Inventory

PLZ-07 122mm SP Howitzer. Unveiled during the 60th anniversary of the PRC in October 2009, it has two variants, the land-based (PLZ07A) and the amphibious (PLZ07B) model. It replaces the older 122mm Type 89 systems. Mounted on ZBD-97 infantry fighting vehicles (IFV), the main armament remains 122 mm. Rocket assisted projectile enhances the range from 18 km with standard ammunition to 27 km.

PCL-09 122mm Truck-Mounted Howitzers. To enable 'shoot and scoot' option and for the added mobility to the firing-platform to keep pace with the mechanised column, China developed the mounted gun systems. It drew its inspiration from 1990s French CAESAR truck-mounted howitzer. Introduced in 2010, PCL-09 or CS/SH1 (Chinese export name) is 122mm howitzer that uses Shaanxi 6x6 military trucks and is adopted alongside PLL-09 SP howitzer, which is based on 8x8 armoured personnel carrier (APC). The PCL-09 fitted with a computerized fire control system, navigation, positioning and digital battlefield management system[122] can fire up to a maximum range is 18 km with standard HE-FRAG projectile and 27 km with an extended-range projectile. The PLL-09 is also capable of firing 122 mm laser-guided projectiles. These are based on Russian Kitolov projectile technology.

PLZ-05 or the Type 05 155mm SP Howitzer. It is a 155 mm SP howitzer developed by China to replace the Type 59-1 130mm. The PLZ-05 was officially unveiled at the 80th anniversary of the PLA in July 2007. It has a 52-calibre barrel and driven by 800 hp diesel engines with a gross weight of 35 tonnes. The PLZ-05 can fire the WS-35 shell having a max range reported to be 100 km.

PHL-03, AR 3 and PHL-16 MLRS. PLA Army has an ageing MLRS PHZ-89 akin to 40 barrelled Soviet GRAD rocket system and 2004 vintage

PHL-03 MLRS which is again a Chinese version of a Soviet BM-30 Smerch. The main role of MLRS is to engage remote strategic targets, such as airfields, command centres, support facilities, air defence batteries, and large concentrations of troops. Since 2010 China has developed longer-range guided rockets for the export customers also besides upgrading its arsenal. The PHZ-11, a tracked version of the SR4 122mm MLRS, mounted on truck chassis, is also called PZL11 in the Chinese Army. It uses the same tracked chassis as the PLZ-05 155mm self-propelled howitzer and the PGZ-09 self-propelled anti-aircraft gun.[123] The latest of the MLRS is the AR3 which can handle several different sized rockets that are stored and fired from pods designed to operate from the same AR3 8x8 heavy truck. PHL-16 is a version of the AR3, that was first publicly revealed in 2019. The PHL-16 uses 370 mm guided rockets with a maximum range of 220 km. The system uses pods with missiles, and it can be configured to use rockets of a different calibre. It can launch tactical ballistic missiles and anti-ship missiles. The previous AR3 also carries pods with 300 mm rockets, Fire Dragon 480 tactical ballistic missiles and TL-7B anti-ship missiles.

WS-35 Guided Munitions. China has made incremental improvements to its artillery and ammunition. It is 18 Kg guided 155mm guided shell. It is the Chinese version of GPS and inertial guidance shell that uses the Chinese GPS (BeiDou) and initial navigation system (INS) for backup. It claims to have achieved a max range of 100 Km and an accuracy of 40 meters. However, no one outside China has witnessed WS-35 in action. WS-35 is developed for the PLZ-05 which is capable of firing rocket-assisted shells.[124]

CM-501GA and CM-501XA Land-Based Mobile Missile System. The Chinese CM-501 system appeared after Israel revealed details of their Spike non-line-of-sight (NLOS) and Jumper missiles during the 2014 Israeli-Hamas War. Chinese CM-501GA, is a precision-guided missile, while CM-501XA, is a loitering munition. The two-metre-long CM-501GA is an NLOS missile is capable of targetting both stationary and moving targets at a distance between 5 and 40 km. It weighs over 100 kg and carries a 20 kg blast fragmentation warhead. Its propulsion system is based on a solid-propellant rocket motor. The missile uses a combined TV/imaging infrared (IIR) seeker for terminal guidance. It is presumed that some form of INS aided by the BeiDou Navigation Satellite System, is used for the non-terminal guidance phases. The manufacturer claims the missile has a circular error of probability of less than one metre when engaging stationary targets, and a hit probability of more than 90 per cent when striking moving ones. The 2-metre-long CM-501GX loitering munition is more like a miniature cruise missile with pop-out wings, and a small jet engine has both naval and land versions. The guidance options such as Satellite/Inertial Navigation System (INS), imaging infrared (IIR), semi-active laser (SAL) homing and in-flight updates for re-targeting coupled with a modular design makes it a versatile system. It is being introduced in two configurations: on a 6×6 APC, and the CSK181 series of mine-resistant ambush-protected vehicles. With an endurance of more than 30 minutes, it is designed to engage targets at a range of 70 km.[125]

Examining the PLA Artillery New Generation System

Magnetized Plasma Artillery. The major challenge facing the artillery is extending the range. The Chinese military published a notice in February 2019 inviting tenders to procure test systems for magnetised plasma artillery,[126] a technology patented with the same name in 2015 by the PLA Academy of Armoured Forces Engineering. The weapon uses magnetism instead of gunpowder to fire shells. The system uses a magnetic field generator to create a magnetic field inside the barrel. When the gun fires the gas inside the barrel will be partly ionised into plasma by the high pressure and heat. The plasma having 'stress anisotropic' characteristic and thermal insulation function then forms about a millimetre casing on the inner wall of the barrel due to the magnetic field.[127] It greatly improves the driving force of the shell and the heat resistance, thus prolonging barrel life. According to Global Times, the reduced friction extends the range of a conventional 155-mm self-propelled howitzer from 30-50 Km to 100 Km besides improving its accuracy. According to National Interest, while the idea may be possible on papers, the main hurdle is the life span of the plasma and whether it is enough during the launch time.[128] The Chinese development challenges the US Extended Range Cannon Artillery programme for its new 155mm self-propelled howitzer (M1299) that has achieved 62 Km range.[129]

Electromagnetic Rocket. For Tibetan contingency, China is developing the world's first electromagnetic surface-to-surface rocket that offers greater fire range. While the conventional rockets rely on explosive powder for the initial push, but the new electromagnetic rockets will be launched using additional electromagnetic force, like the catapult launchers that China and the US are developing for their rail guns. The actual range of the electromagnetic rocket being developed is unknown. China has spared no effort to catch up with the US electromagnetic technology, to turn the new technology into an all-purpose propulsion system for extensive use in ship-mounted weapons and maglev trains and even to replace rockets to launch satellites into space.

WeiShi-2 (WS-2). It is a 400-mm rocket system with variants having a range of 200-350 Km. It was fielded in 2007, but detailed information on the numbers produced is not available.[130] In 2008, it was revealed that sub-munitions are developed for WS-2, including a specialized anti-radar version, which is a rocket containing three UAVs. Once the rocket is fired at the target area, the UAVs are released the same way as other sub-munitions. The seekers would seek out target radar signals as UAVs began to cruise, and once locked on to the radar, UAV would home in and attack. Some have even compared it to Israeli Harpy anti-radar UAVs.

PLA Army Air Defence

PLA Army air defence units comprise active-duty forces and reserve forces. Active-duty units provide air defence for the mobile forces. These units are armed with a mix of tactical anti-aircraft missiles, anti-aircraft artillery, anti-aircraft gun and missile systems, and man-portable anti-aircraft missile systems. An extensive reserve anti-aircraft artillery force, comprising of divisions and separate brigades provides area anti-aircraft artillery protection for China's urban areas and important economic regions.

SAM Systems. The FD-2000/HQ-9 provide a long-range SAM capability, distinct from the medium-range capabilities of the HQ-12/KS-1 series. The FT-2000, a derivative of anti-radiation seeker is meant for engagements of AEW&C/AWACS and stand-off jamming aircraft. China has fielded medium-range HQ-16 SAMs with select air defence units in the PLA Army to upgrade its air defence capabilities comprehensively. It may be a joint PLA-Russian development of the SA-11 Gadfly or SA-17 Grizzly medium-range semi-active radar homing SAM. The indigenous HQ-12 deployed with PLA air defence units replaces the HQ-2 systems. HQ-12 has many variants, these including static rail launchers derived from the HQ-2 design, a 6x6 road-mobile TEL also derived from the HQ-2 launcher and a road-mobile Patriot like box launcher.[131] China manufactures its variant of Russia's SA-15 and is fielding the system with PLA Army air defence units supporting tracked armoured forces.[132] China has domestically designed French Crotale tactical SAM system. This wheeled SAM is being fielded with PLA Army air defence units supporting the wheeled fighting forces. China's tactical SAMs have been replacing outdated large-calibre anti-aircraft artillery in air defence units defending operational and large tactical-level units.[133]

Gun Systems. Most of the towed system (approx. 7000 pieces) of Army Air Defence systems of China is vintage. Its reliance remains on the SAM systems. A modest effort is being made to field modern domestically produced SP anti-aircraft gun system with select PLA Army air defence units to keep pace with manoeuvre units. It also provides mobile coverage to headquarters, troop concentrations, and key logistic areas. Chinese indigenously produced PGZ-04 integrated missile-gun anti-aircraft system is an upgraded version of the PGZ-95, equipped with more effective short-range SAMs.[134] PGZ-07 is gradually getting inducted into many PLA Army armoured and mechanised formations.

Radar Systems. PLA has a large inventory of fire control radars, search and acquisition radars and wide-area surveillance radars for PLA Army Air Defence component. However, its thrust for fielding radars relates to its need for strategic situational awareness. Hence, the Army Air Defence remains relegated and neglected in parts. Most Radars of Soviet and French origins are reverse-engineered like the 1970 French Crotale radars. It has been re-engineered as FM 80 and FM90 and is being also exported. Refer to Table 3.7 for the list of radars.

Table 3.7: List of PLA Army Air Defence Radars

Engagement and Fire Control Radars	*Search and Acquisition Radars*	*Wide Area Surveillance Radars*
• CPMIEC HT-233/HQ-9/10 Phased-array Radar • CASIC SJ-231/KS-1A/HQ-12 Phased-array Radar • CNPIPC/CEIEC H-200 KS-1A/ HQ-12 Phased-array/ Triumphant Mountain • CPMIEC 2FA(B)/ ZD-2(B)/	• NRIET/CEIEC/CETC YLC-2/ YLC-2A/YLC-2V High Guard 3D Long-range Surveillance Radar • CEIEC/JESE JL3D-90A/ 3D Commander • ECRIEE/CETC JY-11/JY-11B HUNTER-1, XINDI • ECRIEE/CETC JY-29/LSS-1 Low	• OTH-B Over-The-Horizon Backscatter Radar • CEIEC Surface Wave-OTH (SW-OTH) Radar

Engagement and Fire Control Radars	*Search and Acquisition Radars*	*Wide Area Surveillance Radars*
HQ-2BE/SNR-75A Gin Sling B/ HQ-2 and HQ2J Guideline • SJ-202 Gin Sling A/KS-1 • Type 341/H/LJP-341 RICE LAMP/Type 342/342C FOG LAMP/ZL-1B SD1/A 723 • CW Tracking and Illuminating Radar • LY-60/HQ-64 Engagement Radar • HQ-7/FM-80FS/FM-90FS/ Type 345 Crotale Engagement Radar • LD-2000 TR47/Type 730/H/ PJ12/LR66 Engagement Radar	Altitude 2D Air Defence Radar • Type 120/K/LLQ120 Self-Propelled Low Altitude Acquisition Radar • ECRIEE/CETC JYL-1 Long-range 3D Air Defence Radar • CETC JY-27 Wide Mat VHF Band Long-range 2D Surveillance Radar • NRIET/CEIEC/CETC YLC-4 2D Long-range Surveillance Radar • CETC YLC-8/8A VHF Band Long-range 2D Surveillance Radar • ECRIEE JY-14/Great Wall Tactical 3D Surveillance Radar • NRIET/CETC YLC-6/6M/STAR 2000 Medium Range Surveillance Radar • CETC YLC-18 High Mobility Medium-Range Low Altitude 3D Radar • LY-60/HQ-64 Acquisition Radar • HQ-7/FM-80SS/FM-90SS Crotale Acquisition Radars	

Source: Air Power Australia. 2014. "PLA Air Defence Radars." 27 January. Accessed June 25, 2020. http://www.ausairpower.net/APA-PLA-IADS-Radars.html.

PLA Army Special Operations Force

PLA Army Special Operations Forces (SOF) are among the "new type" units receiving priority for development. The PLA SOF units came into existence after the 1991 Persian Gulf War. Over the past three decades, these units have expanded, additional Army SOF units raised (including a few small units composed of women). The Army is likely controlling nine SOF brigades (each with 2,000–3,000 personnel), and the two SOF regiments (each of 2,000 personnel) is part of nine group armies and two military districts.[135] Over the past three years, six out of the seven Army SOF groups have now expanded to brigade size. They are part of the 38th, 21st, 26th, 31st, 42nd and 13th Group Armies. The 39th Group Army's SOF Regiment is an exception.[136] The Xinjiang Military District commands a SOF brigade while a SOF regiment is with the Tibet Military District. Reportedly, at least one infantry division of the 16th Group Army and one infantry brigade of the 12th Group Army have been converted into two new SOF brigades and remain affiliated to their group army headquarters.[137] An unknown number of smaller SOF units (likely companies or platoons) is with some infantry and armoured divisions and brigades (refer Figure 3.3 for the SOF organisation).

Numerous PLA publications indicate an increase in new type operational forces such as special operations. The PLA plans to arm SOF with new weapons systems such as lasers, electromagnetic pulse emitters and incapacitating chemical compounds. To improve the situational awareness, planning and decision-making abilities, the SOF has planned to upgrade its command automation systems. The SOF plans to deploy high-tech, light-weight, lethal and non-lethal weapons, surveillance equipment, and communications. A SOF Brigade may have an organisation that may vary based on mission requirements. Western Theatre Command is likely to have an anti-terrorist unit. At the same time, the PLAN SOF may focus on maritime or amphibious direct action or reconnaissance missions and PLAAF Airborne SOF may have pathfinders' units for reconnaissance and securing of drop zones. PLARF SOF missions may include guidance and damage assessments. A UAV unit with the SOF brigade may contain reconnaissance of combat UAVs. A likely organisation of SOF brigade is in Figure 3.3.

Figure 3.3: SOF Brigade Organisation

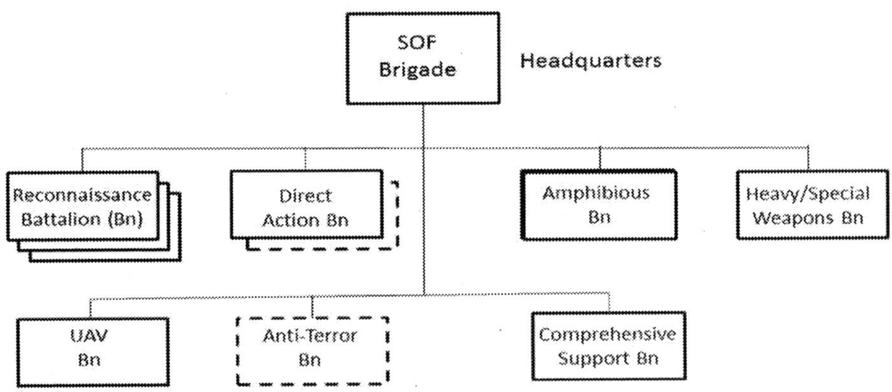

Source: McCauley, Kevin. 2015. "PLA Special Operations: Forces, Command, Training and Future Direction." *China Brief Volume: 15 Issue: 16*. 18 August. Accessed January 15, 2020. https://jamestown.org/program/pla-special-operations-forces-command-training-and-future-direction/.

SOF Doctrine and Employment. SOF doctrine emphasizes its employment as a force multiplier in executing important strategic and operational tasks that cannot be undertaken by the conventional forces or weapons systems. Affiliated currently with the Group Army they are also tasked for theatre objectives during the critical operational phase. The PLA considers the primary mission of SOF units' as reconnaissance, although direct action missions are also important. The PLA doctrine links special operations as one of the links in the system of systems operations. It aims to integrate the other essential campaign activities of information warfare, firepower assault, manoeuvre and psychological warfare. Special operations seek to create favourable environments for main offensive forces by raiding vital areas, paralyzing enemy operational systems and capabilities, besides interfering, delaying and disrupting enemy operational activities. SOF units mainly conduct special reconnaissance, raids, sabotage, harassment, hostage rescue and decapitation missions. China has reportedly sent its two SOF units known as the "Tigers of Siberia" and the "Night Tigers" to aid Syrian government troops against the 5,000 Uyghur Muslim fighters who arrived in Syria, illegally passing through Southeast Asia and Turkey.[138] Hence, China is looking to provide exposure to its SOF in the conflict zone and gain inroads into managing the grey zone using non-state actors.

PLA NAVY: SECURING GLOBAL INTERESTS AND MARITIME DOMAIN

Maritime Role and Strategy

From its inception in 1949 until the mid-1980s, the PLAN's primary strategic concept was one of *"coastal defence."* The events of the Taiwan Strait crisis of 1996 made CMC adopt the offshore defence policy to strengthen its maritime capabilities beyond coastal waters. After spending more than 20 years of naval development under offshore defence, the PLAN strategists advocated a new strategy for the 21st century, termed "distant sea defence." Under this new strategy, the maritime operations would not be bounded by the geographical limits and were to be defined according to China's maritime needs as China has a coastline of over 18,000 km with a complex maritime security situation. China's core maritime interests not only look at preventing the US or allied forces from defeating China's enforcement of maritime claims, control of maritime territory, and defence of the PRC shoreline in a conflict but also look at defending and extending the claims to its EEZ. Taiwan remains China's unfinished agenda with its reunification claim tied to the Great Rejuvenation. It aims to build counter-intervention capabilities to address its A2AD strategy. China has maritime boundary disputes with numerous countries like Japan, North and South Korea, Vietnam, the Philippines, Malaysia, and Brunei. The aggression by the PLAN may result in an escalation in the region as PLAN has numerous engagements against Vietnamese outposts in the Paracel and Spratly islands; the standoff at Scarborough Shoal with the Philippines; and recent imbroglios with Japan over the Senkaku/Diaoyu Islands. (Refer to Figure 3.4).

Figure 3.4: Nation Claim Lines on China's Eastern Seaboard

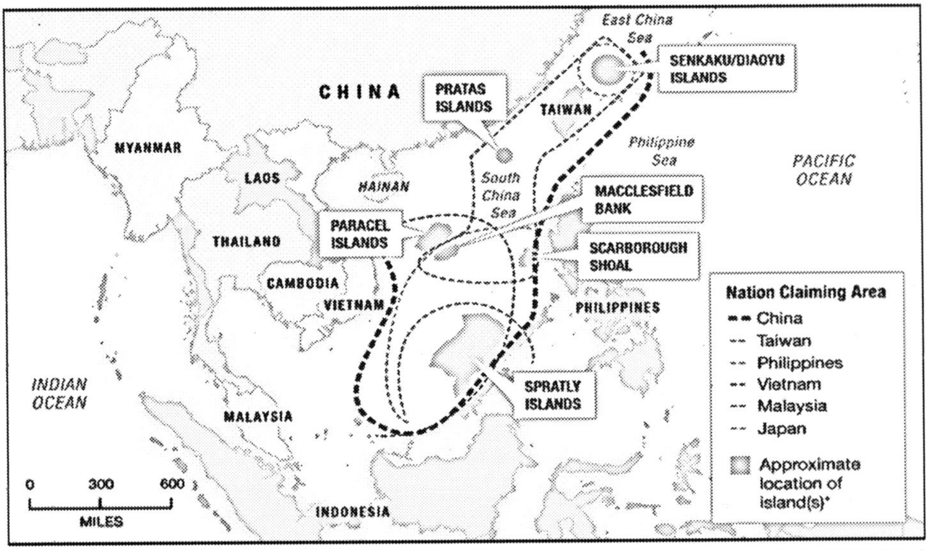

Source: Katie Park/NPR Accessed from https://www.npr.org/sections/parallels/2016/04/13/472711435/a-primer-on-the-complicated-battle-for-the-south-china-sea.

Stability of the maritime region is important for the Chinese leadership as Chinese economic growth is largely dependent on seaborne trade, exploitation of offshore oil and natural gas reserves, and access to fishing stocks and other natural resources. For the PLA, this means ensuring access to key regional SLOCs and extending China's strategic and operational depth.

Given the rapid expansion of China's global presence, the PLA has the task to protect its overseas citizens and economic interests. According to Peoples' Daily editorial of 06 February 2012, many of China's overseas investments are in some of the world's worst neighbourhoods as the Western countries have already occupied most safe investment destinations while Chinese companies invest in dangerous regions abroad. The PLAN, therefore, has to be prepared to engage in rescue operations as part of its non-war military operations which besides building its image also provides it with operational experience. Evacuation of 35,000 Chinese citizens in Libya, 225 foreign nationals and nearly 600 Chinese citizens from Yemen[139] has boosted the confidence of PLAN and the diaspora. According to 2019 NDWP, it has taken concrete steps to address its deficiencies in overseas operations and support by building far seas forces, develop overseas logistical facilities and has commissioned in August 2017 the first PLA Djibouti Support Base.

Maritime Missions

The concept of "forward edge defence" articulated in SMS 2013 establishes the intent for maritime overreach from coast to sea to oceans. Thus, the Indian Ocean and Western Pacific Ocean becomes China's strategic areas of interest given the Indo-Pacific overtones of the US strategy. To enable China to seize strategic initiative it has to radiate its influence through its maritime assets in the form of blue water navy and also look for basing requirements across the SLOCs in these oceans to enable it to control the operations. It relates to the formulations increasingly appearing in Chinese sources: "using the land to control the seas and using the seas to control the oceans."[140] SMS 2013 assigns PLAN eight strategic missions:

- Develop capabilities in the main strategic direction of operations towards Taiwan.
- Contain and resist sea-borne invasions even though remote.
- Protect island sovereignty and maritime rights and interests and contest the Freedom of Navigation Operations (FONOP) undertaken by the US and its allies. SMS 2013 asserts that there is around 1.5 million square km and over 50 islands or reef are under occupation by other states. The PLAN, Coast Guard and maritime militia have an important role to play.
- Protect maritime transportation security to keep the SLOCs secure.
- Engage in protecting overseas interests and the rights of Chinese citizens.

- Engage in nuclear deterrence and counterattack.
- Coordinate with the military struggle on land.
- Protect the security of international sea space.

Maritime Force Development

To achieve the desired strategic missions, the PLAN has evolved force design to facilitate for the following capability building which caters to plug the gaps in certain contingencies and also acts as deterrence:[141]

- Informatise the PLAN to enable synergy across the agencies involved for joint operations. Help in strategic situational awareness for better force deployment or packaging.
- Undertake hardware development to carry out far seas operation and also help in power projection capability. Besides developing large and medium surface combatants, it needs an aircraft carrier for each theatre.
- Develop strategic kill-ware with long-range, precise, smart, stealthy autonomous unmanned systems. It calls for developing nuclear-capable platforms to provide credible deterrence.
- Undertake opinion-shaping as part of 'three warfares' concept to enable regime affinity amongst the island nations in ASEAN and Micronesia as a part to ensure maritime sovereignty and also A2AD strategy.
- Contest and limit conflict through Grey Zone operations to be taken by Militia, China Coast Guard and the PLAN in a measured escalation matrix to ensure effective control along the conflict management phase.
- Creation of strong strategic point including basing and berthing outside of East Asia. It indicates PLAN strategic intentions of dominating the far seas.
- PLAN's continued acquisition and basing of long-range weapons on the ships, submarines, aircraft, or shore-based platforms demonstrates its commitment to non-contact warfare.

Organisational Structuring

The PLAN controls all of China's naval and naval aviation forces as well as marine brigades. It has deployed naval forces in three of China's five geographically oriented theatres. A department of the PLA's Overseas Operations Office under the CMC's JSD has been created to coordinate overseas non-war actions of the PLAN. This department thus enables centralized C2 of overseas forces. The PLAN controls all of China's naval and naval aviation forces. Deputy Commander of each fleet commands its respective aviation force as well as seven marine brigades and has deployed naval forces in three of China's five geographically oriented theatres that conduct day-to-day operations.

North Sea Fleet. Headquartered in Qingdao, the North Sea Fleet is responsible for the Bo Hai, Yellow Sea, and northern portion of the East China Sea. It falls under the PLA Northern Theatre Command's area of operations.

East Sea Fleet. Headquartered in Ningbo, the East Sea Fleet covers the majority of the East China Sea and the Taiwan Strait. It falls under the PLA Eastern Theatre Command's area of operations.

South Sea Fleet. Headquartered in Zhanjiang, the South Sea Fleet is responsible for the South China Sea. It falls under the PLA Southern Theatre Command's area of operations.

Table 3.8: List of Naval Units and Assets

Details	*Northern Theatre Navy*	*Eastern Theatre Navy*	*Southern Theatre Navy*	*Total*
Aircraft Carrier	01		01 (Sanya)	02
Submarine – Nuclear Powered	04		04@+02#	06+04
Submarine – Diesel Powered	18	16	16	50
Destroyers	08	09	11	28
Frigates	12	20	19	51
Corvettes	07	10	11	28
Amphibious Transport Docks		01	03	04
Tank Landing Ships	03	16	10	29
Medium Landing Ships	06	08	09	23
Missile Patrol Craft	18	44	24	86

@Nuclear Powered Ballistic Missile Submarine; #Nuclear-Powered Attack Submarines

Source: US Defense Intelligence Agency, 2019. China Military Power- Modernising a Force to Fight and Win, p.68

As of 2019, the PLAN consists of around 250 surface ships and sixty submarines, and by 2030, it is estimated that the PLAN will consist of some 550 ships: 450 surface ships and ninety-nine submarines. Between 2014 and 2018, China has launched more submarines, warships, amphibious vessels, and auxiliaries than the number of ships currently serving in the individual navies of Germany, India, Spain, and the United Kingdom.[142] China commissioned Eighteen ships in 2016 alone, and at least another 14 were added in 2017.[143] Over 70 per cent of the PLAN fleet in 2017 was considered "modern," up from less than 50 per cent in 2010. China is also producing larger ships capable of accommodating advanced armaments and on-board systems.

China's growing shipbuilding capability has undergirded the rapid expansion of the PLAN. Having entered into the joint venture with Japan and South Korea in the 1990s, today China is the global leader in shipbuilding orders by capturing 43.9 per cent of the global market in 2018, and an impressive 51.8 per cent of worldwide new orders of 2019.[144] The two largest shipbuilding companies of China—China Shipbuilding Industry Corporation (CSIC) and China State Shipbuilding Corporation (CSSC)—produce three-quarters of China's overall shipbuilding output.[145] While the operational standards and technical requirements of naval shipbuilding differ for the commercial ships nonetheless, China's State Council has encouraged this practice in hopes of boosting technology transfers among sectors and help in removing the capacity-building bottlenecks.

To have a greater range of non-military options, China undertook a consolidation of various maritime law enforcement agencies into a single China Coast Guard in 2013. The additional civilian capabilities help to manage disputes in contentious the South China Sea and the East China Sea from blowing into crisis and allows practising of grey-zone warfare with the graded response as part of war control measures.

As part of its assertive design to promote its maritime influence, it endeavours to change the maritime boundary by developing and constructing at least four airstrips on the disputed Woody Island in the Paracel, and on Fiery Cross, Mischief and Subi reefs in the Spratly archipelago. The satellite pictures released May 2018 showed a Chinese H-6K strategic bomber taking part in take-off and landing drills on Woody, and the presence of YJ-12B anti-ship cruise missiles and HQ-9B long-range surface-to-air missiles on Fiery Cross, Mischief and Subi.[146]

PLAN Marine Corps

PLAN Marine Corps (PLANMC) consisting of only two brigades, the 1st and 164th Marine Brigades (each with 5,000 to 6,000 personnel) under the

South Sea Fleet stationed in Zhanjiang, Guangdong is under transformation. The primary focus is on amphibious assault and the defence of outposts in the South China Sea. It is estimated that by 2020 PLANMC will consist of seven brigades with around 30,000 personnel and an expanded mission to include expeditionary operations on foreign soil."[147] According to Dennis J. Blasko and Roderick Lee commentary, post-reforms the number of brigades will swell to a total of eight brigades comprising of four new Marine Combined Arms Brigades, a Special Operations Forces (SOF) brigade, and the core of a Shipborne Aviation (helicopter) brigade added to the previously existing two brigades. The four new combined arms brigades have been formed out of units transferred from the Army, while the SOF and helicopter brigades were created from standing Navy units. A corps-level headquarters for the Marine Corps also has been formed with its first commander being Major General Kong Jun. This new structure probably amounts to a total of approximately 40,000 personnel.[148]

The expanded ORBAT means PLANMC being assigned to eastern Chinese seaboard from Shandong in the North, to Fujian and Guangdong in the East opposite Taiwan, to Hainan in the South China Sea.[149] The expansion is part of redistributing and reorganising existing units and reassigning them to the PLANMC. For instance, in Northern Shandong, a former Army motorized infantry brigade of the old 26th Group Army has been transformed into a new Marine brigade. On Shandong's Southern coast a second new brigade is likely to have been formed from a former Army coastal defence regiment located near Qingdao. The third new brigade created at Fujian has come from an Army coastal defence division at Jinjiang and has probably contributed to the fourth new brigade at Jieyang in Eastern Guangdong province.[150]

Marine combined arms battalions have amphibious mechanised and light mechanised combined arms battalions with few units trained for air assault operations. The equipment is composed of tracked ZBD05 Infantry Fighting Vehicle (IFV), tracked ZTD05 Assault Vehicle, PLZ07 122mm Self-Propelled Howitzer, eight-wheeled ZBL09 IFV, eight-wheeled ZTL11 assault vehicle, and the *Mengshi* Assault Vehicle, with some of them stationed at Djibouti Support base. The PLA Army has transferred approximately 20,000 personnel to PLANMC while retaining some of its Amphibious Divisions stationed in the Nanjing and Guangdong Region. It has restructured them into two combined arms brigades each with an additional combined arms brigade at Fujian, duplication of role assignment maybe probably as part of keeping the force as deterrence for the Taiwan contingency. Alternately, it may be retaining part of the troops till such time the capabilities of the expanded PLANMC is fully operationalized.

The new Marine SOF brigade formed out of the Navy's existing SOF Regiment stationed in Hainan includes the *Jiaolong* (Dragon) commando unit. Of the entire new Marine units within the expanded force structure, the SOF Brigade currently is the most combat-ready. Creation of an independent aviation brigade with organic helicopter transport and attack capability increases the expeditionary warfare capabilities. The new Marine Ship-borne Aviation (helicopter) Brigade has been raised out of elements from all three PLAN independent air regiments.

For far seas missions, the PLAN's fleet of six Type 071 LPDs, the first of which entered service in 2007, is the primary means of moving Marine units over long distances. Each ship carries almost a battalion of infantry, about 20 to 30 vehicles, and two to four helicopters for extended periods. Additional Type 071s are expected to induct into the service besides several new larger amphibious ships like the Type 075 amphibious assault ship (LHA).[151] The expansion of Marine Corps is a significant component of the goal to develop the PLA into a "world-class military" as it provides flexibility to the planners in employing this vital resource in combat or anti-terrorist operations or deterrence missions besides looking at the HADR missions.

PLAN Capability Development

China State Shipbuilding Corporation and China Shipbuilding Industry Company, the two leading state-owned shipbuilding conglomerates, were merged on 26 November 2019 to create a new shipbuilding giant named China State Shipbuilding Corporation. It is now the world's largest shipbuilder by sales with about 20 per cent of the global market.[152] The resource optimisation brought about by the merger will drive China's naval modernisation effort. Cross-Strait contingency and related issues of A2AD remain at the top of the list. The second priority remains the guarding of maritime sovereignty, followed by its ability to influence far seas operations. These operational requirements necessitate the development of a wide array of platform and weapon acquisition programmes, including ASBMs, ASCMs, submarines, surface ships, aircraft, UAVs, and supporting C4ISR systems. China's naval modernisation effort also includes improvements in maintenance and logistics, doctrine, personnel quality, education and training, and exercises.

Anti-Ship Warfare (ASW) Capability Enhancement

Two types of land-based ballistic missiles with a capability of hitting ships at sea—the DF-21D with a range of more than 1,500 km, and the DF-26 multi-role IRBM with a maximum range of about 4,000 km have been introduced as part of ASW. China is also developing hypersonic glide vehicles that, if incorporated into Chinese ASBMs, could make Chinese ASBMs more difficult to intercept.[153] The YJ-18 is an ASCM with a subsonic cruise mode and a supersonic terminal attack and a range of approximately 540 km. Chinese media claims that the missile is equipped with an inertial guidance system that uses BeiDou Navigation Satellite System data and it carries a 300 kg high-explosive warhead or an anti-radiation warhead to destroy electronics at short range. The YJ-18 is deployed on-board the Type 052D Luyang III- the destroyer, the Type 055 Renhai-class Large destroyer and the Shang II-class nuclear attack submarine.[154] The PLAN recognizes that these extended-range weapons require OTH-T capability. To realise their full potential, PLAN is modernising its maritime reconnaissance systems at the strategic and tactical levels. It is linking them with robust communication systems for better sharing of targeting information to launch platforms.

Surface Combatants

Missile Boats. During the past two decades, China has phased out large numbers of Cold War-era patrol craft. For area-denial 60 HOUBEI (Type 022) class missile patrol craft built in the mid-2000s have been added to supplement existing 25 1990s-vintage HOUJIAN and HOUXIN-class missile patrol combatants. The HOUBEI design integrates a high-speed wave-piercing catamaran hull, waterjet propulsion, signature-reduction features, and the YJ-83 family ASCM. Although it may be poorly equipped for offshore patrol duties, the HOUBEI is valuable for reacting to specific threats in China's EEZ.

Corvettes. In 2012, China began producing the JIANGDAO-class (Type 056) corvette (FFL). It provides the flexibility that the HOUBEI lacks. The Type 056 corvette fills the capability gap between the Type 022 missile boat and the Type 054A frigate. The JIANGDAO is tasked to patrol China's claimed EEZ and assert Beijing's interests in South China and East China

Seas. The 1500-ton JIANGDAO is fitted with 76mm, 30mm, and 12.7mm guns, four YJ-83 family ASCMs, torpedo tubes, and a helicopter landing area. It is ideally suited for general medium-endurance patrols and counter-piracy tasks but is not adequately armed for blue-water combat operations.[155] Forty-one Type 056 corvettes inducted into PLAN in the past five years, and an estimated 60 are to be launched.[156] An anti-submarine variant of Type 056A with an active towed-array system is in the planning.

Frigates/Destroyers/Cruiser. Type 054A- JIANGKAI II-class frigate is the backbone of China's patrol missions in the South China Sea. The PLAN also used it in the anti-piracy operations in the Gulf of Aden. By 2018, there were 28 Type 054A frigates in service with the vertically-launched HHQ-16, with more under construction. The PLAN produced a total of six LUYANG II-class (Type 052C) destroyers with the HHQ-9 surface-to-air missile (200 Km) and is now receiving the new LUYANG III-class (Type 052D) destroyer, which carries an extended-range variant of the HHQ-9. Type 052D entered service in 2014 and is part of the PLAN's goal of expanding operations into distant seas. In 2019, there are eleven Type 052D destroyers in active service, while an additional nine are undergoing sea trials or are under fitment. China is also building a new class of cruiser (or large destroyer), called the Renhai-class or Type 055 that reportedly displaces between 10,000 and 13,000 tonnes and is bigger than the US Navy's Ticonderoga (CG-47) class cruisers and Arleigh Burke (DDG-51) class destroyers.[157] Type 055 is expected to perform essential command and control functions. It is likely to serve as the primary escort of China's aircraft carrier strike groups in blue water operations. The first Type 055 cruiser was launched in June 2017, and so far, five have been inducted by 2019.[158]

Amphibious Ships. China's amphibious ship force has remained steady since the 2000s. China built four large YUZHAO (Type 071) class amphibious transport docks (LPD) for expeditionary and OTH amphibious assault capability. It has inherent HADR and counter-piracy capabilities also. YUZHAO can transport up to four of the new air cushion landing craft, as well as four or more helicopters, armoured vehicles, and troops on long-distance deployments. Construction of LHA-Type 075, which will have an estimated displacement of 30,000 to 40,000 tonnes as compared to YUZHAO, 19,855 tonnes, is likely to be produced.[159] Although larger amphibious ships like the Type 071 and Type 075 are more designed for Taiwan-related contingencies but can also be used in conflict scenarios in the South and East China Seas or HADR or anti-piracy tasks.

Submarines and Anti-Submarine Warfare (ASuW)

Conventional Submarines. Similar to the surface combatant force, China's submarine force is also concentrating on a smaller mix of units, suggesting that the PLAN is contented with the current policy. For its diesel-electric force, between 2000 and 2005, China constructed MING-class SS, SONG-class SS, the first YUAN-class (Type 039) SSP while purchasing an additional eight Kilo-class SS from Russia. All of these classes remain operational. Twelve YUAN SSP, China's most modern convention-ally powered submarine, is being supplemented with are currently in use with as many as eight more slated for production. The YUAN SSP has the added benefit of an air-independent power (AIP) system. Reducing the number of different classes is the priority of PLAN for bringing better synergy in operations. The submarine force consisting of six nuclear attack submarines, four nuclear ballistic missile submarines, and 57 diesel attack submarines is likely to grow to more than 70 submarines by 2020.[160] The newest indigenous submarine-launched ASCM, the YJ-18, extends a similar capability to the SONG, YUAN, and SHANG classes. Chinese submarines may be armed with one or more of the following- ASCMs, wire-guided and wake-homing torpedoes, and mines. Wake-homing torpedoes can be very difficult for surface ships to avoid.

Nuclear Powered Submarines. Nuclear-powered attack submarine force continues to be a relatively small percentage of the total number of Chinese submarines. The SHANG-class (Type 093) SSN's initial production run stopped after only two hulls that were launched in 2002 and 2003. After nearly ten years, China is continuing production with four additional hulls of an improved variant. These six submarines will replace the ageing HAN class SSN on almost a one-for-one basis. Post completion of the improved SHANG SSN, the PLAN will progress to Jin (Type 094) class SSBN, which will mark China's first credible at-sea second-strike nuclear capability. Five is expected to be commissioned.[161] Each Jin-class SSBN will be armed with 12 JL-2 nuclear-armed submarine-launched ballistic missiles (SLBMs) with an estimated range of 7,400 km China reportedly is developing a new SLBM, called the JL-3, as a successor to the JL-2.[162]

Pocket Submarine. China's latest nuclear submarine design appears to include a shelter capable of holding a miniature submarine for special operations forces (SOF). Based on the online image, the Chinese Type-93T or Shang-class nuclear attack submarine features in the hangar for the SOF submersible that would allow PLA troops to discretely deployment much like US forces. The pocket submarine can carry nine special forces.[163] Development of small submarines also accelerates China's ability to develop unmanned underwater combat vehicles (UUCVs) that could be used for surveillance, targeting, mine-laying or attacking ships.[164]

China's Aircraft Carrier Programme

China has now two aircraft carrier in service. Liaoning (Type 001), Ukrainian refurbished aircraft carrier entered service in 2012. It can accommodate 30 or more fixed-wing aircraft including 24 fighters. Shandong (Type 001A), is a modified version of the Liaoning design that incorporates some design improvements was commissioned into the PLAN on 17 December 2019 in Sanya on the island province of Hainan.[165] It can accommodate 40 aircraft that includes 36 fighters and has an estimated displacement of 66,000 to 70,000 tonnes.[166]

The Type 002 carrier, with a displacement of 80,000 tonnes to 85,000 tonnes, has commenced. Chinese first two aircraft carriers use ski-jump launch system adopted from Soviet technology. In contrast, the third carrier is likely to feature Catapult Assisted Take-Off But Arrested Recovery (CATOBAR) system for the aircraft launch and recovery. Some reports suggest that the vessel will use an electromagnetic launch system similar to that of USS Gerald R. Ford-class supercarriers. The third carrier is currently under construction at Jiangnan.[167] Based on the Type 002 design China was to start building a Type 003 carrier with a larger displacement. However, the same appears to be on hold.[168]

PLAN Air Forces

The role of the PLAN Air Force has been steadily evolving for the past decade as PLAN's area of interest is increasing. It has allowed the PLAN Air Force to concentrate on an expanded array of missions, particularly maritime strike besides undertaking maritime patrols, ASW, airborne early warning, and logistics. The advent of the Liaoning and Shandong aircraft carriers signals a new age for the PLAN Air Force, which will now evolve into a sea-based component.

Helicopters. The PLAN operates three main helicopter variants: Z-9, the Z-8, and the HELIX. The Z-9C is capable of operating from any helicopter-capable PLAN combatant. The Z-9C can be fitted with the KLC-1 search radar, dipping sonar, and a single, lightweight torpedo. A new roof-mounted electro-optical (EO) turret, unguided rockets, and 12.7mm machine gun pods were seen on several Z-9Cs during counter-piracy deployments. An upgraded naval version, designated as Z-9D carries ASCMs. Another Chinese-produced helicopter, the Z-8, is also based on a French medium lift-helicopter design. Although capable of HADR or logistical support roles, its size limits its deployment on carriers only. In 1999 PLAN inducted nine HELIX Russian made helicopters which are being used for ASW missions. In 2010, China purchased nine Ka-31 AEW helicopters and the E-801 radar system.[169] With the induction of a large number of ships planned in the PLAN inventory, the helicopter fleet will continue to grow in the foreseeable future.

Fixed-wing Aircraft. During the past two decades, antiquated fixed-wing aircrafts such as Nanchang Q-5 Fantan and Harbin H-5 Beagle have given way to an array of relatively high-quality aircraft like Su-30MK2 FLANKER and domestically produced 4th-generation fighter aircraft J-10A Firebird and the J-11B FLANKER. These are equipped with modern radars, PL-8 and PL-12 air-to-air missiles. For maritime strike, the PLAN has relied on the H-6 BADGER bomber, maritime versions of which can employ advanced ASCMs against surface targets. Despite the age of the design, it continues to receive upgrades. Noted improvements include the ability to carry four ASCMs while some H-6 have also been modified as tankers,[170] increasing the PLAN's flexibility and range. The JH-7 FLOUNDER augments the H-6 for maritime strike. It can also carry four ASCMs and two PL-5 or PL-8 short-range air-to-air missiles, providing considerable payload for maritime strike missions. After Y-8, a Chinese license-production version of the ex-Soviet An-12 Cub, China has introduced a Y-9 naval variant that is equipped with a magnetic anomaly detector boom, typical of ASW aircraft. This Y-9 ASW variant features a large surface search radar mounted under the nose as well as multiple blade antennae on the fuselage for probable electronic surveillance. Also present is a small EO/IR turret just aft of the nose wheel and an internal weapons bay forward of the main landing gear. The fact that this aircraft appeared in a primer yellow paint scheme indicates that it was under development and probably has not yet entered service. It has an endurance of around ten hours and can carry 20 tonnes of cargo or about 100 paratroopers.[171]

UAVs. PLAN vessels are also known to operate UAVs and unmanned helicopters for use in support of maritime ISR capabilities to enhance situational awareness. The S-100, purchased in 2010 from the Swedish company Schiebel, has been observed operating off the Type-054 frigate. PLAN is likely to continue to field the WZ-6B unmanned helicopter developed indigenously by the Nanjing Research Institute of Simulation Technology with a range of 200 km and a maximum endurance of six hours.[172] Notably, the PLAN operates the medium altitude long endurance (MALE) BZK-005 or Chang Ying or the Soaring Dragon, which has a maximum range of 2,400 km and a maximum endurance of 40 hours. The BZK-005, designed by the Beihang University's UAV Institute and the Harbin Aircraft Industry Group is thus roughly comparable to the US Global Hawk. It entered service in 2007. China recently unveiled its first prototype unmanned combat aerial vehicle (UCAV), Lijan, which features a blended-wing design and low observable technologies.

Maritime C4ISR. To effectively employ sophisticated naval platforms and long-range weaponry, PLAN has embarked on an advanced maritime C4ISR capability. The ranges of modern ASCMs extend well beyond the range of a ship's sensors. The contested space of the South China Sea and East China Sea space is being used by a large number of navies and coast guards from regional countries as well as several globally deploying nations. To gain a broader view of the activity in its near and far seas, China has turned to more sophisticated sensors. China has launched five Haiyang series of maritime observation satellites with the latest one launched in 2019.[173] Underwater Great Wall Project having a network of sensors, which will include those placed on the seabed integrated with a range of gliders, is currently under development by the China State Shipbuilding Corporation.[174] It facilitates submarines detection. Presence of similar underwater listening devices between Guam and the South China Sea has been placed by PLAN. The skywave OTH radar provides awareness of a much larger area than conventional radars by bouncing signals off the ionosphere. At the same time, China operates a growing array of reconnaissance satellites, which allow it to observe maritime activity anywhere on the earth. Two civilian systems also contribute to China's maritime awareness. The first is a coastal monitoring network for the Automatic Identification System- an automated system required on most commercial vessels by the International Maritime Organisation. China's Beidou system installed on several thousands of Chinese fishing boats provides GPS-like navigation to the boats and their live locations to Chinese monitoring agencies. For system integration, the PLAN is dependent on strategic communication assets.

To gain a broader view of activity in its near and far seas, China requires more sophisticated sensors. The skywave OTH radar provides awareness of a much larger area than conventional radars by bouncing signals off the ionosphere. China also operates a growing array of reconnaissance satellites, which allow observation of maritime activity virtually anywhere on the earth.

Conclusion

China's sweeping military reforms have ushered in substantial changes in the relative status and relationships between different parts of the PLA. The PLARF has been the major gainer in the reforms. The PLA Army, PLAN and the PLAAF lost operational control of their forces to the theatre commands. The division of strategic decision making and operational control with CMC and Theatre Command is likely to help in resource augmentation and better synergy in operational planning. Strategic situational awareness remains the key for the employment of the vital kinetic resources with PLARF and the building of triad with PLAAF and PLAN. Nuclear and conventional deterrence is based on the credibility of the weapon system being displayed or demonstrated.

For PLA, the main strategic direction remains Taiwan followed by social stability, sovereignty and then the overseas interest. The PLA pursued its force development consistently since 2004 when Hu Jintao unveiled the 'New Historic Mission' and has worked on improving the lethality and range of its kinetic weapon systems from tactical to strategic levels. It has created strategic space and ability to exercise effective control along the escalation ladder. Hence, the PLA has been able to move from dissuasive deterrence to a credible deterrence posture, and it has migrated from contingency-based force planning to contingency-cum-capability based force design. The PLA, like the US, want to graduate to a tailored deterrence response doctrine. It is aiming at extending the tactical pursuit to strategic pursuit through the use of long-range systems.

PLA Artillery, PLARF and PLAAF packs a punch in long-distance engagement and can act as Elite Force Sharp Arm during the initial phase of operations. PLAAF and PLAN have improved its force projection capability through its Marine and Airborne Corps and the attached platforms that help it to undertake conventional and unconventional tasks. The expansion of SOF and PLANMC units adds to the force multiplier ratio in the conduct of diverse missions in peacetime or war. Importantly, the belief that SOF forces can achieve diplomatic, political, and military objectives with precision, less risk and cost than the employment of conventional forces, making SOF forces an important weapon available for achieving Beijing's objectives in peace or war. The PLA has been modernising the force with specialised equipment, particularly stealthy assets for air and sea infiltration, as well as develop global intelligence capabilities to realise the potential of this elite force completely.

China's naval modernisation effort has substantially improved China's naval capabilities in recent years. China's navy currently is assessed as having limitations or weaknesses in some regions of ASuW, dependence on foreign suppliers for some ship components. The induction of ASCM and HGV makes the BMD system like THAAD and Patriot ineffective while improving the precision strike. China's submarines are not currently optimized for two missions—ASW and land attack.[175]

The reliance on kinetic long strike systems and power projection systems on the C4ISR systems makes it an essential facet in the execution of the war. With the decision support system tied to sensors and communication system, the growing effort by the PLA is to prevent it from being impaired or degraded so that the freedom to response options is available. Outer-space and cyberspace have an essential role in controlling the operation within the kinetic domain due to the inherent dependency of systems on the need to communicate with each other for precision, guidance and ISR. Hence, it is important to understand how is China defending its outer space and cyberspace.

NOTES

1 Williams, Ian. (2019). "More Than Missiles: China Previews its New Way of War." *Center for Strategic & International Studies*. 16 October. Accessed December 13, 2019. https://www.csis.org/analysis/more-missiles-china-previews-its-new-way-war.

2 Chan, Minnie. *Chinese General's New Job Suggests Army Revamp*. June 25, 2016. https://www.scmp.com/news/china/diplomacy-defence/article/1980861/chinese-generals-new-job-suggests-army-revamp-finished (accessed December 13, 2019).

3 International College of Defence Studies,. n.d. *National Defense Policy.* Accessed December 12, 2019. http://www.cdsndu.org/html_en/to_xygk_orderNo=2701&superOrderNo=2700.html.

4 Ibid.

5 The State Council Information Office of the People's Republic of China,. 2019. "China's National Defense in the New Era." Foreign Languages Press Co. Ltd., Beijing. 24 July. Accessed December 14, 2019. http://www.xinhuanet.com/english/2019-09/27/c_138427541.htm.

6 Ibid.

7 Jinping, Xi. *The Governance of China Vol II.* Beijing: Foreign Language Press, 2017. pp103-104.

8 Office of the US Secretary of Defense. (2017). *Military and Security Developments Involving the People's Republic of China.* Annual Report to Congress, Washington DC: US Department of Defense.

9 Jun Mai, 'Xi Jinping Claims Progress on National Security in Meeting of Secretive Commission', 20 April 2018, available at https://www.scmp.com/news/china/policies-politics/ article/2142505/xi-jinping-claims-progress-national-security-meeting, accessed on 18 May 2020.

10 Office of the US Secretary of Defense. (2017). *Military and Security Developments Involving the People's Republic of China.* Annual Report to Congress, Washington DC: US Department of Defense, pp.126-127.

11 McReynolds, John Costello and Joe. (October 2018). *China's Strategic Support Force: A Force for a New Era.* Study Report, Centre for the Study of Chinese Military Affairs, Institute for National Strategic Studies, Washington DC: National Defense University Press. Accessed January 04, 2020. inss.ndu.edu/Publications.aspx, p.3.

12 "Facts and Figures on China's Military Reform," *Xinhua*, December 19, 2017, available at www.xinhuanet.com/english/2017-12/19/c_136837189.htm.

13 *Xinhua* . "Starting with a New Style Under Fluttering Red Combat Banners – Observing the New Theater Commands.". 02 February 2016. Accessed December 13, 2019. http://news.xinhuanet.com/poli¬tics/2016-02/02/c_1117973365.htm .

14 US Defense Intelligence Agency. (2019). *China Military Power – Modernising a Force to Fight and Win.* Intelligence Report, Washington DC. Accessed December 30, 2019. www.dia.mil/Military-Power-Publications, p.50.

15 Ibid.

16 Ibid.

17 "China Inaugurates PLA Rocket Force as Military Reform Deepens," *Xinhua*, January 1, 2016, http://news.xinhuanet.com/english/2016-01/01/c_134970418.htm

18 Ibid.

19 Ni, Bates Gill & Adam. "The People's Liberation Army Rocket Force." *Australian Journal of International Affairs.* January 22, 2019. https://doi.org/10.1080/10357718.2018.1545831 (accessed January 03, 2020).

20 Xiao, Tianliang. (2015). Zhanlue xue [Science of Military Strategy]. Beijing: National Defense University Press, pp. 367–368.

21 Ibid.

22 China Military Online. (2016). "Cong erpaobing dao huojianjun, zhexie ni yingai zhidao" [From the Second Artillery to the Rocket Force, this you should know]. January 2, 2016. Accessed November 2, 2018. http://www.81.cn/depb/2016-01/02/content_6840120_6.htm.

23 2019. *China displays new hypersonic nuclear missile on 70th anniversary.* 01 October. Accessed January 03, 2020. https://www.aljazeera.com/news/2019/10/china-displays-hypersonic-ballistic-nuclear-missile-191001031803778.html.

24 Chase, Michael S. (2017). "Nuclear Bomber Could Boost PLAAF Strategic Role, Create Credible Triad." *China Brief Volume: 17 Issue: 9 Jamestown Foundation.* July 06. Accessed December 31, 2019. https://jamestown.org/program/nuclear-bomber-boost-plaaf-strategic-role-create-credible-triad/.

25 Eric Heginbotham, Michael S. Chase, Jacob Heim, Bonny Lin, Mark R. Cozad, Lyle J. Morris, Christopher P. Twomey, Forrest E. Morgan, Michael Nixon, Cristina L. Garafola, and Samuel K. Berkowitz, China's Evolving Nuclear Deterrent: Major Drivers and Issues for the United States, Santa Monica, Calif.: RAND Corporation, RR-1628-AF, 2017, https://www.rand.org/pubs/research_reports/RR1628.html.

26 Chase, Michael S. "Chapter 5: PLA Rocket Force: Executor's of China's Nuclear Strategy and Policy." In *China's Evolving Military Strategy*, by Joe McReynolds, 140-171. Washington DC: The Jamestown Foundation, January 2017, p.160.

27 Blasko, Dennis J. (2019). ""PLA Weaknesses and Xi's Concerns about PLA Capabilities."" *U.S.-China Economic and Security Review Commission.* 07 February. Accessed December 26, 2019. https://www.uscc.gov/sites/default/files/Blasko_USCC%20Testimony_FINAL.pdf.

28 Gill, Adam Ni and Bates. (2018). "China's New Missile Force: New Ambitions, New Challenges (Part 1)." *China Brief Volume: 18 Issue: 14 The Jamestown Foundation.* 18 August. Accessed January 02, 2020. http://jamestown.org/program/chinas-new-missile-force-new-ambitions-new-challenges-part-1/.

29 Logan, David C. (2019). "Making Sense of China's Missile Force." In Chairman Xi Remakes the PLA, edited by Arthur S. Ding, Andrew Scobell, Andrew N.D. Yang, and Joel Wuthnow Phillip C. Saunders, 393-435. Washington DC: National Defense University Press, p.402.

30 15 February 2019. *Military Balance.* https://doi.org/10.1080/04597222.2018.1561021, pp.235-236.

31 The basic unit of firepower for nuclear-armed forces is the battalion, while for conventional units, it appears to be the platoon. Logan, David C. 2019. op.cit., pp.402-403.

32 Ibid.

33 Ibid.

34 Ibid.

35 Eric Heginbotham, et.al. op.cit.

36 Fiona S. Cunningham and M. Taylor Fravel, "Assuring Assured Retaliation: China's Nuclear Posture and U.S.-China Strategic Stability," International Security, Fall 2015, pp. 7–50.

37 U.S. Department of Defense, Military and Security Developments Involving the People's Republic of China 2017, Washington, D.C., May 2017, p. 31, https://www.defense.gov/Portals/1/Documents/pubs/2017_China_Military_Power_Report.pdf.

38 Ibid.

39 Eric Heginbotham, et al. op. cit.

40 "New Chinese Missile a More Mobile Deterrent: PLA," *The Straits Times*, August 5, 2017, http://www.straitstimes.com/asia/east-asia/new-chinese-missile-df-31ag-a-more-mobile-deterrent

41 U.S. Department of Defense, Military and Security Developments Involving the People's Republic of China 2017, op. cit.

42 Eric Heginbotham, et al. op. cit.

43 Zhao Lei, "Rocket Force More Versatile," *China Daily*, June 21, 2017, http://www.chinadaily.com.cn/china/2017-06/21/content_29825134.htm.

44 U.S. Department of Defense, *Military and Security Developments Involving the People's Republic of China 2017*, op. cit., p. 31.

45 Ibid.

46 Logan, David C. 2019., op. cit., pp.418-419.

47 The islands running from the Kurils, through Taiwan, to Borneo, roughly encompassing the Yellow Sea, East China Sea, and the South China Sea.

48 State Council Information Office of the People's Republic of China, China's Military Strategy, Beijing, May 2015, http://english.gov.cn/archive/white_paper/2015/05/27/content_281475115610833.htm

49 Elsa Kania and John Costello, "China Quest for Informatization Drives PLA Reforms," *The Diplomat*, March 4, 2017, https://thediplomat.com/2017/03/chinasquest-for-informatization-drives-pla-reforms/

50 State Council Information Office of the People's Republic of China, *China's Military Strategy*, op. cit.

51 Ballistic and Cruise Missile Threats, 2013, National Air and Space Intelligence Centre, Washington DC.

52 ARG 2006-2020. n.d. "DF 41- Intercontinental Missile." *Military-Today.com* . Accessed June 25, 2020. http://www.military-today.com/missiles/df_41.htm.

53 Chan, Minnie. (2017). "Did China test missile that could hit any target in US two days before Donald Trump's visit?" *SCMP.* 09 November. Accessed December 13, 2019. https://www.scmp.com/news/china/diplomacy-defence/article/2119201/did-china-test-missile-could-hit-any-target-us-two-days.

54 MDAA. n.d. "Dong Feng-41 (CSS-X-20)." *Missile Defence Advocacy Alliance.* Accessed December 13, 2019. https://missiledefenseadvocacy.org/missile-threat-and-proliferation/missile-proliferation/china/df-41/.

55 US Defense Intelligence Agency. (2019). *China Military Power – Modernising a Force to Fight and Win*, op.cit., p.92.

56 MDAA. n.d. "Hypersonic Weapon Basics." *Missile Defence Advocacy Alliance.* Accessed December 13, 2019. https://missiledefenseadvocacy.org/missile-threat-and-proliferation/missile-basics/hypersonic-missiles/.

57 Lora Saalman, "China's Calculus on Hypersonic Glide," Stockholm International Peace Research Institute, August 15, 2017, https://www.sipri.org/commentary/topical-backgrounder/2017/chinas-calculus-hypersonic-glide

58 Joshua H. Pollack, "Boost-Glide Weapons and U.S.-China Strategic Stability," *Nonproliferation Review*, Vol. 22, No. 2, February 2016, pp. 155–164.

59 Axe, David. (2019). "Is China's DF-17 Hypersonic Missile Really a Super-Weapon?" *National Interest.* 21 November. Accessed December 13, 2019. https://nationalinterest.org/blog/buzz/china%E2%80%99s-df-17-hypersonic-missile-really-super-weapon-98242.

60 Ibid.

61 Trevithick, Joseph. (2017). "China Shows Off Hypersonic Vehicle Test Model After US Navy Weapon Test, ." 07 November. Accessed December 13, 2019. https://

www.thedrive.com/the-war-zone/15828/china-shows-off-hypersonic-vehicle-test-model-after-us-navy-weapon-test.

62 US Defense Intelligence Agency. (2019). *China Military Power – Modernising a Force to Fight and Win*, op. cit.

63 Ibid.

64 Ibid, p.91.

65 Kelsey Davenport, "China Elevates Nuclear Rocket Force," Arms Control Association, March 3, 2016, available at www.armscontrol.org/ACT/2016_03/News/China-Elevates-Nuclear-Rocket-Force.

66 L.Garafola, Cristina. "Chapter 3: The Evolution of PLAAF Mission, Roles and Requirements." In *China's Evolving Military Strategy*, by Joe McReynolds, 74-100. Washington DC: The Jameston Foundation, January 2017, p.83.

67 Ibid, pp. 75–100.

68 Kao, Ernest. (2015). *China Considered Using Drone in Myanmar to Kill Wanted Drug Lord.* 20 February. Accessed December 30, 2019. http://www.scmp.com/news/china/article/1154217/china-consuidered-using-drone-in-myanmar-to-kill-wanted-drug-lord.

69 US Defense Intelligence Agency. (2019). *China Military Power – Modernising a Force to Fight and Win.* op. cit., p.83.

70 Lin, Ying Yu. (2019). *What Are China's Plans for its Airborne Corps?* 20 April. Accessed January 03, 2020. https://thediplomat.com/2019/04/what-are-chinas-plans-for-military-aviation/.

71 US Defense Intelligence Agency. (2019). *China Military Power – Modernising a Force to Fight and Win.* op. cit., p.83.

72 Ibid.

73 Ibid, p.89.

74 Ibid.

75 Office of the Secretary of Defense, Annual Report to Congress: Military and Security Developments Involving the People's Republic of China 2017.

76 Mulvaney, Dr. Brendan S. (15 February 2018). *China's Military Reforms and Modernization: Implications for the United States.* Testimony, Washington DC: U.S.-China Economic and Security Review Commission. Accessed April 19, 2020. https://www.uscc.gov/sites/default/files/Dr%20Mulvaney%20testimony%20to%20USCC%2015%20Feb% 202018%20PLA%20Air%20Force.pdf.

77 Ibid.

78 US Defense Intelligence Agency. (2019). *China Military Power – Modernising a Force to Fight and Win, op cit.*, p.33.

79 Lei, Zhao. (2016). *PLA Air Force commander confirms new strategic bomber.* September 02. Accessed January 01, 2020. http://www.chinadaily.com.cn/china/2016-09/02/content_26683883.htm.

80 Chase, Michael S. (2017). op. cit.

81 US Defense Intelligence Agency. (2019). *China Military Power – Modernising a Force to Fight and Win*, op.cit., pp.33-34.

82 Ibid, p.88.

83 China Military Power Report 2019 – The Frontier Post. https://thefrontierpost.com/china-military-power-report-2019/.

84 Ibid.

85 Military Balance 2019, op.cit., p.238.

86 2019. *China Finally Closes the Engine Gap: 100% Domestic Jet Fighter Engines.* 30 December . Accessed January 03, 2020. https://china-defense.blogspot.com/2019/.
87 Thomas Newdick, "Wow, China Has a Lot of Different Early-Warning Planes," *War is Boring*, March 16, 2015, https://medium.com/war-is-boring/wow-china-has-a-lot-of-different-early-warning-planes-7e7ac7edae8.
88 Ibid.
89 Ibid. Also see "Why is China's Air Force not equipped with a large number of KJ-2000 early warning aircraft?" Sohu, September 25, 2015,
90 Kania, Llsa B. "China's Strategic Awareness Capabilities." *ONTHERADAR.CSIS.ORG.* Spring 2019. https://ontheradar.csis.org/issue-briefs/china-situational-awareness/ (accessed January 08, 2020). Also see "KJ-200" Baike, https://baike.baidu.com/item/%E7%A9%BA%E8%AD%A6-200/15598551?fromtitle =%E7%A9%BA%E8%AD%A6200 &fromid=4856986.
91 "CETC Releases the "Silk Eye" Radar, Will Be Displayed at Zhuhai Airshow", *Global Times*, October 29, 2018, https://mil.news.sina.com.cn/china/2018-10-29/doc-ihnaivxq2790198.shtml+&cd=10&hl=en&ct=clnk&gl=us
92 "China's new generation of early warning aircraft KJ-500's equipment and platform localization", *Xinhua*, March 13, 2016, http://www.xinhuanet.com/mil/2016-03/14/c_128797638.htm
93 Mike Yeo, "China ramps up production of new airborne early warning aircraft," Defense News, February 5, 2018, https://www.defensenews.com/digital-show-dailies/singapore-airshow/2018/02/05/china-ramps-up-production-of-new-airborne-early-warning-aircraft/
94 "China's strategic early warning balloon program exposed", *Sohu*, February 2017, https://m.sohu.com/n/557067298/
95 Tate, Andrew. 2017. "China integrates long-range surveillance capabilities." *IHS Jane's.* Accessed April 20, 2020. https://www.janes.com/images/assets/477/75477/China_integrates_long-range_surveillance capabilities.pdf.
96 Kania, Elsa B. (2019). "China's Strategic Situational Awareness Capabilities.", op. cit.
97 Ibid.
98 "Attack-1 UAV Fills the Chinese Air Force's Integrated Reconnaissance and Strike Gap", *Xinhua*, November 14, 2014, http://news.xinhuanet.com/mil/2014-11/13/c_1113239224.htm
99 "CETC Showcases World's First Unmanned Early Warning UAV", November 7, 2018, http://www.dgdrpc.com/tiyu/1764.html
100 Office of the Secretary of Defense, Annual Report to Congress: Military and Security Developments Involving the People's Republic of China 2017.
101 Liu Zhen, "Chinese solar-powered drone Morning Star spreads its wings in successful test flight," *South China Morning Post*, October 31, 2018, https://www.scmp.com/news/china/military/article/2171081/chinese-solar-powered-drone-spreads-its-wings-successful-test
102 Zinan, Cao. *China's self-developed commercial drone Feihong-98 completes test flight.* October 17, 2018. http://www.chinadaily.com.cn/a/201810/17/WS5bc6e5dea310eff303282ed8.html (accessed January 13, 2020).
103 "China Unveils a Harpy-Type Loitering Munition," Israel Defense, January 3, 2017, http://www.israeldefense.co.il/en/node/28716.
104 "UAV Formation: Important Forces for Our Military's New-Quality Combat Power", Xinhua, July 30, 2017, http://www.xinhuanet.com/2017-07/30/c_1121402330.htm.

105 Keck, Zachary. (2015). *China Is Building 42,000 Military Drones: Should America Worry?* 10 May. Accessed June 23, 2020. https://nationalinterest.org/blog/the-buzz/china-building-42000-military-drones-should-america-worry-12856.
106 China Power Team. "Is China at the forefront of drone technology?". May 29, 2018. Updated March 20, 2020. Accessed June 24, 2020. https://chinapower.csis.org/china-drones-unmanned-technology/.
107 Kania, Elsa. (2017). "Swarms at War: Chinese Advances in Swarm Intelligence." *Jamestown Foundation.* 17 July. Accessed June 23, 2020. http://moderntokyotimes.com/swarms-at-war-chinese-advances-in-swarm-intelligence/.
108 US Defense Intelligence Agency. (2019). *China Military Power – Modernising a Force to Fight and Win*, op. cit.
109 Majumdar, Dave. (2018). *Why China's New Air Defense System Could be Quite Dangerous.* 16 July. Accessed April 20, 2020. https://nationalinterest.org/blog/buzz/why-chinas-new-air-defense-system-could-be-quite-dangerous-25956.
110 Ibid.
111 Ibid.
112 Panyue, Huang. (2019). *China ready to defend against drone attacks after Saudi Arabia oil hit.* 17 September. Accessed January 01, 2020. http://eng.chinamil.com.cn/view/2019-09/17/content_9624543.htm.
113 Yang, Liu Xuanzun and Liu. (2019). "China ready to defend against drone attacks after Saudi Arabia oil hit." *Global Times.* 16 September. Accessed June 24, 2020., http://www.globaltimes.cn/content/1164603.shtml.
114 "Chinese Large Freighter Plane Enters Military Service," *Xinhua* in English, July 7, 2016.
115 Kenneth Allen and Emma Kelly, "China's Air Force Female Aviators: Sixty Years of Excellence (1952–2012)," *China Brief*, Vol. 12, No. 12, June 22, 2012.
116 Ibid.
117 Saxena, Lt Gen (Dr) V.K. (2016). "Growing Muscle of PLAAF." *Vivekananda International foundation.* March. Accessed April 20, 2020. https://www.vifindia.org/sites/default/files/growing-muscle-of-plaaf.pdf.
118 Military Balance 2019, op. cit., p.233.
119 Panyue, Huang. (2019). *Gyroplane can send stealth missions.* October 09. Accessed January 01, 2020. http://eng.chinamil.com.cn/view/2019-10/09/content_9645570.htm.
120 The Military Balance, 2019, op. cit.
121 Blasko, Dennis J. "The Biggest Loser in Chinese Military Reforms – The PLA Army." In *Chairman Xi Remakes the PLA – Assessing Chinese Military Reforms*, Edited by Phillip C. Saunders, Arthur S. Ding, Andrew Scobell, Andrew N.D. Yang, and Joel Wuthnow 345. Washington, D.C.: National Defense University, p.368.
122 *PLL-09 – 122 mm self-propelled howitzer.* n.d. http://www.military-today.com/artillery/pll_09.htm (accessed December 19, 2019).
123 Defense Global Security army industry. (2020). "New Chinese army PHZ-11 122mm MLRS Multiple Launch Rocket System on tracked chassis." *Army Recognition* . 27 April. Accessed June 25, 2020. https://www.armyrecognition.com/april_2020_news_defense_global_security_army_industry/new_chinese_army_phz-11_122mm_mlrs_multiple_launch_rocket_system_on_tracked_chassis.html.
124 *Artillery: The Chinese Magical Mystery Shell.* November 28, 2013. https://

www.strategypage.com/htmw/htart/20131128.aspx#foo (accessed December 19, 2019).

125 Novichkov, Neil Gibson and Nikolai. *PLA set to adopt new tactical missile system.* March 06, 2019. https://www.janes.com/article/87032/pla-set-to-adopt-new-tactical-missile-system (accessed December 19, 2019).

126 Xuanzun, Liu. (2019). "China to test magnetized plasma artillery." *Global Times Published.* 18 February. Accessed December 2019, 2019. http://www.globaltimes.cn/content/1139224.shtml.

127 Ibid.

128 Ibid.

129 Judson, Jen. (2019). *BAE gets green light to help build extended-range cannon prototype for US Army.* 15 July. Accessed December 18, 2019. https://www.defensenews.com/land/2019/07/15/bae-gets-green-light-to-build-us-army-extended-range-cannon-prototype/.

130 "SCAIC 400 mm WS-2 Multiple Rocket Weapon System," Jane's Armour and Artillery, updated July 22, 2013.

131 Kopp, Dr Carlo. (2014). *PLA Area Defence Missile Systems.* 27 January. Accessed April 20, 2020. http://www.ausairpower.net/APA-PLA-IADS-SAMs.html.

132 US Defense Intelligence Agency. (2019). *China Military Power – Modernising a Force to Fight and Win*, op. cit, p.60.

133 Ibid.

134 Ibid.

135 Blasko, Dennis J. (2015). "PLA Special Operations Forces: Organisations, Missions and Training." *China Brief Volume: 15 Issue: 9.* 01 May. Accessed January 15, 2020. http://jamestown.org/program/pla-special-operations-forces-organisations-missions-and-training/.

136 Ibid.

137 Ibid.

138 Zain Khan, China 'to deploy' special operations forces in Syria, Tactical Talk, 30 November 2017, https://tacticaltalk.net/2017/11/30/china-deploy-special-operations-forces-syria/ .

139 "Yemen Crisis: China Evacuates Citizens and Foreigners from Aden," *BBC News*, April 3, 2015.

140 Academy of Military Sciences. (2013). *The Science of Military Strategy.* Edited by Sun Zhaoli. Beijing : Military Science Press, pp.102, 109.

141 Ibid.

142 China Power Team. "How is China modernizing its navy?" December 17, 2018. Updated May 14, 2020. Accessed June 25, 2020. https://chinapower.csis.org/china-naval-modernization/.

143 Ibid.

144 Xinhuanet. (2019). "China maintains top position in global shipbuilding industry in H1." 20 July. Accessed June 25, 2020. http://www.xinhuanet.com/english/2019-07/20/c_138242350.htm.

145 https://www.amazon.com/Chinese-Naval-Shipbuilding-Ambitious-Development/dp/1682470814 .

146 China is putting troops, weapons on The South China Sea islands, and has every right to do so, PLA official says, South China Morning Post, International Edition Online, 03 June 2018, accessed on 04 February 2019 from https://www.scmp.com/

news/china/diplomacy-defence/article/2148979/china-putting-troops-weapons-south-china-sea-islands.

147 U.S. Department of Defense, *Annual Report to Congress: Military and Security Developments Involving the People's Republic of China 2018*, p.28. https://media.defense.gov/2018/Aug/16/2001955282/-1/-1/1/2018-CHINA-MILITARY-POWER-REPORT.PDF#page=11&zoom=auto,-85,733.

148 Dennis J. Blasko, Roderick Lee, The Chinese Navy's Marine Corps, Part 1: Expansion and Reorganisation, China Brief, Vol. 19, Issue 3, February 1, 2019, https://jamestown.org/program/the-chinese-navys-marine-corps-part-1-expansion-and-reorganization/.

149 Ibid.

150 Ibid.

151 Dennis J. Blasko, Roderick Lee, The Chinese Navy's Marine Corps, Part 2: Expansion and Reorganization, China Brief Vol. 19, Issue 4, February 15, 2019, https://jamestown.org/program/the-chinese-navys-marine-corps-part-2-chain-of-command-reforms-and-evolving-training/ .

152 Legarda, Helena. No. 6, July – December 2019. "China Global Security Tracker." *Mercator Institute for China Studies (MERICS).* Accessed April 22, 2020. https://www.merics.org/sites/default/files/2020-02/200211_MERICS_China_Global_Security_Tracker_No_6.pdf, p.6.

153 Dennis J. Blasko, Roderick Lee, The Chinese Navy's Marine Corps, Part 2: Expansion and Reorganisation, China Brief Vol. 19, Issue 4, op. cit., pp.4-5.

154 Submarine-Launched Variant of China's YJ-18 Supersonic Anti-Ship Missile Emerges - Navyrecognition.com, 2 October 2017.

155 Office of US Naval Intelligence. (2015), op. cit.

156 Franz-Stefan Gady, "China's People Liberation Army Navy Commissions 42nd and 43rd Type 056/056A Corvettes," *Diplomat*, December 19, 2019.

157 "China Naval Modernization: Implications for U.S. Navy Capabilities—Background and Issues for Congress." *Congressional Research Service.* December 20, 2019. https://crsreports.congress.gov/product/pdf/RL/RL33153/228 (accessed January 15, 2020).

158 Ibid.

159 Rick Joe, "The Future of China's Amphibious Assault Fleet," *Diplomat*, July 17, 2019.

160 Office of US Naval Intelligence, op. cit., pp.17-18.

161 Ibid, p.20.

162 Andrew Tate, China conducts probable test launch of JL-3 SLBM, London, Jane's Defence Weekly, 03 June 2019, https://www.janes.com/article/89001/china-conducts-probable-test-launch-of-jl-3-slbm

163 LaGrone, Sam. (2015). *New Chinese Nuclear Sub Design Includes Special Operations Mini-Sub.* 25 March. Accessed January 15, 2020. https://news.usni.org/2015/03/25/new-chinese-nuclear-sub-design-includes-special-operations-mini-sub.

164 Lowther, William. (2015). *Chinese military develops 'midget' sub: reports.* 01 July. Accessed January 15, 2020. http://www.taipeitimes.com/News/taiwan/archives/2015/07/01/2003621999.

165 What do we know (so far) about China's second aircraft carrier? *ChinaPower*, CSIS.org, https://chinapower.csis.org/china-aircraft-carrier-type-001a/

166 Ibid.

167 How is China modernizing its navy? China Power, op. cit.

168 Jeffrey Lin and P.W. Singer, "A Chinese Shipbuilder Accidentally Revealed Its Major

Navy Plans," Popular Science, March 15, 2018.

169 Office of US Naval Intelligence, op. cit., pp.21-22.

170 Ibid.

171 Ibid.

172 "Schiebel Camcopter S-100 operated from Chinese frigate," *Flight Global,* May 19, 2012, https://www.flightglobal.com/news/articles/pictures-schiebel-camcopter-s-100-operated-from-chinese-frigate-372045/.

173 Kania, Elsa B. (2019), op. cit.

174 Ibid.

175 Office of Naval Intelligence. (2015), op. cit.

4

PLA's Non-Kinetic Non-Contact Warfare Capabilities

"Manage the Earth; make our voice heard everywhere in the world."[1]

– Mao Zedong, 1955

PLA STRATEGIC SUPPORT FORCE AND NON-KINETIC WARFARE

Importance of Non-Kinetic Warfare Domains to the PLA

Two decades of American involvement in fighting the counter-insurgency operation provided the window of opportunity to China to force structure its forces to fight the "local wars under the conditions of informatisation". China realised that the development in accuracy and increase in range of the kinetic platforms were all tied to the informationised technology. For a missile to hit a target deep inside the enemy territory or for a PLAAF fighter pilot to have the complete situational awareness in his cockpit was a result of putting systems inside the platforms that can talk to their command and control centres. Two decades of focused capability building process set out by Jiang Zemin and formalised by Hu Jintao in 2004 as part of 'New Historic Mission' has been relentlessly followed. The PLA has completed major mechanisation of its forces. It has now embarked on the mission to achieve informatisation of its strategic capabilities.[2]

Military strategists in China have laid out a "unified field theory" of war in which the kinetic dimension is no longer dominant.[3] The articulation on 'Unrestricted Warfare' by Senior Colonels from the PLA, Qiao Liang and Wang Xiangsui actually in mandarin refers to "Chao Xian Zhan" or "wars beyond rules". It simply illustrates that warfare is not restricted to the military domain, and it can be practised in trans-military or non-military domains also. Technology, as a driver for economic development, has also been associated with security management. The security concerns have aggravated with participation by mega-corporations in the future development of the dual-use technologies like AI, 5G, robotics, unmanned systems and sensors. China is enamoured by the big tech-giants in the US who are not only commercially engaged across the world but are intricately linked to the Pentagon. The pace of development in the technological era is guided by innovation and ability to penetrate the global market. While the world militaries are competing with each other based on the technology-anti-technology platforms; the people led by mega-corporation are fighting for the market share and wealth accumulation. The technology itself is not about a single product, but it is a result of the fusion of scores of technologies. Warfare has extended beyond the preserve of the military. Civil-military fusion is a trend which has been captured by Qiao Liang and Wang Xiangsui in their 1999 book "Unrestricted Warfare". The emergence of information and knowledge domain has virtually blurred the boundary of war. The question one is compelled to ask is "where to fight" as the expansion of battlespace is across multi-domain. "Non-natural space" like electromagnetic spectrum has created a "network space". Similarly, the "atomic space", "nanometer-space" and even "cognitive space" has emerged as the new areas of prosecuting the warfare.

To achieve its millennium goal, China realises that besides strengthening its economy and securing its territorial sovereignty, it has to secure the new emerging sovereign domains of cyberspace, electromagnetic and outer-space. Social stability is another crucial concern for the CPC, and it looks at guarding the people who have been tied to technology. It feels that the information domain is a strategic space created by the western world to undertake influence operations by shaping the opinion and occupying the cognitive space of the leadership. The colour revolution and the Hong Kong 2019 protests have reconfirmed their hypothesis. Non-kinetic domain has gained prominence in Chinese thinking with some inspiration drawn from the text of 'Unrestricted

Warfare' or warfare beyond rules. Strategy to influence has emerged which understands all-pervasiveness of the influence-space and synchronous effort provided by space, cyber and electromagnetic technologies. It aims at phased objectives to control the influence-space through unlimited ways and calibrated asymmetrical response for effective control[4] followed by a recalibrated response to retain the influence. According to 2019 NDWP, China still has a strategic opportunity to develop. Hence, it is more relevant for China to keep the contest and conflict confined to non-contact non-lethal space as it helps in early conflict resolution and minimal employment or diversion of the resource. The reforms ushered in 2016 by Xi Jinping was with an intent to restructure and rebalance the PLASSF to meet the demands of safeguarding China's national security in the new era.

Genesis of PLASSF Creation

The PLA capability and capacity development to a capability-cum-contingency based force has made the US and its allies in Indo-Pacific to assess the balance of power gap. China knows that a large-scale invasion along its coastline is not feasible. It is aware that security threats have increased outwards with an increase in China's economic interests. Hence, while carrying out the reforms, Xi Jinping gave preference to its two significant services- PLARF and PLA Strategic Support Force (PLASSF). However, placing their command and control structures subordinate to the CMC, it ensures political oversight always.

As early as 2007, Chinese strategists have been advocating an independent space force to unify myriad elements of Chinese organisations responsible for space operations. After the formation of the US Cyber Command (USCYBERCOM) in 2009, the call for PLA to establish its equivalent gained momentum. Ye Zheng, the influential PLA information warfare specialist, in 2012, suggested a conceptual and organisational integration of information warfare components into an integrated network-electronic-psychological warfare force that partially resembles the present PLASSF cyber force.[5] The decision was inspired by the USSTRATCOM's (US Strategic Command)[6] structures that dealt with space, cyberspace, strategic EW, and strategic information support. The PLASSF is tasked with space and cyber missions, while also providing the theatre commands with ISR support for joint operations. China established the PLASSF in late 2015 as part of its reform aimed to improve the PLA's ability to fight informationised conflicts and enhance joint operations and power projection capabilities in support of China's strategic aims. According to China's Ministry of National Defence spokesperson Senior Colonel Yang Yujun: "The Strategic Support Force is... mainly formed from the functional integration of various types of support forces with strong strategic, foundational and supportive functions for optimising the military's force structure and improving integrated support capabilities."[7] The PLA's concept of "new-type combat force" is centred on leveraging space, electromagnetic, and network capabilities as key enablers of integrated joint operations across multiple domains of conflict, including land, sea, air, space and network domains. Indeed, the SMS 2013 called for prioritising the development of such combat force in "near space, outer space and network space" that are "able to surpass geographical barriers and directly threaten the centre of gravity and key nodes of an enemy's combat systems."[8]

The PLASSF Salient Structural Features

PLA has taken the two-phased approach to implementing the reforms by 2020. The first phase consists of 'above the neck' reforms that look into the overall design of armed forces and the second phase consist of "below the neck" reforms to reshape and skill the institutions and operations at the operational and tactical levels. The PLASSF was created as part of a broader reorganisation that dissolved the PLA's four former general departments, transforming the bulk of their functions into 15 joint force "functional organs" within an expanded CMC. The reorganisation, the PLASSF, was formed out of these departments' operational units responsible for space, cyber, and early-warning (EW). This move was aimed in part to break the silos within the organisation and remove roadblocks impeding its growth. Salient issues are as under:

- JSD is responsible for planning, coordinating and allocation of PLASSF resources. The five departments under GSD have been rechristened and reshuffled to create new five bureaus. Operations Bureau corresponds to GSD First Department, but the Survey, Maps and Navigation Bureau has been merged with the newly created Battlefield Environment Support Bureau. GSD Second Department has been nominated as Intelligence Bureau, but the Space Reconnaissance Bureau has been moved to PLASSF. The GSD Third Department has also been transferred to PLASSF. The GSD Fourth Department less the ECM Brigades have been restricted to form the Network Electronics Bureau while the ECM brigades have been transferred to PLASSF.

- CMC JSD, therefore, handles the core operations and intelligence analysis, a function that was looked after by the GSD. JSD acting on behalf of the CMC is likely to support strategic, operational plans with issues related to missile strike or defence, situational awareness derived from space and cyber systems, counter-space and offensive cyberwar.
- JSD run by a CMC-member grade officer senior to the theatre commanders is better positioned to have oversight over the theatre's operations due to integrated communications systems and a common operational picture.
- All the launch bases and Telemetry, Tracking and Coordination Bases of General Armament Department (GAD) has been transferred to PLASSF.
- The PLASSF's Space Systems Department (SSD) is formed primarily from units under the former GAD and select elements of the GSD responsible for space-based C4ISR.
- The PLASSF's Network Systems Department (NSD) comes largely from the former Third and Fourth departments of the GSD, which had respectively held the responsibilities for technical surveillance and offensive cyber operations.
- The cyber, electronic, and psychological warfare as interconnected subcomponents of information warfare has been incorporated into the NSD. The psychological domain constitutes a core element of the PLA's concept of the 'three warfares'. The majority of the PLA's information warfare structures and capabilities has been consolidated under a single PLASSF command structure. The GPD's Base 311 (Unit 61716), which engages in the 'three warfares', is most likely now part of the PLASSF.[9] However, the Political Work Department still retains the primary responsibility for political and psychological warfare, as well as the intelligence-related functions outlined in the Political Work Guidelines. The former GPD Liaison Department is now the Liaison Bureau within the new Political Work Department. The changes to the guidelines in 2003 and 2010 emphasised the importance of political officers becoming part of the PLA's warfighting capability.[10]

- The pre-reform major components of the PLASSF is given in Figure 4.1. It also shows how the CMC-JSD has been organised to coordinate strategic forces operation and intelligence with an officer senior to the theatre grade officer.

The post-reform structure of the PLASSF has been captured in Figure 4.2. The headquarters elements are organised into six first-level departments of which four are administrative– the Staff Department, the Political Work Department, the Logistics Department and the Equipment Department. The other two operational departments, like the Space Systems Departments, is responsible for space operations, and the Network Systems Department is responsible for IO. Besides this, they have a Discipline and Inspection Commission.[11] PLASSF senior officers manage at least three 1st-level administrative departments, two systems departments, and at least 12 corps leader-grade or corps deputy leader-grade base commands.[12] The PLASSF is a theatre command leader grade independent military force under the direct command of the CMC. General Gao Jin, a former PLASAF Commander and the president of the Academy of Military Science (AMS), was the first PLASSF commander to oversee the integration of diverse departments. Administratively, the PLASSF operates similarly to the former PLASAF, which was also a force that functioned as a service under the direct command of the CMC.[13]

The PLASSF is required to fulfil the SMS 2013 conceptualisation of a new-type combat force that was to operate in the 'near space, outer space and network space' and able to surpass geographical barriers and directly threaten the centre of gravity and key nodes of an enemy's combat systems. The official phrase summarises the PLASSF's operational responsibilities, "CMC leads, theatres fight, and services build."[14] A new dual-command structure has been created with an administrative chain from the CMC. Though the structure of these departments is mostly opaque, the details will slowly emerge as the transition takes shape. Some of the inferences are:

- The PLASSF appears to have a bifurcated structure, whereby the SSD and NSD act as largely independent, administrative headquarters for their respective forces.
- The Staff Department within the PLASSF headquarters enables the SSD and NSD to independently develop their force structure and training, allowing the CMC to integrate their operations based on strategic intelligence and missions.

Figure 4.1: Pre-Reform Structure of Major PLASSF Component

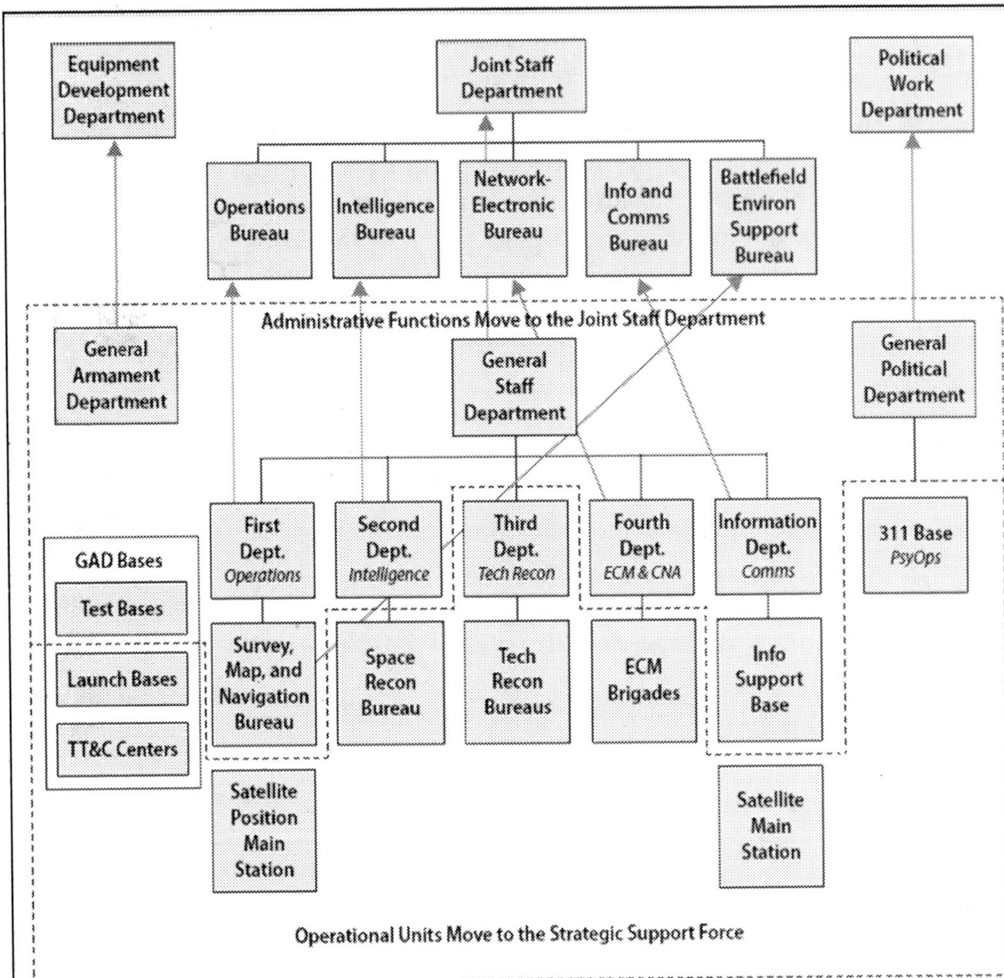

Key: ECM: electronic countermeasures; GAD: General Armament Department; PsyOps: psychological operations; TT&C: telemetry, tracking, and control; GPD: General Political Department.

Source: McReynolds, John Costello and Joe. October 2018. *China's Strategic Support Force: A Force for a New Era*. Washington DC: National Defense University Press. inss.ndu.edu/Publications.aspx.

Figure 4.2: Organisation of PLASSF and Grade Structure

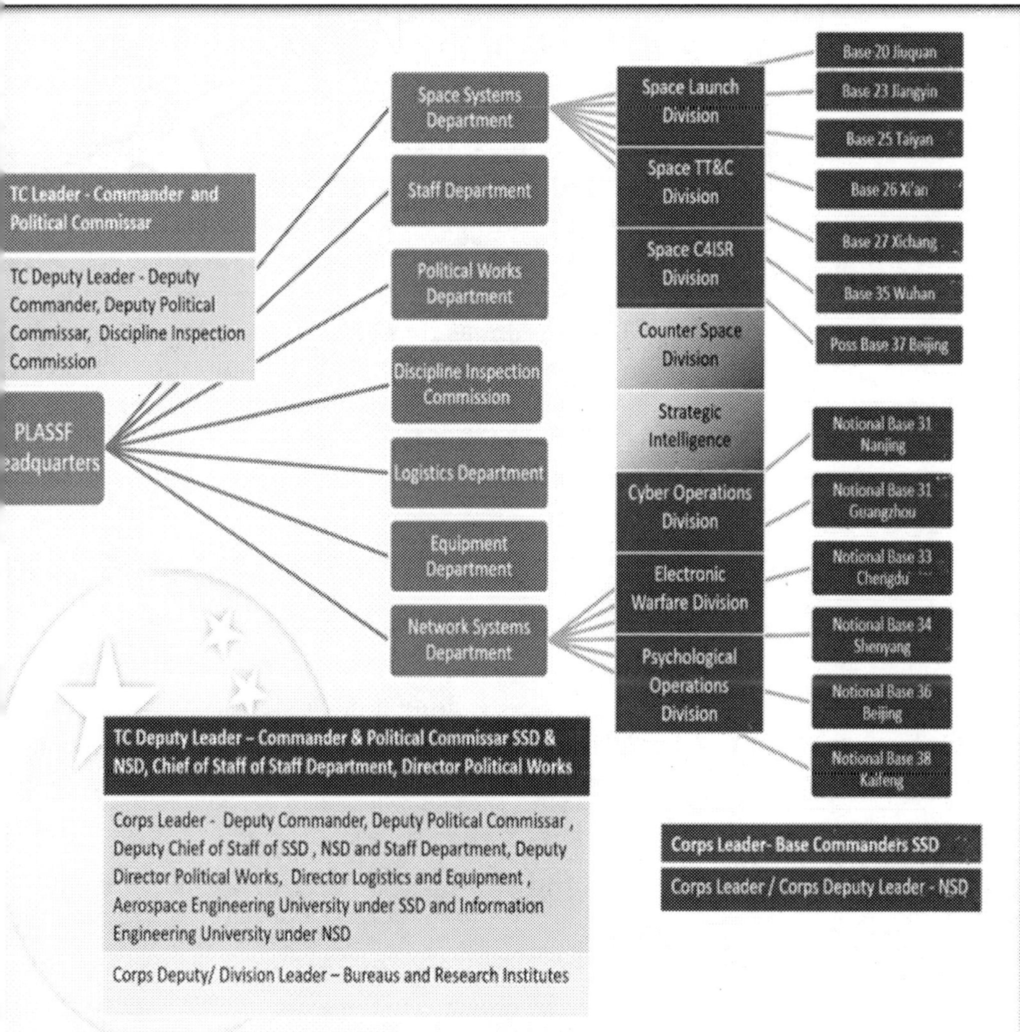

Source: McReynolds, John Costello and Joe. October 2018. *China's Strategic Support Force: A Force for a New Era*, op. cit., p.18. and Stokes, Rachael Burton and Martin. 2018. "The People's Liberation Army Strategic Support Force Leadership and Structures." *Project 2049 Institute*. 25 September. Accessed April 22, 2020.

- Many PLASSF forces appear to be organised as 'bases', a form of corps leader grade unit that is distinct to the PLA.

Usually, an organisation's grade, not its commander's rank, has been the determining factor for its authority in the PLA.[15]

The consequential mystery is regarding the SSD and NSD appearing on the same grade as the PLASSF Staff Department (refer Figure 4.2), limiting the latter's ability to command and direct their operations. According to some analysts, this arrangement may be part of bureaucratic necessity where many of the former GAD launch bases were 'corps leader grade' organisations. The SSD would need to be at least a 'deputy theatre command leader grade' to command them. It means that grade increase that made it the equal of the Staff Department. Alternatively, it may indicate that PLASSF is in a transitional state, and further changes might happen as space and cyber forces move into a more permanent organisational framework.[16]

PLASSF Doctrinal Precepts

According to Alfred D. Chandler, "structure follows strategy". Having looked at the conceptual issues and broad structural framework related to the raising of the PLASSF. The close examination of the doctrinal precepts will help us to understand the rationale of force structuring of PLASSF, its mission and role before delving again about the structures at the functional levels of NSD and SSD.

Information Age Warfare and Integrated Network Electronic Warfare (INEW)

According to SMS 2013, the pros and cons of information determine the choice of methods of warfare. The changes in the form of warfare directly affect the outcome of the war. The PLA has adopted information warfare concepts suited to its organisation by blending its traditional tactics and borrowing concepts from the Soviet military and the US doctrine. It has dovetailed the 'three warfares' strategy into it through modernised and improved psychological and public opinion warfare operations and expanded the role of its legal scholars in justifying military and political actions and territorial claims. INEW is the brainchild of Dai Qingmin, the former head of Fourth Department of PLA GSD before its reform.[17]

INEW forms the backbone of the PLA information warfare as it also recognises it as important social infrastructure. It has expanded electronic warfare and signal intelligence to include cyber. Space assets to create shared awareness through data exchange and indulge in information confrontation where the free flow of information is contested, subverted or denied. Co-opting its 'three warfares strategy' helps it to scale up the operation beyond the operational level and enmeshes all of a national approach to the IO. According to PLA analysts, the information age warfare involves the creation of 'Global Information Grid' like the US with interconnected, end-to-end systems capable of routing analysed information to the information warrior and the policymakers. Hence, the informatisation roadmap aims to create space-ground-service based systems networks by integrating human resources, electronic systems in the theatre and creating space systems.[18] Space has emerged as the edifice for information support, and the PLA is aware of the need for encryption and adequacy of bandwidth to support transmission velocity, volume and veracity. The biggest integrator in the whole systems' configuration – the human talent was put in place in 2011 by the PLA through a dedicated decade long programme, and it is confident to have the requisite talent pool by 2020.[19]

The PLA INEW doctrine has elevated the Soviet doctrine of Radio-Electronic Combat[20] to the strategic level. It has included cyber-attacks and space warfare as part of its offensive operations. INEW is a "systems-versus-systems" confrontation and intends extending the operations beyond theatre to include civil and social infrastructure and the economy. Combat effectiveness is highly dependent on information superiority and protecting information security. The room for struggle is extremely vast and covers all areas related to human cyber and space activities.

PLA has broadly defined information warfare as a "war in which the military groups seize information space and fight for information resources,"[21] in other words, it aims at systems of systems confrontations. IO are those operations designed to deceive, disrupt or otherwise manipulate an adversary's C4ISR systems. Even the conventional kinetic attempts to destroy critical nodes of enemy's C4ISR systems qualify as IO. The three insights of the modern informatised world drive China's IO.[22]

- **Peacetime-wartime integration**. The PLA IO works on

continuous preparation of information battlespace during peacetime to ensure its usefulness during wartime to deter the enemy through a demonstration of dominance at the outset.

- **The ubiquity of cyberspace and the electromagnetic spectrum**. The growth of information across geographical and virtual spaces has an exponential reach and has added to various security threats that need to be guarded.
- **Non-nuclear deterrence**. According to SMS 2013, there is a likelihood of increased limited confrontations that may not escalate to the nuclear level. The IO has utility at all levels – from political, economic to the military, can be disrupted to create large scale chaos and disorder. Hence, non-nuclear deterrence is important to the PLA.

The 2013 lectures by PLA scholar Major General Ye Zheng on the 'Science of Information Operations' provides a glimpse about the secretive Chinese IO. According to him, there are four fundamental principles of IO:

- **IO is offence-oriented**. Information dominance is the fundamental of the "three dominances" of information, air, and space. Once it is achieved, the victory is ensured. Hence, system-of-systems operations aim at disrupting an adversary's system of systems while preserving one's own to gain and retain the strategic initiative and effective control.
- **IO is offence-dominant**. Cyber and intelligence operations rely on techniques and the ability to access systems. Cyber operations are more effective in the initial stages of conflict because once it is used, the surprise is lost.
- **Persistent presence**. It is the cornerstone of information warfare. The advantage in the information domain is based on the priority of timing, blurring the distinction between peacetime and wartime. It aims to be embedded within every adversary's system during peacetime.
- **Information advantage**. It can be achieved through either cyber implant in an adversary's systems or by strategic information support to anticipate, delay, and disable an adversary's ability to defend itself or project power.

Cyberwarfare. It takes place in the electromagnetic spectrum. Hence, there is a great deal of conceptual overlap with electronic warfare. Like other developed military power, China is heavily involved in computer network operation. The US 2018 NDS accusation that China uses predatory methods to promote its economic interests is borne out of the fact that China has used cyberwarfare mechanism to obtain business-sensitive data of the US companies. The two nations have locked horn over system penetration for intelligence collection and mounting of regular cyber-attacks on each other interests. The PLA is looking to develop the asymmetrical capabilities against potential adversaries with a capability of turning the cyber capability into combat capability during hostilities. Securing the network is the most critical aspect of INEW. These networks include the physical infrastructure (like the government facilities, railroad, pipelines and ports), the critical infrastructure (like the energy, banking and finance) and the cyberinfrastructure (like the software, hardware, internet, information service, etc.). They are interdependent and vulnerable to cyber operations that may include network-centric warfare, cyber-physical system attack like 'Stuxnet' type cyber-weapon, cyber espionage and cyber deterrence.

Electronic Warfare. Electronic warfare, according to the PLA analysts, is not inherently strategic. But its combination with cyber network and space gives it a status of "strategic high ground."[23] The PLA used innovative means to expand the Soviet doctrine on "radio-electronic combat," for initiating soft and hard kill options for network system including space-based assets. The PLA, however, apparently intends to conduct these activities at the tactical, operational, and strategic levels of war, envisioning attacks on an enemy's homeland critical infrastructure and points of embarkation. The expansion of worldwide penetration on internet and satellite navigation; however, it poses a question as to what will constitute war in space electronics fields as electromagnetic domain does not exist in isolation. For China, INEW refers to merging the electronic warfare strength at the campaign level with the network warfare strength at the strategic level to ensure dominance across all the phases of operations.

PLASSF Space Warfare Doctrine

The aggressive forays by the US in the space has alarmed China, especially unmanned X-37B space reusable spacecraft operating between the altitude of 850 km[24] is seen as a space weapon by China. It feels that it needs to correct the imbalance but is constrained by technology and economic factors. The SMS 2013 assessment that PLA must protect its interest in outer space and develop space and counter-space capabilities appears to necessitate the strategy for employment of these capabilities. Incorporating 'active defence' and 'informatisation' into its assessment of the changing character of warfare fits the bill. Regarding outer space as a critical domain, the PLA is looking to deploy forward defence guiding ideas to it. It is looking at moving from the platform-centric approach to a system-centric approach and aims to guard its vulnerabilities while displaying an intent to strike if provoked. Thus, practising effective control or war control manoeuvres as space is tied to all domains and across the peace-war continuum. The vastness of space has increased strategic space for 'active defence' compelling China to include 'space operations' as part of the nine main operational activities required to be conducted by it.[25] Expanding strategic space has been captured in the SMS 2013, which defines it as "the area required by a nation or state to resist foreign interference and aggression and safeguard their survival and development."[26] Unlike 'forward defence' where China intends conducting future military operations, strategic space looks at areas of potential interest which it plans to influence with military capabilities including non-war operations. The dynamic nature of strategic space based on expanding threat concerns from the multi-dimensional spaces adds ambiguity to the extent of the space and where it will be contested. The militarisation of outer space is an indisputable fact. China realises that it has to take the lead in this field to improve on its situational awareness and information supremacy and enhance space deterrence capability.[27] It aims to bridge the capability gap through asymmetric system development and restrict the weaponisation of space through international coalition and regulatory norms.

Three Warfares

The doctrine of 'three warfares' has been covered in Chapter 2. However, few issues pertinent to PLASSF is important to be highlighted. According to SMS 2013, the 'three warfares' is a force multiplier to be used in military operations or to manipulate the political or diplomatic landscape alike. The 2003 and 2010 Political Work Regulations assigns the 'three warfares' as a "wartime political work". The GPD of the former GSD was made responsible, however, through the 2016 organisational reforms the Political Work Department, subordinate to the CMC is now responsible.[28] One of its core activity is to select foreign political, business, and military elites and organisations abroad that can comply according to China's interests.

This cognitive contouring allows management of tailored influence operations.

The right of discourse is determined by "information-faith-mind" combination to weave perception and ability to control the narrative.[29] Its application is intended to control the prevailing narrative and influence perceptions in a way that promotes China's interests while compromising the capability of opponents to respond. The focus of each of these activities is fundamental to create and to advance international and domestic legitimacy for CPC's viewpoint. The impact of the operation is controlled by either expanding, diluting or shifting so that the powerful psychological shock can be brought to bear on the enemy leadership and forces. The 2014 NDU paper on the 'Introduction to Public Opinion Warfare, Psychological Warfare, and Legal Warfare' mentions that at the basic level, the 'three warfares' aim at influencing and targeting the adversary's psychology by weaponising the information dissemination mechanism including social media.[30] It is aimed at improving China's soft power and acceptability across the world in non-war military operations and is executed by an amalgam of uniformed PLA and civilian.[31] The public opinion and legal warfare are directed at the strategic level based upon the efficacy of information. In contrast, psychological warfare is often implemented at the campaign and tactical levels.[32] The strategic, doctrinal, and organisational changes in PLA will be pivotal in operationalising the 'three warfares' into a potent element of conflict management and war control.

PLASSF Strategic Missions and Role

The PLASSF Likely Missions

The PLASSF, as the new information warfare force of the PLA, has two primary missions. "First, it is to provide the PLA with strategic information support through space and network-based capabilities, including communications, navigation and positioning, intelligence, surveillance and reconnaissance, and the protection of military information infrastructure. Second, the SSF is to conduct IO, including space and counter-space, cyber, electromagnetic warfare, and psychological operations.[33]

The PLASSF Strategic Role

The creation of the PLASSF signifies the importance accorded by China's military planner to information dominance. It is also a direct recognition that the "strategic frontiers" of space and cyberspace are vital to China's expanding hard power as well as its broader strategic interests, including economic growth and technological development. To achieve information dominance, SMS 2013 calls for the coordinated employment of space, cyber, and electronic warfare as strategic weapons to paralyse or sabotage the enemy's command operational system of systems in the initial stages of a struggle while protecting its own. These concepts are not unique to many modern militaries. The PLASSF's IO campaign is complex and constitutes a multi-dimensional set of manoeuvres that integrates kinetic, space, cyber, electronic, and psychological activities through all phases of conflict. Each discipline of IO has specific strengths at different phases of a crisis or conflict. Psychological and electronic warfare forms the part of the pre-crisis period to raise the political and military risks associated with aggression. Electronic warfare is likely to be used as a key signalling mechanism for the PLA as it bridges the gap of cyber operations, which have a high opportunity cost in terms of blown access when used for signalling, and kinetic strikes, which mark a transition to open warfare. Thus, electronic warfare is the workhorse in Chinese IO and is seen as a double-duty tool for both coercion and information denial. The creation of PLASSF has enabled the unity of command, planning, and force development. The PLASSF can conduct complex, coordinated set of IO in both peacetime and wartime using unified force, integrating cyber espionage and offence, unifying information warfare campaign planning, and unifying responsibilities for information warfare command and control.[34]

Network Security Operations. For the PLA, the information warfare is directed at "the enemy's information detection sources, information channels and information-processing and decision making."[35] Cyber-threat poses dangers not only to the economy and financial services but has the power to collapse governance and social stability, especially when compounded with military confrontations. According to SMS 2013, the extreme distribution of global network allows concealment in attack without revealing the true identity. Ability to attribute impedes the response time, and hence the effective control is not always available. The military confrontation in the network field is essentially based on knowledge and intelligence. Network reconnaissance provides persistent presence to siphon of the non-public information without disturbing the user[36] and convert it into a network attack based on the choice to be exercised. Targeted cyber confrontations are also something the PLA has evolved and is likely to be played based on soft kill option options by hacking or hard kill option through the use of electromagnetic pulse bomb, microwave bomb etc.

Cyber Deterrence. SMS 2013 also talks about cyber deterrence capability development by creating the capability to identify the cyber-attack and have the determination of retaliation. Cyber deterrence is beyond the use of cyber weapons and also looks at the general regulations. Strategic guidance for military struggles in the network field include:[37]

- Maintain the national important information and information network security by creating sound IT infrastructure with core technologies as China fears that the US may control the internet and put China in a disadvantage in online confrontation. So, for China, the goal of the military struggle is to preserve information security of national finance, transportation, energy, and major defence companies.
- Uncertainty and the unpredictability of attack necessitates a good defensive capability as the priority followed by deterrence and cyber combat. The paper claim that China is developing its offensive capabilities to strengthen its deterrent capability.
- It is looking at civil-military fusion for the professional handling of cyber networks. Combat forces are organised by the PLA and specialised in cyber warfare while it advocates local forces, mainly organised within the relevant government departments such as the Ministry of Security and the Ministry of Public Security; private forces to conduct network offensive and defensive. After mobilisation and organisation, it can be used in the network Combat.

Strategic Information Support. Information support, according to Chinese General Gao Jin, is the crucial role of the PLASSF. It is required to provide vital support for safeguarding and raising an 'information umbrella' for the military system that can be integrated with the actions on land, sea, air and space. It forms an essential force for winning the war.[38] The SMS 2013 refers to the PLASSF space force as the "strategic brace support" of space-based intelligence and communications.[39] The PLASSF's draws its strategic information support from the large intelligence and communications assets under space and cyber forces. It also maintains deep technical collection capabilities that are consequential even beyond offence and espionage operations within the cyber domain. PLASSF information support missions can be divided into five primary functions across the military:

- **Centralising Technical Intelligence Collection and Management**. The PLASSF has recomposed a large array of national-level technical collection assets from the former organisations. It includes space-based electro-optical imagery intelligence, synthetic aperture radar, electronic intelligence platforms from the former GSD and GAD. From the former Fourth Department, it has amalgamated electronic support capabilities, and from the former Third Department, it has taken the strategic, long-range ground-based collection systems.[40] The reorganisation places all these collection assets under the same organisation. The advantages accruing out of centralisation is dependent on how well the technical systems, data, and organisational procedures have been integrated. However, the wealth of information processed allows the PLASSF a comprehensive perspective to identify gaps in the collection, assess trends, task-relevant sources and tailor operations and acquisitions to address shortfalls and new challenges. The sheer breadth of what the PLASSF can observe, empowers it to play a pivotal role in the PLA's comprehensive domain awareness and national defence.
- **Providing Strategic Intelligence Support to Theatre Commands**. The theatre command technical reconnaissance bureaus and theatre-subordinate service elements are largely focused on operational and tactical level ISR with limited coverage beyond their areas of responsibility. Comprehensive intelligence picture is not available to the theatre command commanders due to limited-range drones, and shore-based surveillance platforms.[41] The PLASSF with extended global coverage due to space-based surveillance capacity helps to fill the intelligence voids of the theatre command commanders. The PLASSF's primacy in space-based intelligence collection helps it in tagging the foreign military targets, especially the radar and the IR heat signatures, signal parameters, or even imagery profiles. These assist in detecting,

identifying, tracking, and targeting certain operational platforms and weapons systems. The PLASSF is also responsible for joint force early warning, air defence and area surveillance. Besides these tasks, it is also capable of non-kinetic targeting with its cyber and electromagnetic assets as it owns sensors and communications signatures.

- **Enabling the PLA Power Projection**. The PLASSF provides the backbone to the strategic deterrence scheme of the PLA. The strategic intelligence support in the form of space-based surveillance, satellite relay and communications, and telemetry, tracking. Navigation adds to the "information chain", an important subset of the kill chain, of the lethal long-range precision system which is vital to enable and sustain the power projection across two seas and beyond the first island chain. The conventional strike is the most critical component of both the PLA's non-nuclear deterrence posture and its "counter-intervention" strategy. Despite being conducted primarily by the PLARF, it depends heavily on the support operations of the PLASSF. These include initial detection, identification, guidance, targeting, and battlefield damage assessment. Similarly, it has an indispensable role to play in enabling the PLAN and PLAAF to operate in the seas. The PLASSF also provide foundational "battlefield environment support"- a term used by the PLA to describe battlespace related survey, mapping, meteorological, oceanographic, and navigation information.[42] The knowledge-base is a critical factor for command decision making by PLAN. China's increasing fleet of maritime surveillance satellites, dual-use oceanographic and hydrological satellites, and expanding constellation of BeiDou navigation satellites, set to be fully operationalised by 2020, adds to the effectiveness of the PLAN while dealing with A2AD operations.
- **Supporting Strategic Defence in the Space and Nuclear Domains**. The PLASSF's responsibilities for anti-satellite missile operations, ballistic missile defence, and space-based kinetic operations are not explicit. However, its monopoly on space surveillance and early warning gives it a pivotal role in supporting these missions as it can detect, identify, and track objects in space which is the prerequisite for both anti-satellite and ballistic missile defence.

- **Enabling Integrated Joint Operations**. The integrated joint operations hinge on communication and surveillance. The PLASSF's by virtue of its role in strategic information support directly enables this crucial operation by seamlessly integrating disparate units and systems from the PLA's four services. The PLASSF's ability to provide the information umbrella of space-based C4ISR and battlefield environment assessments helps to forge a common intelligence picture among joint forces within each theatre command, a fundamental requirement for fulfilling the PLA's mission of winning the informationised local wars. However, the growing information-dominant system-of-systems integration challenges have become the fundamental requirement for future joint operations.[43]

Strategic Space Deterrence

The SMS 2013 describes two ways the deterrence can be used – firstly, a robust ISR allows for better situational awareness to enable pre-emptive military and diplomatic measures. Secondly, is the application of counter-space measures in the form of limited space operations with warning and punishments to enable war control. China also follows a policy to prevent the weaponisation of space while it works secretively to develop counter-space capabilities. It is implemented through space military forces a basic form of space-military struggle. Hence, SMS 2013 is vocal about raising a space-operational force that provides resilience for space defence at the same time it propagates that China must develop and demonstrate the offensive capabilities periodically.

Space Attack and Defence

SMS 2013 sees a trend beyond air-based deterrent methods. It advocates direct space confrontations, especially with strong enemies. However, The PLA divides the offensive and defensive operations as:

- **Satellite offensive and defensive operations**. It includes the use of ground-based, air-based, space-based weapons to attack enemy satellites.
- **Space anti-satellite operations**. This operation entails interception and destruction of enemy space assets by use of laser and energy directed weapon systems, projectile warfare etc.

- **Space combat platforms**. Platforms like space planes, space stations for the attack on space-based assets.
- **Other Space-based Attack Operations against Ground and Air Targets**. Operations employing the use of laser, particle beam or kinetic energy weapons from space-based platforms to destroy targets on the ground, air or sea.

PLASFF: NETWORK SYSTEMS DEPARTMENT AND CYBER FORCES

President Xi during the PLASSF founding ceremony on 31 December 2015 called it a new type of combat force essential for national security. The PLASSF was formed to consolidate cyber elements of the former PLA General Staff Third (Technical Reconnaissance) and Fourth (Electronic Countermeasures and Radar) Departments and Informatisation Department.[44] Cyberspace remains a preferred operational domain for China as it provides a wide range of choice to orchestrate operations from covert to the overt arena. It includes espionage of adversarial nation-states, commercial enterprises and undertaking of sponsored activities through proxy hacker groups. The Next-generation technologies, such as Artificial Intelligence (AI) and the Internet-of-Things (IoT) introduce new vulnerabilities to the network systems. Building an effective response requires an understanding of cybersecurity and the ability to gauge the multi-vector threat to the integrity of the nation's economy and global trade. The NSD is responsible for executing the PLASSF's network mission, which includes, and potentially integrates, a diverse range of operations, including signals intelligence, cyber cum economic espionage, computer attack, electromagnetic warfare and psychological operations.

NSD Cyber Force

The centralisation of China's strategic cyber forces is a key feature of the NSD as it irons out the operational coordination challenges that arose due to the structure of the former GSD. Reportedly, computer network attack was handled by the GSD Fourth Department (4PLA), while the GSD Informatisation Department handled the PLA counter-network defence operations. The former 4PLA's computer network attack forces are now part of the PLASSF to integrate with the cyber-espionage elements of the former 3PLA. However, the NSD does not appear to have integrated the

PLA's counter-network defence mission, which remains with the JSD Information Support Base under its Network Security Defence Centre.[45]

The NSD retains the headquarters of the former 3PLA along with its bureau-centric structure because in one case the NSD has been addressed as the "SSF Third Department", its former designation.[46] For instance, the 12th Bureau, Unit 61486, headquartered in Shanghai's Chabei District, supports China's space surveillance network[47] with an estimated 20,000 personnel, with their linguists trained at the Luoyang Institute of Foreign Languages.[48] They conduct intelligence-gathering operations targeting the government, defence, research and technology sectors in the US, with specific targeting of space, aerospace, and communications. The former 56th, 57th, and 58th Research Institutes under the GSD which previously provided research, development, and weapon support to the technical reconnaissance tasks have also moved to NSD.[49] Table 4.1 shows the range of activities undertaken by the 3PLA. The PLASSF Information Engineering University, a corps leader-grade organisation, is the training vehicle of 3PLA. Some of the important institutions it may oversee are in Table 4.2.

Table 4.1: Organisation of the Operational Bureaus of the 3 PLA of the NSD

Bureau & MUCD Number	*Location*	*Task*
1st Bureau (61786 Unit)	Beijing	Decryption, encryption, information security
2nd Bureau (61398 Unit)	Shanghai	US and Canada focus
3rd Bureau (61785 Unit)	Beijing	Radio communications, direction finding, emission control
4th Bureau (61419 Unit)	Qingdao	Japan and Korea focus
5th Bureau (61565 Unit)	Beijing	Russia focus
6th Bureau (61726 Unit)	Wuhan	Network attack and defence centre
7th Bureau (61580 Unit)	Beijing	Computer network operations based on the US network-centric concept, psychological and technical aspects of reading and interpreting foreign languages
8th Bureau (61046 Unit)	Beijing	Europe, West Asia, Africa, Latin America
9th Bureau (opaquest Bureau)	Beijing	Strategic intelligence analysis/database management
10th Bureau (61886 or 7911 Unit)	Beijing	CAR or Russia, telemetry missile tracking, nuclear testing
11th Bureau (61672 or 2020 Unit)	Beijing	Russia

Bureau & MUCD Number	*Location*	*Task*
12th Bureau (61486 Unit)	Shanghai	Satellites, space-based signals intelligence collection
Research Institutes • 56th Research Institute • 57th Research Institute • 58th Research Institute		
Organisations associated with Computer Network Defence • PLA's Information Engineering University • PLA Communications Security Bureau China • Beijing North Computation Centre • National Research Centre for Information Security Technology (Network Risk Assessment). • PLA Information Security Evaluation and Certification Centre. • Information Security Research Institute National Information Centre • National Information Security Engineering Technology Centre		

Source: Mallick, PK. September-October 2017. "PLA in Electromagnetic Domain." *India Foundation Journal*, 35-39.

Table 4.2: List of Institutions Under the PLASSF Information Engineering University

• Command Information Systems Academy	• Command Officer Basic Education Academy
• Electronic Technology Academy	• Blockchain Academy located in Shenzhen
• Encryption Engineering Academy	• National Digital Switching Engineering Research Centre
• Luoyang Foreign Language Academy	• National Key Laboratory of Mathematical Engineering and Advanced Computing
• Geospatial Information Academy	• Information Technology Research Institute
• Cyberspace Security Academy	
• Navigation and Aerospace Engineering Academy	

The NSD and Electronic Warfare

Strategic electronic warfare and computer network attack was the responsibility of the GSD Electronic Countermeasures and Radar Department or the 4 PLA. It has now been split. While the headquarter elements of 4 PLA has been reorganised or transferred to the JSD where it has been reconstituted as the new JSD Network-Electronic Bureau (JSD-NEB). In its new form, it likely oversees the management of the cyber and electronic warfare missions across the entire Chinese military, including the PLASSF, theatre commands, and services. The 4 PLA's military academy, the PLA Electrical Engineering Institute has been subsumed by the National University of Defence Technology (NUDT) to become the NUDT ECM Institute.

Meanwhile, 4 PLA's 54th Research Institute, responsible for research and development of operational electronic and network countermeasures, has moved over to the PLASSF, likely under the NSD.[50] At a lower, operational level, at least some of the 4 PLA's ECM units have been reassigned to the PLASSF. The reallocation of the 54th Research Institute to NSD shows that the electronic warfare role has been assigned to the NSD (see Figure 4.3).

Intelligence and Technical Reconnaissance

The Second Department (2 PLA) of the GSD was responsible for gathering military information. The activities included those of military attaches at Chinese embassies, clandestine special agents inserted to foreign countries to obtain military information, and the analysis of information publicly published in foreign countries. The 2PLA oversees military human intelligence (HUMINT) widely. It uses open-source materials while fusing HUMINT, signals intelligence (SIGINT), and imagery intelligence data, and disseminating intelligence to the CMC and other consumers. Preliminary fusion is carried out by the 2PLA's Analysis Bureau, which operates the National Watch Centre that forms the focal point for national-level warning and the regional bureaus carry out in-depth analysis. Aerospace Reconnaissance Bureau and the UAV assets have likely been migrated to PLASSF for better intelligence tasking and coordination. The reforms also substantially reorganised intelligence responsibilities. 2PLA headquarters and its intelligence elements seem to have shifted to the new JSD Intelligence Bureau while the strategic technical collection organisation like the 55th Research Institute and the Aerospace Reconnaissance Bureau has shifted to the SSD of the PLASSF.

The perceived threat from foreign intelligence services, which Chinese believe are the most persistent and pervasive, is the guiding force behind China's cyber actors being tied to economic espionage. Despite advances in cybersecurity, cyber espionage remains a relatively low-cost, high-yield approach to a wide spectrum of intellectual property. It is an area which helps China to keep pace with the developmental economics and security barriers which China needs to create.

The first step by China in raising a cyber-force is by dovetailing cyber reconnaissance, cyber-attack, and cyber-defence capabilities into one organisation. It removes operational bottlenecks. To enable the NSD mission of fulfilling the missions to support theatre commands NSD may

Figure 4.3: Network Electronics Units Post Reform

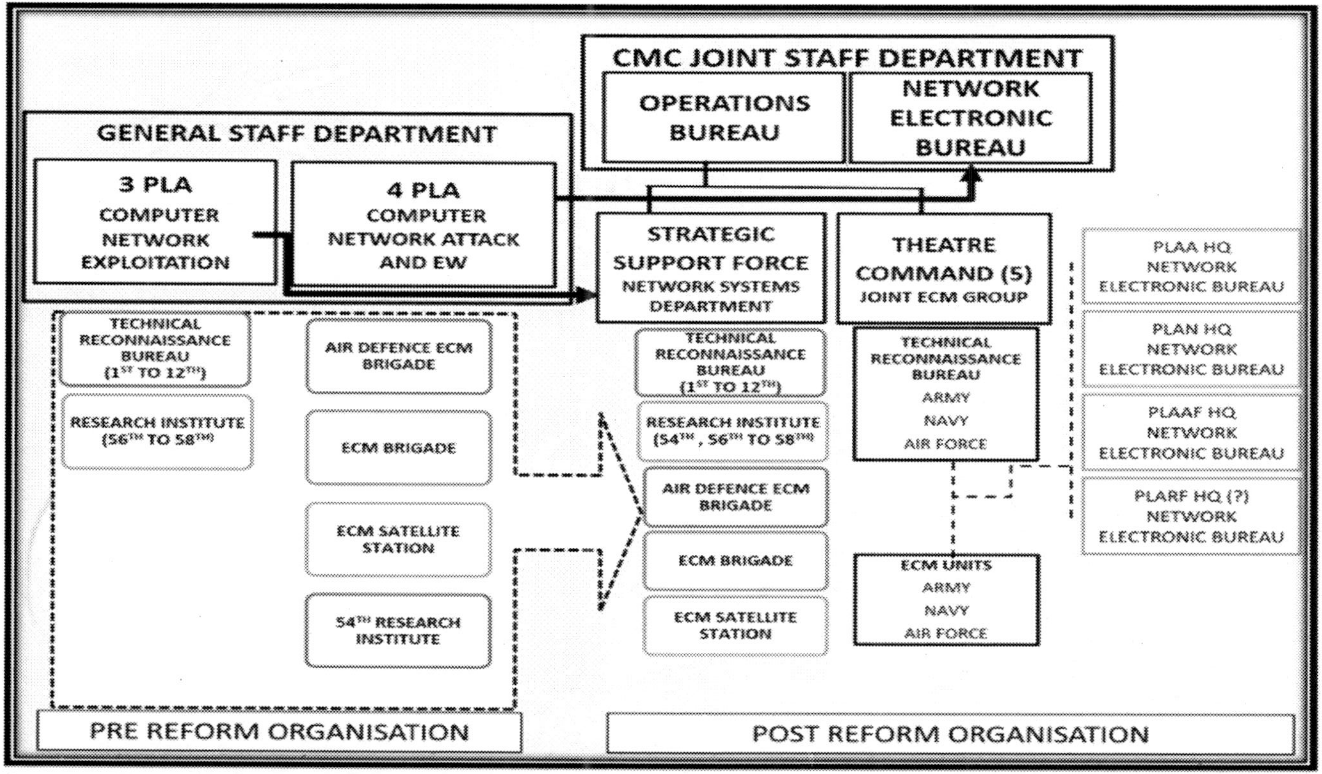

Source: McReynolds, John Costello and Joe. October 2018. *China's Strategic Support Force: A Force for a New Era.* Study Report, Centre for the Study of Chinese Military Affairs, Institute for National Strategic Studies, Washington DC: National Defense University Press. Accessed January 04, 2020. pp.473-475. inss.ndu.edu/Publications.aspx.

Figure 4.4: Pre-2016 and Post- Reform Intelligence Set Up

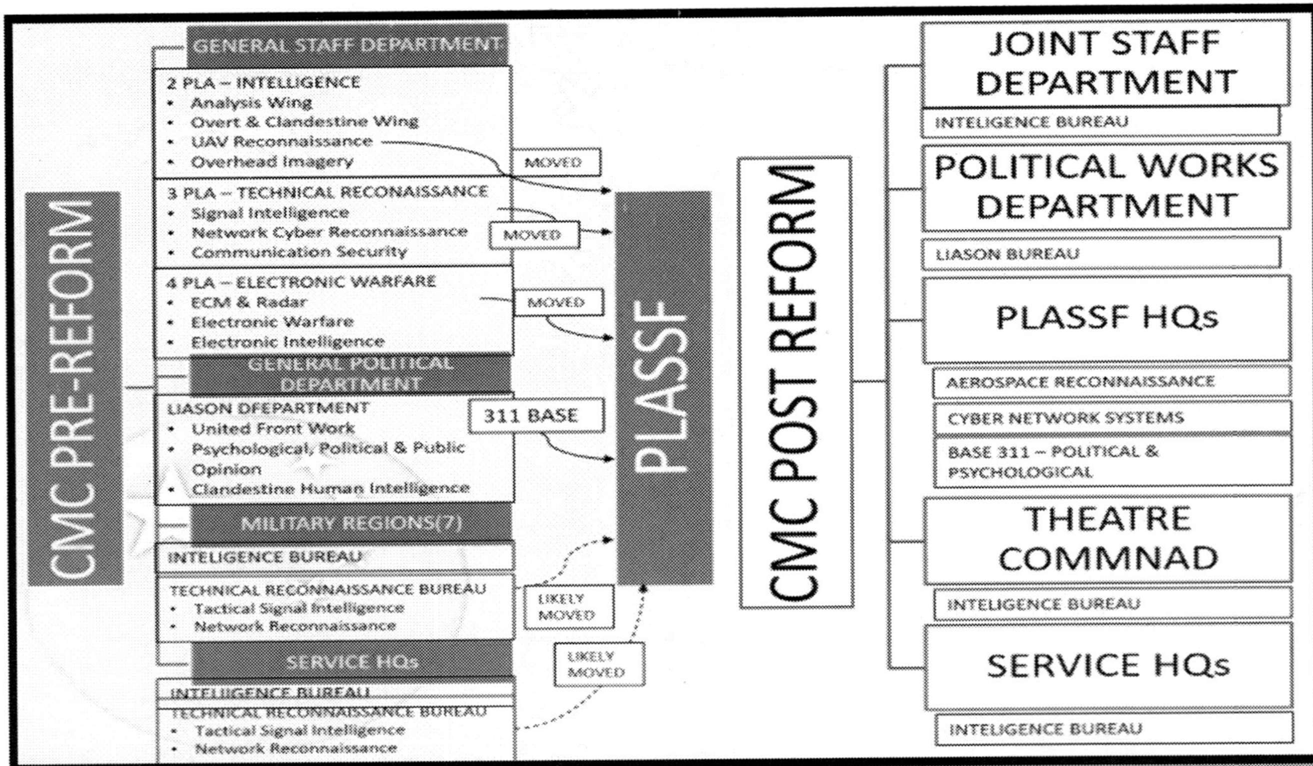

Sources: Peter Mattis, Elsa Kania. 2016. "Modernizing Military Intelligence: Playing Catchup (Part Two)." *China Brief Volume: 16 Issue: 19.* 21 December. Accessed January 05, 2020. https://jamestown.org/program/modernizing-military-intelligence-playing-catchup-part-two/; Third Department, Accessed January 09, 2020. https://www.globalsecurity.org/intell/world/china/pla-dept_3.htm.

use the bases of the newly created Joint Logistics Support Force to organise the loose and geographically dispersed subunits of cyber, EW, and psychological warfare forces it has inherited. It may, therefore, explain the absence of identifiable PLASSF elements under theatre commands.[51]

Military Electro-Magnetic Spectrum Management (EMSM)

National-level policy direction for military EMSM is a joint effort that, as early as 2006, was coordinated by the predecessor organisations of the Ministry of Industry and Information Technology (MIIT) and the PLA JSD. The two successor organisations appear to maintain this shared role. Furthermore, this parallel civilian-military responsibility is mirrored at local levels. According to China's Radio Management Regulations published in 2016 directs the military and local officials to share the division of radio frequencies and resolve both military system and civilian system radio management arrangements report to the National Radio Spectrum Management Centre in Beijing, which itself is subordinate to MIIT. The EMSM Centre also appears to play a role in fostering coordination between provincial and local-area civilian and military officials. Pursuant to its effort to merge military and civilian resources for EMSM, the PLA is actively engaged in creating "reserve frequency management units", which are intended to help the PLA successfully navigate the complex electromagnetic pitfalls of both major peacetime events and potential future conflicts. These units have been employed in recent field training exercises across multiple regions of China.[52] Recent exercise and training activities indicate that these units are, at a minimum, being prepared to monitor for sources of EM interference that could impact PLA and civil defence operations during wartime, natural disasters, or major public events. However, the serious attention is given to these units—and the fact that technical experts from civilian industry, to include the telecom sector, is being actively recruited—suggests that they may be called upon to perform more ambitious roles of the EM interference in the future.

Future Development

The 13th Five-Year Plan of China demands accelerating research on "majorly influential disruptive technologies" and the pursuit of "leapfrog" science and technology developments to win a competitive advantage in the new round of industry transformation. China has stressed on indigenous innovation and the rapid development of strategic science and technology sectors like ICT, high-end manufacturing, alternative energy, and biotechnology. The 2017 National AI Plan describes steps for China to become the "world's major AI innovation centre" by 2030 and calls for the country to accelerate the integration of AI with the economy, society, and national defence. The other plans address the development of various sectors of China's robust Internet ecosystem to include cloud computing, the big data industry, e-commerce, and next-generation broadband wireless communications networks, including fifth-generation (5G) wireless networks.[53] Due to information-sharing requirements with Chinese security services as stipulated in Chinese laws, worldwide expansion of Chinese-made equipment in 5G networks will challenge the security and resiliency of other countries' networks. China is actively pursuing an intensive campaign to obtain foreign technology through imports, foreign direct investment, industrial and cyber-espionage, and establishment of foreign R&D centres. China is investing in the critical technologies that will be foundational for future innovations both for commercial and military applications: AI, robotics, autonomous vehicles, quantum information sciences, augmented and virtual reality, financial technology, and gene editing which are largely ICT dependent.

PLASSF: Space Support Department and the Space Forces

Space Goals

China has clearly outlined its global ambitions of being a leader in space technology and status. According to Xi Jinping, China's space dream hinges on "exploring the vast universe, developing aerospace enterprises, and building a strong aerospace country."[54] Wu Yanhua, administrator of the Chinese space agency in January 2017 claimed that China aims to be a major world space power by around 2030 while China's state-owned space contractor talks of attaining the status of a global leader in space equipment and technology by 2045.[55] These goals are in league with China's aspiration of advancing its national strength. The comprehensive approach of China's space programme helps it to draw important economic, political, and diplomatic benefits. It provides domestic legitimacy, international prestige, and access to collated data derived from international clients using its space platforms.[56] For example, China's Beidou Global Navigation and Surveillance System (GNSS) is a vital component of the BRI Digital Silk Road initiative.[57]

The Digital Silk Road slogan to establish "a community of common destiny in cyberspace," is a ploy by Beijing to shape the political and economic systems in 138 BRI states. China's 2016 space white paper intends establishing a stable and reliable space infrastructure by 2021. It includes upgraded satellite systems and space- ground integrated information networks aimed to remove bottlenecks to scientific advancements.[58] The white paper also announced Beijing's intention of the far side moon probe in 2018 and feasibility studies of a robotic mission to Jupiter. However, the latter programme has not yet been officially approved.[59] China has developed new space and counter-space capabilities and restructured its space entities under PLASSF. China trails the US in satellite assets significantly (refer to Figure 4.5).

Space Role

Pentagon space vision plans to protect US interests, assets, and way of life by building a new age space technology and field new multi-domain systems. The aim is to deter and if necessary, degrade, deny, disrupt, destroy, and manipulate adversaries' capabilities. This new age aims to unlock growth in the US industrial base, expand the commercial space economy, and strengthen cooperation with allies and partners."[60] According to 2019 DIA report, China views space superiority as part of the ability to control the information sphere while Russia sees space as a warfighting domain, and winning the battle in orbit as decisive in future warfare."[61]

Given the strategic competition underway between the US and China, space and counter-space operations thus form an integral part of the PLA campaign. Space situational awareness through surveillance and identification sensors is crucial for China's denial and deception programmes. Predictive modelling of the satellite path allows adversaries to coordinate the concealment of sensitive military capabilities or operations on the ground. The satellite command and data distribution networks expose space systems, ground infrastructure, users, and the links connecting these components to cyber threats. China considers both offensive cyber capabilities and electronic warfare as key assets for maintaining military advantage, and therefore, it is developing cyber capabilities and modernising electronic warfare assets.[62] The increase in competitions in satellite internet, imaging, and power will have fallout in the fields of economy and technology, which may perpetuate into a multi-

Figure 4.5: Comparative Assessment of Space Assets of US, China, Russia and Rest of World

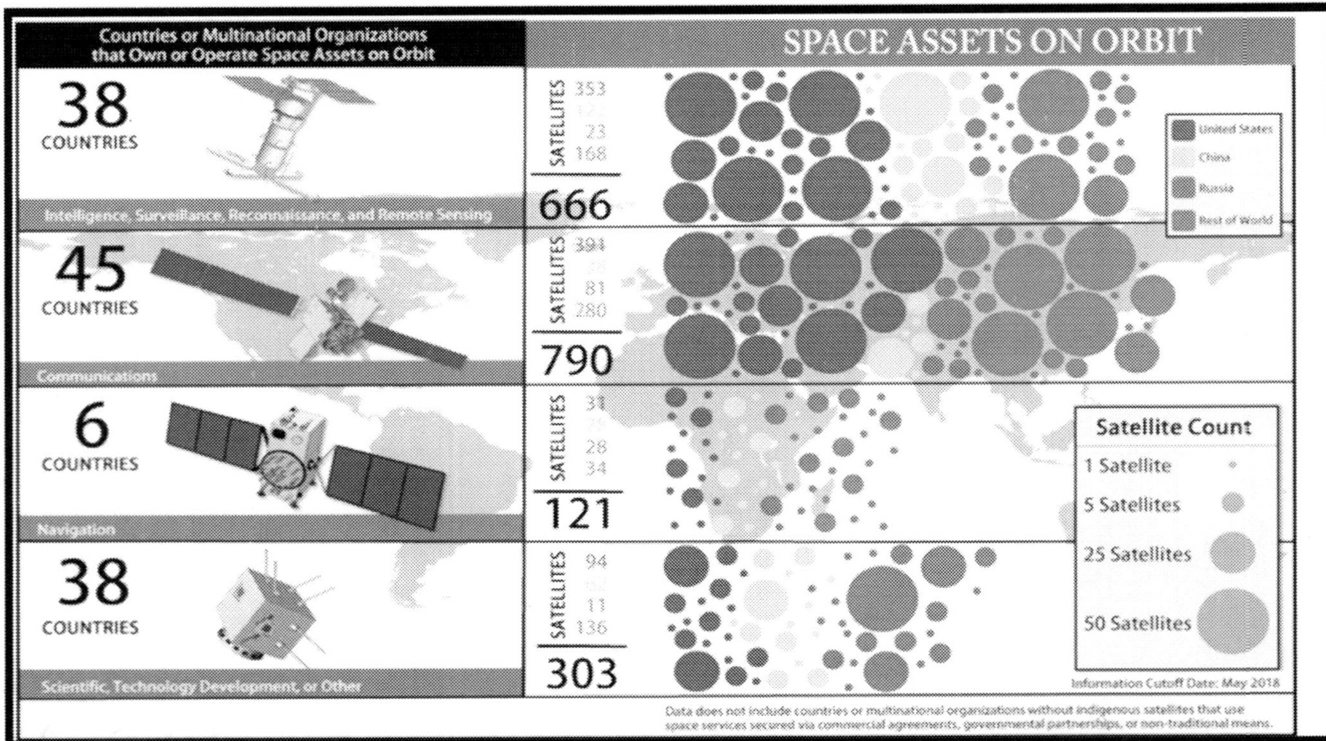

Source: Competing in Space, NASIC Public Affairs Office 4180 Watson Way, https://media.defense.gov/2019/Jan/16/2002080386/-1/-1/1/190115-F-NV711-0002.PDF

domain slugfest. Some of the threats which the PLA is looking at addressing as part of its force development plan are:[63]

- Jamming of global navigation and communications satellites used to command and control of naval, ground, and air forces including manned and unmanned vehicles.
- Weapons like lasers designed to temporarily or permanently blind the target intelligence, surveillance, and reconnaissance capabilities.
- Use of anti-satellite missiles to shoot down satellites in low Earth orbit. China has already demonstrated the anti-satellite missile capability against its defunct weather satellite in 2007.
- The resultant debris due to missile shooting down a satellite can also threaten satellites in nearby orbits.
- China is believed to be testing on-orbit, space-based anti-satellite technologies and concepts like nuclear-electronic warfare for eclipsing communication.
- Physical attacks against ground infrastructures supporting space operations that can adversely affect satellite services and functions.
- Cyber capabilities to target space systems and supporting infrastructure.

SSD Entities

Since 1960s China Central Special Committee comprising of civilian, military, scientific, and engineering leaders have been part of space journey and it reports to the State Council, the CCP Politburo Standing Committee, and the CMC.[64] The Committee coordinates China's strategic R&D including the space domain[65] while the State Council formed a Space Leading Group in 1989 comprising of scientists, industry, foreign affairs, and state planning officials. The PLA plays a role in planning space policy. In 2004 the State Council and the CMC, China's highest-ranking military body, also created a joint leading small group for the lunar probe project that convened at least 14 times from 2004 to 2015.[66] Besides lunar exploration, China has also formed leading small groups for human spaceflight, earth observation satellites, and heavy-lift launch vehicles. The military participation reflects the importance Beijing ascribes to these programmes. Figure 4.6 shows that planning and execution of space policy and research have enmeshed several government entities across the civil,

Figure 4.6: Key Organisations in China's Space Activities

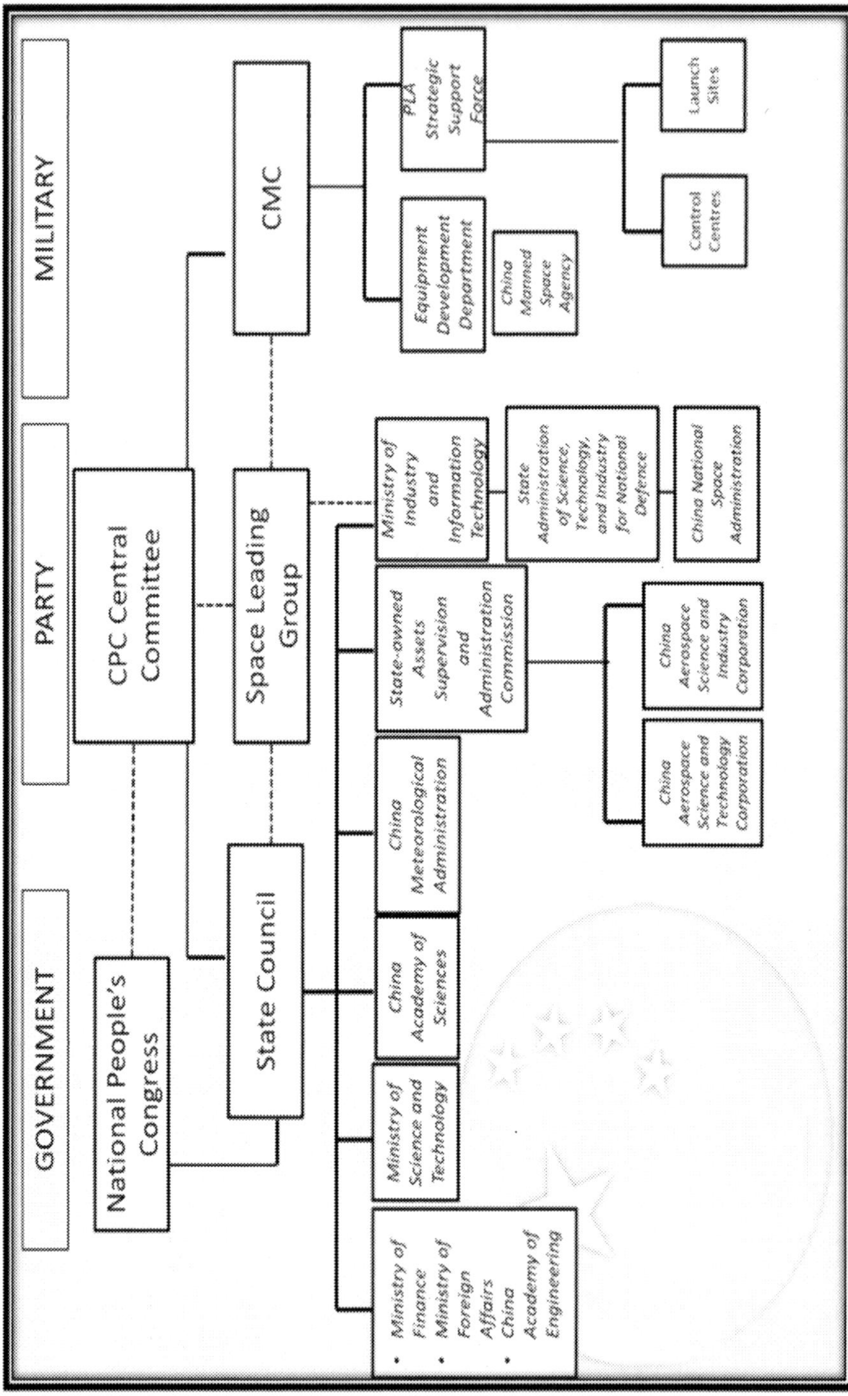

Source: Adapted from Marco Aliberti, *When China Goes to the Moon*. Springer International Publishing, 2015, p.10.

military, academic, and commercial fields. Military entities are heavily enmeshed in China's ostensibly non-military space projects.

Of the known missions of the PLASSF, the space mission has shown creditworthiness. Space units are organised into the newly-established SSD. The former GAD's space mission forms the basis for the SSD, although it also draws units and missions from the former GSD. The SSD has consolidated almost all aspect of PLA space operation, including space launch, support, telemetry, tracking, and control (TT&C) and space ISR.[67] The 2PLA's Aerospace Reconnaissance Bureau and 55th Research Institute also seem to be part of the SSD, where it may now be known as the Aerospace Reconnaissance Command. The Satellite Main Station 61096 from the former GSD Informatisation Department has also been incorporated into the SSD. The former GSD 2PLA is now the new JSD Intelligence Bureau, and the former GSD Informatisation Department is rechristened as JSD Information Communications Bureau.[68] Some R&D-focused institutes may also be housed in the SSD or may have been transferred to the PLASSF's Equipment Department, or some equivalent agencies like China Nuclear Test Base/21st Experimental and Training Base 63650, Aerospace Research and Development Centre and Project Design Research Centre.

The space force was already organised as bases before the creation of the PLASSF. Of the former GAD "test bases" numbering 20 to 33, the five responsible for space operations have been transferred to the PLASSF (refer Figure 4.2) and probably the remaining bases to the CMC Equipment Development Department or the services. These bases seem to have retained their previous numerical designations even under the new system. The creation or designation of a new PLASSF base beyond those five that are known to exist raises the likelihood that more space-related numerical bases may be raised. The new bases may also be responsible for missions like space information support, survey, mapping, and navigation. A newly designated unit like the "35th Base" is designated to look after the space-based survey, mapping, and navigation, including the management of military BeiDou satellites.[69]

China Launch and Tracking Control System Department are responsible through its Xi'an Satellite Control Centre for operating several fixed and mobile TT&C stations in and beyond China. The Chinese locations include Miyun (Beijing), Sanya (Hainan), Kashgar (Xinjiang), and

Kunming (Yunnan), estimated to receive satellite signals encompassing about 70 per cent of Asia. The reach of the China Launch and Tracking Control Department has expanded globally; it has operated stations and established a presence in Karachi, Pakistan; Swakopmund in Namibia, Malindi in Kenya; Dongara in Australia; Santiago in Chile; Alcantara in Brazil; Neuquén in Argentina; and Kiruna in Sweden.[70] The geography of these ground stations and locations may be leveraged for strategic purposes, provoking security concerns in some cases. For example, China's leasing of the ground station in Dongara, motivated by geography advantageous for telemetry, resulted in controversy because of its proximity to sensitive US military facilities. The Neuquén Deep Space Facility in Argentina, built and operated by China to support lunar exploration missions, also possesses potential military relevance.[71]

The articles published by the military researchers affiliated with the GAD 21st Test Base have discussed the use of directed energy weapons (DEW). It suggests that this base may have a mission to research operational uses of lasers or other DEW. It is also aligned with the PLASSF mission to be a "new-type" force responsible for "new-type" capabilities.[72] As a result, the PLASSF now controls the PLA's intelligence satellites and space reconnaissance capabilities, including any future endeavours such as robotic probe missions and international space cooperation.

Space Assets: Satellites

China employs a robust space-based ISR capability designed to enhance its worldwide situational awareness through use of civil and military remote sensing, and mapping, terrestrial and maritime surveillance and military intelligence collection, China's ISR satellites can provide electro-optical (EO) and synthetic aperture radar imagery, as part of electronic and signals intelligence data.

Remote Sensing Satellites. China possesses robust remote sensing capabilities. Of China's satellite constellations, Yaogan, which employs optical and SAR sensors, is the most mature, involving more than 50 satellites.[73] Besides promoting BeiDou, in January 2019 China established a new remote sensing satellite data centre in Fuzhou, Fujian Province that Beijing has billed as part of its Maritime Silk Road, the maritime component of the BRI.[74] China claims the new data centre—which can receive, store, process, and distribute data from 26 Chinese Yaogan remote sensing satellites—will promote information integration between Fujian and Association of Southeast Asian Nations countries, provide services to BRI countries, and promote integration between Taiwan and the Chinese Mainland.[75] The Gaofen series, a sub-meter resolution optical satellite that has been developed by China Academy of Space Technology (CAST), is a clear priority, with six new satellites launched as of mid-2018.[76] Gaofen has been highlighted as a model of military-civil fusion, given the range of defence and commercial applications that it will support, including those under China's BRI. China is on track for the rapid expansion of its remote sensing satellites. The LKW-3 satellite, developed by CAST and launched in January 2018, after launches of the LKW-1 and LKW-2 in December 2017, has also been characterised as intended for remote sensing purposes, potentially as an extension or augmentation of the Yagnon series. Besides, China plans to launch 60 high-resolution optical remote sensing satellites, known as Jilin-1, by 2020.[77] There are at least 13 in space as of 2019, including the latest launched in China's first sea-based launch. By 2020, China intends to create "a global, 24-hour, all-weather earth remote sensing system."[78] This China High-Resolution Earth Observation System (CHEOS) will include EO and SAR satellites, as well as airborne and near-space systems, such as drones or stratospheric balloons. Some of China's big data centres and new overseas satellite ground station near the North Pole in Kiruna, Sweden, completed in 2016, designed for military-civil fusion have also concentrated on making data from space systems, such as remote sensing imagery, more readily available.[79] This China Remote Sensing Satellite North Pole Ground Station, integral to Gaofen, reportedly possesses the potential to "improve China's rapid global remote sensing data acquisition capabilities greatly," with download speeds that are "the fastest in the world."[80] This network of ground stations could continue to expand under the aegis of BRI. In April 2018, China and Finland signed an agreement to cooperate in the research and spatial information acquisition, which will include access to facilities.[81] The 'Space Silk Road' has expanded through multiple partnerships and agreements for cooperation. Even if such collaborations are typically characterised as being oriented toward scientific and commercial applications, these engagements may also support future military operations.

Communication Satellites. China pursues parallel programmes for military and commercial communications satellites (COMSATs). It operates around 30 COMSATs for civil, commercial, and military satellite communications while the PLA operates a small number of dedicated military COMSATs.[82] China's civil COMSATs incorporate turnkey off-the-shelf commercially manufactured components, and China produces its military-dedicated satellites domestically. China uses its domestically produced Dong-fanghong-4 (DFH-4) satellite bus—the structure that contains the components of the satellite—for its military COMSATs. The DFH-4 bus is China's trusted system that has positioned it as a leading competitor in the international COMSAT market. It has contracts with many foreign countries to supply on-orbit satellites, ground-control systems, and training.

Data-Relay Satellite. China is also developing a limited but expanding architecture of satellites for data relay and communications. So far, these include the Fenghuo, Zhongxing, and Shentong series of communication satellites.[83] China launched the first Tianlian data-relay satellite of its China Tracking and Data Relay Satellite constellation in 2008. It has four data-relay satellites in orbit for relaying commands and data to its satellites.[84] The launch of the secretive TXJSSY-1 communications engineering test satellite in September 2015 may have been related to an experimental early warning satellite programme.[85] As of May 2018, the Queqiao data relay satellite, which will support China's mission to the far side of the moon, also has been launched.[86] China has also begun to launch the first in a new array of 320 low-orbit satellites for communications, known as the Hongyan constellation, which has been developed by CASC.[87] There are plans to introduce the Xingyun project, another constellation of 156 low-orbit satellites for narrow-band commercial communications developed by the China Aerospace Science and Industry Corporation (CASIC).[88]

Meteorological Satellites. China has ten domestically produced Fengyun and Yunhai meteorological satellites.[89] The newer satellites have many all-weather sensors concerning atmospheric conditions as well as maritime terrain data for military and civilian customers. The China Meteorological Administration supports civilian and military customers with the delivery of meteorological data and detailed weather forecasts. China's membership in the World Meteorological Organisation grants its free access to global meteorological data from the international organisation's 191 members.[90]

Satellite Navigation System. China embarked on regional satellite navigation system journey on 2000 with the launch of its first BeiDou satellites to create BeiDou Navigation Satellite System (BDS). A regional satellite navigation constellation was established in China by 2012 consisting of ten Beidou satellites. It had even initiated the testing of global constellation similar to the US GPS. By launching the 52nd and 53rd Medium Earth Orbit (MEO) satellite on 16 December 2019 China has completed its global constellation of BeiDou satellites[91] while maintaining a separate regional constellation providing redundant coverage over Asia. With the launch of two more GEO satellites in June 2020, China has completed the deployment of all 30 satellites of the BDS-3 constellation. BDS application is still inferior as compared to GPS in terms of user terminals and software. It aims to replace GPS in BRI administered areas with its BDS. China has promoted BDS at GNSS standardisation work of international organisations including the International Civil Aviation Organisation, International Marine Organisation and International Cospas-Sarsat Programme, a satellite-aided search and rescue initiative. Before 2035, China intends building a global positioning, navigation and timing system with BDS at its core.[92]

Space Launch Assets

China has a large fleet of launch vehicles. The Chang Zheng or Long March and Kuaizhou SLVs are capable of launching the Chinese spacecraft to any orbit. On 16 December 2019, the 12th launch by Long March-3A rocket series rocket in 2019 was completed. The Long March-3 rocket series like the 3A, 3B and 3C rockets can carry a payload of 5.5 tonnes into geosynchronous orbit. It is developed by the China Academy of Launch Vehicle Technology at the China Aerospace Science and Technology Corporation.[93]

China is currently capable of launching space vehicles to any Earth orbit. Still, it has not yet perfected advanced launch vehicles necessary to achieve its most important space goals, such as launching crewed lunar missions.[94] China's 2016 space white paper identified the implementation of new-generation launch vehicles as a major task over five years. Thus, by 2020 Chinese rockets are planned to reach "international mainstream standards" and will be able to provide "diversified commercial launch services" globally.[95] China's plans depend in part on the success of the crucial LM-5 heavy-lift launch vehicle, the lift capacity of which is 27.6 tonnes to LEO and 15.4 tonnes to geosynchronous orbit. The heavy-lift LM-5 and the future LM-9 super heavy-lift launch vehicles are China's most important launch vehicle projects and rely on new technologies, materials, manufacturing techniques, and equipment. China is also working on technology for reusable rockets, which will debut with the LM-8 around 2021; once this technology is mature, other LM versions will likely also adopt it.[96] Refer to Table 4.3 and Figure 4.7 for China's space fleet.

Table 4.3: China's Space Launch Fleet

System	*Propellant*	*Generation*	*Outlook*
LM-2, LM-3, LM-4	Liquid	Legacy	Phase-out by 2025
LM-5 series	Liquid	Next	Heavy-lift for the space station and other payloads
LM-6 series	Liquid	Next	Light-lift for low Earth and sun-synchronous orbit
LM-7 series	Liquid	Next	Medium-lift for human spaceflight and resupply to the future space station
LM-9 Series	Liquid/Solid	Next -2030	Super-heavy carrier rocket for manned Moon mission
LM-11 & Kuaizhou series	Solid	Next	Lift for emergency response

Source: US Defense Intelligence Agency. 2019. *China Military Power: Modernising a Force to Fight and Win*, p.44.

The LM-5 new technology will be used to upgrade other rockets for China's planned moon probe, the first module of the long-term crewed space station beginning in 2020, a Mars probe mission in 2020, and a probe mission to Jupiter in the 2020s.[97] It remains likely that China will complete a crewed lunar mission by the mid-2030s, using either an LM-9 or a similar rocket which is still in a feasibility study stage.

China's commercial space sector is growing rapidly to bridge the wide gap that exists between the private space sector of China and the US. A determined push given by China for the development of private sectors reached its climax in 2019 with domestic players making technology breakthroughs. In August 2019, China tested new Dragon series of the commercial rocket, Smart Dragon-1, developed by the China Rocket Company (affiliated to the China Academy of Launch Vehicle Technology) to meet the market demand to launch small commercial satellites.[98] Chinese private rocket space firms like iSpace, OneSpace and LandSpace have made forays into the commercial business pie of space economy. In July 2019 iSpace's carrier rocket successfully sent satellites into orbit from the Jiuquan Satellite Launch Centre in Northwest China's Gansu Province.[99] The

Figure 4.7: Chinese Space Launch Vehicles

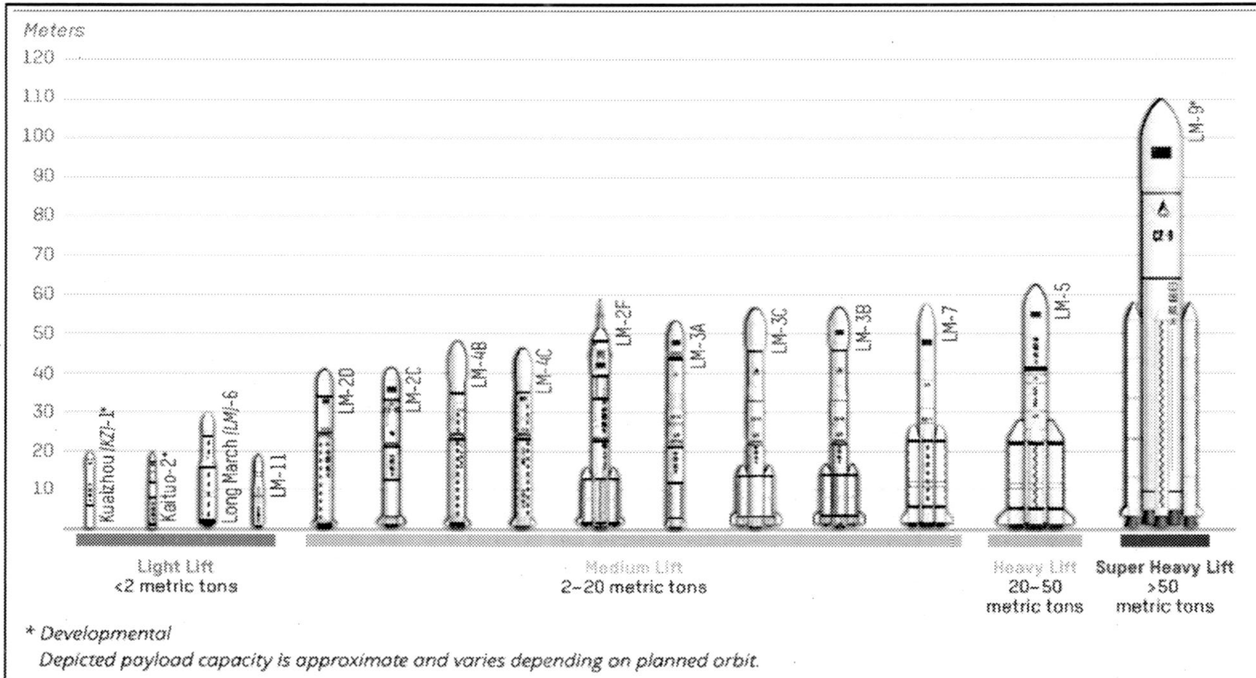

Source: US Defense Intelligence Agency. 2019. "Challenges to the Security in Space." January. Accessed April 29, 2020, p.16. https://www.dia.mil/Portals/27/Documents/News/Military%20Power%20Publications/Space_Threat_V14_020119_sm.pdf.

battlefield for space economy has been drawn, and this time, China wants to promote its commercial companies to outsmart US commercial interests.

The space launch facilities are under the SSD control. Thus, PLA brings in civil-military synergy in space, especially with forays by the private players. The details of SSD launch and control facilities are in Table 4.4.

Table 4.4: SSD Space Launch and Control Facilities

Type of Facility	*Base*	*Location*
Space Launch Facilities		
Satellite Launch Centre	20th Base	Jiuquan
Satellite Launch Centre	25th Base	Taiyuan
Satellite Launch Centre	27th Base	Xichang
Spacecraft Launch Site		Wenchang
Telemetry, Tracking, and Control		
Satellite Control Centre*	26th Base	Xi'an *administers land-based TT&C network for space operations stations like in Changchun (Jilin), Jiamusi (Heilongjiang), Kashi (XUAR), Minxi (Fujian), Nanning (Guangxi) Qingdao (Shandong), Sanya (Hainan), and Weinan (Shaanxi)
China Satellite Maritime Tracking and Control Department**	23th Base	**Manages four space tracking ships (Yuanwang 3, 5, 6 & 7) and two specialised cargo ships (Yuanwang 21 and 22) designed to transport heavy-lift orbital launch vehicles, like Long March 5 or 7 series.
Aerospace Flight Control Centre		Beijing
Space-Based Communications and ISR		
Satellite Communications Main Station#		#Responsible for PLA's satellite communication network. Transferred to PLASSF SSD from the GSD Informatisation Department which is now the CMC JSD Information Communication Bureau.
Satellite Positioning Main Station		35th Base
Aerospace Reconnaissance Bureau$		$Responsible for space-based ISR

Source: Gill, Adam Ni and Bates. 2019. "The People's Liberation Army Strategic Support Force: Update 2019." *China Brief*, Vol. 19, Issue 10, Jamestown Foundation, 29 May. Accessed April 26, 2020.

Counter-space Assets

The PLA is developing a whole range of technologies to improve its counter-space capabilities. China is developing anti-satellite capabilities, including research and possible development of DEW, satellite jammers, and probably the anti-satellite missile systems that were tested in July 2014. China is employing more sophisticated satellite operations and probably is testing dual-use technologies that could be applied to counter-space missions.[100] Refer Table 4.5 for PLA counter-space capabilities.

Table 4.5: PLA Counter-space Weapons Capabilities

Type	*Year*	*Weapons System*	*Comments*	*Kinetic Impact?*
ASAT test	2005	SC-19	First reported test. Failed.	
ASAT test	2006	SC-19	Failed to intercept the target.	
ASAT test	2007	SC-19	The successful intercept of the target.	Created thousands of debris on-orbit.
Missile defence test (suborbital)	2010	SC-19	Successful technology test against a suborbital target. To understand the homing performance of the interceptor.	Yes
Missile defence test (suborbital)	2013	SC-19	Likely another technology demonstration test.	Yes
ASAT test	2013	DN-2	China declared the test as a high-altitude science mission. Proof of Chinese direct-ascent ASATs that could reach targets up to GEO.	No. Possibly done to test timing capabilities.
ASAT test	2014	SC-19	China claimed it as a land-based missile interceptor test, while the US assessed the test as a non-destructive ASAT test	No
ASAT test	2015	DN-3	Do	No
Missile defence test	2017	DN-3	Unsuccessful test of the DN-3 missile interceptor	No
Missile defence test	2018	DN-3	DN-3 midcourse interceptor successfully intercepted its DF-21 target.	Yes

Source: Todd Harrison, K Johnson, TG Roberts, Tyler Way and Makena Young. 2020. "Space Threat Assessment 2020." *CSIS*. March. Accessed 2020. https://aerospace.csis.org/wp-content/uploads/2020/03/Harrison_SpaceThreatAssessment20_WEB_FINAL-min.pdf.

Electronic Warfare. The PLA considers electronic warfare capabilities key assets for modern warfare, and its doctrine emphasise using electronic warfare weapons to suppress or deceive enemy equipment. The PLA routinely incorporates jamming and anti-jamming techniques against multiple communication, radar systems, and GPS satellite systems in exercises.[101] China continues to develop jammers dedicated to targeting SAR aboard military reconnaissance platforms, including LEO satellites. Additionally, China is developing jammers to target SATCOM over a range of frequency bands, including military protected extremely high-frequency communications.[102] According to US Electro-Magnetic Commission report, China and Russia are developing nuclear-electronic device also known as super EMP bomb which when exploded in higher levels of altitude is capable of eclipsing and frying all space-borne devices based on the intensity and altitude of the explosion.[103] It may be part of the Chinese strategy of total information warfare in case of a contingency faced with a technologically superior force in a Taiwan contingency or the East China Sea and as part of technology demonstration against a peer competitor like India in case of a collusive scenario of China with Pakistan and China wishes to bail-out its proxy.

ASAT Weapons. PLA writings emphasise the necessity of "destroying, damaging, and interfering with the enemy's reconnaissance...and communications satellites."[104] It suggests that systems like navigation and early warning satellites could be among the targets of attacks designed to blind and deafen the enemy. Since its ASAT tests in 2007, China has not publicly acknowledged the existence of any new anti-satellite missile programmes. China is likely to field a ground-based laser weapon system capable of countering low-orbit space-based sensors by 2020. By the mid-to-late 2020s, it is likely to field higher power systems that extend the threat to the structures of non-optical satellites.[105]

Orbital Threats. China is developing sophisticated on-orbit capabilities, such as satellite inspection and repair, at least some of which could also function as a weapon. China has launched multiple satellites to conduct scientific experiments on space maintenance technologies, and it is conducting space debris clean up research.[106]

Some questions remain regarding the PLASSF's space mission. For one, it remains unclear whether the SSD will incorporate kinetic anti-satellite capabilities, such as direct-ascent weapons, or those will remain with the PLARF. It is not clear whether the operational units responsible for hydrology, meteorology, mapping, and navigation will be incorporated in the SSD. However, the initial indications suggest that some of these units are now part of the PLASSF. These units were previously under the GSD First Department (1PLA); also known as the Operations Department, Survey and Mapping Bureau (SMB). The 1PLA is now reorganised as the JSD Operations Bureau (JSD-OB) with the new Battlefield Environmental Support Bureau (JSD-BESB) taking the place of the former Survey and Mapping Bureau.

PLA AND THE BIOLOGICAL WARFARE

Biological Weapon Convention and China

After twenty-seven years China acceded to the 1925 Geneva Protocol on 'the prohibition of the use in war of asphyxiating, poisonous, or other gases, and of bacteriological methods of warfare'. China ratified 1972 Biological Weapon Convention (BWC) on the prohibition of the development, production, and stockpiling of bacteriological (biological) and toxin weapons and their destruction after twelve years in 1984.[107] Chinese have been cautious about signing protocols and is secretive about its biological programme. In the absence of literature of Chinese origin, one has to rely on the western source whose complete credibility cannot be guaranteed. Nonetheless, it throws up issues that concern not only the West but the other countries in the world, especially after the spread of COVID-19 contagion that originated in China.

Analysis of PLA Publications and Biological Projects

A review of Chinese publications reveals a growing consensus within the Chinese establishment to use biological warfare as part of Chinese national strategy. Even China's national strategy of military-civil fusion has highlighted biology as a priority. Advances in biotechnology and genetic engineering have exciting applications, including military affairs and the PLA could be at the forefront of expanding and exploiting this knowledge. Few facts connect the dots.

- The importance of biological warfare in future warfare was indicated by Guo Jiwei, a professor in the Third Military Medical University in his 2010 published book 'War of Biological Dominance'.
- Major General He Fuchu, former President of Academy of

Military Medical Science (AMMS) was appointed Vice President of the Academy of Military Sciences in 2015. He is responsible for China's military science enterprise and has talked about biotechnology as the new 'strategic high ground' of national defence with biomaterials and brain control weapons as its important ingredients.[108]

- In 2016, "The Evaluation of Human Enhancement Technology" AMMS doctoral research paper highlighted three methods to improve the combat efficiency of the troops– firstly through the use of Modafinil drug for cognitive enhancement. Secondly, through the use of transcranial magnetic stimulation in which the brain is stimulated. Thirdly, the research indicated the use of a revolutionary gene-editing technology in which the Deoxyribonucleic Acid (DNA) can be edited with remarkable precision to form Clustered Regularly Interspaced Short Palindromic Repeat (CRISPR) or CRISPR/Cas9. The research indicated that this technology could also be used as military deterrence.[109]
- A new chapter on biology as a domain of military struggle was added in 2017 to the "Science of Military Strategy" by the PLA National Defence University.
- Zhang Shibo, a retired general of the PLA National Defence University, in his 2017 book "New Domains of Warfare" talked about offensive capabilities brought about by the modern biotechnological developments.
- In 2016, CMC funded projects on the new concept of biotechnology like brain science, advanced biomimetic systems and materials, human performance enhancement. The China Brain Project calls for "One Body and Two Wings" strategy that looks at brain disease diagnosis/intervention and brain-inspired intelligent technology (two wings).[110]

Biological Warfare Infrastructure. Biotech is an expansive frontier and PLA is aware of the emergence of the bio-informatics as a treasure trove to be protected. The vastness of genome data requires AI and supercomputers to make it happen. The measures and infrastructure involved in biological weapon development and bio-security are of immense strategic importance to China. The important developments which have taken place are:

- PLA's AMMS touted as the cradle of medical talent in China has been credited with developing of Ebola vaccine in 2014[111] and has again been tasked to work on COVID-19 vaccine. Xi Jinping visit to the institute on 03 March 2020 confirms the faith the Chinese leadership poses on this institute to combat the COVID-19 threats. Chinese biotechnology firm Cansino Biologics Inc in collaboration with AMMS, is developing the vaccine for COVID-19.[112] Putting AMMS directly under the Academy of Military Science is to bring synergy between medical science and military strategy. On 07 February 2020, Major General Chen Wei, China's chief biochemical weapon defence expert and director of the Institute of Bioengineering, AMMS has rushed to take over the alleged Wuhan Institute of Virology,[113] which is at the centre of COVID-19 storm. Thus, PLA is seamlessly integrated into all biological weapon development and management programme of China.
- In 2016, the Chinese government launched the 'National Genebank' to safeguard the strategic value of genetic information and boost the genetics industry.[114] BGI Genomics of China has outreach with over 66 countries and has offices in Denmark, and the US. It is the leading global provider of genomic sequencing. The links between BGI's research and military research activities also exist, especially with the PLA's National University of Defence Technology because BGI's bioinformatics has used its Tianhe supercomputers to process genetic information for biomedical applications. BGI and NUDT researchers have also collaborated on research publications, including the design of tools for the use of CRISPR.[115]
- Chinese biological weapons facility existence in the Xinjiang province, near the nuclear testing site at Lop Nor, have emerged frequently in the news. In the late 1980s, an outbreak of haemorrhagic fever at this facility was reported, which may be the result of research of China's offensive biological weapons. The story was captured by Ken Alibek in his book "Biohazard: The Chilling True Story of the Largest Covert Biological Weapons Programme in the World–Told from Inside by the Man Who Ran It".[116]
- The US Department of State 2005 report also identified two

facilities that have links to an offensive biological weapons programme: the AMMS linked Institute of Microbiology and Epidemiology (IME) in Beijing, and the Lanzhou Institute of Biological Produces (LIBP).

Refer to Table 4.6 for the lists of the biological production and research institutes.

Table 4.6: List of PLA's Biological Warfare Research and Production Facility

Factory	*Location*	*Production Details*	*Remarks*
Yan'an Bacteriological Factory	Yan'an, Xishan	Four types of bacteriological bombs • Smoke or aerosol • Paper canister • Malignant bacteria grenade • Tetanus bacteria bomb	Large scale biological research and production site
Dalian Biological Products Factory	Dalian	• Tetanus/cholera mix vaccine • Diphtheria vaccine • Rabies virus vaccine • Typhus vaccine • ABC Vaccine	Large scale biological research and production site
Changchun Biological Products Factory	Changchun	Cultivation and experimentation of various biological agents	
Wuhan Biological Products Factory	Wuchang	Cultivation of various biological agents	
Chongqing Biological Products Factory	Chongqing	Research and cultivation of various biological agents	
Kunming Biological Products Factory	Kunming	Research and cultivation of various biological agents	
Beijing Biological Products Factory	Beijing	Cultivation and research in various bacteria	
Central Biological Products Testing Laboratory	Beijing	Liquid vaccines, testing of antimicrobial products	
The biological warfare production facility	Shenyang, Shanghai, Lanzhou and Guangzhou		

Sources: Croddy, Eric (Spring 2003), "China's Role in the Chemical and Biological Disarmament Regime." *The Nonproliferation Review* 13, p.13; Pinko, Eyal (2020), *On Chinese biological warfare.* 30 April. Accessed April 30, 2020. https://www.israeldefense.co.il/he/node/42583.

Biological Warfare Strategy. According to the Nuclear Threat Initiative (NTI), China owns the required technologies and resources to mass-produce biological agents. The dual-use infrastructure created by China acts as the basis for its offensive biological capability. In November 2018, a Chinese scientist, He Jiankui, of the Southern University of Science and Technology in Shenzhen China announced that he used the gene-editing technique CRISPR-Cas9 to create genetically modified human babies. In 2019, the Chinese government investigated Jiankui for ethics and law violations. He has since been fined 3 million yuan and has been sentenced to three years in jail.[117] But if his breakthrough is successful, then it opens up a new threat era. China has made progressive development to build its biological warfare capacity. China has a penchant for turning the disaster into an opportunity. Hence, it used the 2003 SARS epidemic as an excuse to scout for establishing a BSL-4 laboratory. The absence of any verification procedure for the development of biotechnology in BSL-4 laboratory provided an excellent platform to China to undertake dual-research of vaccine generation and development of biomaterials. The collaboration of PLA and the civil agencies within China on the production of vaccine or handling of genomic information points that PLA is wedded with the various enterprises. The affiliation of AMMS with the Academy of Sciences and appointing one of the former President of AMMS with the Academy of Military Sciences is a pointer that PLA is working secretly into the non-nuclear deterrent domain to safeguard its assets in-depth areas. It may be undertaking vigorous scientific research to prepare for the known and unknown threats on the pretext of defending the society from the micro-organism threats. CMC funded research, and PLA National Defence University publications cement the belief that biological warfare is very much part of the PLA capability development. Punishing of He Jiankui is only to put course correction within the Chinese research community to prevent individual researchers from exceeding their mandate as the CPC wants to have full state control on such technologies. China realised the enormity of threat posed by biomaterials and wanted to bring in draft legislation in October 2019 on bio-security, but COVID-19 has blown the lid. According to Major General He Fuchu, the weaponisation of living organisms will become a reality in the future, non-traditional combat styles will be staged, and the 'biological frontier' will become a new frontier for national defence.

Chemical Warfare

It took four years for China to ratify the 1993 Chemical Weapons Convention (CWC) that called for preventing the stockpiling or production of harmful chemical substances. China has declared that it once operated a small chemical weapons programme for offensive purposes; however, Beijing had consistently maintained that the programme had been dismantled before China ratified the CWC. According to the US 2019 Defence Intelligence Agency report, Beijing had published chemical export control regulations consistent with Organisation for the Prohibition of Chemical Weapons (OPCW) standards way back in 1998. It has updated its chemical control list under the Australia Group chemical control list. China continues to reaffirm its compliance with the CWC as well as its support for the activities conducted by the OPCW. Since acceding to the CWC, China has declared hundreds of dual-use facilities and has hosted hundreds of facility inspections and OPCW-led seminars. China's chemical infrastructure is sufficient to research, develop, and produce some chemical agents on a large scale. It has enough artillery pieces and multi-barrel long-range rocket launchers for delivery. It possesses the expertise to weaponise chemical and biological warfare agents. China also has the technical expertise, military units, and equipment necessary to detect chemical and biological warfare agents. In addition to the ground units identified for the theatre group army, each group army also has an engineering and chemical defence brigade, and a service support brigade.

Conclusion

The creation of the PLASSF epitomises the Xi's New Era thinking. It also reflects Chinese thinking and future strategic posture. The question is whether the PLA is gravitating from the localised informationised warfare to power-projection wars or is it merely trying to keep it local while going global. One thing is but sure that the creation of PLASSF demonstrates the evolution of Chinese military thought on using the information as a strategic resource in warfare and the role it plays in empowering other forces and safeguarding the vulnerabilities. The inclusion of responsibilities for both information support and information dominance in the same organisation and its control with the CMC reflects the weight lifting which these departments will have to do for the CPC. As China continues to develop technologically and operate beyond the first and second island chains, the asymmetric advantages it had relied so far upon as a land-based, technologically inferior power will narrow, and it will have to invest well in keeping abreast with the strategic situational awareness.

China's strategic situational awareness capabilities are robust and multifaceted, yet still constrained by certain technical and operational limitations. From the development of new radar and early warning aircraft to the rapid expansion of China's already extensive architecture of satellites, China has invested in expanding its capabilities for early warning and surveillance in ways that can enhance its readiness and capabilities in a future crisis or conflict. In some cases, it is difficult to assess the technical specifications of capabilities that have remained under development and are still overcoming past challenges in indigenous innovation, including issues of systems integration.

As the Chinese military is tasked to become a "world-class" force by mid-century, continued advances in its capabilities could enable the PLA to leapfrog ahead of the US military in certain domains and technologies. Seeking to establish itself as an "aerospace superpower", China has launched a range of satellites at a rapid pace, quickly expanding its space-based surveillance capabilities, including its capacity to process and glean insights from that data rapidly. The PLA is actively experimenting with unmanned systems for early warning and surveillance, fielding and integrating a growing number of systems that could increase its flexibility in enhancing situational awareness in a crisis or conflict. Meanwhile, the continued increase in PLA's cyber capabilities and persistent presence within the adversaries' system also contributes significantly to Chinese espionage efforts.

The amalgam of information operations by the PLA with the psychological warfare and combining it with the targeted manipulation of public opinion, or media warfare; and legal arguments as part of "legal warfare," join together to form a comprehensive information operations doctrine. The revision of this operational doctrine forms the new "integrated joint operations" for the PLA in the 21st-century to strengthen China's diplomatic and security position.

Biotechnology and communications sectors are two areas that are likely to outpace regulations and increase the likelihood of health and economic surprise. A gene-editing process like CRISPR may lead to the development of microbes that mimics the transmissibility and lethality of smallpox with technology ordered online at a throwaway price with larger global ramifications. China realises the threats posed by such technologies more now, and is actively talking about the bio-security to prevent pandemic resurfacing in China from 'imported epidemic infection'. Hence, akin to the ambiguity and secrecy surrounding China's nuclear weapons and other aspects of military modernisation, Beijing has successfully erected walls to prevent any outflow of information regarding its biological or chemical weapons capabilities, including its potential to produce and mobilise. What remains available in the declassified domain is the PLA's assertion that the use of chemical weapons would be like opening Pandora's box and releasing the evil spirits.

Technologies like AI are likely to be all-pervasive and will be used to enhance platform effectiveness. The non-contact content of non-contact warfare need not be non-lethal. The escalation mechanism and platform configuration underway allow the PLA to turn non-military non-lethal systems to lethal systems within the non-contact domain. The US competitive strategy has compelled the PLA to start putting its doctrine to practice. The use of non-contact warfare to preserve its core interest is, therefore, an imperative that the PLA cannot ignore. The weapon and technology development plan gives the PLA the wherewithal to enlarge the strategic space to seize the initiative. The US declared multi-domain doctrine is something which the PLA will have to confront. However, capability development and application are two separate issues. Hence, it is important to assess how the PLA will play its game not only with the US but also in its periphery.

NOTES

1 Zedong, Mao. *Mao Zedong: selected Writings on Journalism.* Beijing: Xinhua Press, 1983, p.183.

2 The State Council Information Office of the People's Republic of China. (2019). "China's National Defense in the New Era." Foreign Languages Press Co. Ltd., Beijing. 24 July. Accessed December 14, 2019. http://www.xinhuanet.com/english/2019-09/27/c_138427541.htm.

3 Narayanan, Rajiv. *PLA Reforms of Xi Jinping in an Era of Assertive Diplomacy.* New Delhi: USI of India, 2018, p.16.

4 Ibid.

5 Ye Zheng's *Lectures on the Science of Information Operations,* Beijing: Military Science Press, 2013, p.81.

6 Located at Offutt Air Force Base near Omaha, Neb., US Strategic Command is one of eleven unified commands in the US Department of Defence. The mission of USSTRATCOM is to deter strategic attack and global situational awareness of the

commanders. The command's assigned responsibilities include strategic deterrence; nuclear operations; space operations; joint electronic spectrum operations; global strike; missile defence; and analysis and targeting.

7 Opinion of the Central Military Commission on Deepening the Reform of National Defense and the Army, January 01, 2016 18:47:53 Source: Xinhua News Agency, accessed on 09 January 2020, http://www.xinhuanet.com/mil/2016-01/01/c_1117646695.htm

8 Academy of Military Sciences. (2013). *The Science of Military Strategy.* Edited by Sun Zhaoli. Beijing : Military Science Press.

9 Ibid.

10 Ibid.

11 Gill, Adam Ni and Bates. (2019). "The People's Liberation Army Strategic Support Force: Update 2019." *China Brief*, Vol. 19, Issue 10, Jamestown Foundation. 29 May . Accessed April 26, 2020.

12 Stokes, Rachael Burton and Martin. (2018). "The People's Liberation Army Strategic Support Force Leadership and Structures." *Project 2049 Institute.* 25 September. Accessed April 22, 2020.

13 McReynolds, John Costello and Joe. (October 2018). *China's Strategic Support Force: A Force for a New Era.* Study Report, Centre for the Study of Chinese Military Affairs, Institute for National Strategic Studies, Washington DC: National Defense University Press. Accessed January 04, 2020. p.36. inss.ndu.edu/Publications.aspx.

14 Academy of Military Sciences. (2013). *The Science of Military Strategy. op. cit.*, pp. 184-191.

15 Kenneth Allen, "Assessing the PLA's Promotion Ladder to CMC Member Based on Grades vs. Ranks—Part 1," *China Brief* 10, no. 15 (July 22, 2010), available at https://jamestown.org/program/assessing-the-plas-promotion-ladder-to-cmc-member-based-on-grades-vs-ranks-part-1/.

16 Ibid.

17 Mattis, John Costello and Peter. (January 2017). "Chapter 6: Electronic Warfare and the Renaissance of Chinese Information Operations." In *China's Evolving Military Strategy*, by Joe McReynolds, 173-212. Washington DC: Jamestown Foundation., p.185.

18 Tongxinbo, "Zanqu Xinxi Hua Jianshe Chubu Gouxiang" ("The Initial Concept of Theatre Informatisation Efforts"), Junshi Xueshu (Military Art), No. 7, July 1, 2004, p.20 quoted in Wortzel, Larry M. March 2014. *The Chinese People's Liberation Army and Information Warfare.* Carlisle Barracks: United States Army War College Press. http://www.StrategicStudiesInstitute.army.mil/., pp.6-7.

19 Chan, Minnie. (2011). *PLA Eyes Talent Pool to Expand Capability.* 11 April. Accessed April 25, 2020. www.scmp/portal/site/SCMP/menuitem.2af62ecb329dd7733492.

20 US Department of Defense. (1989). "Soviet Military Power: Prospects for Change ." Washington DC.

21 Shen Weiguang, Information Warfare, Zhejiang University Press, Hangzhou. (1990), p.9., quoted by Mattis, John Costello and Peter. op. cit.

22 Academy of Military Sciences. (2013). *The Science of Military Strategy.* op. cit.

23 Mattis, John Costello and Peter. (January 2017). op. cit, p.182.

24 Wall, Mike. (2019). *X-37B: The Air Force's Mysterious Space Plane.* 27 October. Accessed April 23, 2020. https://www.space.com/25275-x37b-space-plane.html.

25 Ray, Kevin Pollpeter and Jonathan. (January 2017). "Chapter 8: The Conceptual Evolution of China's Military Space Operations and Strategy." In *China's Evolving*

Military Strategy, by Joe McReynolds, 265-307. Washington DC: Jamestown Foundation., p.285.

26 Academy of Military Sciences. (2013). *The Science of Military Strategy.* op. cit.

27 The State Council Information Office of the People's Republic of China. 2019. "China's National Defense in the New Era." op. cit.

28 Academy of Military Sciences. (2013). *The Science of Military Strategy.* op. cit., p.131.

29 Ibid.

30 Kania, Elsa. (2016). "The PLA's Latest Strategic Thinking on the Three Warfares." *China Brief Volume 16, Isuue 13, Jamestown Foundation.* August 22. Accessed September 13, 2019. https://jamestown.org/program/the-plas-latest-strategic-thinking-on-the-three-warfares/.

31 Ibid.

32 Ibid.

33 Costello, John. (2016). "The Strategic Support Force: Update and Overview." *China Brief Volume: 16 Issue: 19.* 21 December. Accessed January 04, 2020. https://jamestown.org/program/strategic-support-force-update-overview/.

34 McReynolds, John Costello and Joe. October 2018. *China's Strategic Support Force: A Force for a New Era, op. cit.*, p.41.

35 Wortzel, Larry M. (March 2014). *The Chinese People's Liberation Army and Information Warfare.* Carlisle Barracks: United States Army War College Press. http://www.StrategicStudiesInstitute.army.mil/., p.3.

36 Academy of Military Sciences. (2013). *The Science of Military Strategy. op.* cit., pp.184-191.

37 Ibid.

38 McReynolds, John Costello and Joe. (October 2018). *China's Strategic Support Force: A Force for a New Era. op. cit.*, p.36.

39 Ibid.

40 Annual Report to Congress: Military and Security Developments Involving the People's Republic of China 2015 (Washington, DC: Office of the Secretary of Defense, 2015), p.14.

41 "Prepared Statement of Mark A. Stokes, Executive Director Project 2049 Institute, before theU.S.-China Economic and Security Review Commission," Hearing on Chinese Intelligence Services andEspionage Operations (Washington, DC: U.S.-China Economic and Security Review Commission, June9, 2016), available at www.uscc.gov/sites/default/files/Mark%20Stokes_Written%20Testimony060916.pdf.

42 A good indicator of this change of terminology is the transformation of the former GSD Survey, Mapping, and Navigation Bureau into the Joint Staff Department Battlefield Environment Support Bureau.

43 Zou Weirong, "New-Quality Weapons Decide Victory on the Future Battlefield", PLA Daily, March 11, 2016, available at http://jz.chinamil.com.cn/zhuanti/content/2016-03/11/content_6954336.htm.

44 US Defense Intelligence Agency. (2019). *China Military Power – Modernising a Force to Fight and Win. Washington DC. Accessed December 30, 2019. www.dia.mil/Military-Power-Publications.*p.45.

45 Ibid.

46 McReynolds, John Costello and Joe. (2019). "China's Strategic Support Force : A Force for a New Era." In *Chairman Xi Remakes the PLA*, by Arthur S. Ding, Andrew Scobell,

Andrew N.D. Yang, and Joel Wuthnow Phillip C. Saunders, 437-516. Washington DC: National Defense University Press, pp.460-461.

47 Third Department, Accessed January 09, 2020. https://www.globalsecurity.org/intell/world/china/pla-dept_3.htm.

48 Ibid.

49 McReynolds, John Costello and Joe. (2019). "China's Strategic Support Force : A Force for a New Era." op. cit., pp. 461-463.

50 McReynolds, John Costello and Joe. (2019). "China's Strategic Support Force : A Force for a New Era." op. cit., pp. 473-475.

51 Third Department, Accessed January 09, 2020. https://www.globalsecurity.org/intell/world/china/pla-dept_3.htm.

52 Dotson, John. (2019). "Military-Civil Fusion and Electromagnetic Spectrum Management in the PLA." *The Jamestown Foundation.* 08 October. Accessed January 05, 2020. https://jamestown.org/program/military-civil-fusion-and-electromagnetic-spectrum-management-in-the-pla/.

53 "Annual Report to Congress- Military and Security Developments in China 2019." *US Department of Defence.* 2019. https://media.defense.gov/2019/May/02/2002127082/-1/-1/1/2019_CHINA_MILITARY_POWER_REPORT.pdf (accessed January 10, 2020).

54 Xinhua, "Xi Jinping: Persist with Innovation to Drive Development, Bravely Climb to the Technical Peak, and Compose a New Chapter of China's Aerospace Endeavours," April 24, 2016. http://www.xinhuanet.com//politics/2016-04/24/c_1118719221.htm.

55 Abigail Beall, "Everything You Need to Know about China's Ambitious Space Plans," Wired, November 18, 2017. http://www.wired.co.uk/article/chinas-space-plans; Ma Chi, "China Aims to Be World-Leading Space Power by 2045," China Daily, November 17, 2017. http://www.chinadaily.com.cn/china/2017-11/17/content_34653486.htm; Xinhua, "Towards the Depths of the Cosmos! China Will Carry Out Four Major Deep Space Exploration Missions in the Future," January 30, 2017. http://www.xinhuanet.com/politics/2017-01/30/c_1120394632.htm.

56 Defense Intelligence Agency, Challenges to Security in Space, February 11, 2019, http://www.dia.mil/Portals/27/Documents/News/Military%20Power%20Publications/Space_Threat_V14_020119_sm.pdf

57 U.S.-China Economic and Security Review Commission, Hearing on China's Belt and Road Initiative: Five Years Later, written testimony of Nadège Rolland, January 25, 2018, 5. https://www.uscc.gov/sites/default/files/Rolland_USCC%20Testimony_16Jan2018.pdf

58 State Council Information Office, *China's Space Activities in 2016*, December 27, 2016. *http://news.xinhuanet.com/english/china/2016-12/27/c_135935416.htm* .

59 Ibid.

60 "Final Report on Organisational and Management Structure for the National Security Space Components of theDepartment of Defense." *Department of Defense.* August 11, 2018. https://media.defense.gov/2018/Aug/09/2001952764/-1/-1/1/ORGANISATIONAL-MANAGEMENT-STRUCTURE-DOD-NATIONAL-SECURITY-SPACE-COMPONENTS.PDF (accessed August 18, 2019).

61 "DIA Report Details Threats to America's Space-Based World." *https://dod.defense.gov.* 11 February 2019. https://dod.defense.gov/News/Article/Article/1754509/dia-report-details-threats-to-americas-space-based-world/ (accessed August 18, 2019).

62 "Competing in Space." Department of Defence, *Washington DC.*, December 2018. https://media.defense.gov/2019/Jan/16/2002080386/-1/-1/1/190115-F-NV711-0002.PDF (accessed August 18, 2019).

63 Competing in Space, NASIC Public Affairs Office 4180 Watson Way, https://media.defense.gov/2019/Jan/16/2002080386/-1/-1/1/190115-F-NV711-0002.PDF .

64 Bowe, Alexander. (11 April 2019). *China's Pursuit of Space Power Status and Implications for the United States.* Staff Research Report, Washington DC: US-China Economic and Security Review Commission, p.9.

65 Ibid.

66 Ibid.

67 Costello, John. (2016). "The Strategic Support Force: Update and Overview." *op. cit.*, p.17.

68 Ibid.

69 Ibid.

70 "Namibia and China sign an employment agreement," Republic of Namibia Ministry of Education, March 29, 2012, http://www.moe.gov.na/news_article.php?type=press release&id=60&title=Namibia; "China launches its first fully owned overseas satellite ground station near North Pole," *South China Morning Post*, December 16, 2016, https://www.scmp.com/news/china/policies-politics/article/2055224/china-launches-its-first-fully-owned-overseas-satellite.

71 Ernesto Londoño, "From a Space Station in Argentina, China Expands Its Reach in Latin America," *New York Times*, July 28, 2018, https://www.nytimes.com/2018/07/28/world/americas/china-latin-america.html?hp&action=click&pgtype=Homepage&clickSource=story-heading&module=second-column-region&region=top-news&WT.nav=top-news .

72 Ibid.

73 Ibid, p.17.

74 Wang Yi, "ADASpace set to star in AI satellite constellation sphere," *Global Times*, June 30, 2019, http://www.globaltimes.cn/content/1156263.shtm .

75 *Xinhua*, "China Launches Maritime Silk Road Satellite Data Service," January 15, 2019. *http://www.xinhuanet.com/english/2019-01/15/c_137745521.htm*

76 China National Administration of GNSS and Applications, *Maritime Silk Road Data Service Center Established in Fujian: Data Cover the Hong Kong, Macao, and Taiwan Regions*, January 14, 2019. Translation. *http://www.chinabeidou.gov.cn/fazhan/3258.html*

77 "Gaofen satellite's application for the country's overall capability initially formed", *Xinhua*, April 19, 2017, http://www.cnsa.gov.cn/n6758824/n6759009/n6759041/n6759071/c6780473/content.html

78 The Jilin-1 was developed by Chang Guang Satellite Technology Co. Ltd., which is under the Chinese Academy of Sciences and Changchun Institute of Optics, Fine Mechanics and Physics (CIOMP). "Jilin-1: China's first commercial remote sensing satellites aim to fill the void," *Xinhua*, January 27, 2018, http://www.xinhuanet.com/english/2018-01/27/c_136929344.htm.

79 "China to launch 60 high-resolution EO satellites by 2020," *Geospatial World*, January 29, 2018, https://www.geospatialworld.net/news/china-launch-60-high-resolution-video-satellites-2020/.

80 "The military-civil fusion big data center highlights the effects of aggregation", *China Military Network*, May 3, 2017, http://www.81.cn/gfbmap/content/2017-05/03/content_176276.htm .

81 Ibid.
82 "China and Finland signed a cooperation agreement for the Arctic Space Observation Joint Research Center," Institute of Remote Sensing and Digital Earth, April 17, 2018, http://www.radi.ac.cn/dtxw/rdxw/201804/t20180417_4997963.html.
83 US Defense Intelligence Agency. (2019). *China Military Power – Modernising a Force to Fight and Win. op. cit.* p.41.
84 "Zhongxing-9A Comsat lifts off atop Chinese Long March 3B, Launch Outcome Unclear," Spaceflight, June 18, 2017, http://spaceflight101.com/long-march-3b-zhongxing-9a-launch/ . Rui C. Barbosa, "China returns from Spring break with Zhongxing-6C launch," March 9, 2019, https://www.nasaspaceflight.com/2019/03/china-returns-spring-break-zhongxing-6c-launch/ .
85 US Defense Intelligence Agency. (2019). *China Military Power: Modernising a Force to Fight and Win.* op. cit., p.42.
86 For reporting and speculation at the time of its launch, see: "China Sends an Experimental Satellite Into Space on a Secretive Launch," *Spaceflight Insider*, September 13, 2015, https://www.spaceflightinsider.com/missions/defense/china-sends-an-experimental-satellite-into-space-on-a-secretive-launch/.
87 "China launches relay satellite to explore Moon's far side," *Xinhua*, May 21, 2018, http://www.xinhuanet.com/english/2018-05/21/c_137194776.htm.
88 "CASC Hongyan Low-Orbit Communication Satellite Constellation", China Aerospace Science and Technology Corporation, May 19, 2017, https://www.chinaspaceflight.com/satellite/HONGYAN/HONGYAN.html.
89 "China aerospace giant working on satellite clusters for global communications," *Global Times*, November 2, 2017, http://www.globaltimes.cn/content/1073321.shtml
90 US Defense Intelligence Agency. (2019). *China Military Power – Modernising a Force to Fight and Win.* op. cit., pp.42-43.
91 Ibid.
92 Xiaoci, Deng. (2019). *BeiDou Navigation Satellite System completes deployment.* 16 December. Accessed January 08, 2020. https://www.globaltimes.cn/content/1173712.shtml.
93 Ibid.
94 Ibid.
95 US Defense Intelligence Agency. (2019). *China Military Power – Modernising a Force to Fight and Win.* op. cit.
96 *China Central Television*, "China's Roadmap for Building a Future Space Delivery System: Comprehensively Building a Great Space Power by 2045," November 16, 2017. Translation. http://m.news.cctv.com/2017/11/16/ARTIBsl5lNYrezZ7eeS27JHd171116.shtml
97 Jeffrey Lin and P.W. Singer, "Here's China's Plan to Compete with SpaceX and Blue Origin," *Popular Science*, May 14, 2018. *https://www.popsci.com/chinas-2020-plan-for-reusable-space-launch; Xinhua*, "China Developing Reusable Space Rocket," April 30, 2018. *http://www.xinhuanet.com/english/2018-04/30/c_137147249.htm.*
98 Zhao Lei, "Long March Rocket Launch a Success," *China Daily*, September 29, 2017. *http://www.chinadaily.com.cn/a/201709/29/WS5a0be6b6a31061a738404fe1.html* .
99 Xuanmin, Zhang Hongpei and Li. (2019). *Commercial space industry is soaring*, 25 December. Accessed January 11, 2020. http://www.globaltimes.cn/content/1174817.shtml.
100 Ibid.

101 Annual Report to Congress; Military and Security Develop-ments Involving the People's Republic of China 2017; Office of the Secretary of Defense; May 2017.

102 Annual Report to Congress: Military and Security Developments Involving the People's Republic of China 2018; Office of the Secretary of Defense; 16 May 2018.

103 Wang, H., "Analysis on Anti-jamming Measures of Mobile User Objective System"; Radio Communications Technology, Vol. 35, No. 2; 2009, pp. 46-49.

104 Gertz, Bill. (2019). *China, Russia Building Super-EMP Bombs for 'Blackout Warfare'*. 19 January. Accessed April 27, 2020. https://freebeacon.com/national-security/china-russia-building-super-emp-bombs-for-blackout-warfare/.

105 Li Bingyan, (27 January 2016). Beijing Guangming Ribao: General Trend of the Worldwide Revolution in Military Affairs and the Form of Future War.

106 Wang Shiyong, Fu Youyu, Guo Jin; "Evaluation of high energy laser effecting on remote distance photoelectron sensor system"; Optical Technique, Vol. 28, No 1; January 2002; Gao Guiqing, Xiang Jin, Li Yongxiang, Zhou Yong; "Efficiency research on laser jamming photoelectric detector in early-warning satellite of infrared"; Laser & Infrared, Vol. 40 No. 2; February 2010.

107 US Defense Intelligence Agency. (2019). "Challenges to the Security in Space." January. Accessed April 29, 2020. https://www.dia.mil/Portals/27/Documents/News/Military%20Power%20Publications/Space_Threat_V14_020119_sm.pdf.

108 Verma, Brigadier Vivek. "An Assessment of China's Biological Warfare Capabilities", USI of India, 26 May 2020, https://usiofindia.org/publication/cs3-strategic-perspectives/an-assessment-of-chinas-biological-warfare-capabilities-and-need-for-global-approach-to-bio-security/.

109 Vorndick, Elsa B. Kania and Wilson. (2019). *Weaponizing Biotech: How China's Military Is Preparing for a 'New Domain of Warfare'*. 14 August. Accessed April 30, 2020. https://www.defenseone.com/ideas/2019/08/chinas-military-pursuing-biotech/159167/

110 Ibid.

111 Mu-ming Poo, Jiu-lin Du, Nacy Y Ip, Zhi-Qi Xiong, Bo Xu and Teinyu Tan. (2016). "A comprehensive interpretation of the Chinese Brain Project: from basic neuroscience to brain-inspired computing ." *Neuroview*, Vol. 92, Issue 3, pp.591-596, . 02 November. Accessed June 25, 2020. https://doi.org/10.1016/j.neuron.2016.10.050 and https://www.cell.com/neuron/fulltext/S0896-6273(16)30800-5.

112 Reuters. (2014). *China approves experimental Ebola vaccine for clinical trials*. 18 December. Accessed April 30, 2020. https://www.reuters.com/article/us-health-ebola-china/china-approves-experimental-ebola-vaccine-for-clinical-trials-idUSKBN0JW14020141218.

113 Liu, Angus. (2020). *China's CanSino Bio advances COVID-19 vaccine into phase 2 on preliminary safety data*. 10 April. Accessed April 30, 2020. https://www.fiercepharma.com/vaccines/china-s-cansino-bio-advances-covid-19-vaccine-into-phase-2-preliminary-safety-data.

114 Thompson, Bellie. (2020). *China 'appoints its top military bio-warfare expert to take over secretive virus lab in Wuhan'*,. 20 February. Accessed April 30, 2020. https://www.dailymail.co.uk/news/article-8003713/China-appoints-military-bio-weapon-expert-secretive-virus-lab-Wuhan.html.

115 People's Daily Online. (2016). *China's first gene bank to open in Shenzhen*. 21 September. Accessed April 30, 2020. http://www.china.org.cn/china/2016-09/21/content_39339851.htm.

116 Vorndick, Elsa B. Kania and Wilson. (2019). *Weaponizing Biotech: How China's Military*

Is Preparing for a 'New Domain of Warfare'. 14 August. Accessed April 30, 2020. https://www.defenseone.com/ideas/2019/08/chinas-military-pursuing-biotech/159167/

117 Chansoria, Monika. (2020). *Is China Producing Biological Weapons? Look At Its Capabilities and International Compliance.* 05 March. Accessed Apeil 29, 2020. https://japan-forward.com/is-china-producing-biological-weapons-look-at-its-capabilities-and-international-compliance/.

118 Global Times. (2019). *He Jiankui gets 3-year imprisonment for illegal gene editing.* 30 December. Accessed April 30, 2020. https://www.globaltimes.cn/content/1175208.shtml.

5

China's Approach to Practicing Non-Contact Warfare

"When the wind changes direction, there are those who build walls and those who build windmills."

– Chinese Proverb

WHERE IS THE NON-CONTACT WAR?

Finding the Reason

To make a war one needs to find a reason. If the trade and tariff war was not enough an excuse for the Sino-US conflict, the beginning of the Chinese New Year of Rat on 25 January 2020, brought along the pandemic from the COVID-19 virus. The epicentre of the contagion was Wuhan in China's Hebei province. On 30 January 2020, the WHO declared it a Public Health Emergency of International Concern (PHEIC). In a short span, the contagion has spread across the whole world, affecting millions of people and killing thousands of them. China was able to contain the initial wave of contagion by ruthless enforcement of lockdown, inspection, and surveillance. The same is not true with the western liberal societies who are more divided in subjecting their citizens to discipline of social distancing. The result is that the US has more fatal casualties than it had during the Vietnam War, albeit with a difference, this time fatalities are civilians. The effect by the pandemic has shaken the edifice of the world economy, and according to UN estimates, US$ 2.5 trillion may be required to get it going.[1] The world, having lost the lives and livelihoods, is training its guns on China to uncover the origin of the virus and also stigmatise it as 'Chinese Virus' or 'Wuhan Virus'. The same has not gone down well with Xi Jinping and the CPC which sees it as a ploy to victimise the Chinese people and tarnish its image. China could face trillions of dollars in international lawsuits for its handling of the coronavirus pandemic. When reasons matter much more than the radio or rifle – that's where wars begin.

China's Strategic Objective

The post-COVID-19 world creates a scenario where China may find itself sucked into the inferno, which will impact its credibility, image and influence.[2] It is likely to be contested in the traditional and non-traditional security arena, and the world is set to witness the waves of non-contact warfare. Amidst global destabilisation and the headwinds building within China, the strategic objective for Xi Jinping is clear- to protect the supremacy of the party. The CPC aim will be to prevent the snowballing of crisis. It should be able to localise its impact and defend its interests as far forward as possible while ensuring social stability within its borders. Hence, even during the time of crisis, it will endeavour to minimise the strategic friction and seek strategic opportunity so that its millennium goal of prosperity remains intact.[3] For this to happen, Xi Jinping will need PLA's support, and for PLA, it means that it will have to do the heavy lifting in more area than it is mandated. Whether for COVID-19 impact or the need to counter US dominance, the path taken by China has been constant.

- **Correcting and Controlling the Narrative.** For the CPC, its image is very important to it. It needs to be seen as the champion of the Chinese cause. China recognises that the stigmatisation due to COVID-19 will add another humiliation narrative attributing to the CPC rule. The CPC cannot afford such a narrative when it has been selling the Chinese dream of 'Great Rejuvenation' to its citizen. Hence, employing 'three warfare' strategy is the only choice available to it to control the opinion, legal and psychological space and deflect the origin theory that is being spread and correct the battle of perceptions both locally and internationally. Thus, influence operations become important for China to correct the narrative about the pandemic.

- **Improving Situational Awareness**. Situational awareness is something that China relies on to build response options. It has used technology infusion in governance to secure internal stability. Yet, the gap exists at the global level, which it needs to bridge or create an asymmetric capability to block the access to information to technologically superior powers. Situational awareness efforts are tied to its core areas of interest- Taiwan and internal stability, protecting global interests and image.
- **Localising the Threat.** Global Trends 2025 had indicated that pandemic disease would lead to internal and cross-border tensions, and nations would struggle with their degraded capabilities to administer their control over the movement of populations seeking to avoid infection or maintain access to resources.[4] Pandemic has shown how the governance structures across the world from developed to developing to underdeveloped countries have been stretched. The armed forces are also not immune to the contagion threat. The challenge for China will be to localise the threat of the spread of the second and subsequent wave of pandemic and preserve its forces so that its core interests are not diluted.
- **Force Preservation and Expanding Non-War Military Effort.** China gainfully employed the PLA's capabilities in rescue and surveillance operations while dealing with the pandemic in Wuhan and the countryside. The force preservation remains its primary focus while it looked at expanding its non-war military efforts within the country and along high seas, all directed for ensuring internal stability by assuaging the frayed feathers of the masses.
- **Importance of War Control.** For China, the use of non-nuclear deterrence and the ability to manage escalation control will be crucial to be seen as a responsible emerging world power. This power play will be covertly and overtly applied to limit the expansion of the conflict.
- **Gaining Strategic Space and Opportunity.** China aims to slowly gain strategic space and defend as far forward as possible while denying the space to the adversary by firewalling the critical and vulnerable space. For China, the flow of Shi is important to realise its millennium goal. Hence, it will be looking for the windows of

opportunity to create and build coalition and support and will deploy all means to brave the current oddities.

The intent is the function of capability. Once the capability exists, the intent can change. China having devoted past four decades in building comprehensive national power (CNP) and finds itself at the crossroads where it wants to avoid entering into "Thucydides trap"[5] – where the triptych of fear, anger and emotions may ignite Sino-US conflict. Navigating the non-contact methods of warfare is probably the way out where the principles of 'active defence' and 'three warfares' are likely to be practiced as a low-cost option for contest and preservation of resource diversion. In a globalised world where global disengagements may have been triggered due to pandemic, it is vital to examine how PLA will be used to assist the CPC to contest the non-contact warfare.

CHINA'S INFLUENCE OPERATIONS

Ingredients of Influence Operations

Influencing is the art of communication to change the behaviour of the target audience. Communication has three parts to it – the narrative or the content which one wants to convey, the medium over which it can be carried and the audience. The narrative in case of CPC is controlled, curated and filtered to the masses and global audience so that it is aligned with CPC guidelines and shows the unity of command structure within Chinese society. United Front Works Department (UFWD) under CPC is the agency responsible for coordinating influence operations through narrative build-up both inside China and overseas. The modern world has made communication ubiquitous, and the tools that make them happen have proliferated at an exponential pace. The problem that China encountered at the collapse of the Soviet Union was the rapid growth driven by the internet explosion. The penetration of internet and ability of the western power to throw up new innovative products from social media platforms, to search engines tools to smartphones. The creation of a web of networks which connected not only human to human but human to machine and systems to systems have created huge dependencies within China for economic and societal progress. The cyber dependency created a demand for faster connectivity at the same time it created vulnerabilities. To meet the growing communication demand space technology was ramped up beside the mobile connectivity, which gravitated from 2G connectivity to 5G connectivity within two decades. Behavioural dynamics attributed to social platforms have not only been used to optimise the economic output, e-commerce but has been used to influence and trigger protests in Hong Kong. Facebook – Cambridge Analytica revelation also showed to the Chinese, how opinion-shaping could change governments in democracy.

The IoT has led to the emergence of Big Data and requires AI and quantum computing tools to handle the veracity, velocity and volume of data flow. Thus, overdependence on data and technologies across governance structure and business environment from agriculture to transportation to energy management to financial institutions is guiding the new age competition and conflict. China has taken note of the World Economic Forum 2019 warning that data breaches and cyber-attacks are the top global risks besides natural disasters and climate change. It has initiated measures to secure its data and technologies. Since the data economy is reliant on cyber and space for storage and flow of data, hence, it has tasked PLA to protect and secure the critical domains of cyber and space. Thanks to the data pool generated, the tailored responses targeting the audience are being generated to infuse and sustain a narrative and eclipse it if it turns negative. Thus, China has created structures to deal with the influence operations, which it feels may be targeted to create social instability or harm global interests.

For China, bridging the capability gap through technology infusion and innovation is of strategic importance. Large effort of its agencies is also devoted to influence and obtain key strategic technologies. Measures are adopted by China to acquire technology, and talent for capability development is given in Table 5.1. Some of them may fall within the economic realm, but the data crunching regarding the targeted source is through cyber business espionage and intelligence-based operations.

Table 5.1: China's Modus Operandi to Acquire Technology and Talent for Capability Development

Non-traditional Collectors	Target individuals for whom science and business is the primary profession to acquire technology.
Joint Ventures (JV)	Uses JVs to acquire technology and technical know-how.
Research Partnerships	Seek partnerships with government laboratories to acquire or learn specific technology and soft skills to run such facilities.
Academic Collaborations	Uses collaboration with universities to acquire specific research and gain access to high-end research equipment.

S&T Investments	Sustained and long-term state investments in S&T infrastructure
Merger and Acquisitions	Seeks to buy companies tied to technology and talent
Front Companies	China uses front companies to obscure the hand of the Chinese government and acquire export-controlled technology.
Talent Recruitment	The programme is to influence foreign talent to work for China on key strategic programmes
Intelligence Services	The Ministry of State Security and intelligence units are deployed to acquire technologies.
Legal and Regulatory	China uses the law to disadvantage foreign companies

Source: US National Counterintelligence and Security Center. (2018). *Foreign Economic Espionage in Cyberspace.* Washington DC: Office of the Director of National Intelligence, p.6.

Defending the Battle of Depth

Influence operations include the collection of information across the PIMED of the adversary and selective channelizing of propaganda in concert with the strategic and tactical objective. Traditional techniques of print media, radio, movies, and television have been enmeshed with cyber tools through the internet and social media. The new technologies have carved a qualitatively new landscape of influence operations, persuasion, and, more generally, mass manipulation. The ability to influence is now effectively democratised as any individual or group can script, communicate and influence large numbers of others online. The influence landscape is now significantly more quantifiable. Data tools can disaggregate the response of individuals as well as crowds to influence efforts. It may seem dichotomous, but the influence is also far more concealable now. Users may be influenced by designed information provided to them by strangers, or an interface. Thus, the Internet and social media provide alternate ways of constructing realities for actors, audiences, and media. It fundamentally challenges the traditional news media's function as gatekeepers and agenda setters.[6] Interactions within the information environment are rapidly evolving, and new models are becoming irrelevant faster. The uncertainty targets people's mind.[7] As alluded earlier, social stability is the core interest of China; hence it has regarded the internet penetration into its society and businesses as a western grand strategy to compel China in fighting the battle of depth. This fact has also been captured in the 1995 article on "future military trends" by Gao Heng, a Chinese analyst, who predicted that the RMA brought about by internet will turn "the whole globe into a unified battlefield."[8] China has, therefore used a whole-of-a-nation approach to guard the battle of depth. Most of the actions are concurrent, but the first thing it intends doing is guarding its vulnerability at home by amending the legal framework; secondly, it wants to create situational awareness through cyber defence operation and indigenisation of ICT infrastructure and lastly build deterrent capabilities.

Firewalling Cyber Security through Legal Framework. Before the enactment of the 2017 Cybersecurity Law, China had few laws, rules and regulations related to information security, like the Administrative Measures for Prevention and Treatment of Computer Viruses and the Administrative Measures for Hierarchical Protection of Information Security. The 2017 Cybersecurity Law however legislated:

- All individual information and important data collected or generated in China to be stored domestically.
- The "network operators" are the owners and administrators of networks and network service providers are responsible for cybersecurity under the Cybersecurity Law.
- The critical cyber equipment and cybersecurity products can only be sold or provided after receiving security certifications.
- The State Council defines the scope of critical information infrastructure and protection procedures. It may include the protection of public communications and information services, energy, finance, transportation, water conservation, public services and e-governance or any other critical information infrastructure that may cause serious damage to national security, economy and public interest.
- Enterprises that are capable of operating critical information infrastructure are required to assess the cyber threats under Article 38 of the Cybersecurity Law. Steep penalty provisions have been incorporated to desist the enterprises from compromising data privacy and critical infrastructure security.

Predatory Practices. On 01 December 2019, China rolled out the Cybersecurity Multi-level Protection Scheme ("MLPS 2.0") as it felt that the 2007 MLPS 1.0 provisions were not robust to deal with the newly-developed technologies like mobile applications, Big Data, cloud computing, and Internet of Things ('IoT'). On 01 March 2020 another national standard entitled Information Security Technology–Implementation Guide for Classified Protection of Cybersecurity (GB/T

25058-2019) has become effective. This scheme lays out the technical and organisational Internet security controls, which has to be complied by all companies and individuals in China. All these indicate that the Chinese Ministry of Public Security and other internet security agencies have complete access to regulate the Chinese companies and multi-national corporations operating in China. The goals are firewalling Chinese interests through surveillance and control by the CPC and the PLA. The confidentiality clause inserted in the regulation is to prevent the officials from the Ministry of Public Security to sell or share data with any foreign and Chinese companies for profit. However, the data is available to be used by CPC to bolster its state-owned entities like Huawei, ZTE, Tencent etc. Thus, the data of companies doing businesses in China is at the disposal of the State Council (refer Table 5.2), a practice that the US has declared as predatory.

Table 5.2: Required Steps for Companies to do Business in China

Steps
Pass National Security Reviews for Technology and Services
Store All Data in China
Form Joint Venture to Open Data Center
Obtain Government Approval for Data Transfers
Buy Government-Approved Encryption and Virtual Private Networks (VPNs)
China has Access to Intellectual Property and Proprietary Information

Strengthening Cyber Defence. 'Low cost, high benefit and low risks' is what makes the cyberwar a preferred war according to SMS 2013.[9] It is worrying not only about the US military but the FANG (Facebook, Amazon, Netflix and Google) as it feels that it has the ability and resource to shape the opinion of the society and thus has devised its own sets of tech-conglomerate BAT (Baidu, Ali Baba and Tencent) to provide the Chinese society with an alternate flavour. The intelligence leaks revelation from Edward Snowden in 2013 underscored the sophistication and extent of internet surveillance by the US and its allies against targets worldwide, including in China. The debate about the balance between security and privacy and American complaints about Chinese penetration of commercial, government, and defence networks only emboldened China to set the games of intelligence collection. China's cyberspace operations are part of a multifaceted, multi-pronged technology development strategy.

Developing Domestic IT Industry. Cyber operations though perceived to be inexpensive and effective, have underappreciated institutional costs involved in their employment. Even if the operational barriers associated with ambitious cyber penetrations are overcome, they still retain the flexibility to preserve the benefits that make exploitation worthwhile in the first place. This logic culminates in relentlessly irritating but indefinitely tolerable stability in the cyber domain.[10] Political stability is at the heart of China's cyber defence, and the monitoring of the internet and social media by the government is based on its ability to use the platform to disseminate the CPC curated information. China is suspicious of the "eight King Kongs", the US-dominated top internet companies in China's domestic supply chain that include Apple, Cisco, Google, IBM, Intel, Microsoft, Oracle, and Qualcomm.[11] According to February 2019 report by Beijing Knownsec Information Technology, China faces the highest distributed denial of service attacks in the world in 2018— an average of over 800 million a day. Scanning and backdoor intrusions made up the majority of the attacks, and domestic hackers conducted about 97 per cent. However, a growing percentage came from overseas, mostly from the US, South Korea, and Japan. China's primary mission in cyberspace is to work towards developing the domestic IT industry to safeguard its information security of critical areas. According to the ICT Development Index that is based on eleven parameters of monitoring and comparing developments in ICT across countries, China is ranked 80th among 176 states in 2017. The 5G era and the IoT supports more types of industrial services and has a wider range of applications, makes security issues increasingly critical. The development of the industrial internet has blurred the boundary between the physical and virtual worlds and increased the impact of a future cyber-attacks. China's Office of the Central Cyberspace Affairs Commission claimed that China has 802 million netizens and a digital economy of 27.2 trillion yuan (US$ 3.86 trillion), almost amounting to 32.9 per cent of its GDP. According to him by 2021, China's cybersecurity market may reach 92.68 billion yuan(US$ 11.5 trillion), and related industries have broad prospects to be aided by the 5G era and the AI.[12] Hence, for President Xi Jinping development and security go together like "two wings of a bird and two wheels of an engine." Therefore, he has directed that the "cyberspace should be made clean and chipper"[13] on indigenised systems. China has made steady progress in the fields of 5G technology, computer and mobile hardware and telecommunication.

Reliance on Cyber Espionage and Technical Reconnaissance. China uses cyber espionage to support its strategic development goals—science and technology advancement, military modernisation, and economic policy objectives. NSD within PLASSF with its cyber force architecture based on former GSD 3PLA is primarily responsible for cyber espionage and contribute to its strategic awareness in a crisis or conflict scenario. Unit 61398 in Shanghai, is the most known unit for undertaking extensive hacking campaigns, often stealing intellectual property.[14] The US uses "Titan Rain" as the informal code name for Chinese cyber espionage acts directed against the US Department of Defence since 2002. According to the Air Force's Chief of Warfighting Integration and Chief Information Officer, Beijing downloaded 10 to 20 terabytes of data from the US NIPRNet (Pentagon's Non-Classified IP Router Network)"[15] compromising the data of the US Army Information Systems Engineering Command, The Naval Ocean Systems Centre, the Missile Defence Agency, and Sandia National Laboratories. China has been worried about the Pentagon network backbone- the Global Information Grid and has been persistently scanning it to bridge its situational awareness gap. Acts of cyber espionage are also directed at private companies, especially related to ICT, high-end manufacturing, biotechnology, alternate energy.[16]

Repurposing the Cyber Weapon. Chinese hacking group Advance Persistent Threat (APT3) is known to explore secrets of its adversaries by digitally invading the IT infrastructure owned by the public and private entities across the world. According to Mark Lechtik, Researcher at CheckPoint, China has already laid traps to capture American Cyber-weapons, and they have been doing it since 2016. According to 06 May 2019 New York Times report "Chinese intelligence agents acquired National Security Agency hacking tools, "eternal blue"[17] and repurposed them in 2016 to attack American allies and private companies in Europe and Asia." The paper quoted Symantec's discovery of claiming that the same Chinese hackers which were being followed by the agency for more than a decade had turned the tables on them.

Hackers Group. The emergence of China's hacker community is part of the orchestrated nationalism. It is instigated when there is a sense of national outrage. It was first witnessed when anti-Chinese riots took place in Indonesia in May 1998. An estimated 3,000 hackers self-organised into a group called the China Hacker Emergency Meeting Centre targetted

Indonesian government websites in protests. A year later on 07 May 1999, when the NATO jet accidentally bombed the Chinese embassy in Belgrade, Yugoslavia the Chinese Red Hacker Alliance was formed within twelve hours and then a series of attacks were launched on numerous US government websites. The mechanism was repeated in 2001 when a Chinese fighter jet collided with a US military aircraft over the South China Sea. In this instance, over 80,000 hackers launched a self-defence cyberwar on the US compelling The New York Times to refer it as "World Wide Web War I."[18] The COVID-19 crisis has again given a reason for the state-sponsored group to get active in stealing the COVID-19 related data. According to a report by Qihoo 360, both domestic Chinese agencies and diplomatic missions in countries including Italy, the UK, North Korea and Thailand were attacked by the leading Chinese internet provider.[19] At the same time, US Defence Counterintelligence and Security Agency cyber division detected nearly 600 "inbound and outbound connections" from "highly likely Electric Panda cyber threat actors" targeting 38 cleared contractor facilities, including those specialising in health care technology.[20] China it seems is now prepared to deal with these emerging threats and has devised its mechanism.

Cyber Deterrence

The Stuxnet episode in Iran in 2010 exposed the world to the vulnerabilities in a system. The shift from attrition warfare to system-disruption warfare demonstrated to China the need to strengthen its cyber deterrence mechanism. China is wary of the cyber exercise conducted by the US with South Korea named Ulchi Freedom Guardian exercises as the US had reportedly turned to cyber-enabled methods to disable and disrupt North Korea's missiles. These capabilities included everything from tampering with the production supply chain for the serial production of missiles in North Korea to tampering with and jamming computers or nuclear command and control systems.[21] Since, November 2019, it has started a similar cyber exercise with Taiwan named Cyber Offensive and Defensive Exercise (CODE).[22]

The PLA writers are also fully aware of the importance of the electromagnetic domain for cyber operations and have stated it as 'sixth domain of battle'.[23] A group of electronic warfare (EW) experts from the National University of Defence Technology's Electronic Countermeasure Institute, in the monograph 'Winning Mechanisms' provide the detail of how the PLA can achieve electromagnetic dominance by "guaranteeing the information activity needs of friendly forces in the electromagnetic spectrum while rendering the enemy's information activities in the electromagnetic spectrum ineffective."[24] The authors specifically champion the use of offensive electronic measures like electromagnetic energy, directed energy, sound energy, and other technical means to achieve such goals.[25] The PLA's game plan is divided into four principles and stages recommending the precise release of energy at the critical node in stage 3 and the final stage it recommends combining firepower with the electromagnetic means as it increases damage to critical nodes in the early warning, communications, and "latent-potential warfare system." [26]

The cyber-attacks against the US Office of Personnel Management in 2015 resulted in the stealing of personal information of almost 20 million Americans, including the applicants' fingerprints. According to *The New York Times*, the Obama administration believed that the Chinese government was behind this cyber espionage, and it even contemplated retaliation.[27] Sensing the dangers posed by the cyber-physical attacks and security concerns over data compromises has prompted the US to ban government agencies from procuring products made by five Chinese companies from August 2020 under its 2019 National Defence Authorisation Act. These companies are ZTE, Huawei Technologies, the world's top surveillance camera maker Hangzhou Hikvision Digital Technology, second-place Dahua Technology and Hytera Communications, the global leader in secure wireless networks used by military and police.

China is also developing a nuclear-electronic weapon system that can generate super-electromagnetic pulse (EMP) waves capable of devastating all electronics—from computers to electric grids— to completely blackout the communication in a contingency. The idea originated from the Russian General Slipchenko book on 'Non-contact Warfare' and has been taken up by the PLA as 'Total Information Warfare'. The attacks are regarded as relatively easy to execute, potentially unattributable means of inflicting mass destruction and forcing opponents to capitulate. 2017 EMP commission report, "Nuclear EMP Attack Scenarios and Combined-Arms Cyberwarfare," suggests that in a major conflict with either China or Russia, the first shot in the war could be a space burst of a super EMP weapon designed to knock out US nuclear command and control and weapons.[28] The PLA has focused on countering C4ISR systems through GPS jamming, Joint Tactical Information Distribution System countermeasures and synthetic radar jamming. These capabilities are likely to be coordinated with computer network attack tools on an adversary's command networks.[29]

China has been galloping in getting its data defence and processing in place. The technological advancement in supercomputing gives China an edge over the US. China now possesses 227 of the world's 500 most powerful supercomputers on the planet, well ahead of the US on 109.[30] The PLA is aware that situational awareness is the key to remain ahead in a deterrent battle and battle of defending the depth. The space-based capability development by the PLA is in the direction to strengthen the C4ISR architecture.

Cognitive Security: A New Frontier

China which fears internal stability the most, has been devising the mechanism to promote its party ideology and keep a tab on the group behaviour. Throughout its history, the CPC has used concepts like the "Mass Line" and "social management" to put the idea of political control into practice, through efforts which have carried over into attempts to build a 'spiritual civilisation' and a more 'service-oriented' government. The Party's goal is to embed 'correct' ideological and moral behaviour into individuals and institutions, so they will automatically make choices that uphold Party power. The CPC development of the 'social credit' system is, in this sense, another step in the Party's long exploration of ways to fuse political control and economic prosperity. With the enormous data being generated through the deployment of new technology like 5G, AI and quantum computing, China leads the governance through surveillance. Its ability to contain the blow-back from the citizens in the initial part of COVID-19 pandemic management was eased out by putting the surveillance, inspections and directions in place along with the use of the State Council' Internet and Supervision' portal which was extensively used for getting the feedback from the people.

The massive behavioural data generated during the pandemic is also being ploughed back to create agile governance mechanism. The CPC was able to douse the flak it faced on reprimanding Dr Li Wenliang, the whistle-blower, of the COVID-19 pandemic in China based on social media analysis. The advent of social media has empowered planners to make significant advances in understanding the dynamics of large groups online and use this understanding to forge powerful new techniques to shape the behaviour and beliefs of people globally. Cognitive security (COGSEC) is a new evolving frontier. In the future, researchers, governments, social platforms, and private actors will be engaged in a continual arms race to influence—and protect from influence—large groups of users online. Having seen the Umbrella Revolution and the 2019 Hong Kong unrest, China is aware of social engineering and social deception in the computer security space. Hence, for social communication, it has devised local applications like WeChat and Weibo to keep their citizens away from Facebook and other western social application. Thus, quarantining the population from uncensored access to information and ensuring the social order is retained and regulated.

Controlling the Narrative: Case Study COVID-19 Pandemic

Strategic messaging or narrative build-up is a key instrument of power and statecraft. A theme or a message is required to change the behaviour, even thoughts and preferences. Countries often indulge in inserting their messages to influence their population and the outside world in one way or another. However, only a few nations like China have invested in harnessing the powers of strategic messaging through political warfare tools. Beijing uses strategic messaging to mould perceptions about China and propagate its narratives to fast-track China's policies, thereby creating an uneven playing field that favours China. Equipped with an enormous messaging capacity, China has undeniable advantages when it engages in strategic competition. The instance of COVID-19 pandemic handling by Xi Jinping and the CPC showed their desire to control the story about the origin of the virus and showcase to the world the superiority of Chinese governance. The pandemic has been taken as a case to highlight how the Chinese state goes about narrative management.

Contextualising COVID-19 Handling by China. Reprimanding of Dr Li Wenliang, the whistle-blower of the contagion, by the officials from China Public Security Bureau on 30 December 2019 was an effort to plug the story from going viral and disturb social order. Dr Li had cautioned medics in his WeChat group of spreading of SARSs like virus and asked them to take precaution. The leadership was probably aware of the unknown virus. It hence used the time to secure the supplies of epidemic related medical equipment from the worldwide market, including the US, which exported 2.4 million pieces to China between 24 January 2020 and 29 February 2020.[31] The timing of disclosure is important in China as it helps in pushing the narrative. Despite growing cases in Wuhan, China carefully weighed the pros and cons, and with nurtured support at the WHO reported about the unknown virus on 03 January 2020 and on 09 January 2020 was able to inform WHO the cause being COVID-19. While the flurry of activity was taking place at WHO emergency committee to submit the report, China used the period to ramp up the state machinery in a quasi-warlike mode to deal with the virus which it knew to be pandemic. Almost a week before the WHO declared it as Public Health Emergency of International Concern (PHEIC),[32] Xi Jinping on the Chinese New Year of Rat, 25 January 2020, declared the tough measures to tackle the COVID-19 threat which had Wuhan at its epicentre. The timing and messaging were of importance. It intended to showcase the existence of strong command governance system under Xi. The agile governance narrative was woven to tell the citizen in China and the world community at large that the CPC cared for its people and the willing participation by the people helped in stemming the pandemic outbreak. The WeChat and Weibo were put under vigilance. The local journalists were given ethical lessons of safeguarding national interests while reporting. Blow by blow account illustrates how the themes were curated and presented before the home and global community.

- **Strong Command Governance System under Xi**. A complete lockdown was declared in Wuhan and adjoining areas, and Premier Li Keqiang was made in charge of the Leading Group of Epidemic Control was done to showcase Xi as a strong and caring leader. Thirty-two government ministries were brought under Joint Working Mechanism with daily reporting with effect from 27 January 2020. PLA and PAP were mobilised; the national strategy of pairing the provinces with the affected cities was implemented to source the relief measures. But the most surprising issue was not the appointment of an epidemic expert to deal with the problem, but the nomination of Sun Chunlan, the Vice-Premier to camp in Wuhan to oversee the epidemic control from 27 January 2020 onwards. For the CPC, handling of the narrative was more important, and hence they wanted to use the expertise of Sun Chunlan, who was former UFWD minister,[33] to correct the narrative coming out from Wuhan.
- **Agile Governance**. The uproar created due to lockdown created massive protest on Chinese social media due to lack of testing kits and medical provisioning despite assurances from National Health Commission of China. However, the testing was ramped

up from 300 to 20,000 in a week by getting the private P2 bio-safety laboratories without checking at the efficacy of the kits. But it did assuage the frustration within the people. Two 2,000 bedded hospital was created, and video made viral to showcase the advance methods available within China to contain the virus. The resentment among the people due to compulsory inspection of all residents in Wuhan and brutal forced quarantining was addressed by repurposing the corruption supervision portal with State Council to take the feedback from people and deploying of massive surveillance and monitoring programme through mobile service providers and community-based volunteers from the party and other agencies to monitor the health and access control. The pictures of the volunteers, medics and the state advisories were flashed on a regular interval for the consumption of local and international media.

- **Saluting the Spirit of the People**. The CPC and UFWD have a well-documented procedure to strike a chord of nationalism at times of crisis. Lot of videos showing the strength and resilience of the Chinese community to deal with odds were splashed. Once, the pandemic started taking its toll in Europe and the US, the UFWD was quick to highlight the failures of western administration to deal with the pandemic, and the US stigmatisation of COVID-19 as 'China Virus' was captured to present the victimisation card by the west.
- **Correcting the Narrative**. China having championed the phase one of its campaign against COVID 19 by end April 2020, was ready to redeem its image. However, the credibility and genuineness problem regarding its overtures to help the global community to fight the pandemic was the biggest challenges confronting China. Key issues that posed problems were: a) hiding of the origin and timing of reporting of COVID-19; b) complicity of WHO in delaying the declaration of a pandemic; c) supplies of faulty masks and testing kits and lack of sincerity in sharing the data on the sequencing of the contagion which has impeded vaccine development. d) Using 'wolf diplomacy' to deflect the accusation and justify aggression by creating tensions in the South China Sea and the Ladakh region of India. The role of UFWD has been at the heart of narrative manipulation. Hence, a brief overview of UFWD and soft power projection of

China has been covered to allow the readers to understand the resources which are at the disposal of CPC to correct the narrative.

UFWD: China's Magic Weapon

China's international influence activities groups are the External Propaganda Leading Group, which has a dual bureaucratic identity as the State Council Information Office; the Central Committee Propaganda Department; the Central Committee UFWD; the Central Committee Foreign Affairs Commission; and the Central Committee Education Leading Small Group. Although bureaucratically ranked slightly lower, the Ministry of Culture and Tourism, the Ministry of Education, the newly created Voice of China, and the Xinhua News Agency all exercise policy formulation and oversight roles in their functional domains.

China uses "United Front" work to coordinate influence operations generally focused on the management of potential opposition groups inside China. It is also geared for important foreign influence mission too. It has been existence since 1920, but it was Xi Jinping who has re-energised UFWD and has increased the resourcing and prominence for such efforts within the CPC political system. Xi has referred to UFWD as a magic weapon adding almost 40,000 new UFWD cadres in first few years of his Presidency[34] and established a leading small group on UFWD with himself at its head signifying a direct line of command from CPC Politburo to UFWD. The restructuring of bureaus, strengthening of the cadre, and the overarching guidance at the highest level shows the growing role UFWD is to play within and outside the country in line with China's growing national power. The growing confidence of the Xi government is based on its ability to tighten control over the flow of information. Four more bureaus have been added by Xi to look after the 'new social class', Xinjiang Uyghur Autonomous Region (XUAR) and overseas affairs to the existing UFWD specialised bureaus, each dealing with a targeted group such as China's eight officially-approved non-communist political parties, ethnic minorities, religious groups and Chinese communities overseas (refer to Figure 5.1). Xi-era UFWD activities fall into four primary categories: Firstly, the use of Chinese diaspora to promote CPC foreign policy and suppress any dissent. Secondly, co-opt foreigners to support to provide access to strategic information and technical knowledge. Thirdly, creating global, multi-platform, for pro-CPC policies and fourthly, support the China-centred strategic bloc known as the BRI for building coalition and client-state.

Figure 5.1: United Front Works Department Bureaus and Affiliations

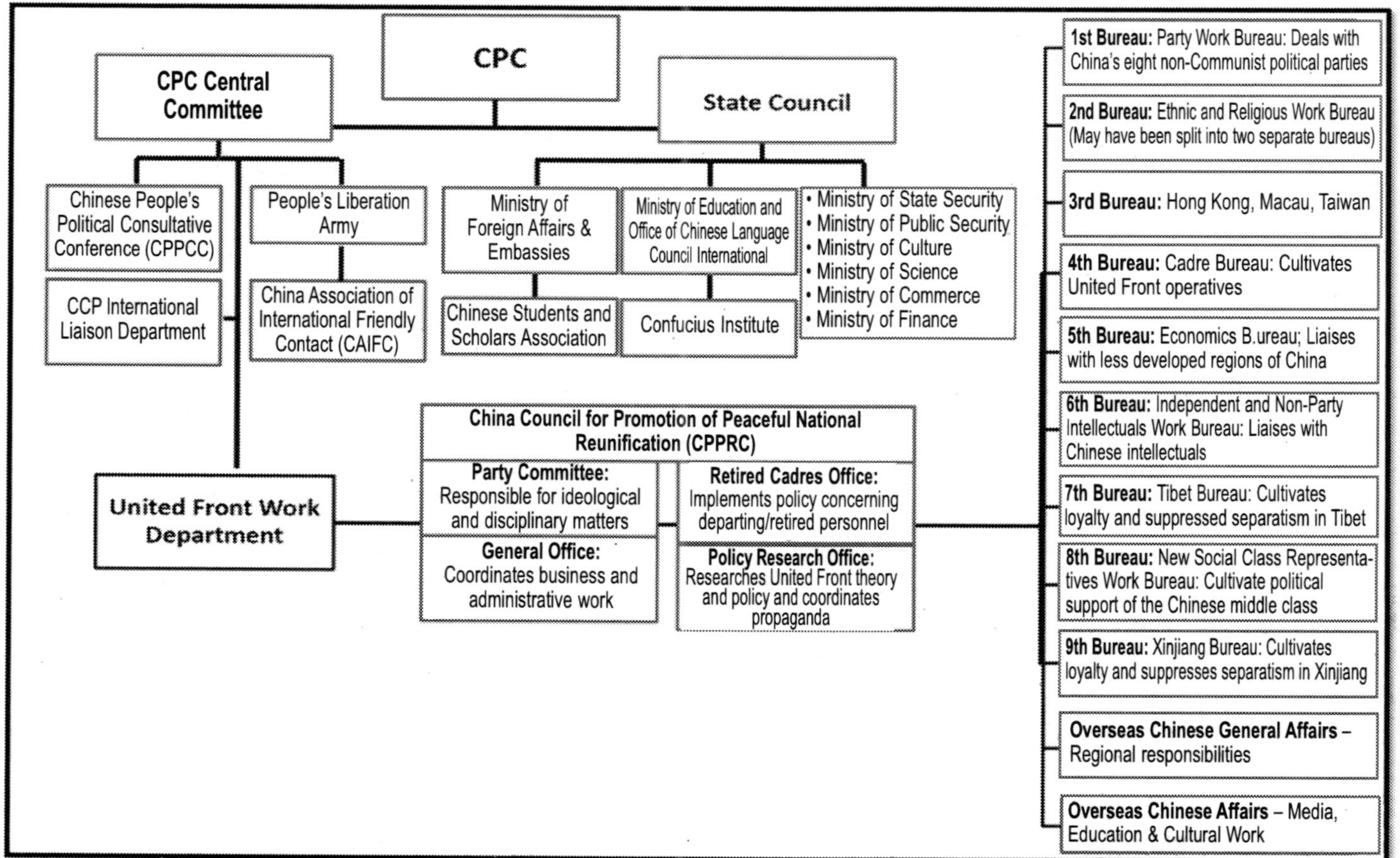

Source: Cole, J. M. (2017, September 26). *China Seeks Vicious Circle of Violence through United Front Activities in Taiwan*. Retrieved January 10, 2020, from Taiwan Sentinel: https://sentinel.tw/china-violence-ufw-tw/.

The UFWD has been actively involved in implementing the Chinese 'three warfares' strategy in concert with the CMC and Ministry of State Security. Figure 5.1 shows UFWD bureaus and affiliations and range of activities it is assigned to conduct. Its Taiwan engagement displays how it attempts to extend conventional war dynamics into the political domain. A slow-moving and surreptitious ploy, the strategy is designed to subdue nations with a dispute with China without ever needing to fight. The 'three warfares' strategy is looking deeply into the fault lines. Social engineering is a concept which can be well utilised for popular mobilisation dynamics using a web of cyber tools, political subversion, creation and preparation of underground militia or workers. The cyber tools provide an excellent means for manipulation and narrative insertion. The defection testimony of China's William Wang Liqian on 23 November 2019 to Australia's counterespionage agency revealed Beijing's modus-operandi of influencing Taiwan's January 2020 elections.[35] Michael Cole, a Taiwan expert and former Canadian intelligence official, believes that the goal of UFWD operations in Taiwan is to create instability and then justify its military intervention.[36]

Beijing's nomination of Sun Chunlan, the Vice-Premier to camp in Wuhan to oversee the epidemic control has more to do with managing the protests and social order due to harsh lockdown measures. She was required to deploy her experience of managing the influence operation as former UFWD Minister. UFWD, along with PLASSF, has already been engaged at monitoring the public health intelligence across the world to hasten its vaccine research. China Daily has already published few sponsored reports on 21 April 2020, less than three months from the declaration of the countdown. For the report to look credible, three institutes were roped in. These were China Watch Institute, Institute of Contemporary Chinese Study- Tsinghua University and School of Health Policy and Management – Peking Medical College. Similarly, the Journal of Science report of 31 March 2020 showed 96 per cent reduction in COVID-19 cases outside Wuhan due to lockdown measures. According to China Daily, China's National Library has been tasked to record the history of COVID-19 battle. To sanitise the adverse foreign reporting, it deported three Wall Street Journalist in February 2020 for writing an article that called it the "real sick man of Asia."[37] The pandemic has thrown open major fault lines within the US and other nations which are being carefully studied by China and will form part of new developing warfare – virtual societal warfare with psychological impacts vectored in leadership choice of response.

Soft Power Projection

Xi Jinping, in 2014, had stressed on a concerted national effort to link China's popularity and likeability to its rise. The CCP leaders have turned to the use of soft power tools to promote Chinese language, educational exchanges, media penetration, and pop culture icons. Some of the activities include:

- **Education Exchanges.** China has more than 541 Confucius Institutes spread across six continents and affiliated with China's ministry of education. The institutes mirror cultural associations like the United Kingdom's British Councils, but it partners with universities. It also runs a Confucius Classrooms programme directed at the primary and secondary institutions in the foreign country. Broader concerns about improper influence over teaching and research, industrial and military espionage surveillance of Chinese abroad, and undermining Taiwanese influence have been dovetailed. The US brought Foreign Influence Transparency Act in March 2018 to regulate the funding in the US academic colleges. China's educational exchange programme through the Scholarship Council provides student financial aid to both the Chinese students going abroad and also to the foreigners coming to China. Around 440,000 international students from 205 countries studied in China in 2016.[38] The Peking University and Tsinghua University are among the world's top fifty higher educational institutions. It also helps it in gaining access and controlling research. Chinese Students and Scholars Associations (CSSA) within the domestic and foreign universities are guided by the CPC members at the embassies and has been involved in promoting party works and reporting against the dissidents.[39] Over the last 40 years, China has become the largest source of international students. A total, 5,194,900 Chinese students have studied abroad, and according to 2017 Ministry of Education report, 1,454,100 students were enrolled in overseas higher education institutions. The rate of returnees after completing higher education stood at 83.7 per cent.[40]

- **Media Expansion.** Besides education, China has put its weight behind its foreign-language news outlets to regulate the narratives about the CCP controlled China. The active engagement and outreach programmes ensures that only curated news item gets to the media. China has scaled up the operations of Xinhua, the government's primary news agency. It has plans of having 200 foreign bureaus by 2020.[41] The 'China Daily' and the 'Global Times' publish English language editions available worldwide. In March 2018, CCTV, CRI, and China National Radio were integrated to establish the China Media Group, also called Voice of China, led by the Propaganda Department of the Central Committee of the CPC.[42] In December 2016, CCTV (the state television broadcasting news service), rebranded itself as China Global Television Network (CGTN). It broadcasts six channels of which two are in English and others are in Arabic, French, Russian, and Spanish. In more than seventy countries it has its reporting teams. China Radio International broadcasts also pitch in with 392 hours of programming each day in almost thirty-eight languages from twenty-seven overseas bureaus.[43] According to a November 2015 Reuters investigation, the media firm also covertly runs a network of more than thirty radio stations in fourteen countries through front companies to mask its influence. Approximately fifty million Chinese diaspora community, primarily in Southeast Asia, are just as much a target audience for Chinese media as the foreigners. As far as the local media is concerned, on 15 December 2019, the code of ethics legislated for the Chinese journalists makes it clear to them to "safeguard the political and the cultural security of the country" besides ensuring social stability.[44] Hence, the domestic media in China is the CPC's mouthpiece, and the truth is the casualty.
- **Controlling Influencers.** Chinese firms have courted Hollywood's film industry to control the influencers. More than half of the ten best movies of 2019 selected by Time magazine were financed by Beijing-friendly firms, such as Tencent Pictures, Sunac Group, Shanghai Road Pictures Film and Television, Media Asia Film, and Bona Film Group. Chinese conglomerate Wang Jianlin, founder of Dalian Wanda and member of CPC acquired US AMC Entertainment for $2.6 billion in May 2012, and

Hollywood studio Legendary Entertainment and theatre Carmike Cinemas in 2016 raising heckles within the US policymakers. According to a report by PricewaterhouseCoopers by 2020, China is set to become the world's largest cinema market, with box office revenue expected to jump to US$15.5 billion by 2023.[45] Chinese firms are seizing the opportunity to shape China's external image, and the US producers have grown cagy of making films that cast China in a negative light, primarily out of a desire to tap into Chinese distribution markets. US Senators like Ted Cruz aims to bring in a bill to reduce Chinese influence in Hollywood.

Influence operations ride on the wealth of intelligence inputs. Regardless of how well new technologies collect and disseminate information and intelligence, they cannot provide perfect situational awareness or perfect information about the enemy or friendly intentions. The force afflicted by influence operations is likely to generate conflict situations with added friction amongst opposing parties and always is likely to lead to unexpected consequences. Friction provides an almost infinite number of outwardly insignificant influences that can impede or derail operations and, when combined with fog, will ensure surprise in warfare will always exist. Countermeasures in multiple forms, including exploiting cyberwarfare to disrupt modern information systems, ensure the fog of war will persist in 21st Century warfare. Thus, China knows that while creating information eclipse at the point of decision, it also needs to create conditions to remain information agile for which it needs to build capacity for uninterrupted situational awareness.

BUILDING SITUATIONAL AWARENESS CAPABILITIES

An internal report by the Chinese Institute for Contemporary International Relations (CICIR), affiliated to Ministry of State Security, warned about the rising global anti-China sentiment in the wake of the COVID-19 outbreak. It concluded that the wave of hostility is more than what was present during the 1989 Tiananmen Square crackdown. The geo-political outcome between Washington and Beijing may result in confrontation.[46] At times of global instability, strategic situational awareness is the most important asset for China to counter any provocation. The PLA is aware of the outreach of the US Global information Grid architecture supported and defended by the USSTRATCOM and knows that the transparency provided to the US forces to target critical infrastructure within and outside

China. China is equally concerned with the need to protecting its global interests and the need for robust regional information architecture to defend its A2AD, border and internal stability threats.

Need for Global Information Grid

Some of the PLA modernisation developments which have challenged US Global Information Grid include the development of hypersonic weapon platform, ASAT, DEW, nuclear-electronic weapon systems, super-computers. The rapid advancement in space, AI and 5G enables it to handle the networks of network and its market share in AI and 5G may create dependency within the US alliance countries thus increasing the threat of collateral damage within US coalition umbrella. Its surveillance outposts in the South China Sea on the artificially created islands also give it a strategic vantage point in the fiercely contested South China Sea and the funnel to China's coastal underbelly. For China, which has recently carried out its reform and aligned its force structure to undertake integrated joint operations, the information grid helps in improving the force application efficacy for both kinetic and non-kinetic operations. It also enables a better command and control and decision support system based on battlespace awareness and transparency of own assets based on a netcentric architecture.

PLASSF has been created to synergise the information operations of the PLA and firewall against the computer network attack, computer network exploitation, electronic warfare measures, physical attack or outsourced attack. Computing, storage and communication survivability is crucial for better situational awareness. According to the 2015 NDWP on 'China's Military Strategy', China aims to optimise its nuclear force structure, improve strategic early warning, command and control, missile penetration, rapid reaction, and survivability and protection. The 2019 NDWP on "China's National Defence in the New Era", talks about safeguarding information and cybersecurity as apart of "national cyber sovereignty." The growing demand for early warning and guidance systems within the PLA is the outcome of concern regarding its capabilities gap, as it knows that any false alarm can trigger nuclear attack or attack by weapons of mass destruction which Beijing can ill afford. Strengthening space situational awareness and freedom to operate in outer space are part of the situational awareness developmental overdrive in the PLA.

Early Warning System

China Electronics Technology Corporation (CETC) has been at the helm of putting China on the map of high-end radar. Project 640 launched in 1964 had laid the foundation of missile defence and development of laser and nuclear EMP systems as part of the nuclear missile defence system.[47] It has developed long-range phased array radars (LPAR) in P Band which has 4000 km range and hence, could be used for ballistic missile tracking. Four of these are located near Huanan, Yiyuan, Hangzhou, and Korla, which gives China adequate early warning.[48] To counter the stealth bombers, it has developed anti-stealth radar-like SLC-7 and YLC-8B. To ensure the survivability of radar systems to electronic warfare measures, it has developed jamming resistant JY 27 A VHF active electronically scanned array (AESA) radars and JL-1 A series help in precision tracking of multiple targets. The quantum radar technology development reported by CETC makes stealth technology redundant. It also allows scanning of high-speed aircraft and the growing space of hypersonic.[49] The low energy emitting makes it difficult to detect. JY 27A AESA radars also happen to be the backbone of China's PLAAF and PLAN airborne early warning and control (AEW&C) systems over KJ series aircraft. The ground-penetrating radar, Eagle Eye-A, built under China Aerospace Science and Industry Corporation is capable of detecting soil diseases, pipelines and even tunnels as deep as six meters underground with a fast response and no harm to the environment. Its integration of AI system and BeiDou satellite navigation and GPS systems allows the efficiency of auto-detection and high precision positioning of underground targets.[50]

Unmanned Surveillance System

The JY-300 (Tian Shao) which has a range of more than 1,000 km and a practical ceiling of more than 5,000 meters, is the world's first unmanned Airborne Warning and Control System (AWACS) aircraft. It integrates radars with the airframe, which means radar antennae are part of the craft's skin.[51] It is likely to have fielded stealthy Shendiao for early warning. Morning Star and Rainbow are being developed for persistent surveillance for months as launch on-demand systems thus providing an alternative to satellites with greater flexibility, including for sea area surveillance.[52]

Space System

China has developed a robust architecture of space systems to support its strategic situational awareness. Though there is a large difference in holding of satellites between China and the US, the Chinese ranks second after the US in terms of the number of satellites that are currently operational. These satellites provide a wide range of sensors that include ELINT, electro-optical (EO) sensors, synthetic aperture radar (SAR), staring camera, stereoscopic imagers, and hyperspectral, among others. The details of various space-based Chinese satellites have been covered in detail in Chapter 4.

Maritime Surveillance

The PLAN with its global commitment and competition along its island chains recognises the importance of a maritime strategic early warning system as critical to its overall national strategic early warning system. The PLAN maritime surveillance capabilities are through the sea- and space-based systems, ranging from the launch of satellites dedicated to that mission to the construction of an 'underwater great wall' of sensors, augmented by a range of underwater sensors and unmanned and autonomous underwater vehicles. China's militarization of the South China Sea has involved the placement of a network of radars on its various installations on features, such as Fiery Cross, Subi Reef, and Mischief Reef, throughout the South China Sea. These radars may contribute to early warning, signals intelligence, and even stealth detection, including via high-frequency arrays that are located on Cuarteron and Fiery Cross reefs. The PLAN has upgraded its capabilities with a ship-based OTH radar to develop a compact version that can allow improved surveillance at much greater distances.

Laser Surveillance System

China has heavily invested in the use of Lidar (a portmanteau of light and radar), Artificial Intelligence (AI) and 5G technology to synergise detection and dissemination processing of the images and intelligence. Lidar uses ultraviolet, visible, or near-infrared light to image objects. It can be used with a wide range of targets, including non-metallic objects, rocks, rain, chemical compounds, aerosols, clouds and even single molecules. However, it has an atrophying effect in fog and murky water. China's new satellite 'Project Guanlan' which means 'watching the big waves' launched in May 2019 at the Pilot National Laboratory in Qingdao in Shandong uses high-powered lasers to spot objects deep underwater up to 500 metres.

It is capable of scanning an area of around 100 Km on land. When used alongside microwave radar, it can scan and identify surface movement and also penetrate through the foliage. A narrow laser beam can be used to map physical features with very high resolution. It brings transparency both on land and sea and exposes weapon systems, including submarines.[53] Riding on its BeiDou Navigation Satellite System, AI and 5G technology, the swathe of Chinese surveillance encompasses from airport scheduling, robot patrol, unmanned aerial vehicles, building and vehicle monitoring and logistics management. The use of such a feature to fuse sensor-shooter integration using AI is a distinct possibility.

Modernising Command and Control Network

The PLA intends achieving networked C4ISR and counter-C4ISR capabilities that enable systems and subsystems to kinetically or non-kinetically defeat or paralyse the enemy's decision support systems. China's advances in space-based capabilities, drone technology, and information processing could provide sufficient means to provide situational awareness and targeting quality data to overseas Chinese forces anywhere in the world by 2030 or 2035.[54] 5G has been developed by Chinese defence academics and engineers to improve battlefield communications with faster and more stable information transmission, increasing the timeliness and integration of information. The increased bandwidth could help the PLA to 'intelligentise' the military, and through this, it seeks to leverage potential applications of AI technologies in military affairs. Chinese aggressive 5G global push to enable massive inter-machine communication in smart cities helps to make similar networking push among sensors and devices could be particularly advantageous as warfare changes from informatised to 'intelligentised'.

Challenges of Systems Integration

In the future, China could employ more integrated strategic early warning systems. In the PLA, the capabilities for various elements of early warning are primarily divided among the PLAAF, PLASSF, PLAN and PLARF. While the PLA has made rapid stride in technology infusion, but it is saddled with legacy equipment, and integration of these systems is a challenge. The efforts of the Chinese defence industry, particularly those of CETC, in providing improved datalinks for real-time sharing and integration of intelligence for enhanced situational awareness have matured. These systems aim to fill a range of kinetic and non-kinetic operations across multiple domains. For example, the anti-missile warfare early warning system is dependent on locating and fixing the ballistic missile ascending and mid-to-end segments, supporting strategic counterattacks and anti-missile interception operations. Designing such a system entails multi-source fusion and comprehensive crossflow of information. PLASSF, as the new informational umbrella and custodian of the situational awareness engine, is responsible for facilitating information transmission, processing, and distribution, and for supporting early warning. Devising hack-free algorithm is an area China is seriously looking at to enable information parity with the US. Thus, it is likely to explore the fields of quantum technologies to provide resilience to its communication, sensor technologies and space exploration.

War Control: An Area of Focus for the PLA

In 2004, Hu Jintao while giving the task to PLA to manage global threats also directed the PLA to improve its capabilities "to respond to crises, safeguard peace, contain war, and win a war."[55] Hence, for peace and stability, the PLA has produced copious writings on the topic since 2008 stressing on the need to develop understanding and implementing escalation control. The NDWP of China has also reflected on controlling crisis and conflict as an essential mission for the PLA. The PLA writings instead of using the term "escalation control" use the phrases "war control," "crisis management," "crisis control," "war situation control," and "war termination." For China to achieve its millennium goals, it must be able to play a leading role in managing conflict and competition.

War Control

PLA views war control as the most critical concept. The 2007 PLA Encyclopaedia defines "war control" as "a set of monitoring and limiting actions aimed at war, undertaken by the people who guide strategy. It includes the conscientious application of greater constraints and limitations on war, encompassing war's initiation, development, scale, intensity, and consequences."[56] An article in 2010 published by three PLA authors at the Shijiazhuang Army Command Academy stressed that in normal situations, restraining crises is of chief importance, winning wars are emphasised when there is no alternative after a failure to contain a crisis, but even then fighting should still strive to contain wartime escalation.[57] According to them, the progression of crisis and conflict passes through a series of stages, as shown in Figure 5.2.

Figure 5.2: Crisis to War Continuum

Crisis → Military Crisis → Armed Conflict → Local War → Total War

Guide for War Control

According to Chinese analysts, the most potentially dangerous state on the continuum of conflict is a middle stage of military crisis and armed conflict stage. A phase of 'quasi-war' have a dual objective of resolving the crisis and preventing the war, and in case the war breaks out then look at winning the war on own terms. Such actions demand clear discerning of intentions and ability to disregard misperception or misinterpretation. The situation where the military activities are taking place the objectives for control are nebulous. The guide for actions in a crisis of conflict is clear.

- The strategic and political objectives should be the primary focus. The military success is related to the ability to support and secure the political objective.
- It reinforces the strategy of pre-emption to "seize the initiative" in the early stages of a conflict.
- Seizing of the initiative is predicated on the ability to preserve strategic and political stability and operational flexibility in response to an adversary's actions without unnecessarily escalating the conflict.

Crisis Management

Zhang Tuosheng, at the China Foundation for International Strategic Studies, contends that the main objective of crisis management is to avert the escalation of a dispute into military conflict and war while trying to protect one's interests. The idea of a principled stand combined with tactical flexibility has long been axiomatic in Chinese approaches to crisis management. The Japanese think tank, National Institute for Defence Studies (NIDS), has supported it. NIDS notes that during the crisis, Beijing tends to firstly stand firm on issues related to its principles, such as sovereignty and territorial integrity, but often behaves flexibly; secondly it promote the appearance that the opponent is always wrong in a crisis, while China seeks to gain the initiative in action; and thirdly, employ military, diplomatic, and economic tools to manage the crisis.[58] The Chinese practice to crisis management is changing, and according to Zhang, China may take recourse to following when confronted with a crisis:

- Use non-military means such as diplomacy, and non-military actions more frequently to send warning signals.
- Place growing importance to act in accordance with international law and seeking legitimacy in actions.
- Strengthen peacetime efforts to build mutual security trust with interested parties.
- More attention to seeking mutual compromise and concessions over disputes and strive for win-win and avoid no-win situations.[59] For instance, the adverse ICJ panel ruling against China regarding its claim in the South China Sea and favour of Philippine sea has been turned over by China courting the Philippine President Duterte. Incidentally, Duterte has made five visits to China since 2016 but none to the US.[60] Duterte's apparent refusal to enforce the ruling against China may have critiques at home, but for China, it serves its purpose especially when the President Duterte talks about of joint exploration in the area of dispute. Beijing's reported establishment of Paracel (Xisha) district and a Spratlys (Nansha) district, to be under the control of the Chinese city of Sansha has not been opposed by Duterte despite the protest from the opposition.[61]

Quasi-war Concept

Some of the PLA texts talk about 'special state' found in the middle stages of the continuum of conflict that lies between peace and war.[62] This 'quasi-war' concept blurs the line between non-war and war activities and objectives. In these stages, militaries are involved in a crisis or conflict but are not yet at war. Such an eventuality aims to create conditions for a political solution while being prepared for war. The method of identifying the intention of the opponent is crucial, especially when kinetic means come into play for creating deterrence. Crisis control methods are dependent on the nature of the crisis, its severity and the intention of the adversary. The SMS 2013 surmises:

- The first option talks about avoiding economic and societal crises from escalating into political crises and non-military crises from becoming military crises. It aims at striving "to control political, diplomatic, and economic contradictions from spreading to strategic conflict."[63]

- The second option looks at limiting the geographic scope of the crisis to prevent it from being spilled over to other areas.[64]
- The third option looks at confining the crisis with the countries directly involved. Zhao and Zhao from NDU argue that it is essential to "keep external forces from intervening so that it will not become multilateral or international in nature."[65]

While in most of the writings, the preference is for using non-military approaches. However, few argue that some crisis may need the use or deployment of military force as deterrence for shaping the perception.[66] Some of the credible deterrence activities suggested includes limited operational actions like blockade or even limited attack.[67] PLA writings have consistently argued that the country should delay the commencement of war until it is equipped to "seize the initiative" and win the war. Thus, the reliance is on developing deterrence mechanism that can be put to practice based on an escalating ladder of conflict.

Practicing War Control

The COVID-19 pandemic has put the Chinese preaching into practice. It is trying to curb the economic and societal crisis brought about by the pandemic from blowing into political crisis despite provocations from the US President. China has deployed the spokesperson from the Ministry of Foreign Affairs to convey the establishment point of view. Xi Jinping is playing the statesman calling the US to improve Sino-US relationship[68] amidst the pandemic crisis and calling for global solidarity[69] to contain the impact of the contagion. China initially tried to localise the pandemic to Hebei province through ruthless surveillance, inspection and intervention programme. While its global impact is still spreading, China has been trying to show the world that it is in control of the situation. Thus, it can guard its core social stability interest. It is aware of the headwinds, and hence, it is trying to project itself to the world as the only nation capable of supporting the worsening health system. The Chinese Foreign Ministry announced on 21 March 2020, while the country was still fighting the pandemic in Wuhan, to help 82 countries, the World Health Organisation and the African Union to fight against COVID-19.[70] The medical supplies China has sent included test kits, masks and protective clothing. However, the poor-quality kits dented its credibility. As regards the PLA posturing amidst the crisis is concerned, it has targeted the US freedom of navigation operations in the South China Sea and near Taiwan while activating its Tibetan border with India in Eastern Ladakh area. The PLA sent out the strategic messaging by sending its aircraft carrier in South China and showing the force preservation capability of the PLA while the US four aircraft carriers were down due to crew affected from COVID-19.[71] In June 2020, seeing China's aggressive design, the US was forced to deploy its three aircraft carriers to the Western Pacific Ocean. China has also activated its front against India in June 2020. According to Brahma Chellaney, strategic overstretch is something China would not like. However, it has to be seen strong to its people, and all its state media is devoted to rallying the CPC points and carry out the coercive diplomacy.[72]

'Active Defence' and Deterrence: Kinetic and Non-Kinetic Options

The PLA see deterrence as a military concept with political and psychological dimension.[73] It is identified as one of three basic ways to use force: war or in case of military deterrence or as a non-war military operation.[74] PLA does not distinguish between the deterrence force and combat force as it believes that it resides within the combat capabilities. China's display of multi-dimensional deterrence posture emphasises the integrated use of a variety of forces to create a global strategic balance and stability and deter local conflicts or war in the conditions of informatisation to safeguard sovereignty and interests. SMS 2013 has noted that the advent of new technologies and its acquisition of operational capabilities have resulted in innovation in its deterrence approach. Disruptive technologies like hypersonic, DEW, EW and biotechnology capabilities are few in the non-nuclear domain. Consistent with its military doctrine, China has executed a series of activities within its 'active defence' strategic guidance in the South China Sea and the East China Sea. Promulgation of ADIZ in the East China Sea has made the US and its allies worry about it being replicated in the South China Sea. General Qian Lihua, former Director at the Ministry of National Defence, has also been vocal about 'active defence' applicability in case of accidental clashes related to territorial and sovereignty issues. The risk assessment based on situational awareness will be critical to war control efforts and deterrence messaging and execution.

Grey Zone Game: Intelligence Process Challenges and Constraints

PLA plays a grey zone game by use of multiple methods that include political and economic coercion, IO through use of cyber and state propaganda machinery, other forms of cyber intrusive and offensive operations and proxy support. As part of proxy support, it uses direct or indirect use of non-state and parastate groups to carry out militarised intimidation or control territory to exert influence or achieve specific security or political outcomes. It also uses State-Controlled Forces to provoke outcomes favourable to state interests by hiding attributions and ratcheting up escalation according to the script. To add a layer to the war control effort, the PLA has consolidated various maritime law enforcement agencies into a single China Coast Guard by amalgamating China Maritime Surveillance, the Fisheries Law Enforcement and other smaller entities under it and provided it with credible capabilities in the form of more than 300 patrol and coastal combatant ships making it the largest blue-water coastguard in the world.[75] It has also arrayed non-traditional forces like a maritime militia to enforce China's maritime sovereignty and undertake grey zone operation. The challenges of increasing contest or conflict in a given space have made global powers to practice creeping coercion by leveraging ambiguity and non-attribution. While in the cyber domain, it is carried out with impunity but its execution by physical methods and means that has worried the security planners. The Commander of the US Indo-Pacific Command declared that "China is now capable of controlling the South China Sea in all scenarios short of war with the US."[76]

China has been employing grey zone tools to promote their influence by using unattributed forces and by exploiting the fault-lines within the targeted country. The leading purveyor of grey-zone tactics in the maritime area is China's irregular maritime militia, dubbed the 'little blue men'. Rear Admiral Zhang Zhaozhong has explained the idea as the "cabbage strategy" which is a strategy of surrounding the contested areas in operational layers with a maritime militia, maritime law enforcement and navy warships working together. To avoid escalation, the warships are positioned the farthest away from the target, but it ensures military presence.[77] The militia, comprising hundreds of fisher-folks in their motorboats as well as China's paramilitary forces, operates mainly out of Chinese-held islands in the South China Sea and has been involved in engaging with the US navy ships and those of neighbouring countries with rival territorial claims. Their activities are consciously kept below the brink of conflict, but effectively demonstrate China's claims over disputed features. China has also accused the US of trying to instigate the privateers to attack Chinese ships by issuing letters of marque – a document authorising privately-owned ships to capture enemy merchant ships. China has termed such actions as "an act of piracy" explicitly prohibited under international laws.[78]

Regardless of grey zone activity type, addressing the grey zone warning elements of temporality, attribution, and intent requires scenario visualisation, the fusing of a multi-modal intelligence analytical package, and mechanisms to make a reasonable judgement in uncertain circumstances. China has been practicing the grey zone game but is aware of the challenges it faces while handling the protests in Hong Kong.

Challenges to War Control Efforts

The Xi administration's political stance of zero tolerance to national sovereignty may impinge on the flexibility of Chinese authorities to pursue compromises in a crisis or conflict. The war control emphasises the potential strategic gains from a crisis or limited clash. Doklam crisis, Scarborough Reef and the Senkaku/Diaoyu Islands are proof that the war control concepts do exist. However, the confidence in controlling escalation in the absence of sound situational awareness architecture may lead to serious miscalculations. Technology is the only panacea to which the PLA looks at. China's civil-military integration is seen to create new efficiencies and a new method to people's war.

Technology for the Future

Chinese leaders recognise the strategic potential of science and technology to enhance economic and military dimensions of national power. One of the national strategic objectives of China is to become a science and technology superpower has pushed the boundaries for the state-owned entities and the private entities in China. The data diversion from an outside source as a monopoly of the state is being monetised for the benefit of the Chinese companies. Rather than depending primarily on the "absorption" of foreign technologies in its quest for indigenous innovation, China intends to accomplish truly disruptive, even "radical" innovation in strategic emerging technologies AI, quantum science, robotics, smart manufacturing and biotechnology. As China promotes a national strategy for military-civil fusion (or "civil-military integration"), it aims to leverage critical technologies for a range of defence applications.

Development of Civil-Military Integration (CMI)

The 2015 NDWP on 'China's Military Strategy' clearly articulated the need for accelerating and diversifying the CMI across key technological areas spanning multiple domains. It also made a case to encourage joint building and utilisation of military and civilian infrastructure in joint exploration of the sea, outer space and air, and collective use of resources like survey and mapping, navigation, meteorology and frequency spectra. It intended to train military personnel in civilian educational institutions, coopt national defence industries and look at outsourcing logistics support to civilian support systems very much in the same form as the US. It seems enamoured by the US research organisations like DARPA and the Pentagon's Defence Innovation Unit Experimental (DIUx) and a study concluded that in the US 85 per cent of the military's core technology comes from the private sector and 80 per cent of firms that supply the US military also sell commercially.

China's 13th Five-Year Special Plan released in March 2016 highlighted CMI strategy to achieve Xi Jinping's vision of creating an 'Innovation-Driven Development Strategy'. Xi's assertion acted as a catalyst encouraging Chinese non-defence companies to begin selling directly to the PLA. Central Commission for the Development of Military-Civil Integration chaired by President Xi was set up in 2017. It resulted in the creation of provincial CMI leading small groups around the nation.[79] It has triggered nation-wide action plan, and CMI has become the prominent component of government initiatives like Promotion of a National IC Industry Development Guidelines (2014), Made in China 2025 (2015) and the Next Generation Artificial Intelligence Development Plan (2017). In April 2017, to demonstrate the PLA's genuine intent to engage with the private sector, the CMC's Equipment Development Department opened tenders on more than 2,000 projects to private companies while simultaneously the CMC's National Defense Intellectual Property Office of the Equipment Development Department declassified over 3,000 defence patents for private sector use. It is the first time that the PLA has declassified patents in the thirty years since the military patent system was created in China. PLASSF by July 2017 had signed the talent and research cooperation agreements with nine research institutions and laboratories, including the Harbin Institute of Technology and Shanghai Jiaotong University, two of the country's leading research universities. The PLAAF Logistics Department signed strategic cooperation agreements with JD.com and SF Express (China's largest e-commerce outlets and logistic companies) to create an intelligent logistics system, including the use of transportation UAVs to maintain supply chains that have been successfully implemented in Shaanxi and Yunnan. On the industry side, two key defence conglomerates that run some of China's most important defence research labs, China Aerospace Science and Industry Corporation (CASIC) and China Electronics Technology Corporation (CETC), have paved the way for greater private sector collaboration. CETC, in collaboration with Wuhan-based Skywalker Technology, made headlines after it successfully launched 119 fixed-wing drone swarm, which is regarded as the core area for AI unmanned systems future operations.[80] In January 2018, the State Council's Development Research Centre published a document outlining the role of legislation similar to the US 1986 Federal Technology Transfer Act and Federal Acquisition Reform Act in the development of dual-use industries.

CMI is ushering Chinese companies into the defence economy. They are being encouraged to acquire and adapt foreign technology through "introduce, digest, absorb, and re-innovate" mechanism. China uses its extensive business and academic presence abroad to obtain foreign strategic technologies and expertise to enrich its growing military capabilities. C4ADS' reviewed 65,727 import records and 429 investment transactions of China over the last three years and found that 1,655 Chinese civilian companies through engagement with the West, acquired foreign technologies and then "re-innovated" them to supply products to advance the PLA's competitiveness.[81] The CMI strategy has brought synergy in Chinese civilian and military industries and driving the pace of the defence-industrial ecosystem. Figure 5.3 provides an overview of the defence-industrial ecosystem in China.

CMI has also been associated with 'Made in China' innovation initiative that seeks international collaborations to advance global scientific engagements. The sensitivity and strategic objectives related to these technologies compel China to engage in cyber espionage that is also directed at private companies. The US National Counterintelligence and

Figure 5.3: China's Defence-Industrial Ecosystem

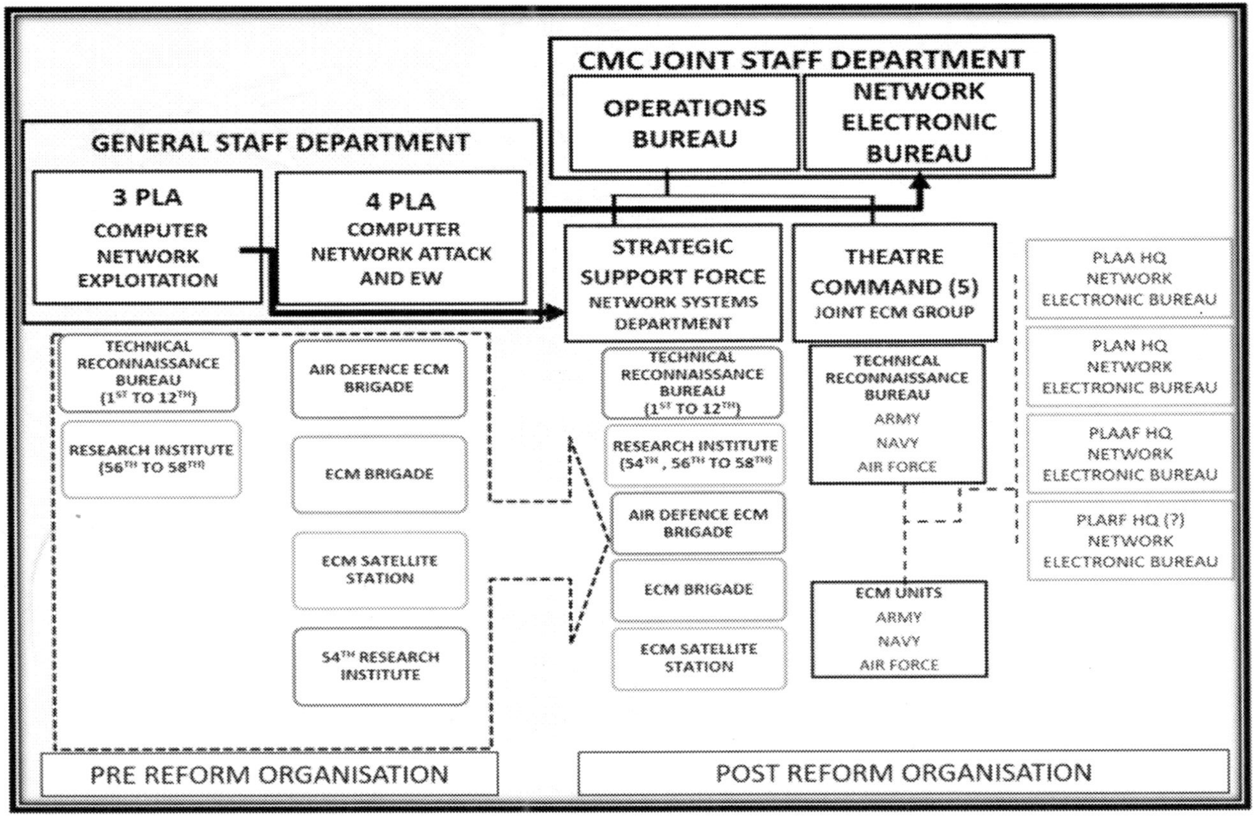

Source: Zhenqi, X. (2017, November 06). *China launches world-record swarm of 119 drones*. Retrieved May 07, 2020, from CGTN.com: https://news.cgtn.com/news/3d4d6a4e3049444e/share_p.html.

Security Centre report captures the areas where China has attempted cyber espionage. Refer to Table 5.3 for details.

Table 5.3: Cyber Espionage for Targeted Technologies

Industry	*Priority Sectors/Technologies*	
Energy/Alternative Energy	• Advanced pressurised water reactor & high-temperature, gas-cooled nuclear power station • Biofuels • Energy-efficient industries	• Oil, gas, and coalbed methane development, including fracking • Smart grids • Solar energy technology • Wind turbines
Biotechnology	• Advanced medical devices • Bio and chemical manufacturing • Biomaterials	• Biopharmaceuticals • Genetically modified organisms • Infectious disease treatment • New vaccines and drugs
Defence Technology	• Aerospace & Aeronautic Systems • Armaments	• Marine Systems • Radar • Optics
Environmental Protection	• Batteries • Energy-efficient appliances • Green building materials	• Hybrid and electric cars • Waste management • Water/air pollution control
High-End Manufacturing	• 3D printing • Advanced robotics • Aircraft engines • Aviation service sectors • Civilian aircraft • Electric motors • Foundational manufacturing equipment	• High-end computer and numerically controlled machines • High-performance composite and sealing materials • Integrated circuit assembly and manufacturing technology • Space infrastructure and exploration technology • Synthetic rubber
ICT	• Artificial intelligence • Big data analysis • Core electronics industries • E-commerce services • Foundational software products • High-end computer chips • Internet of Things	• Network equipment • Next-generation broadband & wireless communications • Quantum computing and communications • Rare-earth materials

Source: 2018. *Foreign Economic Espionage in Cyberspace.* Annual Report, Washington DC: The National Counterintelligence and Security Center, p.11.

Critical Technology

Science and Technology Vision. China's 13th Five Year plan had laid out the objectives to strengthen the development of strategic high-technologies in the deep sea, deep Earth, deep space, deep blue (i.e. information technology). The Made in China 2025 plan, published in 2015, stated Beijing's ambitions to dominate future technologies such as robotics and artificial intelligence. Now, China is currently at the end of its 13th Five-Year plan, and the 14th plan is likely to be unveiled by 2021. Despite the geopolitical headwinds with which China is confronted post-COVID-19 pandemic, China will continue its thrust to invest and improve its dual-use technology capability and work towards developing indigenous technologies. The stressed companies world-wide due to the pandemic may allow China an entry point to scout for technologies it needs badly to bridge its technological gap with the West. Some of the key areas of focus of the PLA have been discussed in this Chapter.

Quantum Technology. China, a late starter to the quantum technology race, is determined to lead the "second quantum revolution." Quantum cryptography and quantum communications are meant to create unhackable new networks, a prerequisite for the information warfare. Touted as the technology of the future; quantum technology is supposed to create innumerable possibilities through its matchless computing capabilities, with impactful applications that include cracking prevalent types of encryption. Chinese researchers claim to have accomplished notable progress in quantum radar, sensing, imaging, metrology and navigation, which enable greater precision and sensitivity. Quantum materials, such as topological insulators, can alter information processing and have innumerable applications to promote clean energy, and it can even be used as a pathway to quantum computing. China's advances in quantum science could alter the future military and strategic balance, perhaps even leapfrogging traditional US military-technological advantages. Quantum research is a long-term vision by China, and it has given it due impetus for its funding. Based on the funding pattern, China will spend more on R&D by 2030 than any other country.[82] Chinese gains in quantum technologies could "offset" key pillars of US military power as conceded by the January 2019 'Worldwide Threat Assessment' report submitted to the US Senate. China's shift in military, governmental, and commercial communications to quantum cryptography networks could frustrate US cyber intrusion and signals intelligence capabilities. It has prompted the US to authorise the National Quantum Initiative Act (NQI) to invest US$ 1.2 billion in quantum information science over five years. US Department of Energy has announced US$80 million in funding for quantum research. 2020 US DARPA budget of US$3.6 billion is devoted to critical technologies like AI and Quantum.[83] The disruptive potential of quantum sciences is evident to China as it may allow greater independence from space-based systems, and the realisation of quantum radar, imaging, and sensing would enhance situational awareness and targeting, potentially disrupting US investments in stealth technologies or deep-sea explorations. It enables PLA to alter the strategic balance and orchestrate a more nuanced non-contact warfare. Some of the technology demonstrators by China include:[84]

- **Long-distance Communication via Entanglement**. On 29 September 2017, a Chinese satellite known as Micius made possible an unhackable videoconference between Vienna and Beijing by delivering a data packet encoded in photons in a delicate quantum state which if intercepted would have destroyed the information and signalling the presence of a hacker. China's likely transition of its military telecommunications to the quantum networks make satellite surveillance difficult.
- **Quantum Radar**. A Chinese company, Electronic Technology Group Corporation, claims it has developed a quantum radar that threatens stealth technology.
- **Submarine Detection.** Chinese National Academy of Science has developed a quantum submarine detector based on an array of sensors known as SQUIDs (Superconducting Quantum Interference Device). It is capable of detecting and monitoring even the brainwaves of a mouse or the electron emissions from deep space hydrogen molecules. A fully functional SQUID array is estimated to have the ability to detect a submarine five or six kilometres, thus limiting the range and effectiveness of nuclear-powered attack submarines.

AI Applications. Close on the heels of the launch of China's ambition New Generation Artificial Intelligence Development Plan 2017, President Xi in his 19th Party Congress address in October 2017 urged the PLA to prepare for the intelligent warfare. A fact which has also been captured in 2019 China's NDWP. Fifteen of 31 provincial-level governments released their own AI plans by the end of March 2018, targeting gross industry output of US$429 billion by 2020, or nearly three times the national target of US$150 billion for the same period.[85] China aims to leverage AI technologies as a guiding concept for future Chinese military modernisation. The various use conceptualised include its application in intelligent and autonomous unmanned systems, AI-enabled analytics, wargaming and simulations, and intelligent support to command decision-making. At present, the PLA is funding a wide range of projects involving AI, and the Chinese defence industry and PLA research institutes are pursuing extensive research and development, in some cases partnering with private enterprises. For instance, to promote intelligent and strong command decision support mechanism, the PLA has embarked on Wargaming simulations through AI. It is aimed to prepare the PLA generals short on war experience to gain experience in handling the complex war control simulations.[86] Phantom1.0 and 'Prophet – Battle Sage' have been the AI war-gaming simulations conceptualised by China Institute of Command and Control (CICC) and the PLA NDU's Joint Operations Academy to enhance the professionalism of the officers and personnel for future warfare.[87] The PLA's initial thinking on AI in warfare has been influenced by the careful analysis of the US military initiatives. However, the approach may progressively diverge depending on the distinct dynamics of AI in impacting the character of warfare fundamentally.[88] The PLA's militarisation of AI will influence the trajectory of strategic stability and may intensify the aggression in the use of non-contact methods of warfare. Some likely AI capabilities are in Table 5.4.

Table 5.4: China's AI Technological Development

Technology	*Application*	*Current Capabilities*	*Key Companies/Institutes*
Machine Learning, which includes Deep Learning	Foundational for other areas of AI	Publication volume by Chinese researchers have grown, but the companies are more focused on commercial gains. China lags in producing chips optimised for machine learning.	National Development and Reform Commission tapped Baidu, Tsinghua and Beihang universities to lead online deep learning lab. Alibaba, Tencent, Baidu; Chips: Cambricon (used in Huawei phones), Horizon Robotics
Natural Language Processing (NLP)	Speech/voice recognition, translation, information extraction, query answering, sentiment analysis	China is leading in chatbots and is developing machine translation for Chinese to languages in BRI countries. iFlytek is a leader in speech recognition for spoken Chinese.	NLP is listed amongst the eight "key technologies" as part of China's AI strategy. Baidu, iFlytek; Microsoft Research Asia is a major player for machine translation and chatbots.
Computer Vision and Biometrics	Facial and image recognition, machine vision (analysing images for surveillance)	Numerous facial recognition companies, including start-ups, powering China's surveillance state. In turn, internet giants like Huawei are integrating this tech for Safe City systems.	Computer vision accounted for 35 per cent of China's AI market in 2017. SenseTime, Yitu, Megvii (Face++), Xloong, Zoloz, DeepGlint, Huawei

Technology	*Application*	*Current Capabilities*	*Key Companies/Institutes*
Robotics	Industrial robots, commercial service robots, and personal service robots	China's domestic sales of industrial robots have increased, but it is heavily dependent on the US, Europe, and Japan for robotics components. It has formed joint ventures with several EU-based firms.	Intelligent Manufacturing Plan, a supplement to Made in China 2025, called for extensive investment in industrial robots. Siasun, GSK CNC Equipment, Effort, Estun, Wuhan Huazhong AVs
Unmanned Autonomous Systems and Autonomous Vehicle (AV)	Passenger vehicles, delivery vehicles, UAVs like drones	It is still behind in developing algorithms that enable successful driving, besides computing platforms, sensors, and systems integration. Drones: DJI controls 70 per cent of the global consumer market	China legalised AV testing in 2017. Launched national strategy in December 2018 emphasising research funding and special test zones. AVs: Baidu, Pony. AI, SAIC; Drones: CETC, DJI

Source: U.S.-China Economic and Security Review Commission. (November 2019). *2019 Report to Congress of the U.S.-China Economic and Security Review Commission.* Washington DC: US Government Publishing Office. Retrieved May 08, 2020, from https://www.uscc.gov, p.234.

New and Advanced Material. Seven areas targeted as 'Strategic Emerging Industries' under Hu Jintao included energy-saving environmental industry, new information technology, biology, high-end equipment manufacturing, new energy, new materials, and new energy automobiles.[89] Developing capabilities in new materials has been part of sustained China's industrial policy. However, over the past decade, the emphasis has expanded from catching up in materials essential in dual-use applications like aerospace to a strategy of accelerating new materials used in disruptive technologies has been gaining prominence. This shift in focus has been accompanied by overseas acquisitions that improve Chinese firms' use of new materials in manufacturing and policy support for materials science research. The new material has usage across all the strategic industries. State funding for materials science has quadrupled since 2008, and Chinese universities have been patenting research aggressively.[90] China now accounts for 58 per cent of global patents in graphene—with most of its patenting activity occurring in the last seven years.[91] China dominates the global supply of numerous critical minerals and metals used in energy storage and other advanced technologies, creating supply risks for materials, components, and end products sourced from China. The Chinese government's approach to establishing dominance in global supply chains has been systematic, requiring coordination between industrial policy, domestic geological exploration, and commercial engagement in resource-rich developing countries, all supported by substantial state funding. According to the US Mineral Commodity Summaries 2019, there are thirteen strategic minerals over which China has more than 50 per cent holdings. These are aluminium (54 per cent), antimony (72 per cent), arsenic (69 per cent), bismuth (80 per cent of refinery production, rather than mine production), fluorspar (62 per cent), gallium (94 per cent), germanium (56 per cent, excluding US production), graphite (70 per cent), magnesium metal (89 per cent), rare earth (80 per cent), tellurium (62 per cent), tungsten (82 per cent), and vanadium (56 per cent). Chinese mining companies have also secured access to critical materials outside of China's borders, such as cobalt and lithium.[92] Thus, China has substantial control of the supply chains for materials used in lithium-ion battery production. It produces 77 per cent of refined cobalt globally and will impact powering requirements of future autonomous vehicles.[93] Besides harnessing energy, China's patenting in metamaterials is highly concentrated in areas with dual-use potential, like antennae, suggesting a research focus on potential military advances. Forty-one per cent of Chinese metamaterials patents through 2017 are in antennae.[94] A brief application of various new materials is given in Table 5.5.

Table 5.5: An Overview of Application of New Material by China

New Material and Category	*Applications*
Metamaterials: Artificial composites with electromagnetic properties that do not occur in natural materials, such as the ability to absorb rather than reflect light or view microscopic phenomena with fidelity not possible in natural lens.	China's stealth aircraft uses it to enhance its antennas and jamming capabilities. China is also reportedly using metamaterials to experiment how its non-stealth fighters appear on radar. Non-military uses of metamaterials may someday include super-lenses to observe viruses or DNA.
Nanomaterials: Materials with an external dimension or internal structure less than 100 nanometres. Generally refined from naturally occurring materials. Well-known examples include graphene and carbon nanotubes.	Current applications include filtration, textiles, cosmetics, environmental protection, and food packaging. Potential applications under development - Graphene lens, a single atomic layer of carbon atoms useful in electronic applications due to its high conductivity, touchscreens or other optical applications due to its transparency. Small amounts of graphene oxide (graphene crystals), mixed into many materials to increase strength or absorption.
Electrical Materials: Organic semi-conductors, polymer-based electronics, and materials used in quantum computation, high-density energy storage, and low power displays.	Fabrication of quantum computers and other advances in electronic computing can break through the storage and speed limitations of silicon semi-conductors. Researchers are pursuing manipulation of carbon nanotubes, exploitation of flaws in conventional semiconductors, or materials that send

New Material and Category	*Applications*
	signals via trapped ions or manipulation of light particles (photonics).
Biomaterials: Any material engineered to interact with a living system; either for a therapeutic function (e.g., tissue regeneration, treating an illness), or to monitor a system and inform diagnosis.	For treatment, application of nanomaterials for transplant and replacement surgery has enabled 3D printing of implants to integrate with the body's systems. Highly conductive biomaterials have been used to reconnect severed nerves. For diagnosis, biosensors like neural implants can gather medical data to tailor treatment to individual patients or model medical experiments computationally with AI.

Source: U.S.-China Economic and Security Review Commission. (November 2019). *2019 Report to Congress of the U.S.-China Economic and Security Review Commission.* Washington DC: US Government Publishing Office. Retrieved May 08, 2020, from https://www.uscc.gov,p.226.

China's Growing Influence in International Standards Setting. In January 2018, China published a white paper aimed at coordinating the AI standards. The white paper was an outcome of 30 institutions and companies' inputs which was taken by Electronic Standardisation Institute, a standards-making body under the Ministry of Industry and Information Technology. The intent is very clear- for global dominance to happen, China must influence global standards-setting bodies in favour of Chinese firms. China's techno-nationalist strategy revised China's Standardisation Law in 2018 to strengthen the role of Chinese standards in international bodies and promote Chinese standards through BRI.[95] Establishing influence in the global standards-making process is central to China's plans to become a world leader in technology. Expanding participation in international standards-making bodies like the Institute of Electrical and Electronics Engineers and International Standards Organisation is with a purpose to wield influence while providing an elevated status to Chinese companies in developing foundational technologies in AI subdomains such as the Internet of Things and 5G. China looks at gaining the leadership positions within the International Telecommunication Union and other bodies focused on connected technologies. The setting of international norms for the application of sensitive technologies and control their proliferation appears to be the game-changer for China. Creating one globe two systems will be the ultimate contest which China has been preparing for and has incorporated CMI as the multipurpose vehicle to navigate the legal labyrinth laid by the US and its allies.

Conclusion

The US caught in its campaign in West Asia, and Afghanistan gave China the critical window to fast pace it's economy. The windfall posts the subprime crisis in 2008 gave China the confidence and muscle to seek coalition partners through its ambitious BRI project under Xi Jinping. China had been bracing with the strategic friction since the time the US had pitched for rebalancing for Asia under Obama. The 2018 US NDS accusing China of predatory economic policy and declaring it as a strategic competitor has vitiated the geo-economic environment. The competitive strategy put into action by President Trump in the form of trade-tariff-technology-currency wars has disrupted global supply chains. COVID-19 originating from China has thrown up multiple challenges at it as the world is grappling with the economic recession. At the time of global concern, both US and China are engaged in a bitter influence operation. The US having lost more than a one hundred thirty thousand civilians to COVID-19 by July 2020, will surely make the Presidential campaign more animated and probably anti-China. More war of words and promises for action against China will redraw the mechanism of competitive strategy. How far the non-contact warfare measures will be put to use will be the test of time and tactics. China having created leverages over its four decades will have to play the game to its gallery at home and abroad.

Though, amidst the chaos due to COVID-19 pandemic, China finds itself securely perched at the home front having braved the initial brunt of contagion attack. However, the external environment seems hostile to China for hiding information about the epidemic outbreak. Hence, it is focussed to advance its agenda of agile governance, influence radiation and image preservation. Situational awareness measures and demonstration of military muscle by both the US and China in the South China Sea is a pointer to the gathering of the storm. As US-China military rivalry continues to intensify, the improvements in the PLA's strategic situational awareness capabilities may be aiming to bring some form of strategic stability. Yet, it may also trigger new risks and challenges. For example, the improved strategic early warning could decrease Chinese anxieties about the risks of a "false negative" and enable more time for decision-making in a crisis in ways that mitigate the risks of accidental escalation. However, the possession of hypersonic may affect decision making. At a time when the world is coping with the threat of health and hunger, the military confrontation is ruled out in the lethal kinetic domain.

However, the non-kinetic non-lethal domain will be keenly contested and may have ramifications for world geopolitical and geo-economic realignment.

The likely Chinese strategy of managing this crisis may be akin to 'influence-beachhead' by China into other countries strategic interests. Its global supply chain and CMI will play a crucial role in its national security and economic competitiveness. The PLA generals having created war-gaming simulations based on AI will like to practice the war-control mechanism. They will do well to keep the health and economic issues within the political realm and avoid the crisis from being spiralling out. As the Chinese saying goes, "*when the wind changes direction, there are those who build walls and those who build windmills.*" Whatever be the outcome of the crisis, India needs to firewall its security concerns.

NOTES

1 UNCTAD. (2020, March 30). *UN calls for $2.5 trillion coronavirus crisis package for developing countries*. Retrieved from https://unctad.org/en/pages/newsdetails.aspx?OriginalVersionID=2315.

2 For scenario refer to my article - Verma, V. (2020, April). *COVID-19 Pandemic and Strategic Implications for China: Building Walls or Wind Mills*. Retrieved from Strategic Perspective, USI of India, New Delhi: https://usiofindia.org/publication/cs3-strategic-perspectives/covid-19-pandemic-and-strategic-implications-for-china-building-walls-or-wind-mills/.

3 Verma, Brigadier Vivek. COVID-19 Pandemic and Strategic Implications for China, USI of India, May 2020. https://usiofindia.org/publication/cs3-strategic-perspectives/covid-19-pandemic-and-strategic-implications-for-china-building-walls-or-wind-mills/.

4 US National Information Council. (November 2008). *Global Trends 2025: A Transformed World*. Washington DC: US Government Printing Office.

5 In the book, 'Destined for War', Professor Graham Allison explains a deadly pattern of structural stress that results when a rising power challenges a ruling one. He draws the inspiration from Thucidyde, the famous Greek historian who in 'The History of the Peloponnesian War' wrote: "What made war inevitable was the growth of Athenian power (rising power) and the fear which this caused in Sparta (the dominant power)."

6 Rand Waltzman, "The Weaponization of the Information Environment," American Foreign Policy Council Defense Technology Program Brief, September 2015.

7 Janis Berzin, Russia New Generation Warfare in Ukraine, National Defence Academy of Latvia, April 2014, p.5..

8 Feng, Guo. (September 1998). "Future Trends in Military." In *Chinese Views of Future Warfare*, by Michael Pillsbury, 85-94. Washington DC: National Defense University Press.

9 Academy of Military Sciences. (2013). *The Science of Military Strategy*. Edited by Sun Zhaoli. Beijing : Military Science Press, p. 191.

10 Lindsay, Jon R. "The Impact of China on Cybersecurity." *International Security*, Vol. 39, No. 3, Winter 2014/15, pp. 7–47.

11 Jinghua, L. (2019, April 01). *What Are China's Cyber Capabilities and Intentions?* Retrieved May 09, 2020, from carnegieendowment.org: https://carnegieendowment.org/2019/04/01/what-are-china-s-cyber-capabilities-and-intentions-pub-78734.

12 Global Times. (2019, August 19). *China to shore up cybersecurity in the upcoming 5G era*. Retrieved January 10, 2020, from http://www.globaltimes.cn/content/1161907.shtml.

13 "Xi Jinping Leads Internet Security Group," Xinhua news agency, February 27, 2014, http://news.xinhuanet.com/english/china/2014-02/27/c_133148273.htm.

14 Wortzel, L.M. (March 2014). *The Chinese People's Liberation Army and Information Warfare*. Carlisle Barracks: United States Army War College Press. Retrieved from http://www.StrategicStudiesInstitute.army.mil/, p.25.

15 Carr, J. (2010). *Inside Cyberwarfare*. Sebastopol: O'Reilly Media, p.4.

16 2018. *Foreign Economic Espionage in Cyberspace*. Annual Report, Washington DC: The National Counterintelligence and Security Center, p.11.

17 EternalBlue is a cyberattack exploit developed by the US National Security Agency. It was leaked by the Shadow Brokers hacker group on April 14, 2017, one month after Microsoft released patches for the vulnerability. EternalBlue exploits a vulnerability in Microsoft's implementation of the Server Message Block (SMB) protocol. The exploit was also reported to have been used since March 2016 by the Chinese hacking group Buckeye (APT3)

18 Carr, Jeffrey. (2010). *Inside Cyberwarfare*. Sebastopol: O'Reilly Media, p.2.

19 Qu, S.D. (2020, April 07). *Hackers target Chinese government agencies, diplomatic missions and WHO amid pandemic*. Retrieved from South China Morning Post: https://www.scmp.com/tech/policy/article/3078808/hackers-target-chinese-government-agencies-diplomatic-missions-amid.

20 Bertrand, N. (2020, April 16). *China-linked 'Electric Panda' hackers seek U.S. targets, intel agency warns*. Retrieved from Politico: https://www.politico.com/news/2020/04/16/china-electric-panda-hackers-seek-us-targets-191220.

21 Panda, A. (2018, December 06). *North Korea, US 'Left of Launch' Cyber Capabilities, and Deterrence,*. Retrieved January 10, 2020, from The Diplomat Online: https://thediplomat.com/2018/12/north-korea-us-left-of-launch-cyber-capabilities-and-deterrence/.

22 Financial Times. (2019, November 04). *US and Taiwan host security exercise to boost cyber defence*. Retrieved January 10, 2020, from Financial Times: https://www.ft.com/content/7d6c78cc-fec8-11e9-b7bc-f3fa4e77dd47.

23 Dotson, John. (2019). "Military-Civil Fusion and Electromagnetic Spectrum Management in the PLA." *The Jamestown Foundation*. 08 October. Accessed January 05, 2020. https://jamestown.org/program/military-civil-fusion-and-electromagnetic-spectrum-management-in-the-pla/.

24 Shan Linfeng, Jin Jiacai, Zhang Ke. *Dianzi Duikang Zhisheng Jili* ("The Winning Mechanism of Electronic Countermeasures"), (Beijing: National Defense Industry Press, 2018), pp.15, 26.

25 Ibid.

26 Yang, Zi. (2019). *PLA Stratagems for Establishing Wartime Electromagnetic Dominance: An Analysis of "The Winning Mechanisms of Electronic Countermeasures."* 01 February. Accessed January 09, 2020. https://jamestown.org/program/pla-stratagems-for-

establishing-wartime-electromagnetic-dominance-an-analysis-of-the-winning-mechanisms-of-electronic-countermeasures/.

27 Putten, S.V. (September 2015). *US Deterrence against Chinese Cyber Espionage.* Clingendael. Netherlands Institute of International Relations.

28 Gertz, B. (2019, January 24). *China, Russia Building Super-EMP Bombs for 'Blackout Warfare'.* Retrieved from Freebeacon: https://freebeacon.com/national-security/china-russia-building-super-emp-bombs-for-blackout-warfare/.

29 Pomerleau, M. (2017, March 22). *Breaking down China's electronic warfare tactics.* Retrieved from https://www.c4isrnet.com/c2-comms/2017/03/22/breaking-down-chinas-electronic-warfare-tactics/.

30 Stilgherrian. (2019, July 28). *China making 'quite significant' strides in supercomputing: Lowy Institute.* Retrieved from ZDNet: https://www.zdnet.com/article/china-making-quite-significant-strides-in-supercomputing-lowy-institute/.

31 Cooper, S. (2020, April 30). *United Front groups in Canada helped Beijing stockpile coronavirus safety supplies.* Retrieved July 11, 2020, from Global News: https://globalnews.ca/news/6858818/coronavirus-china-united-front-canada-protective-equipment-shortage/.

32 United Nations Secretary-General. (2020, April 14). *Statement by the Secretary-General on the World Health Organization.* Retrieved from https://www.un.org/sg/en/content/sg/statement/2020-04-14/statement-the-secretary-general-the-world-health-organization.

33 Bowe, A. (24 August 2018). *China's Overseas United Front Work.* Washington DC: US-China Economic and Security Review Commission, p.22.

34 Ibid.

35 Nick McKenzie, Grace Tobin and Paul Sakkal. *The Moment a Chinese Spy Decided to Defect to Australia.* November 23, 2019. https://www.theage.com.au/national/the-moment-a-chinese-spy-decided-to-defect-to-australia-20191122-p53d0x.html (accessed December 09, 2019).

36 Cole, J. M. (2017, September 26). *China Seeks Vicious Circle of Violence through United Front Activities in Taiwan.* Retrieved January 10, 2020, from Taiwan Sentinel: https://sentinel.tw/china-violence-ufw-tw/.

37 Wu, H. (2020, Februaruy 19). *China revokes three Wall Street Journal reporters' credentials.* Retrieved from Reuters: https://www.reuters.com/article/us-usa-china-media-response-idUSKBN20D0QU.

38 Albert, E. (2018, February 09). *China's Big Bet on Soft Power.* Retrieved June 28, 2020, from Council on the Foreign Affairs: https://www.cfr.org/backgrounder/chinas-big-bet-soft-power.

39 Ibid.

40 *Brief report on Chinese overseas students and international students in China 2017* (2018, April 01). Retrieved June 28, 2020, from moe.gov.cn: http://en.moe.gov.cn/documents/reports/201901/t20190115_367019.html.

41 Albert, E. (2018, February 09). *China's Big Bet on Soft Power,* op.cit.

42 Epoch Times. (2018, June 28). *A translation from the Chinese of a new book, How the Specter of Communism Is Ruling Our World, by the editorial team of the Nine Commentaries on the Communist Party.* Retrieved June 28, 2020, from https://www.theepochtimes.com/chapter-eighteen-the-chinese-communist-partys-global-ambitions-part-ii_2822429.html.

43 Ibid.

44 Shuo, Z. (2019, December 15). *Revised code of ethics for journalists released.* Retrieved June 28, 2020, from ChinaDaily.com.cn: https://global.chinadaily.com.cn/a/201912/16/WS5df6ed76a310cf3e3557e5c6.html.

45 Global Entertainment & Media Outlook 2016-2020. (2016). *China challenges the US for global box office.* Retrieved June 28, 2020, from pwc.com: https://www.pwc.com/gx/en/entertainment-media/pdf/outlook-cinema-article-2016.pdf.

46 Reuters. (2020, May 04). *Exclusive: Internal Chinese report warns Beijing faces Tiananmen-like global backlash over virus.* Retrieved May 05, 2020, from https://www.reuters.com/article/us-health-coronavirus-china-sentiment-ex/exclusive-internal-chinese-report-warns-beijing-faces-tiananmen-like-global-backlash-over-virus-idUSKBN22G19C.

47 Kania, E.B. (2019, Spring). *China's Strategic Situational Awareness Capabilities.* Retrieved April 20, 2020, from Ontheradar.CSIS.Org: https://ontheradar.csis.org/issue-briefs/china-situational-awareness/, p.2.

48 Ibid.

49 Global Times. (2018, June 18). *China can use quantum radar technology to monitor high-speed aircraft from space.* Retrieved from http://military.china.com/zxjq/11139042/20180618/32546024.html.

50 Xinhua. (2018, November 28). *China develops AI radar for underground space detection in cities.* Retrieved May 05 2020, from Xinhuanet: http://www.xinhuanet.com/english/2018-11/28/c_137637800.htm.

51 Lei, Z. (2018, November 10). *Flying radar' is first early-warning drone.* Retrieved May 05, 2020, from China Daily: http://www.chinadaily.com.cn/a/201811/10/WS5be6173ba310eff303287c2c.html.

52 Zhen, L. (2018, October 31). *Chinese solar-powered drone Morning Star spreads its wings in successful test flight.* Retrieved May 05, 2020, from South China Morning Post: https://www.scmp.com/news/china/military/article/2171081/chinese-solar-powered-drone-spreads-its-wings-successful-test.

53 Weston, Phoebe. (2018). *US subs would be sitting ducks for new Chinese 'Death Star' laser satellite that will be able spot them 1,600 ft below the surface.* 01 October. Accessed December 18, 2019. https://www.dailymail.co.uk/sciencetech/article-6226683/Chinas-new-spy-satellite-use-LASERS-light-ocean.html.

54 Cooper, C.A. (2018, February 15). *PLA Military Modernization: Drivers, Force Restructuring, and Implications.* Retrieved June 28, 2020, from RAND: https://www.rand.org/content/dam/rand/pubs/testimonies/CT400/CT488/RAND_CT488.pdf.

55 Hartnett, A.A. (February 2016). *Managing Conflict: Examining Recent PLA Writings on Escalation Control.* Arlington, VA: Centre for Naval Analyses (CAN) China Studies, p.10.

56 Ibid, p.7.

57 Ibid, pp.10-11.

58 Timothy R. Heath, K.G. (2016). *The PLA and China's Rejuvination.* Santa Monica, California: RAND Corporation, pp.23-24.

59 Ibid.

60 Lee, Y.N. (2019, August 27). *Philippine President Duterte says he'll stand up to China – he might not deliver.* Retrieved May 06, 2020, from CNBC: https://www.cnbc.com/2019/08/28/philippines-duterte-in-china-meets-xi-jinping-to-talk-south-china-sea.html.

61 Tomacruz, S. (2020, April 20). *Del Rosario urges Duterte gov't: Protest new Chinese districts in South China Sea.* Retrieved Jul 11, 2020, from Rappler: https://www.rappler.com/

nation/258483-del-rosario-urges-duterte-government-protest-new-districts-south-china-sea.

62 Xiaoli, L. (2009). *Military Response to Significant Sudden Incidents and Crises: Research on Military Operations Other than War.* Beijing: National Defense University Press, p.7.

63 Academy of Military Sciences. (2013). *The Science of Military Strategy.* (S. Zhaoli, Ed.) Beijing, China: Military Science Press, p.113.

64 Jingfang, Z.Z. (2013). *On Control and Management of Military Crises.* Beijing: China Military Science, p.69 .

65 Ibid.

66 Alison A. Hoffman, op.cit. p.53.

67 Ibid.

68 Kuo, L. (2020, March 27). *Xi Jinping calls on Trump to improve US-China relations amid Covid-19 crisis.* Retrieved May 06 2020, from The Guardian: https://www.theguardian.com/world/2020/mar/27/china-prepares-to-seal-itself-off-from-the-world-to-stem-imported-coronavirus-cases.

69 *President Xi's article on global solidarity, cooperation to fight COVID-19 to be published.* (2020, April 16). Retrieved from CGTN: https://news.cgtn.com/news/2020-04-15/Xi-Jinping-calls-for-global-solidarity-to-fight-COVID-19-PI7uEw6zEQ/index.html.

70 CGTN. (2020, March 21). *China announces to help 82 countries fight COVID-19.* Retrieved from CGTN: https://news.cgtn.com/news/2020-03-20/China-announces-to-help-82-countries-fight-COVID-19-P1hcQcQKe4/index.html.

71 Talcott, S. (2020, April 13). *CNN Basically Published A Press Release From The Chinese Military.* Retrieved May 06, 2020, from Daily Caller: https://dailycaller.com/2020/04/13/cnn-press-release-chinese-military-pla-coronavirus/.

72 Chellaney, B. (2020, June 10). *China risks imperial overstretch with post-pandemic aggression.* Retrieved June 28, 2020, from Nikkei Asian Review: https://asia.nikkei.com/Opinion/China-risks-imperial-overstretch-with-post-pandemic-aggression.

73 Blasko, D.J. (January 2017). Chapter 10: China's Evolving Approach to Strategic Deterrence. In J. McReynolds, *China's Military Strategy* (pp. 335-355). Washington DC: The Jamestown Foundation, p.335.

74 Academy of Military Sciences. (2013). *The Science of Military Strategy.* (S. Zhaoli, Ed.) Beijing, China: Military Science Press, p.22.

75 Cordesman, A.H. (August 2016). *China Military Organisation and Reform.* Centre for Strategic International Studies.

76 Kathleen H. Hicks, Joseph Federici and Connor Akiyama. "China in the grey zone." http://www.hybridcoe.fi/. The European Centre of Excellence for Countering Hybrid Threats. April 2019. https://www.hybridcoe.fi/wp-content/uploads/2019/09/Strategic-Analysis-4_2019_rgb.pdf (accessed December 30, 2019).

77 Lu, Zhenhua. *China accused of entering 'grey zone' between war and peace to assert control in disputed waters.* June 28, 2019. https://www.scmp.com/news/china/military/article/3016532/china-accused-entering-grey-zone-between-war-and-peace-assert (accessed December 30, 2019).

78 Zhihao, Z. (2020, April 30). *Chinese military opposes more foreign naval presence in S China Sea.* Retrieved May 06, 2020, from chinadaily.com.cn: https://www.chinadaily.com.cn/a/202004/30/WS5eaab6dca310a8b241153059.html.

79 Christopher K. Johnson, S.K. (17 October 2017). *Xi's Signature Governance Innovation:*

The Rise of Leading Small Groups. Center for Strategic and International Studies. Retrieved May 07, 2020, from https://www.csis.org/analysis/xis-signature-governance-innovation-rise-leading-small-groups.

80 Zhenqi, X. (2017, November 06). *China launches world-record swarm of 119 drones*. Retrieved May 07, 2020, from CGTN.com: https://news.cgtn.com/news/3d4d6a4e3049444e/share_p.html.

81 C4ADS. (2019). *Open Arms: Evaluating Global Exposure to China's Defence Industrial Base*. Washington DC: www.c4ads.org. Retrieved May 07, 2020, from https://static1.squarespace.com/static/566ef8b4d8af107232d5358a/t/5d95fb48a0bfc672d825e346/1570110297719/Open+Arms.pdf.

82 Smith-Goodson, P. (2019, October 10). *Quantum USA Vs. Quantum China: The World's Most Important Technology Race*. Retrieved May 08, 2020, from Forbes: https://www.forbes.com/sites/moorinsights/2019/10/10/quantum-usa-vs-quantum-china-the-worlds-most-important-technology-race/#17c896d272de.

83 Ibid.

84 Ibid.

85 Ibid.

86 Kania, E. (2019, April 09). *Learning Without Fighting: New Developments in PLA Artificial Intelligence War-Gaming*. Retrieved May 08, 2020, from The Jamestown Foundation: https://jamestown.org/program/learning-without-fighting-new-developments-in-pla-artificial-intelligence-war-gaming/.

87 Ibid.

88 Kania, E.B. (2017, November). *Battlefield Singularity: Artificial Intelligence, Military Revolution, and China's Future Military Power.* Retrieved May 08, 2020, from Centre For New American Security: https://s3.amazonaws.com/files.cnas.org/documents/Battlefield-Singularity-November-2017.pdf?mtime=20171129235805.

89 U.S.-China Economic and Security Review Commission. (November 2019). *2019 Report to Congress of the U.S.-China Economic and Security Review Commission*. Washington DC: US Government Publishing Office. Retrieved May 08, 2020, from https://www.uscc.gov, pp.221-224.

90 O'Meara, S. (2019, March 20). *Materials Science Is Helping to Transform China into a High-tech Economy.* Retrieved May 09, 2020, from Nature: https://www.nature.com/articles/d41586-019-00885-5.

91 Cinker, Z. (22 May 2019). What Is Graphene : Graphene on. *American Graphene Summit :Graphene on Capitol Hill*. Washington, DC: National Graphene Association and Nixene Journal.

92 Gold, S.P. (2018, February 11). *There's a Global Race to Control Batteries—and China Is Winning*. Retrieved from Wall Street Journal: https://www.wsj.com/articles/theres-a-global-race-to-control-batteriesand-china-is-winning-1518374815.

93 Thomas, D.M. (2019, April 02). *China is Building the Batteries of the Future*. Retrieved May 09, 2020, from Foreign Policy: https://foreignpolicy.com/2019/04/02/china-is-building-the-batteries-of-the-future-tesla-li-ion/.

94 U.S.-China Economic and Security Review Commission. (November 2019). *2019 Report to Congress of the U.S.-China Economic and Security Review Commission*. Washington DC: US Government Publishing Office. Retrieved May 08, 2020, from https://www.uscc.gov, p.226.

95 Ibid, p.232.

6

Implications for India and Recommendations

"Deliberations should not be unduly delayed once an opportunity for action arises."

– Chanakya in '*The Arthashastra*'

"Victory no longer rests on the ability to inflict massive destruction but on the ability to wrestle popular support from one's opponent."

– General MM Naravane, Indian Chief of Army Staff

TRADITIONAL AND NON-TRADITIONAL SECURITY PARADIGM

Shifting Security Landscape

Non-contact warfare has transformed the security landscape. The force application co-relation has altered the way the countries look to settle political disputes and conflicts. Despite developments in the fields of kinetic lethal systems to fulfil Clausewitz belief on the use of violence, the changing character of warfare has made the professionals ponder on the threshold of violence and use of force. The dynamics get altered while dealing with an adversary with near force parity and nuclear-armed; a place where India finds itself. The unsettled active borders across two fronts and proxy war keeps Indian Armed Forces embroiled in the traditional domain of land, air and seas. The shifting security landscape has added new arena of cyber and space guided by new generation technologies of quantum, AI and 5G. The dilemma for the Indian security planners persists of preparing for the two and half front war scenarios as they look at 'China-Pakistan Collusivity' scenarios besides the internal security situation posed by the non-state actors. Looking from the traditional security situation, this may be the most feasible option. However, the non-contact warfare scenario throws up new challenges which are emanating more in the non-traditional security arena – areas where the armed forces have no jurisdiction or little participation as yet.

Non-contact warfare aims at subverting the politico-eco-social systems. It targets the edifices of national power like finance, industries, commerce, critical technologies, critical resources for new materials, energy grids, transportation, information highway, influence engine within a country like media, academia, political entities, NGOs and societal peace. The armed forces in countries like China, Iran and Pakistan have invested and developed their sub-threshold capabilities as part of their national security strategy to engage their adversaries in a grey-zone conflict or proxy war. The intent is clear – to keep the adversary engaged in an endless battle at the sub-threshold level and prevent the conflict from spiralling out. The operational environment created by them aims at stability at the strategic level while practising continued resistance and offence at the operational and tactical level. Lieutenant General Raj Shukla, Army Commander, Indian Army Training Command, during a seminar on "Changing Characteristics of Land Warfare" conducted by CLAWS (Indian Army think-tank) on 04 March 2020 succinctly explained how the constraining legal factor that distinguishes war and peace is leveraged by the states and non-state actors to wage wars in virgin terrain as they avoid the strength of the adversary's armed forces. They have emerged as the consummate practitioners in the sub-threshold space. So even if the western patterned armed forces, like the Indian Armed Forces, are seemingly at peace, the adversary's wages total war using its full national power and influence at its disposal. Predominantly, the arena chosen are non-kinetic, non-traditional and non-military and the method chosen can vary from public opinion warfare, lawfare, economic measures, psychological warfare, gaining persistent presence within the governance system and critical infrastructure space. They aim to destabilise the adversary, malign its image and hurt the credibility of the government of the day by primarily targeting at the societal peace and economic progress. However, they have invested in building up their strategic capability in Kinetic lethal long-range systems as a means of deterrence.

India's Core Interest and New Sovereign Requirements

In the absence of National Security Strategy, in November 2018, India for the first time released a strategy paper drafted by the NITI Aayog named "Strategy for New India @ 75". The strategy paper serves as a goal documents for the various ministries when India turns 75 in 2022. The goal identified has been to become a US $ 4 trillion economy by 2023 and raise the investment in 11 infrastructure sectors to 36 per cent of GDP.[1] Inclusive rapid growth, balanced development across all regions, states and sectors and bridging the gap between public and private sector performance are the essential themes identified in the paper to meet the aspirational goals. The strategy paper, while being silent on the security front, has made critical recommendations which have security ramifications. The paper identifies areas like technological innovation and essential governance reforms driven by AI to steer Industry 4.0. It has categorically listed the constraints in driving digital connectivity. The two issues highlighted are:[2]

- Only 10 per cent of the Indian internet users are digitally literate.
- Cybersecurity is inadequate to prevent denial of services attack and puts government, banks, and businesses to grave risks.

Industry 4.0 itself has created an operating environment where the blurring of boundaries is altering the state and non-state group participation. The collapse of the barrier between digital and physical, synthetic and organic is taking place. The dual-use technology is merging the civil-military application, and the advancement in biotechnology, neuro-science and life-sciences are altering the doctrinal precepts. The technologies like AI, machine augmented heroes, laser weapon battles in cyber and space, which were so far part of the fiction have started finding their ways in government white paper and strategy formulations. Countries like the US, China and France have articulated their AI strategy and have linked it to the societal benefits and security. In fact, China has gone ahead for "intelligentisation" of their platforms and systems using the combination of so-called private companies like Baidu, Alibaba and Tencent and deploying supercomputers and high-performance semiconductor chips and algorithm. Social benefits from AI deployment has been the Chinese mantra. However, the trajectory of development in lethal autonomous system, creation of algorithmically-driven social-media funnels based on data aggregation and diversion from the world says a different story. It can use the data to create a culturally enclosed echo-chambers as part of their influence platforms to radiate its world view. India, so far, has only been able to devise a working paper under NITI Aayog, "National Strategy for Artificial Intelligence #AIforAll" and yet to come out with an AI strategy. However, Indian Army has identified "AI, BlockChain, Quantum Computing and 5G military applications" to drive strategic-military domain according to Indian Chief of Army Staff in his interview to the 'Force' magazine in February 2020.

It is quite evident that the balance of power syndrome is still guiding the global economy. Strategic autonomy, as part of India's foreign policy, demands that the country should be capable of defending itself. The 'Science Technology Vision 2035' published by the Department of Science and Technology (DST) in 2015 laments in its report that India has paid the price for its strategic autonomy by encountering global technology denial regimes. The technology sovereignty assumes importance as the future game, according to the paper, will now be played by the MNC and patent offices and the policies or strategies formulated will guide the contest. "The tools and tactics of how we fight have always evolved along with technology. We are poised to continue this trend.[3] The new-age technologies have transcended borders and are now embedded within our systems. According to the US Homeland Security Presidential Directive 7 (HSPD 7), there are 18 sectors in the critical infrastructures of the US that are targets of cyber-attack. To take the development down to the economically weaker sections and to improve its governance, India has embraced technology in a big way. While it has been able to alleviate 271 million people out of the poverty over the last decade, but 364 million Indians continue to experience acute deprivations in health, nutrition, schooling and sanitation.[4] While the government of India is keen to push the development agenda, the security landscape necessitates that the society and economy should be insulated from the shocks of threats of war across traditional domains and denial and disruption across the non-traditional domain. What India needs is a whole-of-a-nation approach as alluded by General MM Naravane, Indian Chief of Army Staff.[5] The security threats posed in cyber, space and technological domains makes it imperative to declare them as the new sovereign requirement of the nation.

National Security and Managing Strategic Uncertainties

The national security of the nation is the cumulative sum of its traditional and non-traditional security capabilities. The geo-political-economic issues are required to be tackled through the PIMED (political, intelligence, military, economic and diplomacy) collaborative approach. A nation needs to have a strategic direction and national security doctrine so that all organs within the government can then work towards the attainment of the goals. The world is still wedded to the western concept of strategy where the balance of power has a lot of relevance when discussing diplomacy. The harnessing of hard power with soft power only adds to the great power charm by making it smarter and sharper. The trajectory of the national narrative is dependent on the ability to have a correct strategic picture, and hence, strategic situational awareness needs special attention. A government armed with a clear picture of a problem is better equipped to formulate policy or undertake policy intervention, especially in an area where the national interests are likely to get compromised. The country's pedigree of development and social harmony is reflected in its agile governance and is dependent on its ability to provide effective justice through reasonable law and order apparatus. Technological progress and sound industrial bases provide economic sustainability and further contribute to societal harmony. The world engaged in an endless conflict triggered by the competition is directly affecting the societal well-being and political structures. Range of options provided by the electronic and media platforms is influencing the peace and risk outcomes. Without building traditional and non-traditional capabilities, it is challenging to fortify national security. Hence, the need for a whole-of-a-government approach is essential while devising national security. Development rides on the back of security. Figure 6.1 brings out the requirements for evolving cogent national security to develop a nation and ensure regional stability.

Non-traditional threats like pandemics, war by other means like proxy wars, social engineering, and protests are destabilising the society. Biosecurity, oft relegated topic amidst economic acceleration, has suddenly emerged to the forefront courtesy COVID-19 pandemic. The practitioners of denial and disruptions like the US, Russia and China are themselves mired by the contagion catastrophe. The enormity of devastation and destabilisation has added to the near-term threat to humanity and will test the governance models of each country. However, unabated Sino-US competitive strategy across influence domain, in trade and war and

Figure 6.1: Drivers for National Security and Regional Stability

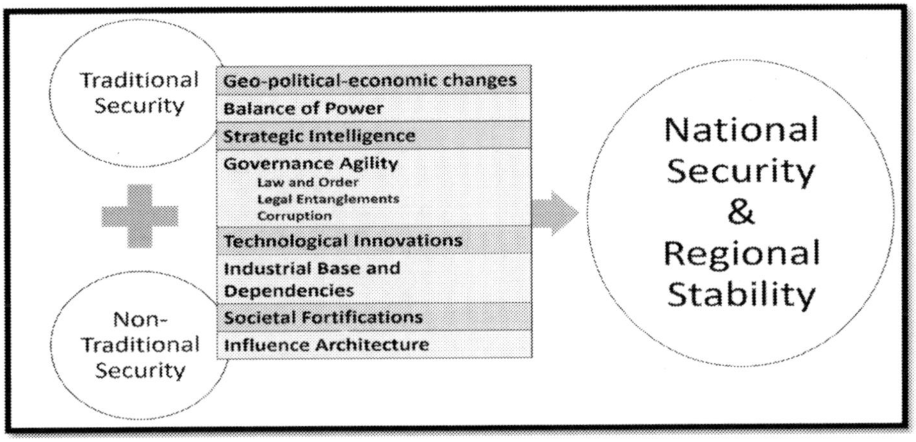

aggression in the South China Sea will continue to add to the long term geo-political-economic-social distress and strategic uncertainties. In an era of blurring boundaries between war and peace and civil and military, the government need to seek answers to the following questions to manage the strategic uncertainties:

- What can cause strategic destabilisation of the country?
- How should India organise to deal with threats and challenges of the future?
- When our adversaries have adopted a sub-threshold doctrine for employment of armed forces in subverting and disrupting our critical systems in the new domain of cyber, space and technology, can Indian Armed Forces continue to operate within the confines of traditional security domains?
- How should India organise its security and defence architecture?

FACTORS THAT CAN CAUSE STRATEGIC DESTABILISATION

Strategic stability is the product of the ability to read the situational dynamics and capability to react with force or deter the adversary of the consequences once the core interests get breached. The shift in the security paradigm and the behaviour of the main adversary have a profound impact on the security profiling of a country and its capability building. While in Chapter 1, the changing character of war has captured the attributes;

however, it is prudent to put in perspective the security paradigm as it affects India.

Security Trends

The new distribution of security responsibility between individuals, companies and institutions of governance has been defining the new approach to international security. Force parity plays a crucial role in the application of force. Examining the game being played by the US and China and the US and Russia, it emerges that the thrust is to increase the strategic space of contest. The reliance is on a multi-domain approach to engage the adversary. However, the approach becomes aggressive when the force asymmetry is significant, e.g. the US and Syria or Russia and Ukraine are concerned.

Exaggerated Threats and Ease of Making War. The increasing reliance on machine killing a specific target, like the US targeted killing of Iranian Major General Qasem Soleimani of the Islamic Revolutionary Guard Corps (IRGC) in January 2020 in Iraq, a third country, brings to question of targeting the leadership of a country from the hidden location. The people who operate the lethal autonomous systems are ever more distant and insulated from the physical dangers, and such precision targeting capabilities have put the world leadership at risk. The retaliation attempt by Iran by using missiles and non-state actors against the US military deployed in Iraq points out that the incentive to strike back is dependent on the dispersed asymmetric capability at the disposal of the country under attack. Swarms of lethal autonomous systems and guidance systems are adding to the concept of exaggerated threats and high-security alertness level, which has the potential to trigger a response on false alarms.

Speed in Processing Information. The decision-making abilities are likely to be challenged due to the increased information processing capacity and the ability to hide cyber-offensive capabilities. The miscalculations may trigger pre-emptive strikes which may spiral uncontrollably. Without strategic communication and trust between adversaries, strategic stability may be challenging to achieve.

Balance of Power and Uncertainties Risks. The technological innovations in niche technological areas are happening at a frenetic pace. The participation by state and non-state groups are scripting new product mix, which has the prospect to alter the balance of power. The waning strategic capabilities by the state or loss of revenue by the non-state group could incentivise risk-taking by state or non-state groups.

Deterrence Disappearance, Pre-emption, and Strategy of Chaos. The investment by nations in strategic intelligence capacity to see underground and underwater has the potential to make triad assets visible to adversaries, thus undermining the second-strike capabilities. Such an eventuality will prompt a review of nuclear doctrine from 'No First Use' to pre-emption, which can adversely affect strategic stability. Alternately, the country may invest in non-nuclear deterrence capabilities in biomaterials, nuclear-electronic attacks or cyber-physical attacks which can plunge the society and governance into chaos.

Grey Zone Threats and Governance Lapses. The grey zone threats need not play in armed forces arena only. The armed forces are part of the national strategic discourse in China and Pakistan, and to a large extent, they are also the drivers of the national objectives. Since they are fused within the state structures, it gives them the unique capability to time and trigger grey zone threats, in non-military non-lethal fields like banking, energy or transportation which has the potential to paralyse the government and make the citizen lose faith in the capacity of the state to guarantee security. Governance failure may trigger destabilisation.

New Arms Race and Proliferation Risks. Strategic stability is related to an arms control agreement. The proliferation of nuclear and chemical weapon system was controlled primarily due to inspection and verification model instituted in them. However, the COVID-19 threat has exposed the biosecurity domain and has highlighted the failure of Biological Warfare Conventions in regulating the biomaterials, which pose a grave threat to humanity. Similarly, the nation-states to draw first-mover advantage in the autonomous system, data and space weaponisation have been reluctant to promote control regime. The dual-use systems developed by state and private enterprises is fraught with the risk of proliferation.

Wider Cast of Private Security Companies. China has expanded its BRI network to over 138 countries.[6] It has been revamping the private security companies to protect the Chinese workforce operating in these countries besides undertaking international obligations of guarding cargo to the project sites. It is also positioning itself to provide cybersecurity along proposed Belt and Road Space Information Corridor which features applications and services related to navigation and positioning, remote sensing, weather, and communications satellites. The Digital Silk Road by China also focuses on the development of communications networks, smart cities, and e-commerce activities, as important components of BRI, that will increase the dependencies of these countries on PLA.[7] Hence, the outsourced security obligations will help China to monitor space and cyber traffic. For instance, China Cityguard Security Service employing over fifteen thousand people and providing security services within China and abroad has been given thirteen contracts to protect infrastructure projects abroad, including in high-risk areas in Pakistan. According to an estimate, the security workers composition is 30 per cent veterans and 50 per cent police officers.[8] China's private cybersecurity company like 'Antiy Labs' is now protecting more than 1.7 billion smart devices and intends having a sizable market share of the global cybersecurity market estimated at US$182 billion by 2021.[9] China has a large number of cybersecurity firms who, besides being employed to check cybercrime, are also engaged in cyber snooping. This growing breed of private security firms tied to China's state system and PLA is likely to vitiate the security landscape and add to the instability and uncertainties.

World Sitting at the Precipice. From government to corporate to individuals, technological innovation is pushing individuals and organisation to adapt to the new sets of innovations and skilling. Transform or turn obsolete is the new age mantra. At the turn of the 21st century, 52 per cent of companies in the Fortune 500 do not exist anymore.[10] The COVID-19 contagion has shown the world how a bio-material if not handled well and with no mechanism to monitor can spoil a century of economic development within months. Crafting stability out of technological innovation is at the cost of the disappearance of personal privacy. The world is moving fast, and we sit astride the most pervasive penetrative platform of the planet created out of the combination of computing power and ubiquitous connectivity. Our network of network systems designed by 5G, managed by the AI and augmented reality has been working to replace the brainpower with machine power. The future seems scary as it tries to unravel the neural network as part of human augmentation project. It creates yet another vulnerability to the human existence of "hackable human". Toby Ord, in his book 'The Precipice', has tried to quantify the probability of existential risks the humanity is likely to face due to natural and manmade catastrophe (refer Table 6.1). The most striking part of the risk landscape is how widely the probabilities vary between different risks. According to the author, the anthropogenic risks are 1,000 times more likely than the natural risks, and within anthropogenic threats, the dangers from future technologies are roughly 100 times larger.[11]

Table 6.1: Existential Risk Landscape and Probabilities

Natural Risk	*Probability in Next 100 Years*	*Manmade Risk*	*Probability in Next 100 Years*
Climate Change	1 in 1000	Nuclear War	1 in 1000
Naturally arising Pandemic	1 in 10,000	Engineered Pandemic	1 in 30
Environmental Damage	1 in 1,000	Unaligned AI	1 in 10
Super Volcanic Eruptions	1 in 10,000	Unforeseen Anthropogenic Risk	1 in 30

Source: Ord, T. (2020). *The Precipice: The Existential Risk and the Future of Humanity*. New York: Hachette Book Group Inc, pp.189-191.

The predictive modelling riding on the computational framework is unfortunately tied to the nation's greed and not to the human need. The competitive strategy, as part of geo-politico-economic dominance, is fraught with the risks of technological disruptions and forced intervention. The challenge for humanity will remain the tracing of ethical technological growth. The ubiquitous communication and surveillance combine ensures tracing through digital tracks. Spoofing, fakery and deep fakery will emerge as new skill sets to cover digital footprints. Privacy will come at a price. The anthropogenic risks increase destabilisation probability profoundly.

China's 'Contagement' Policy

'Contagement' is a portmanteau where containment and engagement are simultaneously used. It is important to gauge the intent of China's contagement policy confronting India. India has moved forward in articulating its national resolve through public declaration in the use of armed forces.[12] It has carried out surgical strike on Pakistani terror camps in 2016 after the Uri attack and again in 2019 after the suicide attack by the Pakistan sponsored terrorists on Indian security forces in Pulwama, it carried out air raids over Pakistan Army operated terror camps. It has also been able to handle the 2017 Doklam crisis against China deftly. It has been an open secret that China and Pakistan have been colluding on nuclear and missile issues, sharing of intelligence and development of weapon systems. They are doing this to embroil and confine the Indian Armed Forces engagement in its traditional domain. Facing strategic contest in the South China Sea, China has trained its guns in South Asia and Indian Ocean region to keep its strategic options open and also contain India's influence in these regions. A multi-pronged strategic oriented drive from the top has been at the heart of China's politico-economic thrust. The PLA and the other organs of the Chinese State-Council and the CPC have been brought under one umbrella to push Beijing agenda.

Strategic Inroads. China has been a silent manipulator and has made strategic inroads into India's strategic space both outside and inside the country and in South Asia-Indian Ocean Region. Within the framework of its 'contagement' policy, China has used the three-fold approach as part of its containment effort. Firstly, the BRI is used to entice cash strapped nations in South Asia and along the Indian Ocean Rim (IOR) states through economic inducement. In the garb of building infrastructure capacities in the host countries it has executed its 'string of pearls' strategy by creating maritime outposts through the development of the ports in Gwadar, Pakistan, Hambantota in Sri Lanka, Kyaukypu in Myanmar and Chittagong Port in Bangladesh.[13] Secondly, it has leveraged dollar diplomacy to make political inroads within the political systems in Sri Lanka,[14] Nepal,[15] Maldives[16] and Pakistan and has been working relentlessly to increase its influence by engaging in anti-India legislations. Thirdly, it has used Pakistan as a proxy against India by proliferating restricted technologies related to nuclear and missiles and would like to create more proxy states by influencing the fragile political structures existing within other South Asian states. Despite India's reservation on development of BRI projects in the disputed Gilgit-Baltistan sector in Pakistan, China has not only gone ahead with the projects but has also been instrumental in paying for the 12,000 security personnel for the China Pakistan Economic Corridor (CPEC). The raising of the Special Security Division (SSD) at Chilas in Gilgit-Baltistan comprising of nine regular battalions and six wings of paramilitary forces akin to Frontier Corps for protection of project and its workforce[17] has been done with twin objective – to guard the restive region along CPEC and to counter India's conventional edge in Pakistan 10 Corps Zone responsible for guarding Pakistan Eastern front along the line of control with India.

Economic Entanglement. On the engagement front, China has tried to entangle India through trade and making inroads into India's communication sectors. It has also been following a pioneering strategy of investing in the Indian start-ups and financial technologies so that it can grow leverages within the systems. Thus, the strategy of engagement hinges on making penetration into India's commercial and critical infrastructure space, leverage financial presence to shore off influence and new ideas that can be redeployed back home and create supply-chain dependencies. China is India's biggest trading partner, but also the most significant contributor to India's trade deficit. While on paper India's trade deficit with China has come down by US$10 billion, from US$63 billion in 2017-18 to US$53 billion in 2018-19. However, taking into account the Hong Kong trade, the deficit stands at US$ 60.1 billion. It has only reconfigured the supply chains.[18]

China's Economic Beachhead Contours. The transactional trade arrangement with China which acquired momentum since 2005 has now given way to the growth of Chinese investments in India since 2014. The investors have targeted areas ranging from infrastructure and energy to newer sectors of interest, such as technology start-ups and real estate. The total current and planned Chinese investment in India has crossed US$26 billion at present. Chinese companies are seeking to establish a long-term presence in India, and their acquisitions in Indian companies give them an enduring stake in the Indian market.[19] The Chinese State-Owned Entities (SOE) and the private sector, along with provincial governments, have emerged as important interest groups in shaping China's diplomacy with India. Xi's government 2018 major restructuring of the party-state architecture has given greater weight to party organs. The foreign policy leading group has been elevated to a Central Foreign Affairs Commission. The delegation of foreign policy deliberation is now with the party's central leading small group for foreign affairs set up under the party's Central Committee. Besides them the other stake holders like the International Liaison Department and the United Front Work Department (UFWD) shape the strategic interests, including the large Tibetan community staying in India. The PLA, assigned with the tasks of guarding global interests, is also a key foreign policy player and a staunch advocate of hard-line[20] with a neighbour with which it has a territorial dispute to settle. The Foreign Affairs Commission is likely to remain an opaque, behind-the-scenes body, out of reach for policymakers. The Indian government will, therefore, continue to have to deal with many Chinese diplomats and government representatives who most likely lack the authority to make decisions on most issues, and the question of engaging with the right interlocutor complicates the negotiations. The biggest driver of this change is the growing weight of strategic commercial considerations in shaping Chinese influence architecture.[21] The establishment of the China International Development Cooperation Agency (CIDCA) points to more centralised control over the ministries of commerce and foreign affairs. Wang Xiaotiao, who headed the BRI as deputy director of the powerful National Development and Reform Commission (NDRC) is in-charge of CIDCA. This indicates that the Chinese development cooperation is also being driven by longer-term strategic interests. NDRC's underlining influence can be gauged by the officials the agency has been able to post in many of China's embassies overseas. For instance, in 2008, businesses belonging to the city or provincial governments accounted for over one-fifth of top Chinese companies investing overseas. In trade with India, three provinces alone accounted for more than half of the US$84.4 billion total bilateral trade in 2017 – Guangdong (US$21.05 billion), Jiangsu (US$13.91 billion) and Zhejiang (US$12.32 billion). Certain provinces have also been tasked with diplomatic outreach activities aimed at specific regions. For instance, Yunnan is the centre for China's South Asia outreach activities and trade fairs, while Guangxi plays a similar role in Southeast Asia.[22] What is clear, however, is that the state sees commercial engagement as one avenue to advance foreign policy and security agenda while supporting the overseas expansion of Chinese companies. Top SOEs and political leadership have a close and symbiotic relationship. More often than not, the head of a major SOE would outrank most officials of the MFA barring the foreign minister, as they are likely to hold ministerial or vice-ministerial ranks. An official policy paper released in March 2019 called on the high-tech and newly emerging industrial sectors to fully implement and fulfil the spirit of the 19th Party Congress and Xi Jinping's vision. The party has co-opted CEOs by appointing them to either the National People's Congress (legislature) or the Chinese People's Political Consultative Conference (a politically advisory body, or upper house), for instance, Pony Ma, Tencent's founder and NPC deputy, Xiaomi's founder and CEO Lei Jun and Baidu's founder Robin Li. By the end of 2016, close to 70% of non-state-owned companies had embedded Party cells or branches in their organisations to align the corporate activities with the national effort.[23] Alibaba, for instance, has played a prominent role in promoting the party's propaganda goals at home. It developed and promoted a widely-used app that tests and ranks users on their knowledge of Xi Jinping's governing philosophy. All party members are obligated to use this app. The app is an example of the close relationship between the tech sector and the party.[24] The economic meltdown due to COVID-19 in February 2020 has sent the stock prices of valued enterprises at a discount world-wide. It has prompted China to use it as an opportunity to increase its stake in India's top financial companies. A part of its plan to create economic beachhead into India. The Government of India has been proactive in reviewing the existing Foreign Direct Investment (FDI) policy for curbing opportunistic takeovers/acquisitions of Indian companies. It amended para 3.1.1 of extant FDI 2017 which has made the "entity of a country, which shares a land border with India or where the beneficial owners of investment into India is situated in or is a citizen of any such country, can invest only under the Government route".[25] The Global Time, China's official English daily has been critical of Indian government policy which they feel are inspired by the US to curb Chinese investment into India which had swollen to US$ 8 billion by December 2019.[26] Hence, while the strategic calm may be seen at the top level, the narrative shows lack of political trust and India-US relation adds to the growing mistrust. The narrative gets fed through Chinese state media as the editorial in Global Times reported that India has been hostile to Beijing's fight against the pandemic.[27]

Information and Communication Space. In 2017-18, almost 60 per cent of India's import requirements of electrical and electronic equipment were met by China.[28] Only Indian IT company to be successful in China is NIIT, which isn't selling Indian IT services or products, but training tens of thousands of young Chinese in IT skills ever year, so they can bolster Chinese IT companies rather than rely on Indian ones.[29] While blocking the entry of foreign players in its critical sovereign cyberspace, China has quietly made significant inroads into Indian technology domain through venture investments in start-ups and penetrated the online ecosystem with its popular smartphones and their applications. In between 2015-2020, 18 of India's 30 unicorns were Chinese funded. TikTok, the YouTube rival video app has 200 million subscribers. Chinese smartphones like Oppo and Xiaomi lead the Indian market with an estimated 72 per cent share, leaving Samsung and Apple behind. Alibaba, Tencent and ByteDance have similarly rivalled the US penetration of Facebook, Amazon and Google in India.[30] The lack of data regulation has allowed Chinese companies to make inroads swiftly. To capture the Indian vernacular content market,

ByteDance has a local team entirely based in New Delhi.[31] A report from Factor Daily found that 44 of the top 100 Android apps in India were developed by Chinese companies, up from just 18 one year prior.[32] According to Telecom Regulatory Authority of India (TRAI), by March 2019, the subscriber base was 1183.51 million out of which, 1161.81 million were wireless subscribers with an overall teledensity of 90.11%.[33] By 2025, the digital applications could proliferate across most sectors of India's economy including new areas of agriculture, education, energy, financial services, healthcare, logistics and retail, as well as government services and labour markets. Core digital sectors such as IT and business process management, digital communication services and electronics manufacturing could increase from US$355 billion to US$435 billion with the additional bonanza of up to US$150 billion as part of incremental economic value in new sectors to help raise output, save costs and time, reduce fraud and improve the matching of demand and supply. The productivity unlocked by the digital economy could create 60 million to 65 million jobs by 2025, many of them requiring functional digital skills.[34] China has been eyeing this vast market and has made a determined push for Huawei to be included as part of India's 5G roll-out plan. However, the Ladakh misadventure by the PLA in June 2020 may cost China dearly. With banning of 59 Chinese applications, Indian government has signalled its intention about future collaborations.

Supply Chain Dependencies. The COVID-19 crisis has shown India the vulnerability of plugging into one supply chain. The dependency on Chinese imports and the associated risk was observed in pharmaceuticals where China supplies almost 70 per cent of active pharmaceutical ingredients (API) requirement for the industry; automobiles providing 10 to 30 per cent of the raw materials and base components, chemicals and textiles. Even, the renewable energy sector which forms the backbone for future energy needs of the country is almost 80 per cent dependent on China for the solar panels. Finally, and potentially most problematically, several micros, small and medium enterprises (MSMEs) are dependent on Chinese imports.[35] Indian Prime Minister in his address to the nation on 13 May 2020 indicated policy directions towards self-reliant India and need for being "vocal for local". However, the determined push by the government has to be supported by the state governments. The policy formulation while looking to make conditions favourable for foreign promoters to do business in India, it's also important for India to guard its sovereign rights and security interests. A beginning to correct the skewed supply chain in pharmaceuticals has been made as the Government of India has decided to promote domestic manufacturing of critical Key Starting Materials (KSM)/Intermediates and Active Pharmaceutical Ingredients (API) in the country. The approved scheme will promote Bulk Drug Parks with a financial investment of US$ 40 billion in the next five years.

PLA Increased Non-Contact Warfare Capability. PLA remains the world's largest armed force with an increasingly modern and advanced equipment inventory. It is likely to complete its major restructuring and reform by 2020. The theatre commands are more or less adapted to the new doctrinal philosophy. The inspection and simulation exercise through which the senior commanders have been put through has helped them to absorb the joint warfare nuances. Most western analysts have questioned the combat experience of these commanders in a total war scenario. However, given the PLA and CPC inclination of minimising the strategic friction, it is evident that PLA would be subscribing to play game in the sub-threshold non-contact warfare domain. It has done well to increase its cyber penetration in India through its mobile sales, supplies of telecommunication equipment, IT hardware and applications. Its investment in space and electronics has helped it to improve its situational awareness. Thus, the persistent presence through cyber and a better situational awareness helps PLA to team up its large non-lethal capability with lethal autonomous systems and missiles.

Given its economic entanglement in India and political influence and financial inducements in India's neighbourhood the PLA plan to intimidate Indian government is on the anvil. Currently, the Indian armed forces may possess dissuasive to credible force capability. However, the burgeoning budgetary gap and China's indigenous production line is likely to tilt the balance in favour of China by 2025 especially in the domain of maritime, autonomous systems, missiles, space and cyber. According to a Chinese saying, "One mountain can accommodate only one tiger." The Chinese look at themselves as the tiger on the Asian mountain and, in their view, there is no place for a second tiger like India. With India joining the western chorus of investigation of COVID-19 origin and will be the crucial player to monitor the progress of the investigation as India sets to head the executive board[36] is likely to intensify the contest between India and China. Some of them have already started manifesting in the form of increased military activities along Ladakh and other regions along the LAC since May 2020, and using the communist government in Nepal to whip up the anti-India sentiment with increased activity of China's International Liaison Department.[37] The challenges for India are ominous.

RECOMMENDATIONS FOR INDIA TO DEAL WITH THREATS AND CHALLENGES

After the outbreak of pandemic, India finds itself in an increasingly destabilised world and society. The external threats posed by the active borders have not diminished as the border with Pakistan is still active with numerous ceasefire violations, and so is the case with China. Our global interests are being tested and influenced by our adversaries. The non-state actors are active too within and outside our country. While the government is grappling with the biggest challenge of modern times, the unpredictable and uncertain internal political and security situation has been challenging all traditional institutions and state structures. The inadequacies while dealing with the challenges within our country are more profound than outside as it has the potential to disturb societal order and peace due to economic threat. In the Indian context, the problems are known, and there are enough expert committee recommendations that are available to guide the developmental and security architecture of India.

Approach to National Security

COVID-19 contagion, whether an engineered pandemic spread as a part of accidental discharge or deliberate act, has happened sooner than later and has impacted the people at large. The impact on people has reverberated across all indices of human development. It has destroyed economic activities, rendered millions jobless, stretched fragile government structures to deal with the disaster of this unprecedented nature, impacted the military's preparedness to some extent, and above all tested the government ability to make an informed policy decision in the absence of factual data. COVID-19 impact is one of the worst-case scenarios a nation can face as part of the future non-contact warfare. Global destabilised environment due to COVID-19 may likely to trigger future disruptions. If the risk assessments (refer to Table 6.1 of this chapter) are any pointer, then the Non-contact Warfare will play a lead role. It makes our society more vulnerable to future shocks, burdens our government and sucks our military into non-military tasks exposing the entire nation to grave risks and undermining the developmental processes which the nation has carefully crafted. Given China's suspicion over Indo-US ties and the swift deterioration in Sino-US relations, China has been expecting a less favourable, if not downright hostile, environment in the post-COVID-19 world. Given, the increase in Chinese non-contact warfare capabilities and the asymmetric threats to India along its borders with collusive support from Pakistan, India would need a multi-discipline approach across PIMED. The broad security architecture based on the national security and defence strategy must work through the NSA and the head of NITI Aayog harmonise the security and administrative interface. It needs to take care of the country's global and societal interests and mitigate internal threats by seamlessly working through PIMED. Refer to Figure 6.2.

Figure 6.2: Broad Framework for National Security Approach

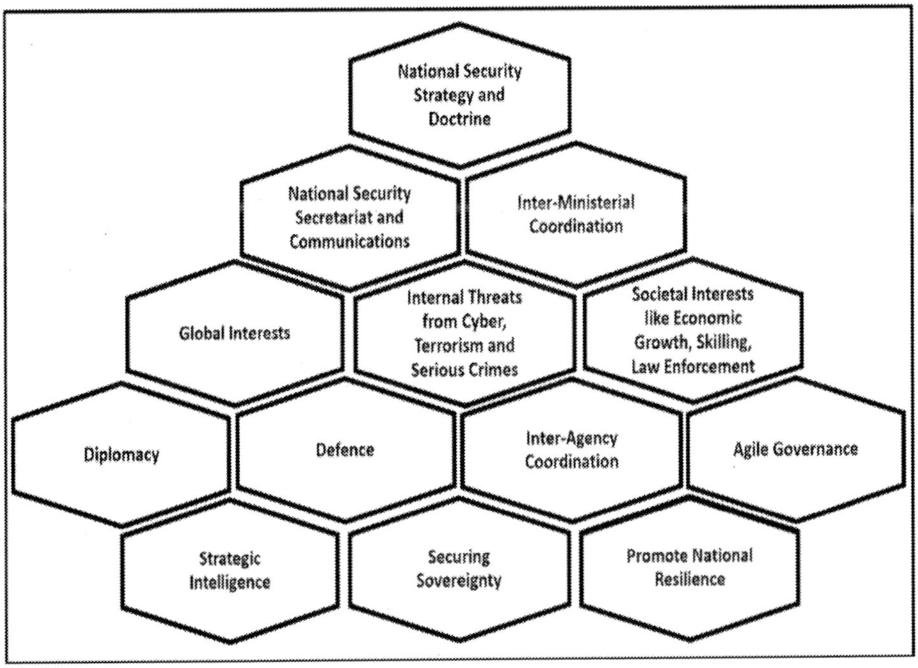

The National Security Objectives should aim at protecting people and sovereignty, enhancing development and increasing influence. According to 2nd Edition of Joint Doctrine of the Indian Armed Forces – 2017 (JDIAF-2017), the National Military Objectives (NMOs) as given in Table 6.2 merits attentions. The force development should look at increasing capabilities in the non-contact kinetic and non-kinetic domains.

Table 6.2: National Military Objectives According to JDIAF-2017

1.	Prevent war through strategic and conventional deterrence across the full spectrum of military conflict, to ensure the defence of India, our National Interests and sovereignty.
2.	Prosecute military operations to defend the territorial integrity and ensure a favourable end-state during the war to achieve stated/implied political objective(s).
3.	Provide assistance to ensure Internal Security, when called upon to do so.
4.	Be prepared for contingencies at home and abroad to render Humanitarian Assistance and Disaster Relief (HADR), Aid to Civil Authority and International Peacekeeping, when called upon to do so.
5.	Enable the required degree of self-sufficiency in defence equipment and technology through indigenisation to achieve the desired degree of technological independence by 2035.

The key recommendations for National Security are:

- **Need for Strategic Security and Defence Review (SSDR).** In the Indian context, the Strategic Defence Review, a blueprint of short- and long-term security threats, as well as possible policy options on a priority basis is supposed to be carried out by the Strategic Planning Group headed by National Security Advisor (NSA). The constitution of Defence Planning Committee (DPC) under the chairmanship of NSA in April 2018 was done with the intent to expedite comprehensive and integrated defence planning in the absence of Chief of Defence Staff (CDS). The DPC was assigned two tasks. One, to analyse and evaluate all relevant inputs relating to defence planning, which includes, among others, the national defence and security priorities, foreign policy imperatives, operational directives and associated requirements, relevant strategic and security-related doctrines, defence acquisition and infrastructure development plans, including the 15-year Long-Term Integrated Perspective Plan (LTIPP), defence technology and development of the Indian defence industry and global technological advancement. Second, to prepare at least five different sets of drafts including: "national security strategy, strategic defence review and doctrines; international defence engagement strategy; a roadmap to build defence manufacturing eco-system; strategy to boost defence exports; and prioritised capability development plans for the armed forces over different time-frames in consonance with the overall priorities, strategies and likely resource flows. Four sub-committees have been created under the DPC to focus on these policy and strategy issues. DPC was also responsible for drawing up a charter of responsibilities for the CDS that was announced by the government on 24 December 2019.[38] The newly formed Department of Military Affairs (DMA) under the current CDS Gen Bipin Rawat has been mandated to look into the tri-service integration. According to the allocation of business rules, Department of Defence under the Defence Secretary still holds the responsibility for the "Defence of India and every part thereof including defence policy and preparation for defence".[39] Hence, the restructuring adds more problems in navigating the strategic contours as policy framing is resident to the department, which lacks expertise in formulating one. In case of prosecution of non-contact warfare which requires an integrated approach, possibly the Coast Guard and Border Road Organisations should be with DMA so that training and operational departmental switch can be avoided. In fact, placing the border management troops along active borders under the Ministry of Defence will ensure better operational and escalation control. It will also promote inter-operability of equipment thus optimising resource and coordination.

- **Defending New Sovereign Requirements**. Space, cyberspace, data, and technology have emerged as a new sovereign requirement and needs to be given due impetus in force planning. The distributed responsibilities to guard them may be detrimental to national security. In the Indian context, the armed forces continue to defend the traditional security front while the aspects of space are handled by ISRO; cyber issues are handled by Ministry of Electronics and Information Technology (MIETY); while technology issues are handled by the Department of Defence Research Organisation (DRDO) and Ministry of Science and Technology besides the National Institution for Transforming India, also known as NITI Aayog. China on its part has reformed its national security architecture. It has created an obscure National Security Commission (refer Chapter 2) by regrouping all components of security apparatus within CPC power structure under the President Xi Jinping to drive the strategic formulation and crisis management. The reorganised PLASSF is responsible for both space and cyber defence and strategic intelligence while

PLARF has looked at strengthening kinetic lethal systems since 2016. A comprehensive cross-ministerial evaluation of national security and defence needs to be undertaken in line with the National Security Strategy. The business allocation for the force assigned to handle the critical infrastructure should be based on threat and capability requirements. India has a well-structured Strategic Forces Command (SFC) to control the long-range nuclear and conventional vectors. In 2019, India made a small beginning by creating tri-service agencies like Defence Space Agency (DSA) to operate the space-warfare assets and the Defence Cyber Agency (DCA) to handle cybersecurity threats. Stove-piped cyber and space organisations must make way to cohesive structures and responsibilities with civil-military integration. Doctrine development and force cohesion take time, and hence the road maps should be drawn to make way to integration.

- **Aligning Structures and Institutions to National Security Priorities**. In 2015, NITI Aayog was formed as a premier policy think tank to the Government of India, providing directional and policy inputs. Apart from designing strategic and long-term policies and programmes for the Government of India, NITI Aayog also provides relevant technical advice to the Centre, states and union territories (UTs). One of the main objectives of NITI Aayog is, to design strategic and long-term policy and programme frameworks and initiatives, and monitor their progress and their efficacy. Given the fusion of security scenario, it is important to look at the constitution and composition of the NITI Aayog. The erstwhile Planning Commission also left the defence and security issues for the ministries to handle on the pretext of secrecy and need to know basis. Even the office of the Indian NSA has three Deputy NSAs with each tasked to look after Intelligence, Internal Affairs and Strategic Affairs with Military Affairs relegated to the Military Advisors with Net Assessment responsibility without sufficient staffing and funding. The structures follow the strategy. Hence, it is evident that the nation looks at a limited role for the Armed Forces. Even, within the Armed Forces, the tri-service integration and integration of the Armed Forces with the Ministry of Defence is incomplete.

Though through the establishment of DMA, some semblance of integration has been constituted. The journey for jointmanship is still a work in progress with the appointment of CDS. The ability to fight non-contact warfare needs more than just jointmanship. It requires integrated structures tailored to deal with threats. The silo-based strategic planning may have helped the nation to deal with Pakistan. But for dealing with an adversary like China, it will be important for India to align the structures and make strategic planning holistically. Net Assessment should be given due impetus and should form the framework for intelligence and ministerial tasking. Even the role of Armed Forces needs to be redefined for non-traditional security space, and forces need to train in new-age skills.

- **Developing Asymmetric Capabilities and Screening Pervasive Threats**. The 2012 Non-Alignment 2.0 Report highlighted the need for three-prong asymmetric capability development for India while dealing with China. It talked of creating asymmetric force by recruiting locals in police and paramilitary force, integration of the frontier region through infrastructure development and lastly creation of Naval Commission for maritime security.[40] Over the past decade, the societal vulnerability tied to ICT has increased exponentially. The new age vulnerabilities riding on ICT and biotechnology, economic inducement and technological ambushes through IPR exploitation need to be safeguarded. Developing the asymmetric capability to guard against the new age vulnerabilities require a new technological and defence enterprise system. Non-Alignment 2.0 report has recommended setting up of Cyber Command with offensive and defensive capabilities.[41] With most of the world-leading military already having cyber commands, India's attempt to raise DCA in 2019 is probably a step towards it. But it needs right mandate, doctrinal push and technological innovations. Besides setting the organisational structures right, there is a need for India to screen deployment of foreign technologies in critical infrastructures like space, telecommunication, energy and transportation to prevent potential disruptions.
- **Civil-Military Integration**. The blurring of security boundaries and technological development brings to focus the need to align

the national security priorities and structures. In China, the PLA and the CPC have been in tandem to devise a strategic plan. The continued CPC rule over the last seven decades has ensured uninterrupted strategic pursuit of national priorities. Hence, in China, the civil-military integration is about PLA embracing the civilian into its architecture. In India, it's the other way around. The Armed Forces have not even been integrated with their parent Ministry of Defence. Hence, integrating them with other ministries will need greater resolve and clear guidelines and business rules. The nature of non-contact warfare demands not only inter-ministerial, inter-agency coordination but a better civil-military integration to allow a plug and play inter-operable system driven by processes rather than personalities.

- **Collaborative Defence Industrial and Technological Base**. Defence eco- systems is supposed to work on niche concepts and ideas. It requires a strong knowledge-based society that is seamlessly integrated across academia, research and development laboratories and industries. The professional advisors and assistance should be embedded in the system. Probably, the creation of greenfield projects based on Defence Economic Zone model would be an ideal way to promote excellence. Alternately, academic institutions, Ordnance Factory Board, Defence Public Sector Undertaking and Private Defence Industry with the defence laboratory and armed forces trial ranges and units should be stitched together. It will help in reducing the incubation period for product development and enable early technological enrichment and breakthroughs. The government directive on offsets and foreign collaboration should be aggressively followed. A sound defence industrial base acts as a net security provider especially, during the time of crisis and snapping of supply chains. India's technological and industrial development road map should look at gaining sovereignty over critical domain areas.

Approach to Guard Global Interests

Defence and diplomacy have to work in tandem to ensure that country's global interests are secured and the influence enhanced. India tryst with non-alignment and strategic autonomy has helped it to steer well out of the ideological morass of the cold war. However, in a pervasive technological world where the standardisations are continually defining protocols; 'the one globe two systems' being attempted by China will push India to make a choice. The key recommendations are:

- **Strengthen Strategic Partnerships**. Prime Minister Narendra Modi in his keynote address at the Shangri-La Dialogue in June 2018 had provided the Indian vision of the Indo-Pacific which puts ASEAN as the centre with extremities extending to the eastern shores of Africa to the west coast of America. Given the huge expanse that the Indian definition of Indo-Pacific covered, it prompted the Ministry of External Affairs (MEA) to create Indo-Pacific wing in April 2019. According to Dr Harsh Pant of ORF, "Act East Policy remains the bedrock of India's Indo-Pacific policy" however, it leaves the larger part of India's western sea-board unaddressed. Also, there are differences between India's vision and the US's strategy for the Indo-Pacific. With the growing geo-political tensions between US and China over trade and technology war and the South China Sea India will have to create a comprehensive security narrative and align its diplomatic effort and defence capabilities to guard India's interest in the region. Post COVID-19, India needs to look at 'Quad'[42] arrangements while protecting its energy and strategic interests in West Asia, CAR and with Russia. India will have to organise its defence forces along the Eastern and Western sea board as two separate theatres; while working towards risk reduction and operational safety measures through a sustained force development and doctrinal framework working in close tandem with Coast Guard and Port Security.
- **Strategic Intelligence and Influence Overreach**. Situational awareness strengthens diplomacy and defence posturing. Hence, India will do well to strengthen its strategic intelligence capability to help it to guard its global interests and take care of security needs related to terrorism and serious crimes with overseas linkages. With increased Chinese threat, it may be prudent for India to develop an intelligence-sharing mechanism with countries like US, Japan, South Korea[43] and even Taiwan or join the 'Five Eye' framework. Defence capabilities based on long-range vectors need deployment of space and cyber-based

capabilities. All these defence intelligence capabilities should get coordinated at the CDS level and shared with the NSA and SPG. Strategic intelligence must eventually create a Regional Information Grid that should help India to secure its supply chains and the diaspora. Health and technological intelligence have emerged as the new need and the capability for the same need to be also developed. India has an extradition treaty with 43 nations and extradition arrangements with 11 countries only which limits India's reach to influence conviction and tracing crimes. The role of the Head of Mission in the foreign countries must be well defined, and the organisational structures should be streamlined to incorporate new requirements of security threats, strategic opportunities, and influence operations.

- **Strategic Developmental Funds**. Preservation of global interests and influence is also related to the security of economic investments. India needs to create enough leverages within world bodies for financial loans and grants. Development Partnership Administration (DPA) in Ministry of External Affairs handling all Lines of Credit through EXIM Bank and grants of projects and assistance under ITEC (Indian Technical and Economic Cooperation Programme)[44] has not been effective despite the progressive increase in Lines of Credit. It is essential to integrate other Indian banks and large corporates to pro-actively undertake strategic resource management and human capital development in the host country.
- **Robust and Dynamic Legal Mechanism and Monitoring System.** Such is the speed, complexity, and ubiquity of innovation today that the regulations process needs to look ahead to manage and monitor the emerging technologies. India should lead the international arms control conventions on technologies that imperil human security. Domestically it should look at unlocking the value chain without compromising security. Hard governance measures of laws and regulations will remain necessary. There is also a need to make more use of faster-moving soft governance mechanisms such as patent procedures, laboratory standards, testing and certification regimes, insurance policies and mechanisms of oversight to deal with potentially dangerous research subjects. These measures require inter-ministerial

coordination to proactively anticipate and adapt to not only technological changes but also to macro-cultural ones, which are a lot harder to predict.

Approach to Internal Security

Politics is at the heart of internal unrest. Protest dynamics across the world during Arab Spring or colour revolutions in some post-USSR Republics or recently in Hong Kong points to the role of media and expansion of societal fault lines existing in a society. Closer home, the stone-pelting incidents in Jammu and Kashmir, left-wing extremism in almost 60 districts and 251 police stations[45] and the spread of anti-Citizenship Amendment Act in February 2020 has shown how agitation can be engineered, and social divide can be created. The matter is compounded by centre-state acrimony on the handling of law and order situation. Law enforcement agencies proficiency and the inability of the judicial system to provide urgent legal recourse are some of the issues which provide ammunition for the perpetration of non-contact warfare. Internal security is an important element of non-contact warfare and needs to be tackled as a security matter and governance issue.

- **Security Matters.** The key issues affecting the internal security rides on intelligence coordination, police and judicial set-up.
  - o **Intelligence Coordination and Follow up.** Rajiv Gandhi's assassination and Mumbai attack have been two major intelligence failure[46] and inadequate follow up actions are some of the major shortcomings which were identified by the IDSA task force for intelligence reforms. The Verma Commission and the Jain Commission reports post-Rajiv Gandhi assassination brought out the lack of coordination between R&AW and IB regarding interpreting the coded LTTE messages. The problem had surfaced between Military Intelligence and R&AW during peacekeeping operations in Sri Lanka also.[47] The office of NSA has brought some synergy in intelligence coordination, and post-Mumbai attack some revamp in intelligence set up has taken place. But the game of one-upmanship continues. Given the expansion of non-traditional threats, the ability of adversaries to penetrate the society and critical systems and structures necessitates inter-agency and inter-force coordination and continuous

monitoring. The Multi-Agency Centre (MAC) has established connectivity between the National Capital, 25 Central Member Agencies and all the State Capitals. In the State Capitals, this network links the Subsidiary Multi-Agency Centre (SMAC), State Police Special Branches and Offices of all the Central and other Counter Terror Agencies. At present total of 429 SMAC Nodes and 251 District Police Offices are connected to the MAC/SMAC Network. However, this link is required to be embedded with all divisional and frontier HQs of Armed Forces and CAPFs engaged in Counter Insurgency/Counter-Terrorism operations at the functional levels. Creating a post of Director National Intelligence working under the NSA with a task of oversight, coordination and policy-centric reporting will help to tie the intelligence with the operational interface.

- **Police and Judicial Reforms.** NITI Aayog paper on 'Strategy for New India @ 75' lists out the need for police and judicial reforms and has given cogent suggestions to make police and judiciary free of encumbrances. However, the Police/law and order is a state subject, falling under List II of the Seventh Schedule of the Constitution of India[48] and bridging the gap, therefore, is the main constraining factor. Given the rising nature of cybercrime with its root outside the country, the nation can examine removing the cyber from the policing duty and hand over to a new civilian entity under the Cyber Command. This helps in bringing the security synergy in handling the internal and external cyber threats.
- **Counter Insurgency and Counter-Terrorism Strategy.** The Ministry of Home Affairs as the lead ministry handling the threats of terrorism must unveil a counter-terrorism strategy. The strategy must lead to policy prescription for coordination aspects between Police, CAPF and Armed Forces. The required legal protection to the forces operating in such an environment should be provided. It is often seen that the subversion of local police personnel in the discharge of duty in a surcharged conflict environment takes place. Hence, mandating a separate corps of investigating and judicial officers assigned to fast pace the justice system in these areas will go a long way in correcting the long pendency of cases in an insurgency or terrorists/

extremists infested areas. In a prolonged conflict scenario, it is observed that an individual gets immune to violence but get rattled by the judicial proceedings. Such measures are essential to not only fix the perpetrators of violence, but also the instigators and planners who remain ensconced in safe havens.

- **Agile Governance.** 'Strategy for New India @ 75' has identified 41 different areas that require either a sharper focus on implementing the flagship schemes already in place or a new design and initiative to achieve India's true potential. However, societal instability firstly due to agitational dynamics caused by anti-CAA protests led to economic disruptions. Further, the COVID-19 contagion tested the agility of the centre-state governance capacity. Given the need to meet the economic and social targets and handling the destabilising effect caused by contagion raises an important question about capacity building in governance. Given the future risk scenario (refer Table 6.1 of this chapter), it is imperative for the government to adapt agile governance model and technique. The key recommendations are:
    - o **Governance Reforms**. Governance is commonly achieved by the creation and enforcement of explicit rules, social norms, guidelines, policies, or the creation of defined command structures. The speed, breadth and depth of the changes brought about by digital technologies are complex and hard to predict and will need more technical support to contain the crisis and deliver goods. COVID-19, for the first time exposed the ministries to the importance of inter-ministerial consultation on an emergent and regular basis. The states and district administrations were also exposed to the importance of correct data compilation to enable resource visibility and societal dynamics and importance of multi-level engagements to mitigate societal stress. It is important to create secure data systems between state and centre for policy intervention, resource positioning and forecasting future course and research. The collaborative approach to governance supported by secure strategic communication is vital for agile governance.
    - o **Strategic Communications.** Strategic communications shape beliefs and influences behaviour. It is an important component of a nation's soft power. The narrative build-up depends on

who is the first to insert the story. The pace of dissemination challenges the population response. The emergence of various strands of communications from diverse, non-official sources is going to affect the populace adversely. Good governance requires good strategic communications as one of its primary functions. Effective strategic communications are must not only between the executive, the judiciary, the legislature, and the populace but also for the diplomatic, security and developmental purposes. Government policies must be communicated to the targeted audience with an understanding of their beliefs, motivations, and interests. The plan must consider the targeted audience, the rationale for the communication, the means of dissemination and the feedback loop. TRAI has already proposed in January 2018 for creation of "Next Generation Public Protection and Disaster Relief Communication Network" which needs to be fast-paced.

- **Civil Service Reforms.** 'Strategy for New India @ 75' has brought about the need for a skill set development to deal with complexities of modern-day governance which require expertise and knowledge base to drive the national objective. The resistance to lateral entry impedes productivity and efficiency.[49] Similarly, about 18 states and seven Union Territories have discontinued the interview system for the lower posts[50] without aiming to build the capacity of officials at the lower posts. Thus, the edifice of agile governance based on a generalist pool of talent will fail to deliver. To enable societal order, it is imperative that civil service reforms at the centre and state level should be implemented.
- **Societal Protection and Oversight Mechanism to deal with Disaster.** Non-contact warfare triggered due to anthropogenic actions like cyber and chemical, biological, radiological, and nuclear (CBRN) fall-out will test the governance capability to deal with the crisis. The society may get affected due to the resultant incapacitation of structures like energy, transportation, and health services. To deal with the COVID-19 pandemic, the Government of India invoked the Disaster Management Act 2005. According to the act, the disaster plan down to each district is required to be made. The success of

the plan is dependent on invoking the system of threat forecasting and continuous monitoring. At the national level there is an institutionalised mechanism existing where the Armed Forces are incorporated in the National Executive Committee, however, at the state and district level the composition has been left at the discretion of state government. Looking at the enormity of response challenges, it may be prudent to incorporate military and CAPF members from the planning stage at the state and district level. Peacetime affiliation for aid to civil authority is part of Armed Forces plan. Given the increased instability that the world and India are likely to face due to geo-politico-economic tensions and increased unforeseen anthropogenic risks, it is important for India to devise "Societal Protection Plan and Oversight Mechanism". This plan should incorporate scientists, technicians, policymakers, security and law enforcement professionals.

Approach to Defence Reforms

There are enough reforms thoughts available with the Ministry of Defence to make the ministry efficient (refer to Table 6.3). What is needed is a determined push to overhaul the security apparatus to improve defence planning, decision-making, defence procurement and defence reforms.

Table 6.3: List of Major Committees Appointed since 1983

- The Arun Singh Committee on Defence Expenditure (CDE), 1983.
- The K C Pant Committee on the NSC, 1989-90.
- The Abdul Kalam Committee on Self-reliance in Weapons Acquisition, 1992.
- The Kargil Review Committee Report, 2000.
- The Group of Minister – appointed task forces on Higher Defence Management, Border Management, Internal Security and Intelligence, 2000-01.
- The GoM chaired by Deputy Prime Minister and Home Minister LK Advani, 2001-02.
- The P. Rama Rao Committee on restructuring the DRDO.
- The Vinod Misra Defence Expenditure Review Committee, 2008-09.
- The Naresh Chandra Committee, 2011-12.
- The Ravindra Gupta Committee on Defence Modernisation and Self-reliance, 2011-12.
- Non-Alignment 2.0, 2012.
- The Dhirendra Singh Committee on Defence Procurement, 2015.
- The Shekatker Committee to Enhance Combat Capability and Rebalance Defence Expenditure, 2016.
- The 10th Finance Commission headed by Vijay Kelkar.
- The Standing Committee(s) on Defence in Parliament.
- The Comptroller and Auditor General (CAG) Reports.

Some of the key recommendations which are borne out of the non-contact warfare compulsions are:

Balance of Power Parity. The Balakote air-strike in February 2019 showed the Indian resolve to retaliate in case of breach of Indian tolerance threshold. The ability to practice warfare through kinetic and non-kinetic non-contact means is thus gaining ground. The unresolved border dispute with Pakistan and China ensures that the bulk of the defence expenditure is devoted to a conventional threat scenario. Given the international security systems and India's priority for development, it is imperative for the security planners to minimise strategic friction. The catalyst to enable strategic stability is to progressively move from dissuasive deterrence to credible deterrence capabilities and generating doctrinal concepts for dynamic and tailored response in the nuclear and non-nuclear lethal and non-lethal domain. It is vital to assess the Chinese flow of 'Shi' and the quantification of force capability and capacity that has a major role in dictating the response.

Prioritise Preparation for War. It is the weakest area of defence planning. Only three out of the last 13 defence five-year plans have been approved by a cabinet committee.[51] The time spent in the vetting of plans by the Ministry of Finance was inordinately delayed. Now as a convention the defence plan is being sent to them for information only.[52] In April 2018, the Defence Planning Committee (DPC) was constituted under the NSA chairmanship to obviate this bottleneck. The mandate given is to create a capability development plan and help obtain budgetary support besides monitoring its implementation. The 13th five-year plan (2017-2022) is yet to get a nod from the cabinet committee. China, on the other hand, has a sustained force development plan for more than two decades. It has been able to attain the milestone "to achieve mechanisation by the year 2020 with significantly enhanced informationisation and greatly improved strategic capabilities" according to 2019 NDWP. The revamped allocation of business rule still grants the Department of Defence under the Defence Secretary the responsibility for the "Defence of India and every part thereof including defence policy and preparation for defence."[53] The role of CDS will, therefore, remain recommendatory, and limited to the military arena as the border roads, and coastguard is assigned to Defence Secretary under the business rule. Given the knowledge base resident in HQ IDS, creating capability development plan should be devolved down to CDS, and the DPC should obtain budgetary support and monitor the implementation of capability development. The remit of CDS as permanent Chairman of Chiefs' of Staff Committee and DMA should help in prioritising the plan for the preparation of war.

Modernise Key Capabilities. The 15-year LTIPP is just an aspirational list which the services want to obtain. Given the dynamics of non-contact warfare and China's strategic capability development, India will need to develop capabilities in the following areas:

- **Space and Cyberspace as Contested Domain**. As already argued, it is important to develop capabilities, including asymmetric capabilities in these critical domains as the pace of development in AI and space will leave a wide capability gap with China. The recommendations of Naresh Chandra Task Force Report 2011 for the creation of Cyber Command and Aero-space Command[54] remains relevant and has also found its resonance in 2012 Non-Alignment 2.0 Report. Aspects of civil-military integration discussed earlier remains key to the success of this reform.
- **Command, Control, Communications, Computers and Intelligence, Surveillance, and Reconnaissance (C4ISR)**. Developing resilient, survivable, combined networks and information ecosystems from the tactical level up to strategic planning is important. Ability to gain and exploit information, denying the same to the competitors is important. Developing attribution capability to hold the state or non-state actors accountable during cyberattacks is crucial as part of non-nuclear deterrence. Execution of electronic ambushes and eclipses need deliberate planning and constant system upgrades. Even, joint exercises with countries with whom we develop strategic partnerships will also help us in augmenting our capability and response options.
- **Unhackable Autonomous Systems**. The development of military and commercial applications in areas of autonomy, artificial intelligence, and machine learning can help us in providing competitive military advantages. To ensure their survivability and safety from being electronically ambushed, it is imperative to invest in quantum communication and code encryption.
- **Precision Long Range Systems**. The ability to hit critical assets in-depth deters the adversary from the coercive policy. At the

same time, it lends options for engagement across the escalation ladder. Hence, developing long-range artillery, rocket and missiles with smart and lethal warheads and multiple payloads is crucial for achieving dominance in operation and tactical environment.

- **Special Operation Force**. The asymmetric force capable of overt and covert operations helps in creating leverages and provide policy options in a grey-zone conflict environment. The force needs to be supported by cutting-edge equipment and communications.
- **Maritime Capabilities**. Given the expanding global interests and China's rapid shipbuilding and naval expansion plan, India must identify the platforms that fulfil our obligations and packs enough punch in defending our interests and influence in the Indian Ocean region.

Professional Military Education (PME), New Education Policy (NEP) and Skill Development. PME, while focusing on bread and butter conventional training, will need to create talent pool in non-traditional security domains too. It will also need to design skill development courses that can be undertaken by the Ministry of Skill Development so that Armed Forces can recruit job-ready individuals and thus can concentrate on imparting advance training. The NEP is focused on creating a talent pool for Industry 4.0. Indian Armed forces as the major user of niche technology should create a human resource development requirement which can get incorporated in the NEP through Ministry of Human Resource Development. Within the services, PME should be used as a strategic asset to build trust and interoperability across the Joint Forces. Based on our strategic partnership development, the professional military and civil courses should be subscribed to cement understanding of each other procedures and culture. National Defence University should be operationalised, and it should act as a fountainhead for ideation of new strategic thoughts.

Technology Development in Critical and Emerging Domains. The 'Science Technology Vision 2035' by DST and 'Defence Technology Vision 2050' by DRDO should bring the academia, researchers, and industry on one page. India, over the last five years, has laid out several initiatives to accelerate investment in transformative ideas and technologies. Technology Demonstrator Fund has been launched by the government to give impetus to the development of projects beyond the proof of concept stage. However, the budgetary provisions are meagre. The piecemeal mechanism has been worked out by respective services within Armed Forces like creating of Army Design Bureau, Army Technology Study Board, Army Management Study Board, and similar mechanism in Navy in the form of Directorate of Naval Design has looked at harnessing the technology. DRDO, on its part, has also tried to partner with industries. However, in terms of patents registration and product roll-out, there is a large gap. In a resource-constrained environment, where feasible, there is a need to make use of more threat-agnostic capabilities. ICT remains the backbone for future development in AI, BlockChain, Quantum Computing and 5G. India will need to look at developing its hardware and operating systems and invest in coding and algorithm development for system protection from cyber-physical attacks. All dual technologies like AI and Biotechnology must be made resident to DRDO, while DRDO and OFB must shed non-core technologies to the Ministry of Science and Technology. The thrust for India to attain technology sovereignty in critical technologies must be outlined through a roadmap.

Evolving Doctrines in League with Developing Technologies. Non-contact warfare is mostly technology-driven. Hence, it is crucial to develop a doctrine against adversary's denial and disruptive capabilities in line with General Naravane's assertion that India should focus on dynamic response below the threshold of an all-out war. While service-specific doctrine exists in some cases, it is vital to create joint doctrine especially on Cyber, Space, AI, Quantum capability development, Autonomous System, Laser and Directed Energy Weapon, Grey-Zone Warfare, information operations. Some doctrine will need to look beyond the scope of jointness and will need an integrated approach across other ministries. Military Operations other than War need a more nuanced look especially in view of the layers over which the non-contact warfare may play out.

Conclusion

Non-contact warfare is changing the traditional force-on-force model and replacing it with a model in which the nation-state collapses due to the engineered crisis directed either against the economy or the population. The centre of gravity is the population specially in a democratic country where the government is at the mercy of their support. As alluded in Chapter 1, the non-contact warfare aims to make the armed forces irrelevant or suck it into secondary tasks, thus compromising the national preparedness. Non-contact warfare will be engaged across multiple domains and will need greater acumen at the strategic level to pace the war control levers.

The emerging COVID-19 crisis should caution our policymakers to start devising people-centric security-driven policy. If preserving the lives and livelihood has to be ensured, then liberties like privacy will need greater scrutiny. The awareness among the people and their ability to grasp the threats from evolving technology will never be able to match the state capabilities. With all modern militaries having declared space and cyber as the warfighting domain, strengthening security frameworks, and putting better situational awareness systems in place is vital. The pervasiveness of technology in the governance and critical infrastructure system will have to be audited and risk levels assigned. While India is aiming for a whole-of-a-government approach and has a strategy to become US$ 5 trillion economy by 2024, the road is fraught with competition and contest. India has to do a serious strategic security and defence review whether declared or confidential. As India climbs the economic growth ladder, it is likely to face strategic friction. A careful and calibrated force development plan with multiple stakeholders' contributions will be essential to absorb the tremors of disruptions and denial.

China has used its military guile and vile to gain more territory in the South China Sea by developing and occupying shoals and reef as artificial islands[55] and has been practising grey-zone warfare by use of militia and coastguard. It has also sunk a Vietnamese vessel in the area as part of strategic messaging to the US and allied forces attempting 'Freedom of Navigation Operations' in the area. Though China is marginalised due to COVID-19 outbreak, yet it has been flexing its muscle in the South China Sea, Taiwan and Tibet. It does not want Taiwan to be part of any WHO health summit. At the same time, it has increased the cyber hacking attempt in the US over COVID-19 related research activities over vaccines and in the US healthcare sector.[56] To prevent any demand for investigation on the origin of the COVID-19 by countries like Australia, China has threatened economic coercion targeting its goods and universities.[57] China is aggressively engaged in protecting its core interests and global interests using non-contact methods.

The world engaged in fighting the global pandemic is also witness to the Sino-US destabilising manoeuvres both in traditional and non-traditional areas. Both are waging influence operations. China has done well to insulate its population from western fed narrative while it is actively engaged in other countries to showcase the efficiency of Chinese governance and technological systems. The competitive strategy put in motion by the US is likely to create global strategic instability and India cannot remain insulated from it.

The immediate question that confronts India is– where is the contest and where does the security problem lie and how well is India equipped to safeguard its population and interests? Should the western-styled military like Indian Army continue to work in its traditional space or should it look for a mandate in non-traditional space? Notwithstanding, India will need to look at the doctrinal approach to security, better civil-military integration, technological innovation, better defence industrial base and robust law enforcement if it has to emerge winner after every contest.

India, which is yet to articulate its National Security Strategy, has a major challenge to adopt and adapt the nuances of Non-Contact warfare. According to Clausewitz, "...the side that feels the lesser urge for peace will naturally get the better bargain." Therefore, India must do a holistic assessment of its threats and vulnerabilities. It can no longer afford to brush aside the much needed administrative and security reforms if it aims at remaining relevant global players. As Chanakya in 'The Arthashastra' said, "deliberations should not be unduly delayed once an opportunity for action arises."[58] As India progresses, the stakes for security will increase exponentially. It will entail a need for better civil-military synergy, ability to safeguard the sovereignty of new domains like data, technology, space and outer space and deep-sea besides traditional security domains and above all creation of asymmetric capabilities. India will do well to manage its fault lines and create alliances and partnership, which will usher in stability and guarantee security. India has to be prepared for Non-contact warfare as it is the future of war, and it needs a whole-of-a-government approach.

NOTES

1 Strategy for New India@75. (2018, November). Retrieved 12 February 2020, from NITI Aayog: https://niti.gov.in/writereaddata/files/Strategy_for_New_India.pdf

2 Ibid, pp 89-90.

3 VAdm Arthur K. Cebrowski, USN, and John J. Garstka, "Network Centric Warfare: Its Origin and Future," Proceedings of the Naval Institute 124:1 (January 1998): 28–35.

4 United Nations Development Programme. (2018, 20 September). *271 million fewer poor people in India*. Retrieved 11 May 2020, from https://www.in.undp.org/content/india/en/home/sustainable-development/successstories/MultiDimesnional PovertyIndex.html

5 Press Trust of India. (2020, 10 May). *India needs 'whole-of-govt approach' for 'strategic uncertainties': Army Chief*. Retrieved 12 May 2020, from Hindustan Times: https://www.hindustantimes.com/india-news/india-needs-whole-of-govt-approach-for-strategic-uncertainties-army-chief-gen-naravane/story-X7UphthriaBEhOJXAZOGVL.html.

6 Green Belt and Road Initiative Centre. (2020, March). *Countries of the Belt and Road Initiative (BRI)*. Retrieved 16 May 2020, from https://green-bri.org/countries-of-the-belt-and-road-initiative-bri.

7 Alessandro, A. (September 2019). *China's Private Security Companies: The Evolution of a New Security Actor*. National Bureau of Asian Research. Retrieved 16 May 2020, from https://www.nbr.org/wp-content/uploads/pdfs/publications/sr80_securing_the_belt_and_road_sep 2019.pdf.

8 Ibid.

9 Zion Market Research. (2017, 18 December*). The report estimates the global cybersecurity market valued at USD 105.45 billion in 2015 to reach USD 181.77 billion in 2021 and is anticipated to grow at a CAGR of 9.5% between 2016 and 2021*. Retrieved 16 May 2020, from https://www.globenewswire.com/news-release/2017/12/18/1263288/0/en/Cyber-Security-Market-Worth-181-77-Billion-by-2021-Zion-Market-Research.html.

10 DXC.technology. (2017, 19 July). *Digital Transformation Is Racing Ahead, and No Industry Is Immune*. Retrieved from Harward Business Review: https://hbr.org/sponsored/2017/07/digital-transformation-is-racing-ahead-and-no-industry-is-immune-2.

11 Ord, T. (2020). *The Precipice: The Existential Risk and the Future of Humanity*. New York: Hachette Book Group Inc, pp.189-191.

12 Burns, J. F. (1998, 05 May). *India's New Defense Chief Sees Chinese Military Threat*. Retrieved 16 May 2020, from The New York Times: https://www.nytimes.com/1998/05/05/world/india-s-new-defense-chief-sees-chinese-military-threat.html.

13 Hongmei He, J. N. (2018, 26 June). *China's assistance for Chittagong port development, not a military conspiracy*. Retrieved 14 May 2020, from The Daily Star: https://www.thedailystar.net/opinion/perspective/chinas-assistance-chittagong-port-development-not-military-conspiracy-1595092.

14 Raman, B. (2010, 23 April). *Chinese Inroads into Sri Lanka*. Retrieved 14 May 2020, from Chennai Centre for China Studies: https://www.c3sindia.org/geopolitics-strategy/chinese-inroads-into-sri-lanka/.

15 Bagchi, I. (2020, 05 May). *Why China's maneuvers in Nepal politics worry India*. Retrieved 14 May 2020, from The Times of India: https://timesofindia.indiatimes.com/world/south-asia/why-chinas-maneuvers-in-nepal-politics-worry-india/articleshow/75562098.cms.

16 Abeynayake, R. (2018, 05 May). *What does China have to do with a Maldives coup? Ask Sri Lankan tourists*. Retrieved 14 May 2020, from South China Morning Post: https://

www.scmp.com/week-asia/politics/article/2144296/what-does-china-have-do-maldives-coup-ask-sri-lankan-tourists.

17 Iyengar, R. (2015, 23 April). *Pakistan Plans 12,000-Strong Security Force to Safeguard Chinese Workers*. Retrieved 14 May 2020, from Time: https://time.com/3832531/pakistan-security-force-china-workers-infrastructure-projects-corridor-12000/.

18 Mallick, M.G. (2019). *Rise of China, History, Technology & Policies: Implications for India.* New Delhi: Vivekananda International Foundation. Retrieved 15 May 2020, from https://www.vifindia.org/sites/default/files/rise-of-china-history-technology-policies-and-implications-for-india.pdf, pp.112-114.

19 Krishnan, A. (2020, March). *Following the Money: China's Inc. Growing Stake in India-China Relation.* Retrieved 14 May 2020, from Brookings Institution India Center: https://www.brookings.edu/wp-content/uploads/2020/03/China-Inc%E2%80%99s-growing-stake-in-India-China-relations_F.pdf.

20 Linda Jakobson and Dean Knox. (2010). New Foreign Policy Actors in China. In *SIPRI Policy Paper No. 26.* SIPRI. Retrieved 15 May 2020, from https://www.sipri.org/publications/publications/2010/sipri-policy-papers/new-foreign-policy-actors-china, p.13.

21 Legarda, H. (2018, 01 August). *In Xi's China, the center takes control of foreign affairs.* Retrieved 15 May 2020, from MERICS: https://www.merics.org/en/blog/xis-china-center-takes-control-foreign-affairs.

22 "India-South China Trade Figures", Consulate General of India in Guangzhou https://www.cgiguangzhou.gov.in/eoi.php?id=South_Chi-na and "India and Eastern China", Consulate General of India in Shanghai https://www.cgishanghai.gov.in/pages?id=3.

23 Kenji Kawase, "In China, Private Companies Walk a Fine Line", Nikkei Asian Review, 23 May 2018 https://asia.nikkei.com/Spotlight/ Cover-Story/In-China-private-companies-walk-a-fine-line2.

24 Echo Huang, "This app is a hit symbol of the uneasy relationship between China's tech giants and the party", *Quartz*, 19 February 2019 https://qz.com/1553407/this-hit-app-is-a-symbol-of-the-uneasy-relationship-between-chinas-tech-giants-and-the-party/.

25 Press Information Bureau. (2020, 17 April). *Government amends the extant FDI policy for curbing opportunistic takeovers/acquisitions of Indian companies due to the current COVID-19 pandemic.* Retrieved 15 May 2020, from Ministry of Commerce & Industry, Government of India: https://pib.gov.in/newsite/PrintRelease.aspx?relid=202359.

26 Hongpei, Z. (2020, 13 May). *India's portfolio investment curbs on China signal bumpy road.* Retrieved 17 May 2020, from Global Times: http://www.globaltimes.cn/content/1188274.shtml.

27 Global Times. (2020, 10 May). *China's diplomatic challenges in a world polarised by the pandemic.* Retrieved 17 May 2020, from http://www.globaltimes.cn/content/1187918.shtml.

28 Ibid.

29 Ibid.

30 Amit Bhandari, B. F. (February 2020). *Chinese Investment in India.* Mumbai: Gateway House, Indian Council on Global Affairs. Retrieved 15 May 2020, from https://www.gatewayhouse.in/wp-content/uploads/2020/03/Chinese-Investments-in-India-Report_2020_Final.pdf.

31 Mallick, M.G. (2019). *Rise of China, History, Technology & Policies: Implications for India.*

New Delhi: Vivekananda International Foundation. Retrieved 15 May 2020, from https://www.vifindia.org/sites/default/files/rise-of-china-history-technology-policies-and-implications-for-india.pdf, pp.119-120.

32 Ibid.

33 Telecom Regulatory Authority of India. (2019). *Annual Report 2018-19*. New Delhi. Retrieved 15 May 2020, from https://trai.gov.in/sites/default/files/Annual_Report_15012020_0.pdf.

34 McKinsey Global Institute. (27 March 2019). *Digital India: Technology o to transform a connected nation*. McKinsey & Company. Retrieved 15 May 2020, from https://www.mckinsey.com/business-functions/mckinsey-digital/our-insights/digital-india-technology-to-transform-a-connected-nation.

35 Roy, D. (2020, 01 April). *Covid-19 exposes Indian industry's supply chain vulnerabilities*. Retrieved 14 May 2020, from The Hindu Business Line: https://www.thehindubusinessline.com/opinion/covid-19-exposes-indian-industrys-supply-chain-vulnerabilities/article31224928.ece#.

36 Jha, D.N. (2020, 20 May). *Union Health Minister Harsh Vardhan to head WHO Executive Board*. Retrieved 21 May 2020, from The Times of India: https://timesofindia.indiatimes.com/india/union-health-minister-harsh-vardhan-to-head-who-executive-board/articleshow/75843069.cms.

37 Chaudhury, D.R. (2020, 02 May). *China Interferes in Nepal to Save the Communist Party Government*. Retrieved May 20, 2020, from The Economic Times: https://economictimes.indiatimes.com/news/international/world-news/china-interferes-in-nepal-to-save-communist-party government/articleshow/75501921.cms.

38 General Bipin Rawat Appointed as Chief of Defence Staff, 30 December 2019, https://pib.gov.in/PressReleasePage.aspx?PRID=1598029.

39 The Second Schedule of Allocation of Business Rules of Government of India, p.44, https://cabsec.gov.in/businessrules/allocationofbusinessrules/secondschedule/.

40 Sunil Khilnani, R.K. (2012). *Non Alignment 2.0: A Foreign and Strategic Policy for India in the 21st Century*. National Defence College and Centre for Policy Research, New Delhi, New Delhi. Retrieved 21 May 2020, from http://www.ris.org.in/images/RIS_images/pdf/NonAlignment.pdf, p.41.

41 Ibid, p.61.

42 The Quadrilateral Security Dialogue (also known as the Quad) is an informal strategic dialogue between the United States, Japan, Australia and India that is maintained by talks between member countries.

43 Press Trust of India. (2019, 14 December). The *Congressional committee wants India, Japan and S Korea at par with Five Eyes on intelligence sharing*. Retrieved 21 May 2020, from The Economic Times: https://economictimes.indiatimes.com/news/defence/congressional-committee-wants-india-japan-and-s-korea-at-par-with-five-eyes-on-intelligence-sharing/articleshow/72587975.cms.

44 Ministry of External Affairs, India. (2020). *Annual Report 2019-20*. New Delhi: Policy Planning and Research Division. Retrieved 21 May 2020, from http://www.mea.gov.in/Uploads/PublicationDocs/32489_AR_Spread_2020_new.pdf.

45 Ministry of Home Affairs. (2019). *Annual Report 2018-19*. New Delhi: Government of India. Retrieved 22 May 2020, from https://www.mha.gov.in/sites/default/files/AnnualReport_English_01102019.pdf, p.11.

46 Institute of Defence and Strategic Analysis. (2012). *A Case for Intelligence Reforms in India*. New Delhi: IDSA, pp22-23.

47 Ibid.

48 NITI Aayog. (November 2018). *Strategy for New India @75.* New Delhi: Government of India, p.178.

49 Ibid.

50 Ibid.

51 Cowshish, A. (2017, 31 July). *13th Five-Year Defence Plan (2017-22): A Re-Run of the past.* Retrieved from Manohar Parikar Institute for Defence and Strategic Analysis: https://idsa.in/idsacomments/13th-five-year-defence-plan-2017-22_acowshish_310717.

52 Kaushal, V. (2018, 14 August). *The Need for a Mid-Term Review of the 13th Defence Five Year Plan.* Retrieved 23 May 2020, from Manohar Parikar Institute for Defence and Strategic Analysis: https://idsa.in/idsacomments/mid-term-review-13th-defence-five-year-plan-vkaushal-140818.

53 The Second Schedule of Allocation of Business Rules of Government of India, p.44, https://cabsec.gov.in/businessrules/allocationofbusinessrules/secondschedule/.

54 Kanwal, G. (2018). Introduction: The Need for Defence Reforms. In G. K. Kohli, *Defence Reforms: A National Imperative.* New Delhi: Pentagon Press and IDSA, p.7.

55 The Economist. (2020, 09 May). *The Pandemic is Driving America and China further Apart.* Retrieved 12 May 2020, from https://www.economist.com/leaders/2020/05/09/the-pandemic-is-driving-america-and-china-further-apart.

56 Cimpanu, C. (2020, 18 April). *FBI says cybercrime reports quadrupled during COVID-19 pandemic.* Retrieved 12 May 2020, from ZDNet: https://www.zdnet.com/article/fbi-says-cybercrime-reports-quadrupled-during-covid-19-pandemic/.

57 Jacobs, E. (2020, 29 April). *China makes economic threats against Australia over coronavirus probe.* Retrieved 12 May 2020, from The New York Post: https://nypost.com/2020/04/29/china-threatens-australia-economically-over-coronavirus-probe/.

58 Rangarajan, L. (1992). *Kautilya: The Arthashastra.* New Delhi: Penguin Books, p.200.

List of Figures and Tables

FIGURES

TABLES

Index